D0154503

The Colombian Caribbean

A REGIONAL HISTORY, 1870–1950

EDUARDO POSADA-CARBÓ

CLARENDON PRESS · OXFORD
1996

Oxford University Press, Walton Street, Oxford OX2 6DP
Oxford New York
Athens Auckland Bangkok Bombay
Calcutta Cape Town Dar es Salaam Delhi
Florence Hong Kong Istanbul Karachi
Kuala Lumpur Madras Madrid Melbourne
Mexico City Nairobi Paris Singapore
Taipei Tokyo Toronto

and associated companies in
Berlin Ibadan

Oxford is a trade mark of Oxford University Press

Published in the United States by
Oxford University Press Inc., New York

British Library Cataloguing in Publication Data
Data available

Library of Congress Cataloging in Publication Data
Data available
ISBN 0–19–820628–3

1 3 5 7 9 10 8 6 4 2

Typeset by Helen Grant
Printed in Great Britain
on acid-free paper by
Bookcraft Ltd.,
Midsomer Norton, Avon

Acknowledgements

This book began as a doctoral thesis completed at St Antony's College, Oxford in 1990. I would like to express my deepest gratitude to Malcolm Deas, whose constant guidance and support has been a major stimulus to my research. His work on Colombian history has inspired many pages of this book.

I owe my special thanks to Darío Jaramillo Agudèlo who has supported me throughout my academic career. I am grateful to Karl Parrish Jr., David Parrish, María Teresa de Gómez, and Felipe Laserna, for giving me free access to their family papers. Diego de la Peña, Julio Tovar D'Andreis, Carlos Daniel Abello, Adolfo Meisel, Gustavo Bell, Ramiro de la Espriella, and Margarita Garrido also provided me with useful materials. Colin Clarke and Marco Palacios made useful comments and suggestions to the manuscript. Jacques Gilard also read the manuscript and made helpful comments. The chapter on cattle benefited from observations by José Antonio Ocampo. Catherine Legrand read and made some useful observations on the different sections on bananas. They, of course, do not bear any responsibilities for the final result of the book.

During all my years of research I have received support and hospitality from many friends and institutions. I want to acknowledge in particular the help of Constanza Toro and Cecilia Inés Restrepo in the *Fundación Antioqueña para los Estudios Sociales*, Arturo Sarabia and Felipe Tovar in the *Cámara de Comercio de Barranquilla,* Gilma Rodríguez in the *Banco de la República,* Moisés Alvarez in the *Archivo de la Gobernación de Bolívar,* Ruth Hodges in the Latin American Centre at St Antony's College, Oxford, and of members of the Bodleian Library in Oxford, the Biblioteca Nacional and the Luis Angel Arango Library in Bogotá, the Biblioteca Departamental in Barranquilla, and the National Archives in Washington. The Banco de la República deserves a special mention for its support to Colombian scholarship, from which I have benefited.

My sojourns in Medellín, Bogotá, Cartagena, and Valledupar were made all the more pleasant by the kindness and hospitality of Horacio and Sonia Vélez, Luis Fernando Criales, Eusebio Carbó, Ricardo Plata, Armando and María Elisa Cuello, and Mauricio Restrepo.

Grants from the Bryce and Read and the Arnold Funds helped me to carry out field work in Washington. My final year of research was made possible by a grant from the *Fundación para la Promoción de la Investigación y la Tecnología*, in Colombia, and a Junior Research Fellowship at the Institute of Latin American Studies (ILAS), University of London. At ILAS, I have benefited greatly from the support and encouragement of Victor Bulmer-Thomas, Tony Bell, and Leslie Bethell. Thanks to the support of ILAS, and the assistance of Helen Grant, I was able to speed up the production of this book. Tony Bell has gone out of his way to be helpful.

I am also grateful for the editorial assistance I have received from Oxford University Press, in particular Anne Gelling, Michael Belson, and Sylvia Jaffrey.

This book would not have been possible without the support that I have always received from my parents, Francisco and Judy Posada. Their enthusiasm for education and their deep *Costeño* feelings have been a constant inspiration. Robin and Beatrice Fawcett have been more than generous and hospitable in seeing this book through the completion. Louise, my wife, has been extremely helpful in editing my work although she does not share the responsibility for any mistakes I have made through my stubbornness in refusing to accept all her suggestions. Her love, understanding, and companionship have encouraged me to finish. To Louise, and to our children, Beatriz Andrea Ramona, Carlos Eduardo Nicolás, and Claudia Louise Ramona, I dedicate this book.

Contents

List of Figures

List of Maps

List of Tables

Abbreviations

ACER	Archivo de Carlos E. Restrepo
ACoHSC	*Anuario Colombiano de Historia Social y de la Cultura*
AEOH	Archivo de Enrique Olaya Herrera
AFL	Archivo de la Familia Laserna
AGB	Archivo de la Gobernación de Bolívar
AGPNO	Archivo del General Pedro Nel Ospina
AJVC	Archivo de José Vicente Concha
AMFS	Archivo Marco Fidel Suárez
ANC	Archivo Nacional de Colombia
APF	Archives of the Parrish Family
ASAS	Archivo de la Sociedad Agrícola del Sinú
BME	*Boletín Municipal de Estadística*
BOLSA	Bank of London and South America Archives
CFBC	Corporation of Foreign Bondholders Council
DB	*Diario de Bolívar*
GB	*Gaceta de Bolívar*
HAHR	*Hispanic American Historical Review*
IARH	*Inter-American Review of Historiography*
IET	Información Económica Trimestral
JIASWA	*Journal of Inter-American Studies and World Affairs*
JLAS	*Journal of Latin-American Studies*
MCR	*Monthly Consular Reports*
MDC	Malcolm Deas's private collection
NAUS	National Archives of the United States
PP	*Parliamentary Papers*
PRGS	*Proceedings of the Royal Geographic Society*
PRO	Public Record Office
RB	*Registro de Bolívar*
RCCB	*Revista de la Cámara de Comercio de Barranquilla*
RNA	*Revista Nacional de Agricultura*
SAS	Sociedad Agrícola del Sinú
UFC	United Fruit Company

Map 1. *Colombia and the Caribbean*

ATLANTIC OCEAN
Eleuthera
Cat I.
Watlings
Long I.
Mariguana
Crooked I.
Caicos Is.
Inagua
Winward Passage
Tortuga
Cap Haitien
La Navidad
Ysabel
Pto. Plata
Haiti
HAITI
S. DOMINGO
S. Domingo
Santiago de Cuba
Port au Prince
C. Tiburon
Kingston
Mona Passage
Mona I.
Puerto Rico
San Juan
Viegues I.
Santa Cruz
St. Thomas
Anegada
Virgin Is.
Sombrero
Anguilla
Saba
St. Eustatius
St. Kitts
Nevis
Barbuda
Antigua
Montserrat
Guadeloupe
Marie Galante
The Saint's Passage
Dominica
Martinique
Bird I.
St. Lucia
Barbados
St. Vincent
Grenada
Tobago
Boca de Monos
Caribbean Sea
Aruba I.
Curaçao
Biren Ayre
Aves
Margarita
Tortuga
G. of Paria
Orinoco Delta
Pt. Gallinus
La Guayra
Caracas
Orinoco R.
Santa Marta
Pto Colombia
Barranquilla
Maracaibo
Cartagena
VENEZUELA
Mulatas I.
G. of Darien
Atrato Depression
Medellin
COLOMBIA
Bogotá
Buenaventura
Cali
SOUTH AMERICA
0 100 200 300 miles
0 200 400 km

MAP 2. *The Colombian Caribbean*

Introduction

In 1926 Arno Pearse warned his fellow Englishmen that if they visited Colombia and began generalizing from what they saw at the Coast,[1] they would obtain 'a very erroneous picture'. It was Pearse's opinion that the 'real Colombia' was in the Andean interior. Rather than the flat coastland with its extremely high temperatures, 'the population consisting mostly of black people of African origin, indolent or even lazy', and the backwardness of coastal towns, Pearse preferred to identify the 'real Colombia' with 'a vast, mountainous country . . . with an agreeable climate . . . [and] a white population much more industrious and enterprising that at the coast.'[2]

His own prejudices and misconceptions aside, Pearse was able to capture not only the existence of two different realities but also to pinpoint the tendency to exclude the Colombian Caribbean whenever attempts were made to define 'national interests', or the 'real Colombia'. In 1881, the prominent *Costeño* politician Rafael Núñez complained about those 'advocates of a national schism', who were constantly on guard against the appointment of any *Costeños* to national public offices.[3] As significant as concern about the distribution of bureaucratic posts were the problems raised by the allocation of public money in a large and diverse country where resources were scant. Under these circumstances, the definition of 'national interest' at the cost of denying regional cleavages became all the more tempting. In 1919, journalists, politicians, and business men organized the *Liga Costeña* to protest against what they perceived as an exclusion of the region from the trends of national development. Occurrences like this, or complaints such as those raised by Núñez, might be considered mere expressions of a recalcitrant parochialism. However, the view that the Coast was alienated from the 'real

[1] The Colombian Caribbean – the region under study in this book – is referred to variously as the Coast, the Atlantic Coast, and the *Costa*. People from the *Costa* are referred to as *Costeños.*

[2] A. Pearse, *Colombia, with Special Reference to Cotton* (London, 1926), 13. On account of its climate and living conditions, the Coast was not appealing to most foreign visitors. C. A. Gosselman observed: 'Had I limited my stay in Colombia to the cities of Cartagena and Santa Marta I would have left the country with an incorrect and unfair opinion about its people, since I do not think that there is a place so different from the provinces of the highlands than the provinces from the Coast'; C. A. Gosselman, *Viaje por Colombia, 1825 y 1826* (Bogotá, 1981), 373.

[3] R. Núñez, *La reforma política* (Bogotá, 1945), (pt. 1), 81.

Colombia' was also developed elsewhere in the country, outside the region. A close look at an influential work by the liberal ideologue Alejandro López, *Problemas Colombianos*, reveals an attempt to define 'national' issues by applying an Andean yardstick. Although his approach might also exclude other regions from his idea of 'national problems', López made a special case of the Coast and explicitly identified it as being alien to the main currents of national development.[4] Thus the significance of the question what was the real Colombia, goes beyond the sympathies and prejudices of a foreign visitor such as Arno Pearse, or of a national ideologue such as Alejandro López. To identify the real Colombia had political, economic and social implications. But was there any one real Colombia?

A Chilean diplomat, having observed the several provinces in the country, concluded in 1903 that 'there has not existed – nor could there have existed – one Colombian community but a number of different communities each isolated from the other'.[5] He exaggerated. Politics and civil wars, education and business had all contributed to the integration of the nation. None the less marked regional differences did exist in Colombia, and posed problems for the consolidation of the nation-state. 'National history is shaped in the regions', Malcolm Deas has pointed out, although he has also observed that the nation should not be neglected in the enthusiasm for regional historiography.[6] Yet it is the need to understand the nature of the Colombian nation, in the light of the country's regional diversity, that makes for the significance of regional histories. To generalize from the experience of the *Costa*, or from any other regional experience, would certainly result in 'a very erroneous picture' of Colombia, as Pearse feared. The picture would be no less erroneous, however, if regions were to be ignored in the

[4] A. López, *Problemas colombianos* (Paris, 1927), 133, 292–4.

[5] *El Nuevo Tiempo*, Bogotá, 28 July 1903, quoted in J. Villegas and J. Yunis, *La guerra de los mil días* (Bogotá, 1979), 20–1. The view that Colombia is a country of regions is now widely accepted by historians. A recent history of the country before independence acknowledges that when 'New Granada' – as it was then called – 'first came under Bourbon rule, it was a mosaic of regions, each isolated from the others by long distances and difficult terrain, and distinguished by cultural differences arising from variations in the local blend of Europeans, Indians and Africans'; A. McFarlane, *Colombia Before Independence. Economy, Society, and Politics under Bourbon Rule* (Cambridge, 1993), 31.

[6] *Aspectos polémicos de la historia colombiana del siglo XIX. Memoria de un seminario* (Bogotá, 1983), 198. See also his *Del poder y la gramática* (Bogotá, 1993), 175–206.

quest of creating the national paradigm. Regions and nation, therefore, should not be regarded as mutually exclusive.

1. The Region in Historical Perspective

Renan's famous address in 1882, 'Qu'est-ce qu'une nation?', has become a common point of reference in stressing the problems faced by any attempt to define a nation and its related concept, nationalism.[7] The definition of region and regionalism poses similar difficulties. Furthermore, where is the line between nation and region to be drawn? The question is particularly relevant to regionalist movements in Western Europe, such as in the Catalan and Basque countries, which have been described as 'unsatisfied nationalisms'.[8] Peter Alter has shown how the existence of particular collective identities places such regionalisms 'in the tradition of nineteenth-century European national movements'. Apart from the 'separatist wings', however, Alter has distinguished regionalist movements by their lack of aspirations to form their own national states.[9] To define regions as parts of a whole might be a good point for departure. There is a need to go further. If nations are identified with 'imagined communities', regions are, in contrast, linked to 'the reality of place', in so far as they are directly concerned with the lives of men.[10] When the organizers of the *Liga Costeña* gathered in 1919, or when mass demonstrations took place on the Barranquilla streets in 1930 to press the central government to invest in the dredging and canalization of the Magdalena river mouth, what was at stake was not a claim for any subjective identity but for the development of a place of 'common living'.[11]

Generally defined as 'areas of distinctive character', regions became the core of their discipline for many a geographer during the first half

[7] E. Renan, *Qu'est-ce qu'une nation?* (Paris, 1882). See also B. Anderson, *Imagined Communities* (London, 1983), 14–16; P. Alter, *Nationalism* (London, 1989), 4–23; E. J. Hobsbawn, *Nations and Nationalism Since 1780* (Cambridge, 1990), 1–13; and A. Smith, *National Identity* (London, 1991), 3–13.

[8] H. Seton-Watson, 'Unsatisfied Nationalism', *Journal of Contemporary History,* 6 (1971), 3–13.

[9] Alter, *Nationalism*, 142. For an essay that explores the evolution of the idea of regions in Europe, see C. Harvie, *The Rise of Regional Europe* (London and New York, 1994).

[10] These expressions have been borrowed from Anderson's *Imagined Communities* and from Charles Fisher's inaugural lecture, *The Reality of Place* (London, 1965).

[11] R. Dickinson, *The City Region in Western Europe* (London, 1967), 5.

of this century. A prolific debate about the concept of region, which seems to have faded away after the 1960s, left, however, a few lessons that can be usefully applied to regional history.[12] First, regions are often clearly distinguishable from each other, which gives them some meaning as an ensemble. However, this does not imply that regions are in themselves completely uniform. Second, although as Joseph Love has noted, 'regions defined by historians have tended to be fixed political units', looking at regions as 'areas of interrelated activities, kindred interests and common organization' can be helpful in appreciating the degree of coherence of a given territory.[13] Third, since the relevance of regions arises form their distinctiveness, the study of their particulars does matter not only for understanding regions *per se* but, more important, for providing additional perspectives to the whole, in this case to national history.

Recent Latin American historiography has been increasingly concerned with questions of region and regionalism. Attention has been paid to problems related to the consolidation of the national state during the nineteenth century, where the focus tends to be placed on the early territorial definition of the republic or around questions such as whether there was nation before state, or to what extent national politics were conditioned by the integration of a national market, or how and when regional élites gave way to a national élite.[14] The study

[12] See e. g. R. B. Hall, 'The Geographic Region: a Resumé', in *AAAG: A Conference on Regions*, 30. 3, (1935), 122–8; P. E. James, 'Toward a Further Understanding of the Regional Concept', *AAAG*, 42 (1952), 195; E. W. Gilbert, 'The Idea of Region', *Geography*, 45 (1960), 157; D. Whittlesey, 'The Regional Concept and the Regional Method', in P. E. James and C. F. Jones (eds.), *American Geography: Inventory and Prospect* (Syracuse, 1954), 21; R. Hartshorne, *Perspective on the Nature of Geography* (London, 1963), 108–5; G. W. S. Robinson, 'The Geographical Region: Form and Function', *The Scottish Geographical Magazine*, 69/2, (Sept. 1953), 49–55; G. H. T. Kimble, 'The Inadequacy of the Regional Concept', in L. D. Stamp and S. W. Wooldridge (eds.), *London Essays in Geography* (London, 1951), 151–174; Dickinson, *The City Region*, 3–13. On the French concept of *pays*, see P. Vidal de la Blache, *The Personality of France* (London, 1928), 13–24. The recent process of European integration has encouraged a fresh interest in the subject from various disciplines. See e. g. L. Bergeron (ed.) *La Croissance Regionale dans l'Europe Mediterranéenne: 18e–20e siécles* (Paris, 1992); and Harvie, *The Rise of Regional Europe*.

[13] J. H. Love, 'An Approach to Regionalism', in R. Graham and P. Smith (eds.) *New Approaches to Latin American History* (Texas, 1974), 140; and Dickinson, *The City Region*, 5.

[14] M. Palacios (ed.) *La unidad nacional en América Latina. Del regionalismo a la nacionalidad* (Mexico, 1983), and his *Estado y clases sociales en Colombia* (Bogotá, 1986), 87–149; B. Roberts, 'State and Region in Latin America: The View from Below', in Cedla, *State and Region in Latin America: A Workshop* (Amsterdam, 1981), 10–31; and essays by B. R. Hamnett and J. Jaramillo Uribe in I. Buisson *et al.* (eds.), *Problemas*

of particular regionalisms, as movements within national politics, has not been popular among scholars though Joseph Love's work on Río Grande do Sul provides one example.[15] There has also been some research on the history of cities which take a regional perspective, such as Guy Thomson's work on Puebla de los Angeles. Indeed regions seem to have found a firm place in Mexican historiography.[16] Yet the most common approach to regional studies among historians of Latin America is to take the region 'as a representative case of the problem under study', or 'as a variant case of a problem', where the region is marginal to the focus of the analysis.[17] Magnus Mörner's stimulating work, *Region and State in Latin America's Past*, follows this approach.[18]

This book places itself within the general current of research that has paid attention to regional analysis in Latin America but slightly differs from the above approaches in the following: first, it looks at the region as an ensemble which merits detailed consideration, although, as already stated, the region is regarded as being part of a whole. Second, it stresses the importance of regional cleavages in the development of the national state but, for the case of Colombia, takes the issue beyond the nineteenth century. Third, although regionalism is regarded as significant, it is considered as but one aspect of an analysis whose main focus is an understanding of the distinctive economic, social, and political features of the region. Fourth, it looks at the role of towns and cities in the integration of the region, but again these remain just one side of the analysis. Overall, this is an attempt to explore how the study of a region can be fruitful in approaching a number of aspects of the history of a Latin American country such as Colombia.

de la formación del Estado y de la nación en hispanoamérica (Cologne, 1984), 305–17 and 339–58.

[15] J. H. Love, *Río Grande do Sul and Brazilian Regionalism, 1882–1930* (Stanford, Calif., 1971); *São Paulo in the Brazilian Federation* (Stanford, Calif., 1980), and 'Federalismo y regionalismo en Brasil, 1889–1937', in M. Carmagnani (ed.), *Federalismos latinoamericanos* (Mexico, 1993), 180–223. See also J. Wirth, *Minas Gerais in the Brazilian Federation, 1889–1937* (Stanford, Calif., 1977), and R. Levine, *Pernambuco in the Brazilian Federation, 1889–1937* (Stanford, Calif., 1978).

[16] G. Thomson, *Puebla de los Angeles: Industry and Society in a Mexican City, 1700–1850* (San Francisco and London, 1988); and E. van Young (ed.), *Mexico's Regions* (San Diego, 1992).

[17] For a typology of regional analysis, see Love, 'An Approach to Regionalism', 142-5.

[18] M. Mörner, *Region and State in Latin America's Past* (Baltimore and London, 1993).

Colombian regional historiography has been hitherto mostly centred on Antioquia, a region which has attracted interest through the prominent role of the *Antioqueño* entrepreneur in regional and national development.[19] However, a rising concern about national diversity has produced a growing literature on regional history.[20] In this context, until recently it was commonly asserted that the Colombian Caribbean had been a region neglected in academic historical research. This assumption has been taken to an extreme by some historians and literary critics, who go as far as to suggest that *One Hundred Years Of Solitude*, by the Nobel Prize winner Gabriel García Márquez, serves adequately to fill the vacuum.[21] However, although there is an immense field yet to be explored, a few scholars have become involved in the study of this significant region. Theodore Nichols was the pioneer of modern scholarly work on the Coast. Written originally as a doctoral dissertation in 1951 but published only in 1973, his *Tres Puertos de Colombia* is a historical geography of Cartagena, Barranquilla, and Santa Marta, focusing on the problems faced by these three ports in their development. Two other geographers, James R. Krogzemis and Le Roy Gordon have contributed to the understanding of two areas of the region, Santa Marta and the Sinú, taking a long historical span. The history of Cartagena has been enriched by Anthony McFarlane's work on the colonial period and Eduardo Lemaitre's massive four-volume study which covers the history of the city up to the 1940s. Aspects of *Costeño* regionalism have been dealt with by James William Park's thesis on Rafael Núñez. Besides these, there has also been a proliferation of articles and essays, of which a good cross-section has been compiled by Gustavo Bell, while Adolfo Meisel Roca has edited a textbook covering the economic and social history of the region since the Spanish conquest.[22]

[19] J. Parsons, *Antioqueño Colonization of Western Colombia* (Berkeley, 1968); R. Brew, *El desarrollo económico de Antioquia desde la independencia hasta 1920* (Bogotá, 1977); *Los estudios regionales en Colombia: el caso de Antioquia* (Medellín, 1982).

[20] See e. g. D. C. Johnson, *Santander* (Bogotá, 1984); Universidad del Valle (ed.) *Sociedad y economía en la Valle del Cauca*, 5 vols. (Bogotá, 1983); and J. Rausch, *The Llanos Frontier in Colombian History, 1830–1930* (Albuquerque, 1993).

[21] See e. g. the bizarre suggestions by Gene H. Bell-Villada, for whom the Colombian Caribbean remains relatively unknown because of 'the vestigial legacy of white chauvinism and Bogotá snobbery', 'the methodological problem posed by a mixed culture', and 'assorted physical dangers', *García Márquez: The Man and his Work* (Chapel Hill and London, 1990), 23, 24.

[22] T. Nichols, *Tres Puertos de Colombia* (Bogotá, 1973); B. Le Roy Gordon, 'Human Geography and Ecology in the Sinú Country of Colombia', *Ibero-Americana*, 39 (Berkeley, 1957); J. Krogzemis, 'A Historical Geography of the Santa Marta Area,

From a regional perspective, however, it is probably Orlando Fals Borda who has produced the most ambitious work on the Coast. After his *Capitalismo, hacienda y poblamiento en la Costa Atlántica*, Fals Borda completed his four volumes of *Historia Doble de la Costa*, which deals with a wide variety of topics from the conquest to the present day, including politics, religion, folklore, and even his own personal involvement in the Colombian peasant movement, although the central theme throughout this undertaking is the history of the struggle for land in the area under study.[23] Fals Borda's *Historia Doble*, however, does not cover the whole region but focuses attention on Southern Bolívar. His wide scope leaves some periods poorly covered, while his focus on agrarian history leads to the neglect of other important aspects. Furthermore, his use of sources seems at times arbitrary and his empirical evidence is scant: two significant objections that Fals Borda has tried to invalidate by legitimizing his work as politically committed to the cause of the popular classes.[24] Despite these shortcomings, Fals Borda has put forward interesting interpretations of several aspects of *Costeño* history.

In the light of the above literature, where does this book stand? How does it aim to contribute to Coastal historiography? First, there has been no previous systematic approach to the region as a whole; the focus has hitherto been placed on particular regional problems, or on cities and subregions. This book intends to look at the history of the Atlantic Coast as an ensemble, taking into account both its internal features and the way it has been externally influenced. In addition, the period covered by this research is of particular interest in understanding the region in relation to the development of the national state. Besides

Colombia', Ph.D. thesis, University of California, Berkeley, 1967; A. McFarlane, 'Commerciantes y monopolio en la Nueva Granada: el consulado de Cartagena de Indias', *ACoHSC*, 11 (Bogotá, 1983), 43–70; E. Lemaitre, *Historia general de Cartagena* (Bogotá, 1983), 4 vols.; J. W. Park, *Rafael Núñez and the Politics of Colombian Regionalism, 1863–1886* (Baton Rouge. La., 1985); G. Bell (ed.) *El Caribe colombiano* (Barranquilla, 1988); and A. Meisel (ed.) *Historia económica y social del Caribe colombiano* (Bogotá, 1994).

[23] O. Fals Borda, *Capitalismo, hacienda y poblamiento en la Costa Atlántica* (Bogotá, 1976); and under the generic title, *Historia doble de la Costa Atlántica: Mompox y Loba* (Bogotá, 1980); *El Presidente Nieto* (Bogotá, 1981); *Resistencia en el San Jorge* (Bogotá, 1984); *Retorno a la tierra* (Bogotá, 1986).

[24] For a critical analysis of *Historia Doble*, see C. Bergquist, 'En nombre de la historia: una crítica disciplinaria de Historia Doble de la Costa de Orlando Fals Borda', *Huellas* (Aug. 1989), 40–56, and Fals Borda's reply, 'Réplica a Bergquist. Comentaríos a la mesa redonda sobre la Historia Doble de la Costa', *Huellas* (Dec. 1989), 23–9.

the focus on the region as such, this book also touches on various themes whose discussion is relevant to the history of other Latin American countries as well. Here I offer what I trust is new information based on manuscript and printed sources which have been hitherto unexplored in studying the Colombian Caribbean.

2. Scope of the Research and a Note on Sources

The paradox of regional history is that it is often singled out as parochial, yet whoever practises it finds himself forever forced to broaden his scope. This is partly the result of misconceiving regions as simple, enclosed units, as if they exist in isolation. However, if a region is to be properly understood, not only does the need to relate it to the outside world become evident, but also the historical research inevitably draws on a wide range of academic enquiry, exploring the fields of geography, politics, sociology, economics, anthropology. Far from being an arrogant assertion, this just recognizes the challenge.

The Caribbean Coast of Colombia is the subject of this study. It tries to look in detail at the social, economic, and political development experienced by this region between 1870 and 1950 within a national context, taking into consideration the external elements that helped to shape its history. Thus it examines what were the achievements and shortcomings of arable agriculture, how the land was increasingly devoted to cattle and how significant this industry was to the regional economy, what links existed between town and countryside, how the Coast was integrated into the national market, how the region coped with transport problems, what influence foreign immigrants and foreign capital had in Coastal development, how local politics related to national politics, and what were the relations between the central state and the region. Although its main emphasis is to identify regional trends, this book also tackles some questions relevant to Colombian historiography and, when appropriate, these are considered in a Latin American context. Given the variety of areas covered, however, it does not attempt to offer definitive answers but it hopes to provide suggestions and to encourage further research.

The student of regional history – be he R. Brew on Antioquia, or C. J. Baker on Tamilnad – can readily illustrate further problems faced in his or her task, when dealing in particular with countries of scarce resources.[25] Archival material is not easily at hand, systematic information is difficult to obtain, data is scant and fallible. In the Colombian Caribbean, these difficulties can appear unsurmountable at a first glance. As the British Vice-Consul observed in 1896, 'unfortunately there are no regular statistics kept by the authorities [in Barranquilla], thus no calculation can be made with any accuracy as to the increase or diminution of the population'.[26] Some contemporary officials did show awareness of the limitations they faced in governing without appropriate information. In 1871, the Magangué Governor acknowledged that when taking over his post he did not find any 'data from my predecessor which would give me an idea of the needs of the province'. Like his colleague in Sincelejo, he had probably to resort to 'his own efforts to trace the history of public administration in the state of Bolívar'.[27] Ignorance about much of the rural world prevailed. In 1919, the *Alcalde* of Lorica pointed out that it was not known locally how much public land – known as *baldío* – had been allocated to private hands nor how much of it still belonged to the state. Production figures were often arbitrary estimates where they did exist. As the Secretary General in Bolívar noted in reference to the town of Morales in 1874, 'it has been impossible even to estimate how many farmers are there or how much they produce'.[28] The *Secretario de Gobierno* summarized the problems four decades later:

> Statistics remain a virgin field among us. We can only count on an ill informed census. We do not have a map of the whole territory of Bolívar . . . nor do we have maps of any of the municipalities; there is no way to compare population density among the different provinces. Neither do we have a cadastral survey of urban and rural property, even less any figure regarding the cattle industry, our main source of wealth.[29]

Problems of this sort were obviously not exclusive to the Coast. In 1939, a First National Assembly of Agricultural Statistics was held in Bogotá, where the General Comptrollor recognized that 'we are

[25] Brew, *El desarrollo económico de Antioquia*, 27–34, and C. J. Baker, *An Indian Rural Economy, 1880–1955: The Tamilnad Countryside* (Oxford, 1984), 15–18. It should be noted, however, that Brew was dealing with probably the richest Colombian region, and Baker with an area where 'from the late nineteenth-century the British rulers began counting things with extraordinary zeal and the resulting heap of statistical data is probably unequalled in the non-western world in this period', p. 16. See also L. González, *Invitación a la microhistoria* (Mexico, 1973), 36–9.

[26] *PP*, 37, LXXXV (1896), 468.

[27] *GB,* 13 Aug. 1871, and *DB*, 9 Aug. 1875.

[28] *GB*, 10 Nov. 1874, and *Bolívar. Gaceta Departamental,* 13 and 14 March 1919.

[29] *Memoria que presenta el Secretario de Gobierno* (Cartagena, 1914), IV.

absolutely ignorant about the volume and value of our agricultural production'.[30] Since Coastal departments were more short of funds than their Andean counterparts, they were bound to face even greater difficulties. Furthermore, it seems that bookkeeping for rural enterprises was generally developed earlier in some Andean regions than on the Coast.[31]

Records were thus deficient in both the public and the private sectors. The reasons for these shortcomings were of a varied nature. There were natural fears of taxation, as US Trade Commissioner Bell observed about statistics on the Colombian cattle industry, while he also noticed 'apprehension concerning possible disturbances, and the difficulties encountered in obtaining accurate returns in this broken and undeveloped country'.[32] Besides these, mixed cropping – a common practice in many rural areas of the tropics – added further obstacles to any attempt to calculate productive acreage and agricultural output.[33] Even if the government was willing to gather information, a scant and sparse population in a large territory did little to ease such a task amidst recurrent financial crisis. Poor finances was not the only explanation. Culture, attitudes towards the past, also conditioned the slow development of a written tradition. 'There is no sense of history,' Luis Striffler observed about the San Jorge region, 'the new generation scarcely remember its parents and never the grandparents'. . . [34] In addition, successive civil disturbances undermined any systematic attempt to accumulate information. Nor were environmental conditions very encouraging. To escape from the boredom of the journey on his way to Ríohacha, the French geographer Eliseo Reclus looked for his books. 'To my surprise,' he exclaimed, 'when I open my books, apparently untouched up to now, I found them almost without pages, like empty boxes. During my pilgrimage in Santa Marta, in just a few weeks, the termites had destroyed everything'.[35]

To acknowledge these problems by no means implies that the region has been left without any significant written sources to trace its history.

[30] *Primera asamblea nacional de estadística agropecuaria* (Bogotá, 1939), 9, 48–9. On the problems of rural statistics in Colombia, see also C. Lleras Restrepo, *La estadística nacional. Su organización, sus problemas* (Bogotá, 1938), 217–47.

[31] Administrator to Manager, Marta Magdalena, 29 Oct. 1933, ASAS/C/120:17.

[32] P. L. Bell (Department of Commerce), *Colombia: A Commercial and Industrial Handbook* (Washington, 1921), 139.

[33] On the problems of statistics in the rural tropics, see P. Hill, *Development Economics on Trial* (Cambridge, 1989), 30–50.

[34] L. Striffler, *El Río San Jorge* (1880) (Montería, 1958), 77, 80.

[35] E. Reclus, *Viaje a la Sierra Nevada de Santa Marta* (1861) (Bogotá, 1949), 74.

In spite of the many shortcomings, local officials did leave valuable records of their experiences in office. An increasing concern with information encouraged some improvements and even some systematic efforts to develop public records. In 1934 the *Alcalde* of Mompox even boasted of the achievements of his Bureau of Statistics.[36] Private accounts and papers, though scant, are also available but their unearthing is often a time-consuming process. Newspaper and journal collections, together with rare pamphlets and some written memoirs provide substantial data. Given the constraints of local sources, the importance of the outsider's view – national personalities, foreign consuls, and travellers – goes far beyond the useful supplementary insight.

All in all, however, the existing information is still scattered and fragmented and often not easily accessible. Some periods are better covered than others. Some areas are hardly documented at all. Few local archives are properly equipped for research, even if not closed to the public altogether. Official memoirs are rarities distributed among several, often distant libraries, private and public alike. This book attempts to overcome these difficulties by placing together pieces of information from a wide variety of sources of different origins. The result, as C. J. Baker called his study on Tamilnad, 'is something of a tight-rope act'. It is hoped that the final picture will prove worth the effort.

[36] M. F. Obregón, *Memoria de gobierno* (Cartagena, 1934), 196.

Prologue
The Colombian Caribbean: An Overview

The Colombian Caribbean, defined here by the borders of the former sovereign states of Bolívar and Magdalena, covers an area of 132,279 square kilometres, or over 11 per cent of the national territory.[1] The region is bounded on the north by the Caribbean Sea; on the south by the slopes of the Andes.[2] This prologue provides a general introduction to the Colombian Caribbean, its geographical setting, and its population. It does not set out to offer a comprehensive historical geography or demography of the region, but intends to highlight some regional features that are relevant to the rest of the book: the pattern of population settlement along waterways and by the sea, the physical circumstances that constrained agricultural development and trade, the diversity of a relatively scant and sparse population, and the loose nature of social relations.

1. Sea, Rivers, and Marshes

The Caribbean coastline contains numerous bays and creeks suitable for the anchorage of ships, determining, together with the Magdalena river, the commercial importance of the region to the Colombian

[1] Bolívar and Magdalena, sovereign states under the federal period (1863–86), became *Departamentos* after 1886. A small territory, with Barranquilla as its capital, seceded from Bolívar, first in 1905 and finally in 1910, to form the *Departamento del Atlántico*. The Guajira, which was part of Magdalena, was given the status of *Intendencia* first in 1898. This book will variously refer to these administrative subdivisions of the *Costeño* region: Bolívar, Magdalena, Atlántico, and Guajira (see Map 2).

[2] For contemporary geographical descriptions of the region see: J. J. Nieto, 'Jeografía histórica, estadística y local de la Provincia de Cartajena, República de la Nueva Granada' (1839), *Boletín Historial,* 34–6 (Apr. 1918); F. Pérez, 'Jeografía física y política del Estado de Bolívar' and 'Jeografía física i política del Estado del Magdalena', in *Jeografía de Colombia* (Bogotá, 1863), 2 vols.; J. Gnecco Laborde, *Nociones de geografía del departamento del Magdalena* (Bogotá, 1896); F. J. Vergara y Velasco, *Nueva Geografía de Colombia* (Bogotá, 1901), 474–80, 514–48 and 791–5. See also E. Guhl, 'Ambiente geográfico humano de la Costa Atlántica', *Revista Geográfica*, (pt. 1) (Barranquilla, 1952), 139–72, and C. Angulo Valdés, 'El departamento del Atlántico y sus condiciones físicas', *Revista Geográfica*, ibid., 9–29.

economy. As F. Loraine Petre observed in 1906, Magdalena and Bolívar were the 'chief gateways' for the country's foreign trade.[3] 'The principal reason for national unity', Reclus described the Magdalena river, referring to the role it played in integrating a country otherwise broken by the abrupt topography of the Andes.[4] The Magdalena flows from south to north through a valley which lies between the eastern and central cordilleras, and reaches the sea after traversing 1,020 miles. With its tributaries – the Cauca, San Jorge, Nechí, Cesar, and Lebrija rivers – the Magdalena forms a vast hydrographic system covering a significant proportion of the northern and central provinces of Colombia, thus providing one of their most significant means of transport. Additionally, the Sinú river runs independently through the Bolívar plains before flowing into the Caribbean (see Map 2). In 1863, Felipe Pérez described the Bolívar territory as a 'massive flooded plain'. 'A rare country in the world', he also called it in observing the numerous marshes which were formed by the floodplains of the rivers Magdalena, Cauca, Sinú, and San Jorge. During the rainy season, when some of these marshes took on the aspect of 'internal seas', several natural canals were ready to provide further water communication to a major portion of the region.[5]

Sea, rivers, and marshes – as outlets for trade, and sources of fresh water and food – conditioned the location of the most important settlements on the Coast. By the mid-nineteenth century, a large proportion of towns with more than 2,000 inhabitants were situated by the sea, rivers, canals, and marshes: Cartagena, Santa Marta, and Ríohacha on the Caribbean; Peñón, Sitionuevo, Cerro de San Antonio, Campo de la Cruz, Santo Tomás, Soledad, Margarita, Remolino, Mompox, and Barranquilla on the Magdalena; Chimá, Lorica, and Montería on the Sinú; Valledupar on the Goataporí; Magangué on the Cauca; Ciénaga de Oro on a channel of the San Jorge; San Juan de Córdoba on the Ciénaga Grande.

The development of seaports was determined by the physical conditions of their bays and, more importantly, by their access to the Magdalena river, the main artery for Colombian trade. Although they possessed good harbours, Portete and Bahiahonda, in the Guajira, were only visited by smugglers. The main port in the Guajira was Ríohacha, but 'the anchorage is too dangerous and unsuitable for ships with a

[3] F. Loraine Petre, *The Republic of Colombia* (London, 1906), 153.

[4] E. Reclus, *Colombia* (Bogotá, 1958), 186. [5] Pérez, 'Jeografía de Bolívar', 9.

deep draft'.[6] To the south-west, the bay of Cispatá near the mouth of the Sinú river was at times considered appropriate for the development of a modern port. Alexander von Humboldt, however, had observed that it 'afforded a very bad anchorage; and in a rough sea, and with a violent wind, we found some difficulty in reaching the coast in our canoe'.[7] Yet the main obstacle to the commercial use of all these bays was their remoteness, and lack of easy communication with the most populated centres of the country.

It was their proximity to the Magdalena river that offered advantages to Cartagena, Santa Marta, Sabanilla, and Puerto Colombia, although these ports too faced geographical difficulties. The bay of Cartagena was praised for its superior natural harbour, 'protected from the swell of the sea by a series of islands very similarly arranged to those comprising the harbor of New York'.[8] Santa Marta also possessed a deep bay with a good harbour, 'perhaps the safest of the Atlantic ports', 'being easily entered by day or night without the necessity of a pilot'.[9] Both ports, however, had troubled access to the Magdalena river. Since colonial times, Cartagena had been linked to the Magdalena by means of the Canal del Dique, a waterway of 135 km. which fell into neglect after the independence wars, and 'soon became filled up with sediment and overgrown with brush and bramble'.[10] Attempts were made to ameliorate the conditions of the canal and steam navigation was finally introduced, but the Dique continued to be a problematic route. Communications between Cartagena and the Magdalena were improved after 1894, when a railway linked the seaport with the river at Calamar. In turn, communications between Santa Marta and the Magdalena river were also inadequate. The most common route during the nineteenth century was by horse to Pueblo Viejo, and from there by small boats through the various narrow canals that were part of the river delta. Surprisingly, first Sabanilla and later Puerto Colombia, despite their shortcomings as mere open roadsteads, became the main ports for the country's foreign trade. Their advantage lay in their close proximity to the Magdalena and their connection with the river port of Barranquilla, which was strengthened after the completion of a railway

[6] Reclus, *Viaje a la Sierra*, 90; Pérez, 'Jeografía del Magdalena', 15–7.

[7] A. von Humboldt, *Personal Narrative of Travels to the Equinoctial Regions of America* (London, 1853), iii. 207.

[8] New Granada Canal and Steam Navigation Company, *Remarks on the Canal or "Dique" of Cartagena, New Granada and its Navigation by Steam* (New York, 1855), 5.

[9] Petre, *The Republic of Colombia*, 159; and *PP*, 49, XCVIII (1904), 618.

[10] W. Scruggs, *The Colombian and Venezuelan Republics* (Boston, 1905), 30.

in 1871 and a long pier at Puerto Colombia in 1893. However, the lack of a proper harbour in both Sabanilla and Puerto Colombia was an increasing obstacle. Just ten miles distant from the Caribbean, Barranquilla aspired to become both a river- and a seaport but sand bars at the mouth of the Magdalena impeded the entrance of vessels and steamers (see Map 2). In spite of these geographical barriers, there is little doubt of the significance of these river- and seaports for the development of the country. 'It is hardly too much to say' – Petre pointed out in 1906 – 'that Cundinamarca, Tolima, Santander, Boyacá, and Antioquia would be starved into barbarism if once the ports at or near the mouth of the Magdalena were closed against them'.[11]

Sea, rivers, and marshes were not only important as outlets for trade, they also afforded other basic resources. The availability of fresh water was obviously a primary condition for human settlement. Seaports such as Santa Marta and Ríohacha benefited also from being next to small rivers, the Manzanares and the Ranchería. When Gosselman visited Santa Marta in 1825, clear fresh water from the Manzanares was distributed in the streets, in large earthenware jars. The majority of the coastal population drank muddy water from the rivers, canals and lagoons, sometimes 'filtered through a porous sandstone into an earthen vessel, and sometimes drunk in its crude state'.[12] Exceptionally Cartagena, which had no fresh water in its immediate vicinity, had to resort to cisterns and tanks which filled during the rainy seasons. 'As water is scarce in Cartagena', Saffray observed, 'trading in this commodity is a most lucrative business'.[13] Cartagena, however, could bring in fresh water from sources just ten miles distant, as it did when a modern aqueduct was built at the end of the century.

Fish was afforded in plenty by the sea, rivers, and lagoons. 'The river abounds with every species and variety of fish . . . usually found in tropical waters', Scruggs noted during his trip on the Magdalena, in one of the most common observations by foreign travellers to the region.[14] Among fishing activities, diving for oysters in search of pearls was popular, particularly among the Guajiro Indians for whom pearls were a precious commodity.[15] In addition, in some areas, the seashore

[11] Petre, *The Republic of Colombia*, 152.

[12] Scruggs, *The Colombian and Venezuelan Republics*, 34; and Gosselman, *Viaje por Colombia*, 49.

[13] Doctor Saffray, *Viaje a Nueva Granada* (Bogotá, 1948), 34.

[14] Scruggs, *The Colombian and Venezuelan Republics*, 45.

[15] See Pérez, 'Jeografía del Magdalena' 14; J. A. de Barranquilla, *Así es la Guajira. Itinerario de un misionero capuchino* (Bogotá, 1953), 51.

was a rich source of salt, whose collection gave employment to a significant number of people; the salt monopoly was one of the most important revenues of the public treasury.[16]

2. The Lowland Plains

With the exception of the Sierra Nevada de Santa Marta – an isolated massif which rises near the coastline to an elevation of 5,775 metres, where the peaks are perpetually covered with snow[17] – the topography of the region is characterized by what is called 'the Atlantic *llanuras*', a series of lowland plains which 'form a perfect whole, whose component parts are easily linked one to each other'.[18] Nineteenth-century geographers generally classified these lands as *llanuras bajas*, *sabanas*, and *serranías*. Periodically exposed to floods, the *llanuras bajas* refer to the marshy, swampy lands, including the *playones* – which are 'flooded during the rainy season and later, after being sun-dried, are covered by abundant pasture to feed the cattle during the summer'.[19] *Sabanas* were the Coastal prairies, previously forested, flood-free lands. During his journey from Valledupar to the Magdalena river, Dawe passed 'through heavy forest land, which, however, was soon replaced by more open lands with extensive sabanas of fine short grass'.[20] *Sabanas* and *playones* complement each other to afford grazing land for cattle during the distinctive wet and dry seasons typical of the Colombian tropics. These lowlands gradually merge with the *serranías*, the rising hills on the frontiers of the Andes.

To the casual nineteenth-century observer, particularly those who travelled on the Magdalena, these lands appeared as a uniform, thick, impenetrable forest, interspersed with small cultivated patches.

[16] M. T. Dawe, *Account of a Journey down the Magdalena River, through the Magdalena Province and the Peninsula of Goajira* (Bogotá, 1917), 18.

[17] The *Sierra Nevada* remained an unknown territory for the vast majority of the population on the Coast. See Reclus's observations in his *Viaje a la Sierra*, 60. In the 1940s, when the anthropologist Gerardo Reichel-Dolmatoff carried out his field work on the Kogis, the *Sierra* was essentially 'an indigenous territory', scarcely populated and hardly known to its neighbours. G. Reichel-Dolmatoff, *Los Kogi* (Bogotá, 1985), i. 39. For contemporary descriptions of the Sierra, its population, and its resources, see also F. A. Simmons, 'On the Sierra Nevada de Santa Marta and its Watershed', *PRGS*, 1 (London, 1881); and G. Taylor, 'Settlement Zones of the Sierra Nevada de Santa Marta, Colombia', *Geographical Review*, 21 (1931), 539–58.

[18] Reclus, *Colombia*, 314.

[19] Pérez, 'Jeografía del Magdalena', 19.

[20] Dawe, *Account of a Journey*, 29.

However, the vegetation varied with the rainfall throughout the region, from the dry and semi-arid Guajira to the extreme tropical conditions of the Atrato.[21] In the semi-desert of the Guajira, amidst 'scrubby parched vegetation', the divi-divi – useful for tanning – was found in abundance. To a large extent, however, the vegetation in this area consisted 'of cacti and dwarf thorny leguminous trees'. A few miles down to the south-west, approaching the Sierra Nevada, the arid Guajira gave way to 'an impressive scene of tropical luxuriance', where Thomson found wild cacao trees of promising potential for an export industry.[22] Further south, at Ríofrio, he also came across 'admirable' banana plantations where irrigation played an important part due to the low levels of rainfall. Tropical fruits were abundant in this area as in most parts of the country: apart from bananas, pineapples, mangoes, guavas, water-melons, oranges, and the like. 'What a large quantity of delicious fruits', Gosselman had exclaimed after visiting the market at Santa Marta.[23]

From Santa Marta to Barranquilla – and wherever the flooded lowlands prevail, as in the terrain between Cartagena and Comisario – the mangrove tree dominated the vegetation. Away from the coast, towards the south, the countryside had all the appearance of extraordinary fertility: 'there all the plants acquire remarkable proportions, and the constant humidity of the soil naturally produces all the advantages that elsewhere are only obtained through artificial irrigation'.[24] This tropical forest abounded in indigo, rubber, ceiba, cedar, fig, *guayacán*, *caracolí,* among many other species, of which the palm-tree 'bears off the crown of beauty'.[25] Timber and rubber extraction attracted early capitalist ventures in the region. Amadeo Truchon, later French vice-consul in Cartagena, originally settled in the region to exploit Brazil-wood and *bálsamo de Tolú.* Around 1886, Geo D. Emery – an American company with headquarters in Montería – exported more than 3,000 tons of timber annually from the

[21] Rainfall varies significantly within the region. While near Santa Marta annual average precipitation often does not exceed 14 in., in the Cartagena district it is about 26 in., and further south the rainfall increases: more than 40 in. in the Sinú and more than 60 in. in the Cesar. See Bell, *Colombia*, 33.

[22] (*sic*, no Christian name given) Thomson, 'Report on an Excursion to the Sierra Nevada de Santa Marta to Investigate the Cultural Capabilities of the District', *PP*, XC (1893–4), 139–46.

[23] Gosselman, *Viaje por Colombia*, 57.

[24] Striffler, *El río Sinú*, 99.

[25] *RB*, 9 Sept. 1889; Consul L. Schnare, 'Forest Resources on the Cartagena District', Cartagena, 19 Jul. 1926, NAUS/ 821.6171/1–2.

Sinú.[26] Alongside these relatively large-scale operations, independent woodcutters were to be found along the river banks selling logs for fuel to the steamers. The Caribbean lowlands were thus of a varied nature. Wherever conditions were appropriate, and the soil was tilled, the land could afford all those tropical crops observed by Juan and Ulloa during the eighteenth century: cotton, corn, cacao, sugar cane, plantains, tobacco and rice.[27] In addition, coffee was grown on the slopes of the Sierra Nevada, albeit in very small quantities. When the British geographer F. A. Simmons visited the area in the late 1870s, Villanueva, 'an enterprising little town', was thriving from coffee production.[28]

The mining prospects of the region did not appear to be promising. In the 1820s, there was a brief gold rush in Simití when 'large quantities of gold were sent to the market in Mompox'.[29] Five decades later, expectation of El Dorado in Simití had vanished. Gold-diggers had emigrated to Antioquia. Simití took on the aspect of a ghost town.[30] In 1888, after pointing out that in Bolívar not one single mine had been the source of great wealth, the *Secretario de Gobierno* advised against thinking about 'the unknown and unstable', and appealed instead for 'sustainable wealth through the encouragement of agriculture'. Yet in the neighbouring department of Magdalena there were rich veins of copper and coal. In 1865, 'immense coalfields' in the Guajira province had been discovered by an English engineer, John May, raising high expectations. However, they were not commercially exploited until more than a century later.[31]

[26] J. Exbrayat, *Reminiscencias monterianas* (Montería, 1939), 23; L. Striffler, *El Río Cesar*, n. d. (possibly 1881), 11; Fals, *Capitalismo, hacienda y poblamiento*, 51–2.

[27] G. Juan and A. de Ulloa, *Voyage to South America: Describing at Large the Spanish Cities, Towns, Provinces, on that Extensive Continent* (London, 1806), 69–79, 83. For a general description of agricultural conditions in tropical environments, see G. B. Masefield, *A Handbook of Tropical Agriculture* (Oxford, 1970).

[28] F. A. A. Simmons, 'Notes on the Topography of the Sierra Nevada de Santa Marta', *PRGS*, 1 (1879), 711.

[29] J. P. Hamilton, *Viajes por el interior de las provincias de Colombia*, (Bogotá, 1955), 62.

[30] *GB*, 10 Nov. 1874; *Memoria del Secretario de Gobierno* (Cartagena, 1888), 219.

[31] *The Republic of Colombia* (New York, 1896), 96–7; R. de la Pedraja, 'La Guajira en el siglo XIX: indígenas, contrabando y carbón', *Desarrollo y Sociedad*, 6 (June 1981); *PP*, LXI (1868–9), 6.

3. Bountiful Tropics?

'Nature, as a generous mother, everywhere dispenses its magnificent gifts without much labour'. The statement comes from Reclus but similar sentiments were echoed by many an outsider who visited the region, overwhelmed by first impressions of the tropics.[32] 'What luxuriant vegetation! What great fertility!', J. Crevaux exclaimed on passing through Calamar in 1881. 'When nature is so prolific', E. Hopkins observed, 'man is not compelled to till much the ground for his sustenance', and he concluded, 'hence the rich and extensive tracts of land watered by this great river are comparatively neglected'.[33] True, under conditions of low population density and with access to land and water resources in the region, it was possible to pursue a life of basic subsistence without nature posing too many obstacles. To exploit resources successfully on a commercial scale was a different matter. Furthermore, not all tropical conditions were so bountiful, even for the most simple existence.

To start with, a large proportion of the region, as already observed, was exposed to periodic floods – the *crecientes*. 'The Cauca, Sinú and San Jorje river basins,' Pérez noted, 'are rendered completely useless as a consequence of floods'.[34] When Wirt Robinson travelled up the Magdalena in 1892, 'the country was inundated in all directions, and no high land was in sight'.[35] Places such as Magangué, most settlements along the rivers, were at the mercy of floods. In 1862 the *creciente* forced some populations to resettle: San Estanislao was moved to Arenal, San Benito de las Palomas to Repelón, Paloquemado to 'the highlands of one Señor Riquet'.[36] In 1879 floods destroyed plantations in the province of Mompox, 'causing starvation among the poorer classes'.[37] Under permanent threat from the *creciente*, some villages and towns on the rivers developed far away from the banks.[38] In addition, the channels of the rivers were changeable. Mompox, one of the most important trading centres on the Magdalena during the colonial period, was left isolated after the mainstream of the river took

[32] Reclus, *Viaje a la Sierra*, 68.

[33] J. Crevaux, *Voyages dans l'Amérique du Sud* (Paris, 1883), 389, and J. D. Powles, *New Granada: Its Internal Resources* (London, 1866), 7.

[34] Pérez, 'Jeografía de Bolívar', 15.

[35] W. Robinson, *A Flying Trip to the Tropics* (Cambridge, Mass., 1892), 50.

[36] P. M. Revollo, 'Inundaciones del Río Magdalena', *Revista Geográfica*, 2. 1 (Dec. 1952), 31–2.

[37] *DB*, 15 July 1880.

[38] Striffler, *El río Sinú*, 86.

another course in the mid-nineteenth century. Captain Cochrane, who visited Mompox in 1823, described a bustling town engaged in river transport: 'we found men busily employed in constructioning champans for the commerce of the river'. Mompox was also, according to Cochrane, 'the grande *rendez-vous* of the bogas, where numbers on the banks of the river amount to nearly 10,000'.[39] However, in 1852 the Governor of the province warned of the pressing need to build a dam to avoid the river changing its course. The resources for such a project were not at hand and in the late 1860s, despite a few efforts to prevent it, the main river had moved to the *Brazo de Loba*, encouraging the development of Magangué at the expense of Mompox.[40] The vagaries of the Magdalena made navigation difficult and determined recurrent changes in the geography of the region. Frederick Von Schenck had first travelled on the Magdalena in 1878. Two years later, he made another journey when he observed: 'Conditions of navigation have not improved at all since my first journey, but I did find that the river bed had changed, especially after Magangué. Everywhere I saw new *playones* and new islands. On one bank, a large stretch of forest land had disappeared; on the other, immense alluvial deposits appeared.'[41]

The lack of control over water resources – the proliferation of floods, swamps, and marshes – in conditions of high temperature went hand in hand with disease: yellow fever, malaria, gastrointestinal infections, and the like.[42] The 1879 *creciente* in Mompox province caused economic disaster, but what followed was even more destructive: once the river returned to normal level, all sorts of illnesses followed, 'and the poor paid their debt to the land, which claimed the lives of their parents, children and friends'.[43] Permanently exposed to disease, natives might develop resistance. But nationals from the highlands and foreigners commonly feared death. 'The air stinks with plague', Gosselman pointed out during his stay in Cartagena.[44] Surrounded by marshes to the east and north, the insalubrity of Cartagena was typical

[39] Capt. C. S. Cochrane, *Journal of a Residence and Travels in Colombia During the Years 1823 and 1824* (London, 1825), 103–8. See also Gosselman, *Viaje por Colombia*, 109; D. E. Peñas Galindo, *Los bogas de Mompox* (Bogotá, 1988), and Fals Borda, *Mompox y Loba*, 44A–49A.

[40] J. M. Pérez, *Esposición del gobernador de Mompós* (Cartagena, 1853), 7; *Informe del Presidente Constitucional* (Cartagena, 1871), 51.

[41] F. von Schenck, *Viajes por Antioquia en el año de 1880* (Bogotá, 1953), 9.

[42] L. Cuervo Márquez, *Geografía médica y patológica de Colombia* (Bogotá and New York, 1915), 62–4; 90–3; 109–11.

[43] *GB*, 15 Jul. 1880.

[44] Gosselman, *Viaje por Colombia*, 33.

of this sort of environment. In 1897 and 1900, Cartagena suffered from epidemics of yellow fever but, according to the US Consul, it only attacked Colombians from the Andean interior and foreigners.[45] Some of these diseases were transmitted by mosquitoes, among the many insects that were a torment to daily life. 'I would be happy to be cold, soaked to the skin, anything to avoid feeling, hearing or seeing those torturing insects', Reclus noted during his journey on the Ciénaga Grande. Several plantations on the rivers Buritaca and Goachaca, in Northern Magdalena, had been abandoned in 1878 'partly because of the insupportable plague of ticks and flies'.[46]

Other insect pests directly attacked the crops. In 1878, an invasion of locusts made its first appearance in Montería causing the ruin of harvests and scarcity of food. In 1880 the calamity spread to the Magdalena department, where it was reported that 'misery and hunger were obligatory guests'. A year later, when it appeared 'as though the country had been burnt over by a devastating fire', Rosa Carnegie-Williams noticed the locusts 'swarming in all directions over the country'.[47] The destruction was immense. Production of grain was severely curtailed, causing famine. 'Owing to the high price of corn', *The Shipping List* reported in Barranquilla, 'the raising of poultry has almost ceased to exist . . . Eggs, like those in the "magician show", have become "invisible" '.[48] In 1882, the US Consul in Ríohacha reported that judging 'by the damage these insects have done, and still continue to do, a very precarious future awaits the poor of these countries'.[49] While the government freed import restrictions to relieve food shortages, the population was powerless against the plague, resorting to palliative measures used in other tropical regions. Father Revollo recalled how he joined the struggle against the plague during his early years in Ciénaga:

[45] US Consul to Assistant Secretary of State, Cartagena 12 Oct. 1897 and 15 Mar. 1900, NAUS, Despaches from US Consuls in Cartagena, Colombia, microfilm T192/12. 'During the English attack on Cartagena . . . in 1742, the English force spent only two months laying siege to the city, but its losses from disease alone were two-thirds to three-quarters of its more than 12,000 men'; see P. D. Curtin, *Death by Migration: Europe's Encounter with the Tropical World in the Nineteenth Century* (Cambridge, 1989), 2.

[46] Simmons, 'Notes on the Topography of the Sierra', 694.

[47] US Consul to Assistant Secretary of State, Sabanilla, 25 Jul. 1881, NAUS, Despatches from US Consuls in Sabanilla, Microfilm T426/5; and R. Carnegie-Williams, *A Year in the Andes or a Lady's Adventures in Bogotá* (London, 1882), 45–6.

[48] Quoted in *MCR* (Jul–Oct. 1883), 198.

[49] *MCR* (Mar. 1882), 456.

The bells at the church sounded in prayer and warning; people shot into the air to frighten away the wretched little creature; the boys made noises with drums and tin cans. In the town, a large quantity of sacks of locust's eggs were purchased, which were either buried in the ground or thrown into the river: all to no avail, the terrible plague claimed whatever God chose.[50]

The government intervened by attempting to create jobs for those directly affected by the locust, after recognizing that there were no resources available to attack the plague itself.[51] By 1889, the swarms seemed to have migrated elsewhere; but in 1909 they were back. Near Magangué, Hiram Bingham saw 'millions upon millions of these large brown grasshoppers . . . Evidently the country has much to suffer from them yet'.[52] In 1914, locusts were again causing destruction in Bolívar, where only the Alcalde of Sincé was reported to have attempted to eradicate them, although with a primitive system and little success.[53]

Under these tropical conditions, the heat – that *chaleur insupportable* which provoked Crevaux's complaint in August 1881 – was probably a minor problem.[54] Climatic influences on the rhythm of life were witnessed by Robert Cunningham Graham in 1917. 'Even the dogs were sleeping' when he arrived in Palmito at the hottest hour of the day, while, 'the occasional horses, standing saddled under reed-thatched shelters, rested on a hind-foot and were too listless even to switch their tails against the myriads of flies that buzzed them'. It was the sacred siesta, so well described by Tuerto López's poem *Tedio de la parroquia*.[55]

Bountiful tropics? When Luis Striffler first visited the Sinú, during the mid-nineteenth century, he felt enchanted by the exuberant vegetation of the region. Yet while he praised the apparent abundance of nature, he lamented the few efforts made by men to develop its resources. Striffler had come to the Sinú employed by a mining company. Together with some other French colleagues, they felt themselves 'predestined to transform the Sinú'. They settled in Higuerón, where they established their headquarters and soon were

[50] P. M. Revollo, *Memorias* (Barranquilla, 1936), 50. See Masefield, *A Handbook of Tropical Agriculture*, 140–1.

[51] *Mensaje del Presidente constitucional* (Cartagena, 1883), 13.

[52] H. Bingham, *The Journal of an Expedition Across Venezuela and Colombia* (London, 1909), 263, 266.

[53] *Memoria que presenta el Secretario de Gobierno* (Cartagena, 1914), 227, 263, 266.

[54] Crevaux, *Voyages dans l'Amérique*, 381.

[55] R. Cunninghame Graham, *Cartagena and the Banks of the Sinú* (London, 1920), 193–4, and C. E. Colon, *La rebelión poética de Luis Carlos López* (Bogotá, 1981), 83–4.

busily organizing a digging operation with new imported machinery, building houses, and even planning agricultural ventures. Their enthusiasm vanished as they learnt the facts of tropical life. 'Soon the river burst its banks'. Striffler expressed surprise at the sudden changes in climatic conditions. Rains increased in frequency, while 'the river started to bring up a large number of wooden posts and trees, and all of the sudden one could not see the water that roared under that mobile layer'. The 'golden dream' gave way to a nightmare: 'Flying insects, eager for blood, multiplied to such an extent that neither by night nor by day could we rest outside the tent . . . Even worse were the multitude of species that came to bother us . . . horseflies . . . which left on us bloody bites . . . Everything had changed: that Eliseus of the Upper Sinú had turned into a real hell.'[56] Such problems were aggravated when the French engineers found they could not cope with the lack of discipline among the native labour force, and reached their peak when a sudden flood destroyed the machinery. 'The French declared unanimously that the country . . . was unexploitable,' Striffler wrote later with frustration. Soon the camp was abandoned and the French engineers were back in their homeland.

Striffler was exceptional in his obstinacy, for he stayed in the region for another three decades. However, it only required a closer look at living conditions to learn that more often than not life in the Colombian Caribbean entailed 'unremitting and persistent toil'. 'Since I set my foot on the Colombian Coast', Miguel Cané observed, 'I have understood the anomaly of having concentrated national development in the Andean highlands, nine hundreds miles from the sea'.[57]

4. Peoples of the Coast

When, on his arrival in 1514, Pedrarias Dávila, first Governor of Castilla de Oro – a territory covering the Coast from Santa Marta to the Darién – sent an expedition to explore the mainland, the Spanish conquerors encountered 'up to a hundred Indians, who were to meet us with great ferocity . . . with their bows and arrows, and fighting

[56] Striffler, *El Río Sinú*, 117.

[57] M. Cané, *En viaje, 1881–1882* (Paris, 1884), 131–2. For living conditions in the tropics see P. James, *A Geography of Man* (Boston, 1949), 116.

valiantly to show that they would resist us to the end'.[58] Fernández de Oviedo, the chronicler of this encounter, referred to them as *Caribes*, as the natives from this land generally came to be known, a name also linked to the ferocity of the tribes that fought to the death the Spanish invasion. *Caribes* was a misleading name, and not all natives from the Coast died fighting the Spaniards; but Oviedo's account illustrates some of the features that characterized the conquest in this region. Indians such as the Chimilas, Guajiros, and Zenúes, strongly resisted the invaders. Some of these tribes remained in a state of war throughout and even beyond the colonial period; others managed to escape to remote areas, like those who sought refuge in the impenetrable Sierra Nevada. Decimated and dispersed by prolonged warfare, only a few were fully integrated into the new social order. After the first century of Spanish presence, those who had been incorporated into the colonial dominion, through the institutions of *encomienda*, *resguardos*, and *reducciones*, were well on their way towards acculturation.[59]

The establishment of an administrative jurisdiction at Santa Marta was followed by the emergence of a few important Spanish settlements in the region. Spanish colonization moved southwards, following the coastline and the Magdalena river route.[60] However, discouraged by the harsh living conditions, most Spaniards moved to other inland provinces. All the same, among the main colonial centres, Cartagena and Mompox rose to prominence, the former becoming the leading port of the viceroyalty, and one of the largest centres for the slave trade in the Atlantic.[61]

Slaves of African origin supplied labour to the plantations, river

[58] Quoted in G. Reichel-Dolmatoff, *Datos histórico-culturales sobre las tribus de la antigua gobernación de Santa Marta* (Bogotá, 1951), 6.

[59] See Reichel-Dolmatoff, *Datos histórico-culturales*, 3–46; Gordon, *Human Geography and Ecology in the Sinú*, 8–46; Krogzemis, *A Historical Geography*, 6–19; A Julián, *La perla de América: Provincia de Santa Marta* (1787) (Bogotá, 1980), 144–5, 151; Fals Borda, *Capitalismo, hacienda y poblamiento*, 15–18. For the weakness of the *encomienda* during the 17th century, see T. M. Vázquez, *La gobernación de Santa Marta (1570–1670)* (Seville, 1976), 45, 89–107.

[60] Fals Borda, *Capitalismo, hacienda y poblamiento*, 18–22.

[61] See N. del Castillo, *La llave de las Indias* (Bogotá, 1981); E. Lemaitre, *Breve historia de Cartagena* (Bogotá, 1979); J. Palacios Preciado, *La trata de negros por Cartagena de Indias* (Tunja, 1973). For the importance of the *Cartagenero* merchants at the end of the 18th century, see A. McFarlane, 'Comerciantes y monopolio en la Nueva Granada; el consulado de Cartagena de Indias', *ACoHSC* 11 (1983), 43–69. For Mompox, see Fals Borda, *Mompox y Loba.*

navigation, and domestic households.[62] However, shortly after the arrival of the first African slaves, some managed to escape from their masters, settling on the *palenques*, communities of runaways that sprung up on the marshy lands of the southern Coastal provinces.[63] Established *palenques* encouraged further runaways but they also provided the slaves with a bargaining tool: '[They threatened] their masters that they would leave them and settle in the *palenques* if too much was demanded from them'.[64] In several instances, the Spanish authorities had to come to terms with the runaways, granting them official freedom. On other occasions, colonial officers managed to crush the *palenques* and return the blacks to prosecution or to slavery. Undoubtedly, the long history of *palenques*, which has been documented elsewhere, passed through various stages.[65] Suffice it to say here that slavery coexisted with, and was conditioned by, the spread of runaway communities which in the long run were accommodated in colonial society.

Alongside the *palenques* in the southern provinces of the Coast, and away from the main colonial centres, settlements spread outside the control of the authorities. Formed originally by Indians escaping *encomiendas*, black runaways, white fugitives, and adventurers, these communities gradually produced a complex pattern of miscegination. Antonio de la Torre y Miranda led one of the several expeditions organized by the Spanish Crown at the end of the eighteenth century, as part of the Bourbon effort to regain control over the colonial territories of the viceroyalty in the region. By 1794, de la Torre y Miranda had on his own account managed to resettle 41,133 people – who had hitherto lived scattered in the woodlands 'beyond the king and the law' – in forty-three new villages and twenty-two parishes. There de la Torre found a diverse population, among them Indians, 'who mixed with

[62] A. Meisel Roca, 'Esclavitud, mestizaje y hacienda en la provincia de Cartagena, 1533–1851', *Desarrollo y Sociedad*, 4 (July 1980), 242–63. In the late 18th century, most slaves in Cartagena province were urban slaves; see A. McFarlane, 'Cimarrones and Palenques: Runaways and Resistance in Colonial Colombia', in G. Heuman (ed.) *Out of the House of Bondage: Runaways, Resistance and Marronage in Africa and the New World* (London, 1986), 131.

[63] Evidences of *palenques* are dated at least from 1540. See R. Arrázola, *Palenque, primer pueblo libre de América: historia de las sublevaciones de los esclavos de Cartagena* (Cartagena, 1970), 12.

[64] Quoted in Arrázola, *Palenque, primer pueblo libre*, 83.

[65] See Arrázola, *Palenque, primer pueblo libre*; A. Escalante, 'Notas sobre el Palenque de San Basilio', *Divulgaciones Etnológicas*, iii. 5 (1954), 208–31; M. del C. Borrego Pla, *Palenque de negros en Cartagena de Indias a fines del siglo XVII* (Seville, 1973); McFarlane, 'Cimarrones and Palenques', 131–51.

mestizas, blacks and *mulatas*, propagated vast numbers of mixed races very difficult to identify'.[66] Miscegination was not exclusive to these southern provinces and occurred throughout the region, as elsewhere in the viceroyalty, characterized by its early *mestizaje*.[67] Groups of Spanish settlers – usually at the highest level of society in the main colonial centres, and some Indian and Black villages, such as San Basilio de Palenque, remained largely untouched by miscegination. However, the general legacy of the colony was a thoroughly mixed population. By the end of the eighteenth century, it was estimated that more than 60 per cent of the Coastal population was of a mixed race.[68] 'A rapid amalgamation of colour is taking place', a British report observed in 1843, 'and ere long there will scarcely be a family on the coast of pure unmixed blood'.[69]

[66] A. de la Torre y Miranda, 'Noticia individual de las poblaciones nuevamente fundadas en la provincia de Cartagena', in J. P. Urueta (ed.), *Documentos para la historia de Cartagena* (Cartagena, 1894), iv. 43. See similar descriptions in G. Reichel-Dolmatoff (ed.) *Diario de viaje del P. Joseph Palacios de la Vega entre los indios y negros de la Provincia de Cartagena en el Nuevo Reino de Granada, 1787–1788* (Bogotá, 1955), 14, 38–40, and Arrázola, *Palenque, primer pueblo libre*, 98. See also P. Moreno de Angel, *Antonio de la Torre y Miranda: Viajero y poblador* (Bogotá, 1993), and M. Lucena, 'Las nuevas poblaciones de Cartagena de Indias, 1774–1794', *Revista de Indias* (Sept.–Dec., 1993), 761–81.

[67] J. M. Samper, *Ensayo sobre las revoluciones políticas y la condición social de las repúblicas colombianas* (1861) (Bogotá, 1984), 5, 78, 80, 84.

[68] F. Silvestre, *Descripción del Reyno de Santa Fe de Bogotá*, (1789), (Bogotá, 1968), 49–51. According to Silvestre the overall distribution was: Whites (11%), Indians (18%), Slaves (8%), and *Libres* – freemen of all colours (63%). These figures, however, do not include the Guajiros, whose numbers were unknown. They were still unknown well into the 20th century: 'the census in the Guajira is perhaps one of the most complicated and difficult to accomplish in the Republic'; *Informe del Ministro de Gobierno* (Bogotá, 1912), 95. An estimated figure of 40,000 was given by the government in 1925; in *Memoria del Ministro de Gobierno* (Bogotá, 1925), 134.

[69] *PP*, 31, LXIV (1847), 331. 'A native of the banks of the Magdalena . . . is an approximation toward the mestizo – half negro and half Indian, but neither you nor he will ever know the exact proportions in which the blood of three races are mingled in his veins', in Holton, *New Granada*, 69. A detailed study of the ethnic composition of the *Costeño* population, and its historical behaviour during the period, is beyond the scope of this book. The information about race in the censuses is patchy and unreliable. But a look at the 1918 census suggests a very similar picture to that given by Silvestre for the end of the colonial period, with a large majority of the population classified as *mestizo*. Peter Wade, who has emphasized the greater impact of black culture in the Coast, refers to the region as having an 'ambigiuous status' as far as racial identity is concerned. Most approaches to the subject would agree with Wade's assertion that 'the Caribbean Coast developed a tri-ethnic mix with strong black and Indian heritage in the lower classes and some purer black and indian enclaves'. See his *Blackness and Race Mixture* (Baltimore and London, 1993), 58, 79–83.

Population was scant overall. By 1789 there were just over 180,000 inhabitants on the Coast. In 1778 Antonio de Narváez y la Torre had identified the scarcity of population as the main cause of economic stagnation in the Santa Marta province.[70] Attacks by buccaneers and unsubdued Indians had previously motivated migration to other provinces. It was, however, primarily the lack of economic opportunities which forced people to move elsewhere and discouraged new colonial settlements. For one thing, labour was in short supply. The number of tributary Indians was extremely small. Slaves were expensive. Spanish, and Europeans in general, found the climatic conditions unsuitable. And '*mulatos, zambos* and free blacks, *mestizos* and the rest of the common folk of mixed race (who make up most of the population) . . . managed to live easily without working'.[71] It was thus a vicious circle which, according to Narváez y la Torre, could be overcome by supporting an active population policy based on the increase of African slaves. His was a costly suggestion for, as he acknowledged, 'only a few could afford to buy four slaves, and even less the requisite number to establish a sugar-mill'.[72] Narváez y la Torre thought that only the Crown could provide the funds for such a project. Whether or not his plan could have been economically viable remains an open question. Soon the wars of independence and subsequent legislation undermined slavery. Furthermore, as Meisel has shown, it seems that the institution of slavery was in rapid decline at the end of the eighteenth century. Between 1778 and 1825 the number of slaves in Cartagena province fell by half. By 1851, when slavery was finally abolished, there were over 2,200 slaves left in the region, most of them women and old men.[73]

During the first half of the nineteenth century, population growth on the Coast suffered serious setbacks due, in particular, to the independence struggle and an epidemic of cholera. Between 1832 and 1851, Bolívar and Magdalena had the lowest rates of growth, besides having the lowest population density (1.7 inhabitants per sq. km.), among Colombian departments.[74] In the following two decades,

[70] Antonio de Narváez y la Torre, 'Relación o informe de la Provincia de Santa Marta y Ríohacha' (1778), in A. B. Cuervo (ed.), *Colección de documentos inéditos sobre la geografía y la historia de Colombia* (Bogotá, 1892), ii. 175–202.

[71] Ibid. 186–8, 192.

[72] Ibid. 198.

[73] Meisel, 'Esclavitud, mestizaje y haciendas', 261; and M. Urrutia and M. Arrubla (eds.), *Compendio de estadísticas históricas de Colombia* (Bogotá, 1970), 18, table 5.

[74] Urrutia and Arrubla, *Compendio de estadísticas*, 18, table 13.

population growth recovered. By 1871, when the Coastal population was 323,949 representing 11.9 per cent of the national total, there were just over 2.5 inhabitants per sq. km. in the region. Population grew slowly and unevenly throughout the region. Already reduced by the independence wars, Cartagena lost about a third of her population as a consequence of the cholera. In 1871 Cartagena's population was only half that of 1835.[75] Mompox, also a town of colonial prominence, suffered a similar decline, and so did Ciénaga de Oro, San Estanislao and Barranca-Nueva. Other settlements, such as Santa Marta, Ríohacha, and Sabanagrande, tended towards demographic stagnation.[76]

At much the same time, however, the population was growing at a significant rate in Ciénaga, Villanueva, Barranquilla, Carmen, and Sincé. It seems that the changes brought by, first, independence, and later the liberal reforms of the mid-nineteenth century, led to the rise of some provinces at the expense of others, and to a relatively intense internal migration. By 1850, Ciénaga, 'that little town of Indians, blacks and christianized *mestizos*', as described by Antonio Julián in 1789, was already larger than the neighbouring colonial city of Santa Marta.[77] Barranquilla, an insignificant village during the colony, was the largest Coastal town by 1870. In 1869 the governor of Barranquilla blamed the newcomers for the rising crime rate, and a year later he suggested the building of a new prison to tackle the growing social problems, which he related to 'that floating population which flows into the larger cities, some looking for jobs, some to hide or disappear into the crowd, to escape from their responsibilities elsewhere'.[78] More research needs to be done to obtain a better picture of population movements within the region. Suffice it to say here that during the period under study, the coastal population rose from 11.9 per cent of the national total in 1870 to 16.7 per cent in 1950 (see Table P.1).

Without adequate resources, the degree of social control that the state could exercise over a small population, scattered throughout a vast territory, was limited. This was repeatedly acknowledged by

[75] For the cholera in Cartagena, see M. E. Corrales (ed.), *Efemérides y Anales del Estado soberano de Bolívar* (Bogotá, 1892), iv. 24–40.

[76] *Anuario Estadístico de Colombia* (Bogotá, 1875), 30, 31, 39.

[77] Julián, *La perla de América*, 151; *Anuario Estadístico de Colombia* (Bogotá, 1875), 39.

[78] F. Agudelo, *Informe dado por el Gobernador de Barranquilla* (Cartagena, 1869), 20, and *GB*, 28 Aug. 1870.

TABLE P.1 *Coastal Population, 1870–1950*

	1870	1905	1918	1928	1950
Atlántico	50,647	104,674	135,792	242,810	428,429
Bolívar	191,057	300,129	457,110*	642,777	991,458
Magdalena	82,255	123,548	234,047	355,396	509,739
Costa	323,959	528,351	826,950	1,220,983	1,929,629
Colombia	2,707,952	4,533,777	6,303,077	7,851,000	11,548,172

Sources: *Anuario Estadístico de Colombia* (Bogotá, 1875), and censuses for 1905, 1918, 1928 and 1950.

government officials.[79] More often than not, the authorities had no choice but to rule with leniency. 'In this province,' the Governor of Ríohacha observed in 1843, 'especially where there are no men of wealth, and where one could correctly say that everyone is poor, any officer who tries to force people to fulfill their duties would be regarded as a tyrant'.[80]

The attitude of the authorities toward unsubdued natives such as the Guajiros reflected how weak the state was, even during the colonial period. 'It is very important to pacify these Indians', Francisco Silvestre noted in 1789, and he added, 'although it should be done slowly and prudently.' 'I fete them and offer them gifts', de Narváez y la Torre explained, describing his policy of fostering the development of trade in the area, and surely aware of the failures of the military campaign against the Guajiros a decade earlier.[81] In 1843, the Governor of Ríohacha reported the 'active, regular and lucrative trade' established between *Riohachero* merchants and the Guajiros.[82] This peaceful coexistence was often disturbed. In the late 1870s, Simmons described how Colombian officials had been driven out of Soldado, their headquarters burnt, and communications between Ríohacha and the province cut. According to Simmons, those living between Barrancas and Ríohacha were under periodical threat by the Guajiros, 'besides costing the nation thousands a year to keep a train of cowardly, useless officials, who spend most of their time in Ríohacha

[79] *Informe del Presidente del estado soberano del Magdalena* (Santa Marta, 1868), 5.

[80] *Memoria del Gobernador de Ríohacha* (Ríohacha, 1843), 5.

[81] Silvestre, *Descripción del Reyno*, 51; Narváez y de la Torre, 'Relación', 189. See also A. Kuethe, 'La campaña pacificadora en la frontera de Ríohacha, 1772–1779', *Huellas* (Apr. 1987), 9–17.

[82] *Memoria del Gobernador de Ríohacha*, 6–7.

annoying their more industrious neighbours'.[83] Despite their recurrent uprisings, the Guajiros kept in contact with merchants in Ríohacha, actively trading in pearls, hides, divi-divi, alcohol, and guns.

Whether one looks at the Guajiros or at the proliferation of *palenques* and free communities in the southern provinces of the region during the colonial period, what emerges is a picture of a weak state attempting to accommodate itself to a hostile environment, under conditions of scarcity. There developed a tradition of resistance to the authorities, encouraged by distance and difficult communications, which persisted long after independence. In sections of the lower Magdalena valley, as von Schenck had observed in 1880, 'the authority of judges and town-mayors is almost non-existent; they are appointed to meet a formality'.[84]

The weak presence of the state usually went hand in hand with a weak church. At the end of the eighteenth century, Father Joseph Palacios de la Vega had witnessed the feebleness of the Catholic church throughout a large part of the region where, despite his catechizing efforts, few significant inroads were made. A century later, von Schenck observed: 'Only a few traces of catholicism, and not very clear ones, remain in the conscience of these people. In the central part of the Magdalena there are still some little half-ruined churches from the time of the Spaniards, but they are rarely visited by a priest.'[85] The lack of influence of the church was reflected in many facets of social life, from family organization to politics. Free unions were more common than marriages. Native-born priests were rare. Tolerance was preferred to religious fanaticism. The idea of another life was often absent: 'men have the feeling that nothing will be left of them when they die, and therefore they do not have to worry about their reputation; eager to live, to enjoy life; the present is their only concern'.[86]

Thus Coastal society by the mid-nineteenth century could be characterized by the loose nature of its social institutions, a pattern already established during the colonial period which was further deepened in the republic. Loose official control over semi-isolated settlements did not make life easier for those living in primitive conditions; but it did produce distinct social relations. Those coming

[83] Simmons, 'The Sierra Nevada de Santa Marta', 715. In the mid-1920s the Guajiros were again in rebellion, causing widespread concern; *El Tiempo*, 21 Dec. 1925; I. Torres Giraldo, *Los inconformes* (Bogotá, 1973), iv. 36; *Memoria del Ministro de Gobierno* (Bogotá, 1925), 134.

[84] von Schenck, *Viajes por Antioquia*, 12.

[85] Ibid. 12.

[86] Striffler, *El río San Jorge*, 80.

from the Andean interior were quick to notice a contrasting regional behaviour: 'People from these lands,' Felipe Pérez pointed out during his trip on the Magdalena, 'far from possessing the courtesy, much less the gentleness, of those from the centre and north of the republic, behave on the contrary with the insolence of insurgent races'.[87] According to the American Minister, William Scruggs, people from the lowlands were 'ready to assert [their] fancied equality upon all possible occasions'.[88] Labour relations were usually conditioned by what Pérez labelled as 'insolence', or what the American Minister despised as 'fancied equality'. In the 1870s, Striffler visited a plant at Cartagena, where a Frenchman was employed as carpenter. The advantages in employing a Frenchman instead of a native were clear to Striffler: 'he knew how to respect his superiors, something unheard of among the creoles on the Coast, for whom familiarity has wiped out any vestige of social distinction'.[89]

Under these circumstances, the few haciendas established with any success near the main urban centres were far from sharing the dominant features that the literature usually ascribes to them.[90] Slavery was not replaced here by the 'feudal' hacienda. What was striking for those who visited the region in the mid-nineteenth century was the lack of control that any *hacendado* possessed over a scant and dispersed labour population. The writer Anthony Trollope, who did not hide his contempt for 'the boom of Utopian freedom' during his brief stay on the Coast in 1859, visited an estate near Santa Marta. 'Since the emancipation in 1851', Trollope pointed out, 'it had become impossible to procure labour; men could not be got to work; and so bush had grown up, and the earth gave none of her increase'.[91] In the 1870s, Striffler visited Southern Magdalena, and his account also left little doubts as to how loose social relations were, due both to the scarce population and to general poverty: 'the *hacendados* do not now have

[87] F. Pérez, *Episodios de un viaje* (1864/5) (Bogotá, 1946), 32.

[88] *MCR* (Jan.–May 1883), 536. See similar observations in *PP,* LXXIV (1874), 367.

[89] Striffler, *El río Sinú*, 121.

[90] For the significance of free-wage labour and small independent farmers on the Coast during the colonial period, see O. Fals Borda, 'Influencia del vecindario pobre colonial en las relaciones de producción de la Costa Atlántica colombiana', *El agro en el desarrollo histórico colombiano* (Bogotá, 1977). Meisel has supported the hypothesis of a 'feudalization' of haciendas during the 19th century, but without empirical evidence; Meisel, 'Esclavitud, mestizaje y haciendas', 275–7. For a critical and suggestive view, see G. Colmenares, 'El tránsito a sociedades campesinas de dos sociedades esclavistas en la Nueva Granada. Cartagena y Popayán, 1780–1850', *Huellas,* 29 Aug. 1990), 8–24.

[91] A. Trollope, *The West Indies and the Spanish Main*, (London, 1859), 243, 246.

slaves to take care of their estates; the *capataces* – foremen – today are free to do whatever they wish; men are very scarce since the country is poorly populated'.[92] Scarcity of labour, among other factors, loomed large in the development of agriculture, the focus of the following chapter.

[92] Striffler, *El rio Cesar,* 10.

1
Agriculture

1. Introduction

In 1869 the Governor of Barranquilla observed that, given the scarcity of labour and the limited knowledge of farming methods, developing agriculture in the province was a most difficult task.[1] Concern about the slow pace of agricultural growth was widespread among local officials, who regarded underpopulation and backward technology together with poor means of transport as the main obstacles to improved farming. In addition, adverse physical conditions discouraged agriculture.

Scarcity of labour was an acute problem, particularly when efforts were made to develop agriculture on any large scale. Labour was expensive. Proposals to encourage immigration – such as the one suggested by F. J. Balmaseda, President of the Central Board of Agriculture in Bolívar, in 1879 – were frequent and as frequently they failed.[2] Attention was also paid to technological problems, but fallow systems prevailed up to 1950, despite efforts to implement annual croppings. It was believed that with education it would be possible to abolish the *cultivos errantes* – slash-and-burn agriculture. In 1871 a *Sociedad de Agricultura* was active in Cartagena, and in 1879 Agricultural Boards were already established in 26 municipalities by the Bolívar government, while a specialized library in farming methods was organized. An official agricultural journal, the *Gaceta Agrícola*, was published in Cartagena between 1879 and 1882. Together with *El Agricultor* of Ciénaga, and the *Escuela Agrícola de Cundinamarca* of Bogotá, these were the only specialized agricultural journals published in Colombia during the second half of the nineteenth century.[3] In 1879, evening farming schools were opened in various towns. An urgent appeal for trained personnel was made by Balmaseda

[1] F. Agudelo, *Informe dado por el Gobernador de Barranquilla* (Cartagena, 1869), 19.

[2] *Informe de Francisco Javier Balmaseda, Presidente de la Junta Central de Agricultura* (Cartagena, 1879), 9.

[3] J. A. Bejarano, 'La historia de las ciencias agropecuarias hasta 1950', *Ensayos de historia agraria colombiana* (Bogotá, 1987), 145–6; 'Decreto que reglamenta la Junta de Agricultura i Fomento del distrito de Santo Tomás', Santo Tomás, 31 Dec. 1878, AGB, 1878–9.

to the Legislative Assembly: 'In this State we have neither agronomists or veterinaries, nor do we have mechanics nor engineers who could build our bridges and roads; pity us, we have only politicians and *literati*'.[4]

Few improvements were accomplished during the nineteenth century, in spite of the above efforts. Measures adopted by the Council in Carmen forbidding the burning of land were ignored, as were the ploughs distributed by the Central Board of Agriculture. As long as land was available in plenty, the cultivator preferred the fallow system: burning the land before planting and moving to another plot after one or two harvests. Communal forms of landholding, the existence of *baldíos* (public land), and the confusion over land ownership were identified as the causes of *cultivo errante* by Balmaseda.

With the exception of a few plantations, agriculture during the nineteenth century was thus developed in smallholdings, as in 1870, when good agricultural prospects had encouraged the cultivation of rice, maize, cacao, sugar cane, plantains, and even coffee in the Cartagena province. According to the Governor, returns were not higher due to transport difficulties.[5] Cultivation of the land took place near the rivers for preference, to ensure access to market when weather conditions made this possible. Official concern was focused on the dredging of canals, although the construction of railways raised significant expectations at the end of the century and a few efforts were made to clear primitive roads. In 1879, the demands from most of the Agricultural Boards were for the improvement of communications: from Carmen, a better road to María la Baja; from Ciénaga de Oro, the dredging of *Caño de Martínez*; from Sincelejo, a railway to Tolú; from Santa Rosa and Santa Catalina, a road to Cartagena.[6]

In addition, adverse climatic conditions, floods and plagues discouraged cultivation at different times and places. Periodical invasions of locusts devastated the crops. Without an appropriate infrastructure, farmers were at the mercy of nature, depending entirely on the regularity of dry and rainy seasons. As a consequence of a drought in Barranquilla province in 1870, grain and other food became 'unbearably expensive'. Weather conditions, however, were localized phenomena. While the drought affected plantations in Barranquilla province, a generous rainy season encouraged crops in Cartagena.

4 *Informe de Balmaseda*, 3–5.

5 *GB* , 8 Aug. and 4 Sept. 1870, 15 Aug. 1873, and 10 Nov. 1874.

6 *Informe de Balmaseda*, 10–13.

During heavy rains, floods became a serious threat, not only to agriculture but to human life as well: destruction of crops and the spread of diseases also meant hunger and migration. Floods in areas such as the Sinú were perceived as permanent obstacles to agriculture.[7] Under these circumstances, the development of agriculture faced serious obstacles, exacerbated always by the lack of sufficient financial resources. Canalization of waterways, drainage and irrigation projects, immigration programmes, improvement of roads and railways: they all required significant amounts of capital that were often beyond the region's capabilities.

This chapter sets out to analyse the circumstances under which *Costeño* agriculture developed by looking individually into the history of various crops: rice, tobacco, cocoa, sugar, bananas, and cotton. In each case, attention will be paid to their different means of cultivation, their changes in location over the period, their responses to market conditions, their impact on the regional economy and, in general, to the factors that either encouraged or constrained their development. A concluding section takes issue with the prevailing view in the literature that tends to ascribe the lack of Colombian agricultural development to the existence of a backward social structure. It will be argued that the development of farming in the Coast faced other more significant problems, such as those already outlined. Moreover, in spite of the many obstacles, the state of *Costeño* agriculture was far from being stagnant. Before turning to an analysis of the individual commodities, it may be useful to take a glance at the eating habits of the region.

2. The Regional Diet

Travellers' descriptions of the eating habits in the region vary according to time and place, but they rarely fail to mention plantains, rice, yucca, cheese, beef, and fish as the food staples in the Coast, while often admiring the choice of tropical fruits available.[8] A soup made out of a mixture of vegetables and meat was a common dish among the popular classes: 'Le *sancocho* . . . le bas de l'alimentation', as H. Candelier learnt after his first encounter with *Costeño* cooking in

[7] *GB*, 8 Aug. and 4 Sept. 1870, 15 Aug. 1873 and 10 Nov. 1874.

[8] See e.g. C. V. R. Bonney (ed.), *A Legacy of Historical Gleanings* (Albany, N.Y., 1875), 448; Carnegie-Williams, *A Year in the Andes*, 38; A. J. Duffield, *Recollections of Travels Abroad* (London, 1889), 46.

the 1880s.[9] For Candelier, it was not an appetizing meal: 'Le bouillon était un peau d'eau chaude jaunie, sans goût, et le bœuf, découpé en petits morceaux composé d'os pour la majeure partie, était entouré des légumes, bananes, yucca, que je voyais pour la première fois'. He was not much impressed either by what followed: 'Puis, ce fût des œufs frits baignant dans la graisse, de la viande effilochée avec les doigts, une assiette énorme de riz.' 'Quelle horrible cuisine', was the judgement of another Frenchman, J. Crevaux, in 1881. According to G. Bolinder, 'the food was uninviting, even in the homes of those fairly well-off', when he visited Valledupar at the beginning of the twentieth century.[10] It does not seem that patterns of food consumption changed much over the years. True, in the main ports, in closer contact with foreign influences, there developed a slightly more sophisticated demand for imported foodstuffs. Rafael Núñez had always at his disposal, indeed next to his desk, English biscuits and jam and Dutch cheese. However, his regular meals followed the common diet: for lunch he had soup, fish, and *bocadillo de Vélez* – a local dessert. His supper differed only slightly.[11] Núñez's was an austere diet and others preferred beef rather than fish. Nevertheless, both were local products, as it was the case with most food consumed in the region. Imports of wheat for the production of flour, together with other grains during periods of shortages, were significant exceptions.

Information about nutrition levels according to social strata is practically non-existent, but doubtless there were wide differences. In 1922 the *administrador* of Marta Magdalena – a large cattle estate in Southern Bolívar – considered that the ration given to labourers 'was hardly sufficient to keep them alive and healthy, particularly when considering weather conditions and the fact that about 60 per cent of labourers have to share their rations with their families'.[12] Yet the accounts of most observers painted a different picture of life in the countryside, a more plentiful one, where people survived easily 'subsisting upon fish and the fruits which grow everywhere in wonderful profusion'.[13] It was the availability of food, under circumstances of low population density and relatively easy access to

[9] H. Candelier, *Río–Hacha et les Indiens Goejires* (Paris, 1983), 23.

[10] Crevaux, *Voyages dans l'Amérique du Sud*, 382; and G. Bolinder, *We Dared the Andes* (London, 1958), 22, 93.

[11] D. Lemaitre, *Soledad Román de Núñez: Recuerdos* (Cartagena, 1938), 100.

[12] Administrator to Manager, Marta Magdalena, 2 Sept. 1922, ASAS/C/123:44, and ASAS/C/83:12.

[13] W. E. Curtis, *The Capitals of Spanish America* (New York, 1888), 236.

water and land resources, which endured well into the twentieth century, that was often identified as the main reason for the limited supply of labour. As an American Consul reported in 1883, 'laborers . . . may abandon you at any moment, as there is plenty of fish in the river and plantains on the trees'.[14] Demographic pressures, land enclosures, and the development of urban centres gradually undermined the conditions for any sort of simple subsistence. None the less, even up to the 1920s employers in Bolívar complained about the persistently high labour turnover.[15]

All in all, there is little doubt that beef, plantains, and fish were widely available, and in general, relatively cheap.[16] In certain rural areas, fishing was a seasonal and complementary activity to agriculture. In towns like San Antonio, where 'in front of all the houses there [were] *bocachicos*, *bagres* and *sábalos* being dried by the sun', the only occupation for the inhabitants was fishing. In Jegua, there were a few banana plantations, but of little importance, 'its population being largely involved in fishing, after providing for their own needs, they would exchange the surplus for plantains and manioca – their daily bread'.[17] In the mid-nineteenth century, as a consequence of floods, mosquitoes, and disease, a group of seasonal fishermen decided to move to the middle of Ciénaga Grande to establish the fishing villages of Nueva Venecia, Buenavista, and Trojas de Cataca.[18] Villages like these, which derived their livelihood from fishing alone, were indeed exceptional. None the less, on both the Caribbean Coast and the rivers, considerable numbers of the population were engaged in fishing, at least during part of the year. As M. T. Dawe observed in 1916, 'the principal industry along the Cesar river, particularly along the lower part is fishing . . . and fishing affords a livelihood to a large number of people in this region'.[19] If fish was to be had, hard times became more bearable. The Prefect of Mompox visited Simití in 1874, already a ghost town after the decline of gold-mining, where during his stay all food supplies but fish were acutely scarce: 'during the eleven days I spent there, not a calf or a pig was slaughtered; people lived on insipid

[14] *MCR* (July–Oct., 1883), 687.

[15] L. Schnare, 'The Labor Situation in the Cartagena Consular District', Cartagena, 20 Aug. 1926, NAUS/ 821.504/19.

[16] See a brief analysis of beef consumption patterns in the following chapter. For plantains, see respective section on bananas in this chapter.

[17] Striffler, *El río San Jorge*, 25, 40, 27.

[18] Krogzemis, 'A Historical Geography', 96–102.

[19] Dawe, *Account of a Journey*, 31.

fish from the swamps. There were no plantains, no *yuca*, no *ñame* . . . Corn was available but at a very high price'.[20]

During two particular seasons, the *subienda* and the *veranillo de San Juan*, fish were abundant, offering opportunities to the fishermen to make a bit of money and providing a cheap staple for the consumer. Fish was generally dried in the sun, and then taken to market. When Reclus arrived at Pueblo Viejo, 'it was market day: blacks and Indians came in and out of the huts offering their catch and shouting at the top of their voices'.[21] Fishing was carried out in a primitive way, using traditional nets although at times dynamite was used in offshore fishing. There is little evidence of attempts to organize and modernize the fishing industry. In 1936, a co-operative of fishermen was formed at El Banco with the purpose of marketing the catches of its members and making loans. Fishermen from the region joined the co-operative which marketed their products in Santander del Sur, Antioquia, Magdalena, Santander del Norte, and Bolívar. A more ambitious project was launched in Cartagena in 1947: with the participation of Swedish capital, the company *Icopesca* was founded to fish on a large commercial scale.[22]

If there was one significant exception to a picture of self-sufficiency in food in the region, that was the production of grains, rice and corn, particularly the former. However, it seems that cultivators in Bolívar attempted to extend their rice production during the 1870s. In view of its widespread cultivation, the American Consul in Cartagena considered that there were good prospects for the import of rice machinery, such as separators, cleaners, and polishers. A small amount of rice was even exported.[23] This expansion was curtailed by the locust invasion, which recurrently destroyed the crops. In 1883 *The Shipping List* reported how 'the corn and rice fields have not yet recuperated from the devastation, and thousands of people are in absolute poverty'.[24] 'These insects' – the American Vice-Consul in Ríohacha observed – 'destroy all hopes of raising grain' . . . if we judge by the damage these insects have done, and still continue to do, a very

[20] *GB*, 10 Nov. 1874.

[21] E. Reclus, *Mis exploraciones en América* (Valencia, 1910), 69.

[22] US report, Bogotá, 19 Nov. 1937, NAUS/ RG151, Colombia, 304, fish; IET, 1st, 2nd and 3rd Trimester 1949; and Bank of London and South America, *Fortnightly Review*, 15 (6 May 1950), 89.

[23] E. W. P. Smith, 'American Trade in the United States of Colombia', *MCR*, (1880–1), 95.

[24] *MCR* (July–Oct. 1883), 198.

precarious future awaits the poor of these countries'.[25] Even the better-off suffered. On 29 April 1883, Doña Manuela de Burgos begged her uncle to send a bag of rice to her at the Hacienda Berástegui: '. . . There are days here when we cannot eat rice because it is not available. I do not know how to be poor and I cannot survive without this staple'.[26]

To tackle the problem of scarcity during the years of acute hardship of the 1880s, the government allowed free entry of food supplies. Rice from Rangoon, imported through British firms, initially provided for the needs of the population.[27] From being self-sufficient, the region had become a net importer of rice. Although domestic production did not cease altogether, it took a long time before rice cultivation could again catch up with the internal demand. Initially discouraged by the effects of the plague and later by its frequent recurrence, many farmers stopped cultivating grain. Some even shifted away from agriculture. However, some persisted. The need to import rice was a cause of frustration: 'shame on us for importing rice from India', the *Secretario de Gobierno* from Bolívar lamented in 1888.[28] More than 33,000 bags of rice were imported through Barranquilla in 1899/1900, although a significant proportion of these imports was to supply the markets of the Andean interior.[29] In 1913, when more than 15,000 tons of rice were imported through Cartagena, D. Martínez Camargo was encouraging local farmers to grow rice in the Sinú Valley. With the outbreak of the war, production on the Coast increased while imports fell to 8,600 tons in 1916 and to 4,000 by 1917. A reduction in prices after the war discouraged production, so imports rose again to 13,000 tons in 1920.[30] Between 1929 and 1933, as a consequence of both the World Depression and government policies, the acreage of rice planted in Colombia more than doubled. In 1937/8, when 116,000 acres of rice were planted, more than 40 per cent of national production came from Coastal departments. Production had grown steadily to substitute imports, even leaving some surpluses for exports.[31] However,

[25] *MCR* (1882), 456.

[26] Quoted in R. Burgos Puche, *El General Burgos* (Bogotá, 1965), 86.

[27] *MCR* (Jan.–May, 1883), 166.

[28] *Memoria del Secretario de Gobierno* (Cartagena, 1888), 218.

[29] *PP*, 45, LXXXI (1901), 587.

[30] *RNA* (Dec. 1913), 202–7.

[31] See US Tariff Commission, *Agricultural, Pastoral and Forest Industries in Colombia* (Washington, 1945), 25; *Boletín de la Unión Americana* (Jan. 1934), 36; Oakley, 'Rice Production', Cartagena, 4 Jan. 1944, NAUS/ RG166: NAR, Colombia, box 180; L. A. Scopes, *Economic and Commercial Conditions in Colombia* (London, 1950), 31.

production was by then increasing more rapidly in other areas of Colombia, as shown in Table 1.1.

TABLE 1.1 *Rice Production in Coastal departments, 1931–1946 (tons)*

Year	Atlántico	Bolívar	Magdalena	Total Coast	Total Col.
1931	91	21,230	1,014	22,335	40,157
1932	54	21,197	1,197	22,935	51,340
1934	595	22,313	2,572	25,480	54,852
1937/8	255	34,795	1,685	36,735	77,005
1939/40	255	34,795	1,685	36,735	77,005
1942	425	32,950	2,200	35,575	87,518
1946		25,332	1,103		118,211

Sources: 'Rice Production in Colombia', NASU/ R6151: Bureau of Foreign and Domestic Commerce, Colombia, 1934, file 128X; and NAUS / RG166, NAR, Colombia, entry 5.

The bulk of the harvest in the region came from Bolívar – the single largest producer among Colombian departments, where at least 20 per cent of the land was 'ideally suited for rice growing'.[32] Traditional rice-growing areas such as Majagual and San Onofre remained the leading producers in 1936; but by 1944, when more than 50,000 acres of rice were planted in Bolívar, half the harvest was produced in the Sinú Valley, despite damage caused by the changes in the course of the Sinú river. Rice then ranked second in importance in Bolívar to the cattle industry, although weather conditions and poor transport were still identified as barriers to its development.[33]

Rice was also grown in considerable quantities in Magdalena but up to the 1930s significant imports from the Far East supplied the internal demand. With the decline of banana production in the 1940s, some cultivators shifted to rice but it was not until the 1950s that suitable areas of that department became important sources of production.[34] By 1942, Barranquilla was 'the center of the rice trade in the country'.[35]

[32] K. Oakley, 'Annual Economic Report', Cartagena, 19 Nov. 1942, NAUS/ RG166, NAR, Box 174.

[33] Oakley, 'Rice Production', and IET, 4th Trimester, 1946, and 1st Trimester, 1950.

[34] G. Castañeda Aragón, *El Magdalena de hoy* (Santa Marta, 1927), 107; J. Bonivento, *Aspectos socio-económicos del departamento del Magdalena* (Bogotá, 1963), 156.

[35] Wylie, *The Agriculture of Colombia*, 87.

Merchants from Barranquilla were actively involved in rice imports, although as opportunities presented themselves they also became interested in its production. In 1919, some rice importers asked the *Cámara de Comercio* in Barranquilla to support a petition to the central government, for the lowering of tariffs. The Chamber of Commerce refused to endorse the petition, arguing that 'it is a well-known fact that there are currently many rice plantations. Quite a few people have devoted time and capital to this industry'.[36]

By and large, however, rice was produced by cultivators on small plots – squatters in *baldíos*, sharecroppers, and farm owners – using primitive techniques: thrashing out the grain 'by a process that has been in use for two hundred years'.[37] In the 1940s, mechanization, artificial irrigation and the use of fertilizers was just beginning. The means of cultivation clearly varied from province to province. In San Onofre, for instance, where cultivators had tenancy arrangements with landowners, the land was 'cleared by the use of *machetes* . . . the crop was harvested by hand and carried by *burro* to the nearer rice mill at Berrugas'. In 1944, it was estimated that the cultivator himself consumed one-third of his crop, sold another third to a private mill, and the remainder in the local market. Sometimes it was stipulated that the landowner would receive part of the yield at current prices. After the harvest, the cultivator usually left the land planted with grass before moving to another plot.[38] Including San Onofre, there were 5,575 cultivators growing rice in 22,420 acres in Achí, Magangué, Majagual and Sucre in 1944. In these five municipalities, it was reported that 42 per cent of the land planted with rice was owned by the cultivators, 33.5 per cent was farmed by share-croppers, and 24.5 per cent was state-owned. It seems that rising prices had motivated cultivators, although in 1946 the *Informe Económico Trimestral* pointed out that 'the benefits do not reach the producer but are diluted among the middlemen', while the recently founded *Instituto Nacional de Agricultura* attempted to protect the farmers.[39]

36 *RCCB* (31 Aug. 1919), 8–11.

37 Smith, 'American Trade', 95.

38 Cartagena, 16 Oct. 1944, NAUS/ RG166: NAR, Colombia, box 180.

39 Oakley, 'Rice Production'; IET, 4th Trimester, 1946, and 2nd Trimester, 1949, and A. Machado, *Políticas agrarias en Colombia, 1900–1960* (Bogotá, 1986), 87.

3. Tobacco After the Export Boom

In 1857, when sales of tobacco from Ambalema – the richest producing region in the country – reached their peak in Bremen, tobacco exports from Carmen accounted for just one-fifth of the total national trade. Known generally as Carmen de Bolívar, after the main district of production, this tobacco was extensively cultivated in several areas of the Coast. By 1862, Carmen exports almost equalled those of Ambalema; and in 1863 Carmen tobacco took the lead in Colombian tobacco exports.[40] As shown in Table 1.2, while tobacco from Ambalema was in decline, production of Carmen went up from 33,000 *serons*[41] in 1865 to 70,000 *serons* in 1869. By 1888, Bolívar was producing more tobacco than the rest of the country together.[42]

In Magdalena, Reclus observed how a group of Italian immigrants, hired by Joaquín de Mier, had soon left his employ to grow tobacco independently near Ciénaga, where its cultivation was already on the increase.[43] Since the mid-1850s its cultivation in this area had expanded. In 1875, tobacco was said to be the only export article cultivated to any extent within the Santa Marta district. By then, however, tobacco exports from Santa Marta had rapidly declined. Although efforts were made to encourage tobacco cultivation 'under the direction of experienced hands from the island of Cuba', they proved unsuccessful.[44]

While in Magdalena, cultivation of tobacco for export was practically abandoned in the late 1870s in favour of other crops, sugar, cacao, and later bananas, in Bolívar tobacco remained an important commodity. Production for export flourished until the mid-1870s. After 1876, tobacco exports lost their significance in the country's overall balance of trade, but production in Bolívar continued to reach the world market while also responding to a growing internal demand. During the *Guerra de los Mil Días*, at the turn of the century, tobacco was the

[40] J. A. Ocampo, *Colombia y la economía mundial, 1830–1910* (Bogotá, 1984), 234, 239, 240; Tobacco was a government monopoly up to 1850. See J. P. Harrison, 'The Colombian Tobacco Industry, from Government Monopoly to Free Trade, 1778–1876' (Ph.D. thesis, unpublished, University of California, 1951).

[41] Bags of tobacco; weight fluctuated but averaged 59 kg.

[42] *PP*, 36, C (1888), 638.

[43] Reclus, *Viaje a la Sierra,* 70.

[44] *PP*, 35, LXXVI (1875), 371, and 27, LXV (1873), 54.

'only product still cultivated', according to P. E. Franco, a combatant who spent a few days in the producing district of Ovejas.[45]

Both as an export commodity and as an article of internal trade, tobacco played a significant role in the regional economy during the second half of the nineteenth century. In the main districts where it was produced, tobacco meant cash for the cultivators and commercial

TABLE 1.2 *Production of Colombian Tobacco, 1865–1896 (serons)*

Year	Ambalema	Girón	Palmira	Carmen	Total
1865	27,000	7,500	2,500	33,500	70,000
1866	34,000	7,000	4,000	43,000	89,000
1867	21,500	3,500	2,000	60,000	87,000
1868	35,000	5,500	6,500	47,000	94,000
1869	16,000	6,500	7,500	70,000	100,000

Sources: *PP*, 29, LXV (1871), 213.

movement for local merchants. Any fall in prices severely hit local economies, as in 1871 when trade diminished, 'as planters today cannot afford any luxury items, or even provide for their basic needs'.[46] Provinces such as Carmen and Magangué almost doubled their populations between 1850 and 1870. The town of Carmen itself experienced one of the highest rates of growth on the Coast during this period. In 1871, Carmen had more income-tax payers than Barranquilla, although *Barranquilleros* were paying twice as much tax.[47] During these successful years, business prospects were so attractive that the Governor of the Province was in difficulties to appoint the directors of the few provincial schools. Carmen officials felt that the province was contributing so much to the finances of Bolívar as to demand fiscal decentralization. However, after the boom years, the rhythm of growth in Carmen slowed down. Production continued but was forced to adapt to declining prices while being exposed to abrupt fluctuations in the market. Development stagnated. A project to build a railway to link Carmen with a port in the Magdalena river, which temporarily revived hopes among tobacco

[45] *Memoria del Secretario de Gobierno* (Cartagena, 1888), 213, 217, and P. E. Franco, *Mis andanzas en la guerra de los mil días* (Barranquilla, 1964), 90.

[46] *GB*, 13, 20 Aug. 1871.

[47] *Anuario Estadístico de Colombia* (Bogotá, 1875), 31, 32; *GB*, Jan. 1871.

producers, never came to anything. None the less, while it was booming the tobacco trade integrated a wider market bringing together cultivators and merchants from several Coastal districts and even from the interior, involving thus a greater degree of circulation of money. The leaf was originally bought in the producing areas by traders who advanced cash to the cultivator, in general small-holders.[48] It was then sold in the Magangué fairs. Tobacco was brought to the fairs by merchants of whom J. Delgado and E. Mathieu of Magangué, P. Blanco of Mompox, and P. Vengochea of Barranquilla were examples: they sold in the fair to the main exporting houses of Cartagena, Barranquilla, and Santa Marta. Exporters of tobacco were among the top income-tax payers in Cartagena in 1871; although there were also exporters with lesser incomes.[49] By 1873, however, the bulk of tobacco – a total of 4,938,261 kg. – was exported from Barranquilla, while only 413,600 kg. were shipped from Cartagena. Barranquilla, by then, thanks largely to the tobacco trade, had consolidated itself as the leading port of Colombia. Its position by the Magdalena river had helped to strengthen its commercial links with trading and production centres such as Magangué and Carmen.

During the first half of the twentieth century, Carmen tobacco continued to find its way onto the international market. Exports from 1900 to 1917 averaged approximately 3,900,000 kg. a year. Considerable demand from Europe, particularly from Germany and the Netherlands but also from France, had given exports an impetus. Exports to Europe came to a standstill during the First World War, and though resumed after the conflict was over never regained the intensity of the pre-war period. Between 1931 and 1937 tobacco exports averaged approximately 1,400,000 kg., and in 1938 reached 5,017,042 kg. According to Harrison, the collapse of tobacco from the East Indian colonial economy in 1946 gave an unusual advantage to the tobacco from the Coast and in 1949 some 4,000,000 kg. of Carmen tobacco were exported.[50]

[48] Harrison has pointed out how this marked an important difference between Carmen tobacco and the other areas in Colombia, where the relationship was established between the planter and the landlord. See Harrison, 'The Colombian Tobacco', 249. See also *PP*, 49, XCV (1898), 18. In Mompox province, tobacco was produced in *baldío* land; see *DB*, 15 July 1880.

[49] *GB*, 1 Jan. and 5 Mar. 1871, and 18 July 1873.

[50] Oakley, 'Economic Survey of Cartagena', and Harrison, 'The Colombian Tobacco', 231.

Two developments lent additional significance to tobacco during the twentieth century: its relevance to public finance in the *Departamentos* and the growing internal demand. In 1909, Congress allowed the *Departamentos* to charge a tax on tobacco consumption. Although according to the law taxation was not to be imposed either on cultivation or on exports, its effect was to create governmental control over the production and trade of the leaf. Local governments counted the tobacco plants and distributed scales among the excise control-posts established in the several producing districts. Internal barriers were erected and taxes levied if tobacco was taken from one *Departamento* to another.[51] In the traditional state of penury of local finances, the *Renta del Tabaco* became one of the most important sources of departmental income: in 1916, the *Renta del Tabaco* was the third most important source in Bolívar, and in 1933 was still among the three most important sources. In places such as Carmen or Corozal, the *Renta del Tabaco* produced more than all other taxes put together.[52]

There were 5,267 cultivators of tobacco in Bolívar in 1937. About 3,800 ha were devoted to the leaf and the *Secretaría de Hacienda* had registered 34,400,100 tobacco plants.[53] In 1948, the *Información Económica Trimestral* reported the existence of 4,038 *cultivadores propietarios,* who sold their crops in advance to merchants. As during the nineteenth century, the local government showed concern about cultivation techniques; but apart from a project to establish an experimental farm there is no evidence of any significant changes in the way tobacco was cultivated during the period.

A growing domestic demand for cigars and cigarettes had stimulated the production of tobacco during the twentieth century, which by the 1940s was among the most important industrial sectors in Colombia. Tobacco from Bolívar was sold in Magdalena, Atlántico, Antioquia, Cundinamarca, and Tolima. In 1934, Bolívar accounted for about 43 per cent of the national production of the tobacco leaf.[54] One of the

[51] *Mensaje e informes del Gobernador* (Cartagena, 1917), 13–19; R. Varela Martínez, *Economia agrícola de Colombia* (Bogotá, 1949), 163.

[52] *Memoria que presenta el Secretario de Hacienda* (Cartagena, 1914), 69, 74–5; *Mensaje e informes del Gobernador*, 26; *Informe del Secretario de Hacienda* (Santa Marta, 1919), 16–19; *Informe al señor Gobernador* (Cartagena, 1934), app.

[53] F. Prado Villanueva, *Informe del señor oficial de estadística de la oficina de tabaco* (Cartagena, 1937), 42.

[54] See Wylie, *The Agriculture of Colombia*, 110; Contraloría, *Síntesis estadística de Colombia, 1939–1943*, 190–2; and *Anuario general de estadística* (Bogotá, 1934), 544.

largest buyers was the *Compañía Colombiana de Tabaco*, from Medellín, which established an agency in Carmen. Cigars and cigarettes were also produced on a small scale in Ovejas, Colosó, Carmen, Toluviejo, Zambrano, and Cartagena, where there were eighteen cigar factories in 1937, 'besides a large number of little local factories of some importance', together employing about 3,500 people.[55] Practically all the tobacco leaf used in these factories was produced in Bolívar; only small quantities were brought in from Santander and Tolima. However, there was already a growing preference for foreign cigarettes: in 1937, more than 1,000,000 packs of Camel and Chesterfield were imported into Bolívar.[56]

4. Sugar: Competition at Home

Sugar cane was widely cultivated throughout the region on a small scale mostly for domestic purposes, although some quantities of cane products were occasionally exported. In 1873, merchants from Cartagena established a modern mill designed to produce sugar for external markets. Cultivation of sugar cane expanded, and was expected to be 'a most lucrative operation if a sufficient supply of labour could be obtained for the purpose'.[57] Expectations were soon frustrated, since the product was not competitive abroad. Sugar exports during the 1880s were derisory and by the 1890s they had ceased altogether: 'The scarcity of labour prohibits any possibility of an export industry in any cane products'.[58]

The cultivation of sugar cane was thus limited to meet local requirements: the manufacture of molasses for rum distilleries and *panela*, a brown sugarloaf. The use of primitive sugar mills – *trapiches* – for extracting the juice from the cane, 'with wooden rollers worked by mule or ox power', was widespread in the region.[59] Before the introduction of the official monopoly of alcohol, rum distilleries were numerous, demanding significant quantities of molasses. *Panela* was a popular product which answered

[55] Prado Villanueva, *Informe*, 44–6; M. F. Obregón, *Memoria de Gobierno* (Cartagena, 1934), 224.

[56] *Memoria del Secretario de Hacienda* (Cartagena, 1937), 37–9.

[57] *PP*, 27, LXV (1873), 46, and 35, LXXVI (1875), 361, and *Revista de Colombia* (Bogotá, 31 May 1873).

[58] *PP*, 47, XCI (1911), 5. See also *PP*, 35, LXXVI (1875), 372; and 35, LXXXIII (1887), 617.

[59] *GB*, 25 Oct. 1873, and *PP*, 36, C (1888), 640.

several purposes besides replacing sugar: 'It is healthy and cheap. It is said to be the panacea for coughs and diarrhoea. It makes a very cooling drink when mixed with water, and many families never use any other drink'.[60] Prices of molasses and *panela*, 'subject to very great fluctuations in the home market', conditioned the expansion of sugar-cane cultivation. In 1904, prices dropped more than 50 per cent, 'and the cost of labour remaining the same, many sugar planters have been obliged either to abandon their plantations or turn their cultivations into bananas or pasture'. Imports of sugar, particularly for the consumption of the better-off and to meet the requirements of the food-processing factories in the main urban centres, were growing.

A turning-point in the development of the industry occurred in 1909 when, supported by protectionist measures, the *Ingenio Central Colombia* in Sincerín by the Dique Canal, produced its first harvest, *zafra*: 5,082 tons of sugar, of which 1,903 were exported to the United Kingdom and 1,304 to the United States. This large sugar estate, 'equal to the very best estates of Cuba', was established by the cattle traders Vélez Daníes and Co., in partnership with fellow merchants from Cartagena.[61] By 1933, there were about 3,000 ha under cultivation in Sincerín and 2,000 employees during the grinding season. The example of Sincerín was later followed by similar ventures but without the same initial success. In 1919, A. and T. Meluk, a firm of Syrian immigrants established in Cartagena, organized the *Empresa Sautatá*, in Chocó; in 1928, the *Empresa Azucarera Berástegui* was established by the Burgos, a family traditionally involved in cattle-raising, and the commercial house *Pombo Hermanos*; D. Vélez, a *Cartagenero* merchant, founded the *Ingenio Santa Cruz* in the early 1940s.[62]

Although production was rising, by 1933 both Sautatá and Berástegui were heavily indebted, mortgages exceeded the value of the properties and wages of employees were in arrears. Berástegui managed to survive under financial constraints during the 1940s, when it also faced

[60] *MCR*, (Oct.–Mar. 1887/88), 243.

[61] *PP*, 47, XCI (1911), 2; *Revista de Colombia* (Bogotá, 15 Nov. 1910), 333 –4; Colombia, *Misión de Rafael Reyes a los Departamentos de la Costa Atlántica y Antioquia* (Bogotá, 1908), 27; *RNA* (Apr. 1913), 754–8.

[62] US report, Cartagena 5 May 1933, NAUS/ RG84: Cartagena consulate, correspondence, 1933, vol. 7; Contraloría, *Geografía económica de Colombia: Bolívar* (Bogotá, 1942), 311, 332–3.

TABLE 1.3 *Sugar Production in Bolívar, 1909–1948 (selected years, tons)*

Year	Sincerín	Berástegui	Sautatá	Sta. Cruz
1909	5,082			
1925			687	
1927	10,187		2,000	
1928	8,312		2,062	
1930	7,875	937	2,437	
1932	10,687	4,375	3,125	
1933	8,125	5,312	1,875	
1940	10,586	5,000		
1946	4,318	4,830		1,050
1948	5,689	3,341		1,800

Sources: *D. and C. R.*, A. S. 4671 (London, 1911), 2; US Consul, Cartagena, 5 May 1933, NAUS RG84: Cartagena consulate, correspondence, 1933 (7); NAUS / RG166: Agriculture, Colombia, Box 57; IET, Cartagena, 1946–50.

severe labour problems, and it finally went bankrupt in 1950.[63] Sincerín, Berástegui, and to a lesser extent Sautatá and Santa Cruz refined the bulk of sugar in the region and played a significant role in the market. Sugar-cane continued to be widely cultivated throughout the Coast. In 1942, out of the 15,000 ha devoted to sugar cultivation 3,900 were controlled by these four *Ingenios*, the rest being grown in small plots where sugar was converted in primitive fashion into *panela*, or into molasses which was sold to the departmental liquor monopoly for the production of alcohol.[64]

It seems that sugar production grew during the 1920s but remained stationary during the 1930s and declined in the 1940s. Yet by 1942, Bolívar produced 22 per cent of Colombia's entire output.[65] The region was still not self-sufficient. In 1946, when the Coast had the capacity to produce about 11,000 tons of sugar, consumption reached 18,000 tons. Sugar from the Andean regions of Valle del Cauca and Santander supplied the deficit, as well as imports from Peru and Cuba.[66] *Ingenios*

[63] Burgos Puche, *El general Burgos*, 425, 353–426.

[64] Contraloría, *Geografía económica de Colombia: Bolívar*, 331. For *panela* production in Magdalena and Bolívar in 1941, see 'Colombian Sugar Mills', Bogotá, 4 Dec. 1941, NAUS/ RG166, entry 5, Box 56.

[65] K. Oakley, 'Economic Survey of the Cartagena Consular District', Cartagena, 10 November 1943, NAUS/ RG166: NAR, 1942–5, Box 174.

[66] IET, 1946.

were slow in modernizing machinery but physical conditions did not favour Coastal production in the face of increasing competition from Valle del Cauca, where, as in Peru, sugar-cane could be grown and processed all the year round.[67]

5. Vain Attempts to Exploit Cacao

Commercial exploitation of cacao was never as important as that of tobacco and sugar, but it raised expectations during the 1870s and 1880s and some capital was invested in its cultivation. A wild type of cacao grew in several areas of the Coast. Few efforts, however, had been made to grow it employing modern methods. In 1879, C. Martínez Ribón published his *Nuevo método para el cultivo del cacao*, with several recommendations as to how to grow the plant.[68] By then cacao plantations in Bolívar were on the increase.

In 1882 Augusto Dangau, a French citizen working in Cartagena as a commercial agent, founded the *Sociedad del Cacaotal Marta Magdalena*. Claiming some land as *baldíos* in the Sinú region, the company was established with a capital of 300,000 French francs and the aim of planting 100,000 cacao trees.[69] Due to mismanagement and adverse physical conditions, the cacao enterprise was a failure, although in 1893 there were still 30,000 cacao trees in Marta Magdalena. However, by then the firm was gradually moving into the more profitable cattle business. A final blow to cacao in Marta Magdalena came in 1910, when floods from the Sinú river destroyed the remaining trees.[70] In addition, local capital was directly involved in cacao plantations. In 1893, there were 350,000 cacao trees planted on over thirty different estates in the Sinú, some of these the results of joint ventures.[71] Nevertheless scarcity of capital and careless management were still the rule on the plantations. Most of the farmers

[67] Wylie, *The Agriculture of Colombia*, 91. On the Coast, production of sugar-cane was limited to 4 or 5 months a year, due to climatic conditions. In contrast, sugar in Valle, as in Peru, could be harvested all the year round. R. Thorp and G. Bertran, *Perú, 1890–1977* (London and Basingstoke, 1978), 41.

[68] *El Agricultor*, 6 Oct. 1879 and H. L. Román, *Memoria del Gobernador* (Cartagena, 1894), 20.

[69] *El Agricultor*, July 1883; J. Exbrayat, *Reminiscencias monterianas* (Montería, 1939), 23; J. Berrocal Hoyos, *La colonización antioqueña en el departamento de Córdoba* (Montería, 1980), 58.

[70] Exbrayat, *Reminiscencias*, 25.

[71] 'Documentos importantes', *El Agricultor*, May 1894.

were cultivating cacao as additional trees alongside plantains, and yields were generally low.

While in the interior cacao was basically produced for the domestic market, its cultivation on the Coast was for export. According to Thompson, cheap transport gave an advantage of $3 per *arroba* to Coastal cacao over that from Tolima in the European market.[72] As was the case in the Sinú, it was in the late 1870s when greater attention was paid to cacao as a commercial commodity in Magdalena. As in the Sinú too, French interests were here involved in cacao production. The *Compagnie Inmobiliere et Agricole de Colombia*, whose land would be sold later to the United Fruit Company, was established in the 1870s to exploit tobacco and cacao near Ciénaga.[73] In 1894, Penon & Co. from Paris established Don Diego – an estate formed originally with 3,600 ha of *baldíos* – with the purpose of exploiting cacao. By then French immigrants had agreed to produce cacao in *La Esperanza*, near Dibuya. In 1916, however, just 80 of its 4,500 ha were devoted to cacao. The main interest of the company had turned then into the exploitation of rubber, and in 1943, *La Esperanza* was rented to the Chicle Development Inc., a subsidiary of a Delaware concern.[74]

There is thus strong evidence that cacao was regarded as a commercially attractive crop in both Bolívar and Magdalena during the last two decades of the nineteenth century, where some local capital and entrepreneurship was also involved. G. Rapalino started to grow cacao in San Cirilo in 1885, after some hesitation due to his initial belief that sugar-cane was more profitable. In 1894, Rapalino planted 5,000 cacao trees and was satisfied with the results: in a farm without irrigation, he was able to produce 6 kg. of cacao per tree.[75] Cacao in Magdalena was planted alongside bananas and, according to R. Echeverría, scarcity of labour impeded the extension of its cultivation. Despite these efforts however, in the Sinú farmers shifted from cacao to more profitable activities, and in Magdalena the quick returns from bananas soon led to the abandonment of cacao trees.

[72] Thompson, 'Report on the Excursion', 145.

[73] R. Herrera Soto and R. Romero Castañeda, *La zona bananera del Magdalena* (Bogotá, 1979), 3.

[74] Consulado General de Colombia, Paris, 'Escritura Pública No.5', Paris, 13 Jan. 1927, Bogotá; Notaría Pública del Circuito, Ríohacha, 'Contrato de Víctor Dugand y Enrique Lallemand, para el fomento y explotación de unos terrenos, Escritura Pública No. 25', 14 Apr. 1891, AFL.

[75] 'Documentos importantes'.

6. Bananas: Five Decades of Export Success

Land originally devoted to cacao, tobacco or sugar was from the early 1880s gradually given over to bananas. Local growers and foreign companies felt the commercial benefits of a crop that could produce fruit, with relatively little investment, less than a year after being planted. Between 1892 and 1899, when the United Fruit Company was formed, banana exports from Santa Marta already averaged approximately 380,000 bunches per year.[76] *El Agricultor*, a journal in Ciénaga, voiced the local enthusiasm for the expansion of banana cultivation. Exports suffered slightly during the *Guerra de los Mil Días* but between 1903 and 1908 shipments from Santa Marta rose from 478,448 to 2,202,850 bunches p.a. In 1908 President Reyes, whose administration had encouraged its production, toured the Coast to inspect at first hand the banana's success, while the Liberal leader Rafael Uribe Uribe praised the virtues of the fruit in a lecture to the *Sociedad de Agricultores de Colombia*.[77] Exports grew steadily during the following years. By 1936, Colombian bananas constituted 8 per cent of the international market, making Colombia the second banana-exporting country after Honduras. (See Table 1.4). The next decade, however, was one of decline. In 1941 exports had fallen to 2,500,000 bunches and by 1942 they were at a standstill, due principally to the war and an outbreak of Sigatoka disease.[78] Some recovery took place after the war, but until 1950 exports did not reach earlier levels.

As one of the main staples of the Coast, the banana had also become an important article in local trade with the growth of cities. In 1921, large plantations of bananas near Cartagena were supplying its local

[76] On the United Fruit Company see: F. U. Adams, *Conquest of the Tropics* (New York, 1914); S. Crowther, *The Romance and Rise of the American Tropics* (New York, 1929); J. T. Palmer, 'The Banana in the Caribbean Trade', *Economic Geography*, 8 (1932), 262–73; C. M. Wilson, *Empire in Green and Gold. The Story of the American Banana Trade* (Henry Holt and Co. n. p., 1947); C. D. Kepner J. and H. Soothill, *The Banana Empire* (New York, 1935); T. P. McCann, *An American Company, the Tragedy of the United Fruit Co.* (New York, 1976). For the activities of this company in Colombia, see J. White, *Historia de una ignominia* (Bogotá, 1978); Herrera Soto and Romero Castañeda, *La zona bananera*; Botero and Guzmán Barney, 'El enclave agrícola en la zona bananera'.

[77] Colombia, *Misión de Rafael Reyes* and *RNA* (May 1908), 5–105.

[78] Oakley, 'Banana Report', Bogotá, 12 Aug. 1942, NAUS/ RG166, FAR, NR, 1942–5, Colombia, Box 176, App C; W. Dawson, 'Data Concerning Colombian Banana', Bogotá, 5 Mar. 1937, NAUS/ 821.6156/216; White, *Historia de una ignominia*, 123.

TABLE 1.4 *Colombian Compared to Central American Banana Exports 1893–1946 ('000 bunches)*

Country	1893	1898	1900	1910	1920
Costa Rica	1,278	2,331	3,420	9,097	8,652
Guatemala	193	186	121	1,226	3,300
Honduras	1,400	1,701	2,040	n.d.	n.d.
Panamá	1,055	2,058	2,838	3,644	4,248
Colombia	201	420	269	3,844	6,294

Country	1925	1930	1935	1940	1946
Costa Rica	8,349	5,834	2,909	3,215	5,692
Guatemala	5,350	4,874	5,595	8,195	10,649
Honduras	14,500	29,084	10,410	14,564	14,338
Panamá	3,417	3,540	5,768	5,865	5,190
Colombia	9,918	11,034	8,167	4,539	2,000

Sources: F. Ellis, *Las transnacionales del banano en Centroamérica* (San José, 1983), 41, 53, 55. Nichols, *Tres puertos*, 255.

market. Some 25,000 bunches of bananas were shipped weekly from Ciénaga to Barranquilla in 1942.[79] None the less, as already shown, the impetus to grow bananas on a large commercial scale stemmed essentially from the external demand at the end of the nineteenth century.

Thus between 1891 and 1941, exports of bananas from Magdalena had experienced an important trade cycle. Their production was concentrated around Ciénaga, Aracataca, and Fundación in an area that came to be known as the *Zona Bananera*.[80] (See Map 3). Although regarded as an enclave, due to the dominant presence of the United Fruit Company, local growers and entrepreneurs had a considerable

[79] Bell, *Colombia*. 154; Oakley, 'Banana Report'. It is impossible to estimate domestic production since 'bananas are grown in almost every garden for home consumption or sale in local markets', see Wylie, *The Agriculture of Colombia*, 67. As Grunwald and Musgrove have observed, 'most of the world's bananas are consumed where they are produced', see J. Grunwald and P. Musgrove, *Natural Resources in Latin American Development* (n. p. 1970), 364.

[80] For geographical descriptions of the banana zone, see Krogzemis: 'A Historical Geography', and C. F. Jones, 'Agricultural Regions of South America', *Economic Geography*, 5 (1929).

MAP 3. *The Banana Zone, as Sketched by Griffith Taylor*

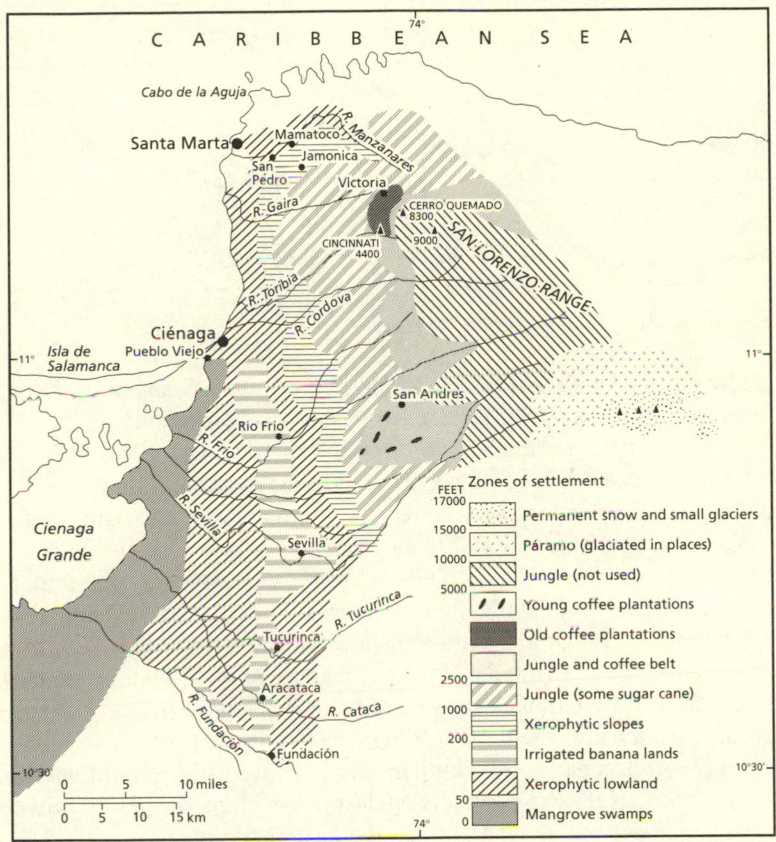

Sources: G. Taylor, 'Settlement zones of the Sierra Nevada de Santa Marta, Colombia', *Geographical Review*, 21 (1931), 547

share in the production stage of the business. In 1908, when the United Fruit Company had 1,229 ha under cultivation, there were 283 other farms growing bananas in an area of 3,821 ha, accounting for some 75 per cent of total production. As illustrated in Table I.5, the bulk of growers had plots of between 1 and 20 ha, although farms above 50 ha, including the United Fruit's, accounted for around 60 per cent of the total land devoted to banana cultivation.

TABLE 1.5 *Banana Farms and Growers, 1908*

Size (ha)	Growers	ha
1–5	173	482
5–20	74	724
20–50	19	661
50–100	12	847
100–500	5	1,107
500 +	1	1,129
Total	284	5,050

Source: Colombia, *Misión de Rafael Reyes*, 45–9.

Most of the small and medium-size farmers in 1908 appear to have been local growers, either private owners or squatters on *baldíos*, and a few of them were members of immigrant families. Two British citizens, L. Bradbury and M. Carr – pioneers in the industry – were among the largest growers, after the United Fruit Co. and some Magdalena planters. Capital from Barranquilla was also invested in banana production: Evaristo Obregón & Co. had 100 ha under cultivation in 1908 while Senior & Wolf had 75 ha. During the following decade, United Fruit expanded its plantations. By 1920, the American company owned 6,000 ha of the 12,000 ha that were devoted to bananas while national growers still contributed 50 per cent of the production, most of them on holdings ranging in area from 1 to 10 or 15 ha.[81] Additionally, the company itself leased land to cultivators, who also received loan contracts against future crops. In 1933, United Fruit had leased out about 4,500 ha. By the time of the crisis in 1943, it had sold 3,000 ha to the lessees.[82] Compared to Central America, with the exception of Costa Rica, in Colombia a greater proportion of the fruit was produced by local growers.[83] As a consequence of labour unrest, direct production of bananas by United Fruit diminished during the 1930s. By 1936, some 80 per cent of the company's exports were purchased from 482 producers who cultivated 14,425 ha of bananas. In

[81] L. Sawyer, 'The Banana Industry in Colombia', Santa Marta, 8 May 1920, NAUS/821.6156/44, and *RNA* (1921), 229.

[82] Oakley, 'Banana Report'.

[83] V. Bulmer-Thomas, *The Political Economy of Central America since 1920* (Cambridge University Press, 1987), 35.

1938, the American company purchased 8,346,984 stems from national growers while 1,605,793 stems were produced on its own farms.[84]

Production was, however, tied to the controls that United Fruit exercised over the marketing of the fruit. Its dominant position in the international trade, strengthened by an outstanding infrastructure, guaranteed the quick delivery of the produce to the retailers.[85] As S. Pérez Triana had himself experienced in a failed attempt to introduce bananas to the US in the 1880s, the product 'is extremely short-lived; if it is not promptly eaten it rots and therefore loses any value'.[86] Linked to the quick shipment of the fruit was its transportation from the plantations to the port. Gradually the American company managed to obtain control over the Santa Marta Railway, originally a British concern whose prosperity as early as 1907 was 'almost entirely dependent on the development of the banana trade'.[87] As significant as the control of the transport system for the success of the enterprise was the organization of a distribution network for bananas: its subsidiary, the Fruit Dispatch Company, had 54 branches in the United States and Canada in 1927, while through Elders and Fyffes the United Fruit Company had a strong foothold in the British market.[88]

Since the company had a virtual monopoly on both transport and distribution, and provided working capital, it could persuade most cultivators to sign contracts which enabled United Fruit to fix prices, while dissuading competitors to enter the market. These contracts were 'in reality loans, advanced after blow-downs or to enable new producers to get a start, secured by all fruit grown by the contractor over a period of years for which the company guarantees a specified price'.[89] Such contracts were a recurrent source of resentment among cultivators, who felt they were losing out through a decline in real

[84] Dawson. 'Data Concerning Colombian Banana'. R. H. Hammer, 'Memorandum', Bogotá, 20 May 1942, NAUS/ 821.6156/317.

[85] United Fruit Co., *A Short History of the Banana and a Few Recipes for its Use* (Boston, 1904).

[86] *RNA* (30 Oct. 1908), 265. See also Hammer, 'Memorandum', 3. 'Prior to 1899, one hundred and fourteen banana concerns organized and went into business. Of these only 22 survived and out of the 22 only four were of any size'; see Crowther, *The Romance and Rise,* 173.

[87] *PP*, 38, XCV (1910), 19.

[88] P. Reynolds, *Banana Chart Manual* (New York, 1927), 8. Over 83% of the British registered company Elders and Fyffes, which controlled the banana market in the United Kingdom, was held by United Fruit. *PP*, 12 (1926), 251. See P. N. Davies, *Fyffes and the Banana: A Centenary History, 1888–1988* (London, 1990).

[89] 'Difficulties of the United Fruit Company in Colombia', Washington, 17 Dec. 1930, NAUS/ 821.6156/129.

prices. It was the company's claim, however, that 'the small planters who attend strictly to business have no complaints to make about prices . . . It is simply the large planters who refuse to work and want to live extravagantly'. According to the Vice-President of United Fruit, in 1919 the company had ceased to extend any money to cultivators because it had suffered losses of $600,000 on loans 'to so-called gentlemen planters who blew the money living high in Colombia or at the Waldorf Hotel in New York'.[90] It was probably a temporary decision, for loans from the American company continued to be a major source of working capital until 1933, when the Government began to give credit through a co-operative. The largest growers, members of the *Sociedad de Agricultores del Magdalena*, were requesting further loans in 1931.[91] However, *bananeros*, owing $3,000,000 to the American company, refused to pay, alleging that United Fruit was charging interest of eight per cent while it was obtaining the money in American banks at six per cent. In 1943, banana growers still owed some $2,000,000. The company had little hope of ever collecting the money.[92]

On several occasions competitors tried to break the monopoly of United Fruit: merchants from Barranquilla jointly with the Atlantic Fruit Co. in 1912, the Santa Marta Fruit Co. in 1920, The Atlantic Fruit and the Cuyamel Fruit Co. in 1928, the English Firm Robert Brinning & Co. in 1930. If ultimately these efforts produced no practical results, in terms of finding new markets for the product, they could have some immediate consequences, as happened in 1928: first, planters who had not previously been able to borrow money from the United Fruit Co. or contract the production of their plantation were now 'approached and offered very good terms to accept money and contract for a term of 5 years'; and second, local planters were made more aware of international prices and of the possibilities of better opportunities for their own product.[93]

[90] Letter from District Officer Manager, Boston, 9 Oct. 1919, NAUS/ RG151: 331.2/ Bananas/Colombia.

[91] *RNA* (May–June 1931), 418–9; Cotie, 'Banana Industry', Santa Marta, 12 Apr. 1928, NAUS./ 821.6156/60; and Kepner and Soothill, *The Banana Empire*, 290.

[92] Oakley, 'Banana Report'; *La Sociedad de Agricultores contesta a la United Fruit Company*, leaflet, Santa Marta, 30 July 1931.

[93] I. Manning, 'Activities of Atlantic Fruit Co.', Barranquilla, 2 Mar. 1912, NAUS/ 821.6156/4, and similar reports in files 821.6156/5, 7, 8, 62–4, 75, 79, 106.

TABLE 1.6 *Production Cost and Yield of an Acre Planted with Bananas, 1922 ($US)*

Cost per acre of good banana land, served by the railroad	400.00
Initial cost, per acre, of clearing land, lining, hoeing, planting, etc., and taking care of plants until bearing, including cost of seed	100.00
Maintenance cost of taking care of plants after bearing, cleaning, pruning, etc., including harvesting and transportation of bananas to delivery station, per acre/year	70.00
Wages paid to labourers on banana plantations	1.00 to 1.50
Cost of production, per count bunch,	
1st year of bearing	0.60
2nd year	0.35
3rd year	0.35
subsequent years	0.30
Yield per acre,	
1st year of bearing (count bunches)	60
2nd year	80
3rd year	100

Source: American Consul to Allen, Santa Marta, 31 Aug. 922, NAUS/ RG84: general correspondence, 1922 (II).

Without risking capital on transport or on the uncertainties of the market, the producer who could secure sales to the United Fruit Co. was involved in a profitable business. 'With production costs averaging less than nineteen cents per count and a price of 0,50', the American Consul pointed out in 1920, 'it is evident that private owners are engaged in a lucrative agricultural enterprise.' 'It's a goldmine!' exclaimed R. Varela Martínez after calculating profits between $400 and $470 yearly per hectare in 1921. M. Dávila Pumarejo, one of the largest Magdalena planters, also gave his figures in a 1931 newspaper: in regions unaffected by hurricanes it was possible to secure annual returns of 70 per cent and in areas with risky climatic conditions annual returns of 25 per cent were still possible. In 1937, while the average cost per bunch to the producer was calculated at $0,355, United Fruit was paying $0,73 per bunch.[94] (Table 1.6 provides production cost figures estimated by the American Consul in 1922).

[94] R. Varela Martínez, 'Estudio de la región bananera', 231; Sawyer, 'The Banana Industry'; M. Dávila Pumarejo, 'La industria del banano'; Dawson, 'Data Concerning Colombian Banana'.

From its early years, the banana economy attracted labour from other areas of the Coast and even from the highlands of the Colombian interior. In spite of this migration, scarcity of labour was an acute problem, particularly during the first decades of this century. In 1908 Uribe Uribe had observed how the struggle to secure labour among planters had had a 'demoralizing effect', as planters competed with each other offering increases in salaries and other perks 'only to secure six hours of poor labour'. According to President Reyes, a labour force of 60,000 was required to cultivate 20,000 hectares of bananas, and in 1915 there were an estimated 15,000 workmen in the Banana Zone. Whatever the needs of labour, they were soon attended to: expectancy of higher wages and new economic opportunities led to a massive influx of people. Migrants came from all over Colombia and also from abroad, but they originated mostly from other areas of the Coast. Immigrants had the most diverse origins. A glance at the employees in Colombia – General Benjamín Herrera's farm in Aracataca – is illustrative: its accountant was from Norte de Santander; two administrators, one from Bucaramanga and the other from Lorica, Bolívar, managed the farm in 1914, when the bulk of the permanent workers were from Barranquilla, although there was a Spaniard among them; the servants came mainly from Barranquilla, but also from Usiacurí, Atlántico; and R. Rubio, in charge of the farm shop, came from Bogotá.[95] Some migrants took up permanent residence in the region, but seasonal migration was significant.[96] Immigrants also came from the Bahamas and Aruba, although in general attempts to introduce an organized foreign labour force failed: in 1916 United Fruit employed just over 100 British West Indians. In contrast with some Central American banana regions, the bulk of the workforce in the Coast overall remained native.[97]

[95] A. Luna Cárdenas, *Un año y otros días con el General Benjamín Herrera en Aracataca* (Medellín, 1960), 113, 159, 169, 195; C. Arango, *Sobrevivientes de las bananeras* (Bogotá, 1981), 38.

[96] W. J. Sullivan, *Report on the Commercial and Economic Situation in the Republic of Colombia* (London, 1925), 58, and C. LeGrand, 'El conflicto de las bananeras', *Nueva Historia de Colombia*, 3 (Bogotá, 1989), 186.

[97] See Uribe Uribe, 'El banano', 100; 'List of British West Indians Employed by the United Fruit Company', 1916, PRO, FO/135/395. Labour immigration, mostly from the West Indies, played a significant role in the development of banana plantations in Central America and Panama. See Bulmer-Thomas, *The Political Economy of Central America*, 11–16, and P. I. Bourgois, *Ethnicity at Work: Divided Labor on a Central American Plantation* (Baltimore and London, 1989), 45–110.

The single largest employer was the United Fruit Company, which by 1920 provided jobs to a total of between 2,500 and 3,000 people in its twenty-five farms distributed in the districts of Aracataca, Sevilla, and Ríofrio. Labour was contracted in two different ways: those involved in the planting, cleaning, and upkeep of plantations were paid on a daily wage arrangement, while those involved in the cutting of the fruit were paid on a piece basis per stem.[98] Some were employed directly by planters, others through middlemen, following a long-established practice in the region. Overall, what emerges from the available information is evidence of a variety of labour arrangements, frequent in the Colombian rural world. The case of one labour leader in the zone as described by Ignacio Torres Giraldo – 'a semi-proletarian named Salas Salas: employed as cutter at the farm La Guaira, but at the same time ranch-owner as a *colono* – squatter' – was probably a frequent pattern.[99] Wages paid by the American company were higher than those paid by local planters, and in any event banana wages were high by Colombian standards.[100] According to A. Pearse, the average wage on the plantation was above $2 a day, 'but a man who works well and longer than five hours can earn as much as $5'. 'This has spoilt the population', Pearse concluded, 'for owing to their few needs . . . they have too much money to spend on drinking and riotous living.' General Herrera thought otherwise. For him, the banana boom had brought an 'entrepreneurial spirit' to Ciénaga, 'where a large proportion of the population had hitherto limited its aspirations to fishing for their daily needs and a lazy siesta in a hammock'.[101] Salaries evidently varied throughout the period. It seems that wages, after a period of rise, declined in the late 1920s and early 1930s. In 1934, as a result of a strike, wages were slightly increased.[102] Wages in the industry obviously also varied according to the nature of the job. The loading of bananas onto trains and ships was also labour intensive,

[98] L. Cotie, 'Banana Industry'.

[99] I. Torres Giraldo, *Los inconformes* (Bogotá, 1974), v. 31.

[100] A critical report by a Commission from the *Cámara de Representantes* recognized that wages were higher than in other Colombian regions and foodstuffs were cheaper. This Commission also pointed out that labour conditions were better in the American company than in plantations owned by nationals. See *Informe que rindió a la honorable Cámara de Representantes la Comisión designada para visitar la zona bananera del Magdalena* (Bogotá, 1935), 13, 33, 34.

[101] Pearse, *Colombia, with Special Reference*, 61, 62, and *RNA* (1913), 75.

[102] US Consul, 31 Aug. 1922, RG84, 1922(2); Oakley, 'Banana Report'.

and wages had to be more attractive.[103] In all events, labour conditions were far from homogeneous. Seasonal employment was probably the rule for a significant proportion of settlers.

Accommodation to the new social circumstances, where banana exports had given way to rapid growth and subsequently to an expanding population, was the source of conflict. In 1916, the Governor of Magdalena felt powerless to guarantee public order. A year later, a general strike broke out: 'the mob was in charge', the Atlántico Governor informed the President, 'if there was no bloodshed, it was because the authorities, feeling impotent, decided to stay away. Isolated in a region in revolt, there was nothing else for the Governor to do'.[104] Dissatisfaction with the United Fruit Company turned into bitter disputes, most prominently in 1924, 1928, 1929, and 1934. Social tensions reached their peak in 1928, when a general strike motivated by labour conflicts and resentment from banana producers, combined with political agitation in the midst of rising unemployment, led to clashes with the Army and a violent outcome. The 1928 strike – later popularized in García Márquez's *One Hundred Years of Solitude* – had far-reaching political consequences, and became a landmark in Colombian labour history.[105]

There has been a tendency to restrict studies of the banana industry in Colombia to disputes between labourers and the American company, particularly the 1928 strike and its suppression. It is undeniable that there were specific issues relevant to workers employed by United

[103] For the relatively better working conditions in the loading of bananas onto trains and ships, see: Bradshaw to Olaya, 30 July 1931, 821.6156/152; A. Giron's personal recollection in Arango, *Sobrevivientes de las bananeras,* 33; and Torres Giraldo, *Los inconformes*, iv. 65.

[104] Magdalena and Atlántico Governors to Concha, Santa Marta, 30 Oct. 1916, and Barranquilla, 14 Jan. 1918, AJVC, Boxes 31 and 1.

[105] A detailed analysis of this strike, and of the social movements in the banana zone in general, have been the subject of a vast literature and is beyond the scope of this book. For different interpretations of the banana strikes, mostly focusing on 1928, see White, *Historia de una ignominia*, 73–122; C. LeGrand, 'El conflicto de las bananeras', 184–217; Herrera Soto and Romero Castañeda, *La zona bananera del Magdalena*, 21–84. Labour leaders, banana workers and farmers, the government, and the head of the Army have also produced their own accounts of the 1928 and 1934 strikes: Arango, *Sobrevivientes de las bananeras*, 51–118; Torres Giraldo, *Los inconformes*, iv. 101–35, and v. 27–34; *Memoria del Ministro de Gobierno* (Bogotá, 1929), pp. X–XII; C. Cortés Vargas, *Los sucesos de las bananeras* (Bogotá, 1979). See a selection of texts from various participants in Valdeblánquez, *Historia del Departamento del Magdalena*, 235–74. A complete collection of newspaper clippings related to the 1928 strike is in NAUS/RG84, American Embassy, general correspondence, 1928 (7).

Fruit which were the cause of recurrent conflict. Despite their significance, however, these issues should not overshadow the complex social picture that emerged from sudden economic growth in Northern Magdalena. Furthermore, there is scope for readdressing the impact of the banana industry on the Coast from a long-term perspective, within the wider context of agricultural history in the region.[106]

The extent to which labour earnings on the plantations and incomes from banana production contributed to other sectors of the economy is a question that will be treated in Chapter 5. Suffice it to say here that banana exports had given rise to rapid and unprecedented growth in Northern Magdalena. Cultivators shifted from less successful crops to a more profitable commodity. Land hitherto unexploited was now given over to growing bananas for the market. An expanding population settled in the area, motivated by the expectations of high wages and new economic opportunities, which were sometimes met with frustration but often also with success.

After five decades, these signs of economic growth came to an abrupt halt during the early 1940s. In 1939 the first effects of the Sigatoka disease were felt in the plantations. A campaign to prevent the spread of the pest accomplished little. The crisis was deepened by the war. In 1943, when the American Consul from Barranquilla visited Santa Marta and the banana zone, the aspect was 'one of desolation': farms had been virtually abandoned, export activity ceased, unemployment remained a serious problem, despite some labour emigration. By 1946 some recovery had taken place, but exports of bananas did not reach previous levels. To overcome the crisis, the government started to implement a programme encouraging the cultivation of other crops.[107]

106 Even the events of 1928 need a thorough re–examination. Asked in a 1990 interview about the number of casualties during the strike, the writer Gabriel García Márquez replied: 'There was talk of a massacre. An apocalyptic massacre. Nothing is sure, but there can't have been many deaths . . . It was a problem for me . . . when I discovered it wasn't a spectacular slaughter. In a book where things are magnified, like *One Hundred Years of Solitude* . . . I needed to fill a whole railway with corpses. I couldn't stick to historical reality. I couldn't say they were 3, or 7, or 17 deaths. They wouldn't even fill a tiny wagon. So I decided on 3,000 dead because that fitted the dimension of the book I was writing. The legend has now been adopted as history'; Dan Weldon, *My Macondo*, Great Britain/ Channel Four Production, 1990, courtesy of the British Film Institute, London. Indeed this figure of 3,000 dead, popularized by *One Hundred Years of Solitude*, is now commonly accepted by literary critics and Colombian history textbooks.

107 American Consul to State Department, Barranquilla, 13 Nov. 1943, NAUS/ 821.6156/326; C. Lleras Restrepo, *Memoria de Hacienda* (Bogotá, 1942), 134–7.

7. Cotton: The Struggle for Self-Sufficiency

The commercial exploitation of cotton in the nineteenth century was restricted to the vicinities of Barranquilla, Cartagena, and Santa Marta. Merchants from these ports encouraged its cultivation in response to international prices. Cotton exports went up first in 1830s and then in the 1860s, following the outbreak of the American civil war, and the consequent opportunities offered by the European market.[108] These were, however, short 'booms' and the volume of trade remained limited throughout the century. Cotton was a cash crop, cultivated at the demand of local merchants who were in contact with world markets. Traders in the region lent money to planters, cleaned the cotton, and packed it for export. In 1839, there was already a steam machine in Barranquilla to clean the fibre; and in 1867, 'four new large steam gins' were in 'active operation'; in 1890, Senior, De Sola & Co. founded El Impulso, a modern establishment with three steam gins which claimed to clean daily 100 *quintales* of raw cotton.[109]

During the second decade of the twentieth century, cotton growing received a fresh impetus from the internal demand of a growing textile industry: a significant expansion of production only took place after 1910 with the establishment of the Fábrica de Tejidos Obregón. A wealthy family from Barranquilla originally engaged in commerce, the Obregóns moved into the textile industry and became directly involved in the cultivation of cotton. Their own 1,000 ha plantation was not as significant in the growth of the industry as their role in distributing free seed, advancing money to cultivators, and purchasing crops.[110] A further attraction to cotton growers was the ready demand for the fibre from other emergent textile factories in Medellín, Samacá, Cartagena, and Barranquilla. In 1917 better prices for raw cotton could be obtained in Barranquilla than on the international market.[111] Production

[108] Nieto, 'Geografía histórica, estadística y local', 34–41; Ocampo, *Colombia y la economía mundial*, 361–3; and S. Montenegro, 'Producción de algodón en Colombia', unpublished mimeo, 1983, 1–8.

[109] A. Martínez and R. Niebles, *Directorio Anuario de Barranquilla* (Barranquilla, 1892), 390 and 109; E. Grau, *La ciudad de Barranquilla en 1896* (Barranquilla, 1896), 97 101; *MCR* (May–Aug. 1895), 47–52.

[110] 'Data Concerning Cotton Growing', Santa Marta, 12 Oct. 1921, NAUS/RG84, General correspondence, 1921 (3).

[111] Bell, *Colombia* 199. See also J. A. Tood, *The World's Cotton Crops* (London, 1915), 203; *British and Latin American Trade Gazette* (London, 20 Oct. 1920), 355.

grew significantly. During the 1920s, when the national production of cotton was supplying around 80 per cent of Colombian textile demand, the bulk of raw cotton came from the Coast. By the early 1930s, however, it had become evident that levels of national production could not keep pace with the growing demand from the textile industry, though production slightly increased after the mid-1930s. During the following decade, output of Colombian cotton almost doubled, but the Coast's share of national production diminished to about 60 per cent.[112] While other provinces in the country had apparently reacted more promptly to market opportunities, cotton production in the Coast seems to have stagnated. Yet a closer look shows a more dynamic picture: within the region, the geographical pattern of cotton cultivation was undergoing changes.[113]

It is impossible to give a complete overall picture of the dimensions and changes in the cultivation of cotton during the period under study. However, the available information shows that during the first decades of this century, the cultivation of cotton took place in the same areas as in the nineteenth century, the main centre of growth being the province of Barranquilla, situated in what came to be known as the Atlántico department after 1905. In 1925, Atlántico still produced 60.8 per cent of the national crop, but in 1937 this percentage had declined to 33.5 per cent and in 1950 to 30 per cent.[114] In the meantime, cultivation of cotton had been gradually extending in the Santa Marta province, particularly to the east of the Magdalena River, and in the provinces of Valledupar and Padilla, which would become one of the strongholds of cotton growing after 1950. In 1937, 18.5 per cent of the national crop came from the Magdalena department; in 1950 this figure was nearly 30 per cent. The pace of cotton growth in Bolívar was apparently slower, although in 1936 the *Secretario de Hacienda* reported a considerable increase in the harvest.[115] More significant development took place at the end of the 1940s. The *Informe Económico Trimestral* prepared by the Cartagena branch of the Banco de la República

112 Annual Report, Bogotá, 23 Mar. 1937, PRO: FO371/20624.

113 P. Leurquin, 'Cotton Growing in Colombia: Achievements and Uncertainties', *Food Research Institute Studies*, 6/1 (1966), 143–80; H. G. Porter, 'Cotton in Colombia', *Foreign Agricultural Service* (Dec. 1971), 1–20; and A. H. J. Helmsing, *Firms, Farms, and the State in Colombia* (Boston, 1988), 201–35.

114 E. Penso Urquijo, 'Aspectos agroecónomicos', *Revista Geográfica*, 1/1 (Dec. 1952), 111; Y. Soler and F. Prieto, *Bonanza y crisis del oro blanco, 1960–80* (Bogotá, 1982), 32–9.

115 *Memoria del Secretario de Hacienda* (Cartagena, 1936), 54–5.

reported in 1948 that the cultivation of cotton 'showed great promise in the Sinú, where it had raised hopes for the agricultural development of the region'. Growth continued in 1949. Good harvests had raised high expectations: 18,000 ha of cotton were planted in the Sinú in 1950.[116]

A detailed analysis of local data provides a more precise picture of what seems to have been a highly changeable pattern in the use of land, due to climatic conditions and price fluctuations. After the harvest of 1919, when its price went up to four pesos per *arroba* (1 *arroba* = 12.5kg.), planters from Magdalena were encouraged to grow cotton. In various reports written at the request of the US Consul in Santa Marta, mayors from several municipalities in Magdalena recorded both the initial enthusiasm and the later discouragement of cotton growers after the abrupt fall of prices in 1921. In Sitionuevo, from a yield of 150,000 *arrobas* in previous years production went down to 50,000 *arrobas* in 1921 and slid further to 39,480 *arrobas* in 1922. In Salamina, some 500 ha were planted in 1921, but a year later production was at a standstill. The case of El Piñón is also illustrative: 470 ha were under cultivation in 1919 and 1920, 197 in 1921, and in 1922, 'a further fall in prices led to the abandonment of the plantations'.[117] These are only rough indicators of cotton development on the Coast before 1950. None the less, they do show that cultivators in the region did respond to market opportunities, albeit unevenly: while traditional cotton areas such as Atlántico seemed to lose out, new provinces gradually emerged as promising cotton producers.

What went wrong in the traditional cotton belt? Why did it take so long for cotton growing to take off in other suitable areas of the Coast? A brief survey of the general conditions of the cultivation of cotton in the region might help to answer these questions. Cotton had been generally cultivated on a small scale by individual owners or tenants. According to A. Escalante and E. Penzo, the bulk of cotton planters were peasants who were permitted by their landlord to cultivate land during a period of two or three years, after which they had to hand it back as pasture.[118] Cotton was just one of a variety of products planted in small plots, along with maize and yucca. However, small landowners, such as one Francisco Silvera, who in 1950 planted 8 ha of

[116] IET, 3rd and 4th trimesters, 1948; 3rd trimester, 1949, and 4th trimester, 1950.

[117] These reports are in NAUS/RG84, Santa Marta, General correspondence, 1922 (2).

[118] Escalante, 'Geoeconomía del algodón', 85–7; Penso Urquijo, 'Aspectos agroeconómicos del Atlántico', 110.

cotton in Baranoa, seem also to have played a significant role.[119] Furthermore, evidence of free labour, particularly during the picking seasons, suggests the existence of a considerable number o independent farmers, either owners or renters. In 1950, more than 10,000 cotton growers were members of the Cooperativa Algodonera del Atlántico, a co-operative founded in 1936 and sponsored by the government to protect the interests of small planters.[120] Medium-sized plantations of between 80 and 90 ha were found in the Sinú by 1950, when most growers in this newly developed cotton region were paying rents between $10 and $15 monthly per hectare.[121] Cotton plantations of 1,000 ha, like that owned by the Obregóns, were indeed exceptional.

During the nineteenth century, the cotton cultivated on the Coast was of a perennial type, yielding crops for 4 or 5 years, although in some cases, 'only one crop is taken from a piece of ground, and then the squatters leave it for another virgin piece'.[122] Cotton-picking was also carelessly done; the cotton became 'ingrained with sand and leaves', damaging its quality and affecting its price. Once harvested, cotton was brought by 'donkeys and mules . . . to the outskirts of cities where runners meet the cargoes and bargain for their masters in the stores'. Often bargaining was not necessary; having been sold in advance, the crop belonged already to the trader.[123] Methods of cultivating cotton did not change significantly during the first half of the twentieth century, although some new seeds from Peru and Mississippi were introduced. Cotton of a hybrid perennial type, more likely to 'harbor and perpetuate various insect pests and diseases', was still the common rule.[124] Plagues, such as the one in Altántico in 1935, caused recurrent damage to the harvests. Production must have been severely hit in 1938 when representatives of all cotton interests met the Atlántico Governor to press for a campaign to prevent the spread of insects attacking the crops. As a result of this meeting, it was ordered that all cotton trees over 3 years old should be destroyed. Nevertheless, perennial-type cotton persisted until the 1960s, although annual

119 Escalante, 'Geoeconomía del algodón', 88; International Institute of Agriculture, *World Cotton Production*, 27.

120 Leurquin, 'Cotton Growing', 155.

121 Escalante, 'Geoeconomía del algodón', 82.

122 Bonney, *A Legacy of Historical Gleanings*, 459. See International Institute of Agriculture, *World Cotton Production and Trade* (Rome, 1936), 27. For a description of the type of cotton found on the Coast, see G. Watt, *The Wild and Cultivated Cotton Plants of the World* (London, 1907), 46, 109, 213.

123 *PP*, 37, LXXC (1896), 471; and 45, LXXXI (1901), 585–6.

124 Dawe, *Account of a Journey*, 17.

varieties of the fibre were finally introduced at the end of the 1940s in the Sinú.[125] Similarly, little attention was paid to insecticides before the 1940s, when in the Sinú some technological improvements were introduced through their purchase, though these represented no more than 5 per cent of the estimated cost of production.[126] Machinery was also scarce. Picking was done by hand, and so carelessly that, 'probably 20 if not 25 per cent of the whole crop is left in the fields'.[127] As serious as the plagues were the floods and erratic rains in a region where, unlike other successful cotton-growing areas such as Egypt or Peru, no major work had been undertaken either to control river courses or to build irrigation canals.[128] In 1927, Casteñada noted how cotton plantations near the banks of the Magdalena river were always at the mercy of floods. Likewise a US consular report observed the damage produced to the 1933 crop by 'an unexpected drop in temperature' while the forecast for the 1934 crop was shadowed by floods along the Magdalena river. Floods in the Sinú river region reportedly destroyed half the crop in 1950.[129]

Attempts to grow cotton on a large commercial scale faced, in turn, the pervasive problem of scarcity of labour. High wages in other production areas in the region worked to the disadvantage of cotton, which required intensive labour particularly during the picking seasons. Immigrant labour from the interior, originally employed by cotton planters, was 'soon attracted to the banana region of Magdalena Department where higher wages are paid'.[130] The cost of labour made Coastal cotton uncompetitive on the world market. Low rates of productivity added to the final cost in relation to the world supply. Pearse was 'astonished' to learn that while women did not pick more than 25 pounds of seed cotton per day, in Texas the average was

[125] *La Prensa*, 5 and 8 Jan. 1938; and *Memoria del Ministro de Agricultura* (Bogotá, 1962), 309.

[126] Leurquin, 'Cotton Growing', 170.

[127] Pearse, *Colombia, with Special Reference*, 98.

[128] In Egypt, the expansion of cotton cultivation during the 19th century went hand in hand with 'a vast programme of public works'; E. R. J. Owen, *Cotton and the Egyptian Economy, 1820–1914* (Oxford, 1969), 47. In Peru, another large cotton producing country, the increase in cotton area in the early 20th century was 'due both to new irrigation projects and a reallocation of cultivated land'; Thorp and Bertram, *Perú 1890–1977*, 57. Both countries had also experienced achievements in technology and pest controls.

[129] Castañeda, *Monografía del Magdalena*, 58, and IET, 4th trimester, 1950.

[130] Barranquilla, 15 June 1924, NAUS/RG166, Colombia, Box 132.

between 75 to 100 pounds. According to Escalante, one of the main problems in developing cotton in southern Bolívar was that labourers only worked 4 hours a day.[131]

By 1932 Barranquilla was said 'to be the only place in Colombia where all manufacturers in the republic come to purchase cotton'.[132] *Barranquillero* merchants, who also controlled the gins, had originally sponsored the industry which gradually developed significant links with the economy of the Coast. Their degree of involvement in the trade of native cotton was clearly manifested when, in 1932, the Barranquilla Chamber of Commerce urged on the national government the adoption of a higher import duty on raw cotton.[133] The issue of tariffs became a major subject of debate between cotton growers and textile industry throughout the 1930s and 1940s. As mere protectionist measures failed to raise production levels to meet the growing domestic demand, textile manufacturers complained about both the high costs and the low quality of national raw cotton. In addition, textile entrepreneurs blamed the practices of middlemen and their obsolete ginning-mills.[134] In 1932, textile interest from Medellín joined forces to found the Algodonera Colombiana, SA, a stock company which aimed to purchase the commodity directly from cotton growers on behalf of its associates. A year later, when Algodonera Colombiana acquired a ginning mill at Sitionuevo, the company bought 609,874 *arrobas* of raw cotton on the Coast.[135] Conflicts over tariffs and prices often had a regional undertone, although since the mid-1930s, the Obregóns had taken sides with their Medellín and Samacá colleagues. None the less, in 1941, a project in Congress to raise custom duties for raw-cotton imports received ready support from *Costeño* Senators while it was opposed by their *Antioqueño* counterparts.[136]

Since the early 1930s, the government had started to intervene in the cotton market and to arbitrate conflicting interests. Protectionist measures were followed by initiatives to improve technology, provide credit facilities, and fix minimum prices for the fibre. In 1935, an experimental farm was established in Atlántico. A year later, the

[131] Pearse, *Colombia, with Special Reference*, 94, 113; Escalante, 'Geoeconomía del algodón', 85.

[132] American Consul to Secretary of State, Barranquilla, 15 Feb. 1932, NAUS/RG84, 1932, (15).

[133] Ibid.

[134] *El Tiempo*, 24 Oct. and 8 Dec. 1935.

[135] R. Phelan, 'Cotton Production and Consumption in the Barranquilla Consular District', NAUS/RG166, NAR, Box 132.

[136] *La Prensa*, 19 and 21 Nov., and 12 Dec. 1941.

government sponsored the organization of the Cooperativa de Algodoneros del Atlántico, a union of growers whose membership had reached 11,100 by 1947, when it had 62 agencies operating all over the cotton areas on the Coast. The role of the Cooperativa in strengthening the bargaining position of growers and in promoting the expansion of cotton cultivation was impressive.[137] Recognizing the dimension of the cotton industry and its importance to the national economy, the government had established a Junta Nacional del Algodón in 1938 and started to fix minimum prices for the fibre, while its imports were also restricted.[138]

To sum up, cotton cultivation on the Coast expanded significantly during the second decade of this century in response to increasing demand from the textile industry. During the 1930s, cotton production lagged behind textile needs despite protectionist measures aimed at substituting imports. Although the area planted with cotton expanded in the region, the obstacles to overcome were multiple: pests, floods, untimely rains, shortages of labour, transport problems, and low levels of productivity, all discouraged rapid accommodation to market opportunities. Problems were exacerbated in Atlántico, where the climate and quality of soil did not favour cotton growers. It was remarkable that they managed to stay in the business at all. They were able to do so mainly for three reasons. First, as smallholders they could probably save on labour expenses by employing family members in the picking seasons. Second, their location, near Barranquilla – the centre of cotton trade, was a great advantage against potentially more productive but distant areas which faced higher transport costs. Finally, their organisation around the Cooperativa Algodonera del Atlántico had strengthened their bargaining position while allowing them greater access to credit facilities. As new areas in the region were brought under cotton cultivation, Atlántico lost its relative advantages. This happened, however, after a long campaign sponsored by the government, and reluctantly backed by the textile industry, to introduce new types of cotton, control pests, and regulate abrupt price fluctuations. While Atlántico lost out, cotton growing shifted to other areas in the Coast, where its development after 1950 not only helped to substitute imports but also even led to a new period of exporting.

137 *Mensaje del Gobernador* (Barranquilla, 1936), 13.

138 *El Tiempo*, 21 May 1938.

8. Conclusions: The Shortcomings of Costeño Farming

Between 1870 and 1950, the Coast had thus experienced the cultivation of a variety of crops with mixed results. A period of rapid expansion in tobacco cultivation during the nineteenth century, motivated by external demand, was followed initially by a sharp decline and later by slight upward trends, although in the long run tobacco production tended to remain stationary. While attempts to grow cacao met with failure from the start, the cultivation of sugar-cane, even on a large commercial scale, had some success, though its achievements were short-lived. The growth of rice and cotton faced multiple problems, yet both crops were accommodated to regional conditions and their development – though uneven throughout the period – was significant to the economy of the Coast. The level of expansion of banana production after the turn of the century, encouraged by the input of foreign capital and a ready demand abroad, was impressive. By 1950, however, after five decades of success, the prospects of bananas as a major export commodity were bleak. The overall accomplishments were few but this was far from being a static situation.[139] Changes in location and shifts in crops were occurring throughout the period. Some rural entrepreneurs attempted relatively large-scale commercial cultivation and made efforts to introduce new techniques. The region experienced years of prosperity and decline. Furthermore, the successes had some national impact. By 1932, the Coast produced, among the most important regional commodities, more than 80 per cent of Colombian cotton, 20 per cent of her tobacco, 42 per cent of her rice and 34 per cent of her sugar, besides by far the largest and commercially most significant proportion of banana production.[140]

Taken as a whole, however these experiences seem to have brought more frustration than reward. Increases in output and acreage were small. Technological transformations were slow to come. Returns, with the possible exception of bananas, were not encouraging. Whether one looks at the experiences of tobacco and sugar, or at cotton, rice, and even bananas, agricultural growth in the Coast faced serious obstacles and, in spite of some progress, this situation changed little throughout the period under study. The 1920s, however, have been singled out y some historians as crucial years when the agrarian question became a

[139] For an exceptional observation on the poor quality of the soil in the Atlantic plains, see Ospina Vásquez, *El plan agrario*, 17 and 19.

[140] *Anuario General de Estadística* (Bogotá, 1934), 544–6.

barrier to Colombian development. The rigidity of agricultural supply is seen as the first expression of an agrarian problem. The deadlock in Colombian agricultural development has been analysed almost exclusively in terms of a backward agrarian structure conditioned, first, by the concentration of land ownership and, second, by the lack of mobility of the labour force and the existence of an indentured peasantry which lived outside the money economy.[141] How does the Coast fit into this picture? To what extent was the agrarian structure the main obstacle to increases in agricultural output? How rigid was the agricultural supply? In the light of the information offered in these chapter some tentative conclusions emerge.

For one thing, it would be misleading to think of the Coast as a region of conspicuous traditional latifundia, as it has often been portrayed.[142] Haciendas of colonial origins such as Berástegui – usually given as the typical example of the *Costeño* latifundia – seem to have been the exception rather than the rule. Moreover, Berástegui itself suffered fragmentation between 1880 and 1930, following financial crisis and family divisions, as will be shown in the next chapter. There were landowners who could claim property rights with titles of colonial origins. More often than not, however, land in such cases was held jointly, after inheritance or acquisition of land shares in a particular market hitherto neglected by historians. Consider the example of the Playones de Punta de Palma in Plato. In 1926, some twenty different individuals from different families claimed property rights as *comuneros* over a plot of approximately 4,000 acres based on colonial titles. Some of them might have been inheritors but, at least since 1881, share ownership had also changed hands as some *comuneros* sold their

[141] J. A. Bejarano, *El régimen agrario de la economía exportadora a la economía industrial* (Bogotá, 1979), 181–235; 'Orígenes del problema agrario', in M. Arrubla (ed.), *La agricultura colombiana en el siglo XX* (Bogotá, 1976), 33, 43, 46, 66, 69, 73, 75, and 'Contribución al debate sobre el problema agrario', in *El agro en el desarrollo colombiano* (Bogotá, 1977), 33–7, 46, 50–2, 60–4; D. Fajardo, *Haciendas, campesinos y políticas agrarias en Colombia, 1920–1980* (Bogotá, 1986), 39–40; Machado, *Políticas agrarias en Colombia*, 23–4; LeGrand, *Colonización y protesta campesina*, 134–5.

[142] See e. g. S. Kalmanowitz, *Economía y nación* (Bogotá, 1986), 164, and L. Zamosc, *The Agrarian Question and the Peasant Movement in Colombia* (Cambridge, 1986), 11.

rights.[143] This market in *acciones de tierra* seems also to have been a feature of the Cesar region.[144]

Some large estates also evolved as a twentieth-century phenomena, after claims on *baldíos* or purchases of land, or a combination of both processes. In 1916, the Hacienda La Esperanza could count on 816 ha, most of the land having been acquired by its owners, V. Dugand and E. Lallemand, through a series of purchases. In 1896, for example, they had bought 300 ha from J. Pereyra who, in turn, had acquired the land in different plots from six different individuals in 1891. One of these sellers, L. Tamayo, had bought his plot from D. Peña in 1887 who, in turn, had bought it from F. Noriega. To La Esperanza, Dugand and Lallemand added 1,034 ha that they were allocated by the state as *baldíos*.[145] One of the largest single landowners during the twentieth century was the United Fruit Company. This was, however, a highly localized phenomena with successive changes over the years, following what appears to have been an active land market. Furthermore, as we have seen, the American company shared the production of bananas with small- and middle-sized independent holders, and it also leased a significant proportion of its own land to tenants, while it was obliged to tolerate the presence of squatters, although the land invaded was considered of marginal importance.

It does not seem that large tracts of land were easily available on the market. In 1920, R. Elliot, on behalf of an American company interested in acquiring some 5,000 ha for grazing purposes in Magdalena, asked Consul Sawyer in Santa Marta for advice. The Consul's reply was far from being encouraging. In the western part of the department, Consul Sawyer answered, the holdings were not large, 'and in order to reach the extension of land desired, long drawn out proceedings would be necessary'. To the south, the Consul acknowledged the existence of large tracts but he considered that they were 'somewhat remote from markets' and also much of the unoccupied land belonged to the government. To the east, the extent of *baldíos* was large and 'were you to buy or rent land in that section,

143 'Indice archivos notariales, Plato, Magdalena', 32, 59, 69, 75, 93, 409, Oxford, MDC.

144 See e. g. Archives of the Notaría Unica, Valledupar: 'Protocolo', 2, 1930, files 163 and 214; Palmera and Mejía to the American Consul, Valledupar, 31 May 1921, in NAUS/RG84, Santa Marta. Correspondence, 1921 (3).

145 'Notaría pública del circuito, Ríohacha': 'Escrituras públicas Nos. 25 (1891), 72 and 73 (1893), 11, 14, 17, 27, 82 (1896), 95 (1899), and 27 (1906); and 'Notaría Segunda Barranquilla': 'Escritura pública No. 1331 (1916)' , in AFL.

titles would probably have to be carefully investigated'. Finally, Consul Sawyer pointed out that 'in government publications much comment regarding the immense grazing possibilities in these different sections is to be noted', but, he added: 'the indifference of the government and the tendency to interpose all kinds of obstacles in the way of developing its agricultural resources, would seem to make the understanding rather questionable'. To conclude, the American Consul advised Mr Elliot, 'before venturing into this section', to contact one J. Cannon in Mompox, who had some experience in these matters.[146] The Consul's advice was probably of little comfort. As representative of the American Colombian Corporation, Cannon had bought in 1910 a vast tract of land – 1,100,000 acres – known as *Tierras de Loba*, whose titles claimed colonial origins. By 1921, Cannon had been able to establish his headquarters in *Las Cabezas*, where the company had 1,500 'head of an inferior grade of cattle' but where there were also 'a good many settlements and numerous single houses scattered all over it, and most of these settlers claim the land and improvements they have made and are ready to go to the law to retain them'.[147] Cannon's pretensions to such a vast area had to face the counterclaims of a large population of settlers who saw themselves either as owners or as *colonos*. Besides, San Fernando and Barranca de Loba, among other *municipios,* also challenged the company's claims.[148] There followed a long dispute with an unfavourable outcome. In the face of strong opposition from a large population and the local authorities, the American company could not take effective possession of what looked on paper to be an impressive tract of land.

Wherever one observes agricultural development on the Coast, the presence of smallholders – either as independent farmers or tenants, and whether or not they were in conflict with expanding estates – was significant. In some cases, the cultivator entered into an arrangement with the landlord whereby he was allowed to till the land for a fixed period, after which he would return it as pasture and then move to another plot. Given the availability of public land, however, it seems likely that the largest proportion of cultivators were established as freeholders or squatters. As demographic pressures mounted, the

[146] Consul Sawyer to Elliot, Santa Marta, 28 Oct. 1920, NAUS/RG84, Santa Marta, correspondence, 1920 (3).

[147] NAUS/RG84, Cartagena, general correspondence, 1921 (7).

[148] Colombia, *Ministerio de industrias: Anexos a la memoria de 1924* (Bogotá, 1924), 175–86; A. N. C., Baldíos, vol. 37, files 192–7, 328–334, and vol. 46, files 220–8; LeGrand, *Colonización y protesta campesina*, 113.

chances of independent cultivators acquiring *baldíos* may have dwindled away. In 1919 *municipios* such as Córdoba, in the province of Carmen, could count on 10,000 ha of *baldíos*, while at the same time the *alcalde* acknowledged that there was a general shortage of labour.[149] In addition, the number and significance of established small- and medium-sized landowners should not be underestimated. They might initially have received the land as *baldíos*, then accumulated more land over the years or simply kept it and passed it on to their heirs. In 1852 Augustín Cotes was officially granted 50 ha of *baldíos* near Dibuya. His wife inherited this and added to it another 50 ha, which were later sold to Francisco Pacheco Triana. In turn, Pachecho's heirs sold the land in 1891 to Rafael Pereyra.[150]

This picture is not intended to suggest a highly fragmented agrarian structure, or to deny the existence of conflict over land tenure, but its complexities defy some of the generalizations hitherto assumed in analysing agricultural development on the Coast. On the one hand, it seems that there was a relatively active land market in which a process of exchanges, divisions, and amalgamations of estates was taking place. On the other hand, in so far as public land was available, possibilities for independent landholding were present. The process of allocation of *baldíos* was bound to be plagued with conflict, as has been shown by Catherine LeGrand but, as LeGrand herself has also pointed out, settlers were well aware of their own rights and ready to resist arbitrary dispossession. Some of them might have succumbed to the short-term temptations of a cash offer and some might have been forced to give up their claims but, in both cases, they could still move to a new settlement. In spite of conflicts, however, many a settler was also able to retain his holdings, as happened in the Tierras de Loba and in the banana zone. One sure result of the process of granting *baldíos* was a highly confused map of property rights which subsequently gave rise to considerable uncertainties among land-holders of all sizes.

As in many other tropical regions, most cultivators of smallholdings short of capital tended to spread their risks by growing a wide range of products: tobacco, rice, sugar-cane, corn, yucca, plantains.[151] A fraction of the *sementera* was usually devoted to cash crops, leaving also land

149 *Bolívar: Gaceta departamental*, 17 Mar. 1919.

150 'Notaría pública del circuito, Ríohacha: Escritura pública No. 27 (1986), in AFL.

151 See e. g. P. James, *A Geography of Man* (Boston, 1949), 95–6; C. J. Baker, *An Indian Rural Economy, 1800–1955. The Tamilnad Countryside* (Oxford, 1984), 208; P. Hill, *Development Economics on Trial* (Cambridge, 1989), 32.

for pasture, and efforts were increasingly concentrated on those products in higher demand by the market after they had proved adaptable to local conditions. Gradually, there emerged some degree of regional specialization such as tobacco in Carmen, rice in San Onofre and Majagual, cotton in Atlántico and eastern Magdalena, bananas in Ciénaga and Aracataca. Even if they produced for the market and kept a portion of the land for subsistence crops, small cultivators were often forced to supplement their income by working as labourers on larger estates, or to seek employment outside agriculture. Some gave up farming altogether. A locust plague prompted migration to the French canal works in Panama during the 1880s. Floods in 1939 had impelled cultivators to leave the land.[152] These movements were sometimes temporary, as in 1908 when labourers from other Coastal areas affected by drought and the locust pest went in search of work to the banana zone; conditions seemed to have improved some months later, and many labourers were reported to have gone back home. In any event, a large proportion of the rural population had no choice but to alternate agriculture with other occupations, since a vast extent of the coast was subject to periodical floods.

Whatever the conditions of the smallholders, there is little doubt that a significant number of them were cultivators in their own right. Tenancy agreements were spreading, but tenants were far from being bound to specific haciendas. Throughout the period under study, the impression received is one of a highly mobile rural population. It was precisely the possibility of setting up independent holdings which made labour scarce and gave rise to the early appearance of wage labour. Scarcity of hands was a real obstacle to any attempt to develop agriculture on a large commercial scale. Labour was not only scarce but became relatively expensive as other activities besides agriculture – oil exploration, public works, and even local industry – also competed for it. Undoubtedly, some influential landowners were anxious to obtain labour by coercive means. In 1892 and 1908, some laws were passed to establish semi-servile institutions, the *matrícula* and *concierto forzoso*. There is little evidence, however, that they were effectively implemented, and their existence rather showed the landowners' degree of concern about the scarcity of labour.[153] Furthermore, as will be shown in the following chapter, most labourers

[152] *Informes del Gobernador* (Santa Marta, 1939), 46.

[153] See description of these institutions in Fals Borda, *Historia de la cuestión agraria*, 106.

were in a position to demand payment in advance, which has erroneously been interpreted as a form of debt peonage. What emerges here is the early existence of a labour market driven by free wages. Given the high degree of geographical mobility together with the development of a land market, the link between a presumed pre-capitalist rural structure and low agricultural output, as traditionally suggested in Colombian historiography, is thus open to question, at least in the case of the Coast.

Without disregarding the need to understand the dynamics of social changes and their relation to economic development, this chapter has also attempted to show how the shortcomings of *Costeño* farming cannot be exclusively linked to a particular agrarian structure. Low population density was at the root of the real problem of labour shortage, a burden to farming. Together with low rates of productivity and inferior technology, the result in most cases was high labour costs relative to other Colombian regions and countries. Communication difficulties should not be underestimated either, as the slow pace of transport development did little to ease the cost of reaching the market. Further disadvantages were imposed by physical conditions. Serious periodical floods and drought often meant that, in order to bring the land under cultivation, significant investments in either drainage or irrigation, or both, had to be made on a scale which was probably beyond the financial capabilities of the country. With the benefit of hindsight, what appears most striking is the way Coastal agriculture adapted to scarce resources and managed, in the long run, to keep pace with demand. Furthermore, the general argument that agricultural output was stationary in the 1920s is highly debatable if applied to the Coast. Not only bananas, but also cotton, sugar-cane, and rice were responding to market conditions, despite the serious obstacles described above. However, the most significant expansion in Coastal agricultural was taking place in developing pasture for livestock, towards which the scant resources of the region were increasingly directed. There was a steady growth in this area throughout the period, motivated mainly by a national demand for beef. It is thus to the study of cattle production, its features and significance to the Coast, that this book now turns.

2
Cattle

1. Introduction

'Cattle here are the symbol of capital', Luis Striffler observed when he travelled around the Cesar region in the 1870s. The importance of the livestock industry as a source of regional wealth was evident to many a contemporary observer. Stock-raising was, in fact, a widespread activity in Colombia. In 1921 US Trade Commissioner Bell compared the significance of cattle to the national economy to that of coffee.[1] On the Coast, where coffee growing was confined to a few insignificant plantations, Bell's remark becomes all the more relevant.

Stimulated mainly by an internal demand for beef, and to a lesser extent by exports of hides and live cattle, herds grew steadily during the nineteenth century despite the recurrence of civil wars. In the 1870s the Governor of Lorica reported how increasing demand from Santander and Antioquia had pushed up cattle prices in the Sinú. In view of the prospects for stock raising in the region, the President of the Agricultural Board asked the Legislative Assembly to encourage its development. 'This industry has experienced a remarkable growth, which in turn has benefitted public wealth in the province', the Governor of Chinú pointed out in 1880. The Governor calculated that there were 100,000 head of cattle in his own province alone while observing that the expansion of the industry had brought an active land market.[2] At the end of the nineteenth century there was little doubt that the most important industry in Bolívar was cattle. It has been estimated that there were over one million head of cattle in the Coast at the beginning of this century. By the 1920s this number had doubled, representing 35 per cent of Colombia's cattle population. In the 1940s the Coast supported between 3.5 and 4 million head of cattle.[3]

[1] Bell, *Colombia*, 139; Striffler, *El río Cesar*, 77.

[2] *DB*, 20 Aug. 1880; *GB*, 26 Aug. 1874; and *Informe de Balmaseda* 13, 15, 17, 18.

[3] R. K. Oakley, 'Cattle Raising and Related Industries in Department of Bolívar, Colombia', Cartagena, 31 July 1944, NAUS/ RG166/ NAR, Colombia, Livestock. Figures are scarce and unreliable, making it practically impossible to trace with accuracy the development of herds. Besides the general backwardness of statistics and the natural fears of taxation, ranchers were wary of censuses since cattle stocks were the main targets of opposing armies in domestic disturbances.

In spite of its significance, the livestock industry has been neglected in the historiography. Moreover, the few references to it tend to undervalue its importance, blaming cattle for the backwardness of *Costeño* economy and society. Cattle ranchers are portrayed as irrational economic agents, with the assumption that land devoted to pasture could have been put to better use. In addition, the cattle industry is almost exclusively linked to the existence of large estates, whose interests conflict with those of a peasantry involved in farming. This chapter aims at revising these and other stereotypes about the industry in the overall context of the region's history. It will examine first the structure of the market to show that, far from being a monopoly of the few, the cattle industry was a widespread activity that, while integrating the region through the different stages of cattle production, encouraged the early formation of a national market. A detailed study of a cattle hacienda will serve to illustrate how the industry was organized to meet the demand for beef in the Andean interior. This section is followed by an analysis of the role played by the exports of livestock, and the frustrating attempts to develop a meat-packing industry. A final section looks briefly at hides, milk, and cheese. Following the lines of the previous chapter, I argue in the conclusion that, contrary to prevailing interpretations, cattle raising was an industry that adapted well to a region of scant resources. But before moving further, this introduction looks at the geographical and technological conditions under which cattle developed in the Colombian Caribbean.

Unlike the Argentine *pampas* and the Venezuelan *llanos*, the Coastal plains where cattle grazing took place were not 'open range' country. Historical geographies of the region have shown how most of the area which came to be known as savannah was previously forested.[4] As the industry prospered, dense forests were removed by burning and clearing the land which was eventually to be pasture. However, this ecological transformation was gradual and did not cover the whole grazing area. Vast portions of the lowlands were flooded for about half the year, though in the other half they provided excellent pasturage. As Cunninghame Graham noted, 'in the rainy season [the River Sinú] overflows its banks for a considerable distance on both sides, leaving a thick deposit of alluvial mud. Then the grass grows luxuriantly and the

[4] Gordon, *Human Geography and Ecology of the Sinú*, 57–70, and Krogzemis, 'A Historical Geography', 46–7. See also L. O. Yoder, 'The Cattle Industry in Colombia and Venezuela', M.Sc. thesis, University of Chicago, 1926, 33.

cattle fatten quickly'.[5] Savannahs and *playones* often complemented each other, conditioning the seasonal movement of herds. Transhumance was thus a basic feature of the cattle economy. 'In January,' Vergara y Velasco pointed out, 'the cattle rancher's family migrates to the swamps . . . Men from the savanna live alternately in two households.' When Cunninghame Graham visited the region, 'the plains were desolate, for all the cattle had been moved into the swamps along the banks of the San Jorge and the Magdalena'.[6] The movement included not only the herds but often also the rancher, his employees, and their families.[7]

Despite the introduction of barbed-wire fencing in the 1870s, enclosure was a gradual process and open fields remained the general rule in several areas of the region well into the twentieth century. In 1921, enclosures were still exceptional in Southern Magdalena, where communal land and *baldíos* were abundant. According to cattlemen from Valledupar, poor breeding went hand in hand with the lack of enclosure.[8] Similarly, the expansion of 'exotic' grasses such as *pará* and *yaraguá*, which were introduced in 1875 and 1906 respectively, was also gradual. In 1924, it was estimated that the area planted with such grasses did not exceed 250,000 ha. Natural grasses were still the rule. Furthermore, pasture was, in most cases, the only source of food for cattle.[9] Innovations were also slow in stockbreeding. During the centuries following the introduction of Iberian stock, a creole race known as *costeño con cuernos* – 'horned coastal' – had emerged through natural selection, adapted to tropical environment.[10] It was not until the end of the nineteenth century, that the first crossings with imported stock – 'Aberdeen Angus' and 'Red Poll' – took place,

[5] Cunninghame Graham, *Cartagena and the Banks of the Sinú*, 8–9; Striffler, *El río San Jorge*, 33, 44, 46; Dawe, *Account of a Journey*, 29.

[6] Vergara y Velasco, *Nueva geografía*, 543; Cunninghame Graham, *Cartagena and the Banks of the Sinú*, 235.

[7] R. K. Oakley, 'Observations Regarding Livestock Industry in Parts of the Department of Magdalena', NAUS/ RG166, NAR (n. d., 1944?), Colombia, Livestock.

[8] Palmera and Mejía to the US Consul in Santa Marta, Valledupar, 31 May 1921, NAUS/ RG84: Santa Marta Consulate, correspondence, 1921 (3). In 1942, there were few fences in some important cattle areas in the Coast; Wylie, *The Agriculture of Colombia*, 121.

[9] L. Schnare, 'Cattle Raising in the Cartagena Consular District', Cartagena, 19 Dec. 1924, NAUS/ 821.6221/2; G. M. Roseveare, *The Grasslands of Latin America* (Cardiff, 1948), 126–7.

[10] C. J. Bishko, 'The Peninsular Background of Latin American Cattle Ranching', *HAHR*, 32/4, (Nov. 1952), 491–515; L. Lorente, 'La ganadería bovina en Colombia', in A. Machado, *Problemas agrarios colombianos* (Bogotá, 1986), 331–68.

producing the *Romo-sinuano* which became popular among some cattle ranchers in Bolívar. Crossbreeding with *zebú,* a race resilient to the harsh arid regions, started in 1905. However, it was considered that the *zebú* produced a coarse beef and its import was prohibited by the government between 1931 and 1939. In 1935, several cattlemen attempted crossbreeding with European stock but without much success.[11]

2. Landowners, Cattle-Owners, and Cattle-Dealers

When Striffler travelled through the region, he noticed the existence of large cattle-owners and land-owners such as O. Trespalacios, 'the master in the Valley', or J. Pumarejo, 'member of an old family of patriots, the richest in the country'. Yet he also observed the activities of a certain Morales, a self-made man who had 'his modest fortune scattered among the large estates'. Morales belonged to the same category as another cattle-owner, 'one Palacio: . . . he was probably the richest in town, but his larder was no better stocked than that of a poor man. Palacio was a man of the people; he owed his wealth to hard work, having perhaps started as a foreman on a hacienda . . .'.[12]

Some traditional families such as the Trespalacios and Pumarejos consolidated their wealth through the cattle industry. However, the expansion of livestock also gave way to an emergent group of local entrepreneurs who found in cattle both profit and a source of social mobility. The Colombian sociologist Orlando Fals Borda has referred to them as 'unpolished old men, wearing sandals and crumpled hats', and he cites as a 'classic example' the case of the Indian C. Ramos, a semi-illiterate 'who managed to build an agrarian empire in Chinú, San Marcos and Caimito'. Fals Borda also points out the cases of C. Támara and P. Herazo, among others: they all shared that 'tradition of austerity that characterized many *nouveau riche Costeños*'.[13] The rise of some did not prevent the fall of others. The case of the Burgos family, and their Hacienda Berástegui – which has often been given as

[11] *RNA* (Mar.–Apr., 1925), 261; (May 1939), 336–7; *Revista de Ganadería* (Jan. 1939), 22.

[12] Striffler, *El río Cesar,* 10, 34, 77, 78.

[13] Fals Borda, *Retorno a la tierra*, 78, 86, 153A.

the example of a typical *Costeño* hacienda which concentrated land and cattle between 1870 and 1930 – is worthy of attention.[14]

Of colonial origins, the hacienda had been inherited by the priest J. M. Berástegui at the end of the eighteenth century, and he in turn, left it to his five illegitimate children.[15] The new generation enriched the land with artificial pastures, fenced off the hacienda, and incorporated new land; thus Berástegui grew from 8,000 to 12,000 ha between 1870 and 1880. The Burgos were pioneers in the introduction of *pará* grass, oil exploration, and sugar plantations. They were also prominent in politics. Cunninghame Graham, who visited many farms, large and small, during his journeys across the Sinú, found Berástegui to be exceptional, 'for we sat down to dinner in a dining room, and conversation was less local in its character, for the owners of the place had travelled widely, had been in Paris, and spoke French and English fluently'.[16] There was definitively something about this hacienda that made it different from the rest, even in the somewhat patriarchal relations between the owners and their dependents which did not escape Cunninghame Graham's attention. However, since the mid-nineteenth century, the owners of Berástegui had been much in debt, and repeatedly used the land – either by renting or mortgaging it – as a means to overcome their recurrent financial crises and to launch new ventures. If it is true that the Burgos managed to acquire more land during the 1870s, after 1880 not only had no new land been incorporated into the hacienda but the existing estate was gradually being fragmented, and by 1930 the hacienda had been sold. In the meantime the Burgos had been losing herds. They finally reduced their business to renting their land to neighbouring cattlemen, although they also tried unsuccessfully to develop a sugar *ingenio*. 'What was left to this poor rheumatic old man?', a journalist asked in 1935 about the fate of General F. Burgos, one of the owners of Berástegui, and he answered: 'Not even a hectare of land. He lives in misery, awaiting death on someone else's estate'.[17]

[14] Fals Borda, *Capitalismo, hacienda y poblamiento*, 35–7, and S. Kalmanowitz, 'El régimen agrario durante el siglo XIX', in *Manual de Historia de Colombia* (Bogotá, 1980) II. 276.

[15] The history of the hacienda is well documented through family correspondence in Burgos Puche, *El general Burgos*; see in particular p. 127, 182, 192, 296, 302, 342, 353, 420–5. See also my essay in A. Meisel and E. Posada, *Por qué se disipó el dinamismo industrial de Barranquilla. Y otros ensayos de historia económica de la Costa Caribe* (Bogotá, 1993), 137–47.

[16] Cunninghame Graham, *Cartagena and the Banks of the Sinú*, 510.

[17] A. Díaz, *Sinú, pasión y vida del trópico* (Bogotá, 1935), 87.

Certainly large herds and ranchers like those to be found in Argentina and in the American West were exceptional in the Colombian Caribbean. In the San Jorge region personal fortunes were not large: 'There are just ten ranchers who own herds of about 500 head of cattle; only one of them is really wealthy'. In the Cesar, Striffler was impressed by the dominant presence of 'massive wild herds' which 'have no known owners and become the property of anyone who can catch them'.[18] Following the expansion of the cattle industry, some ranchers did manage later on to accumulate herds of between 10 and 15,000 head of cattle. However, cattle-raising was never exclusively a large-scale operation. Cattle-owners were not always landowners and the number of small ranchers remained significant.[19] Sometimes tenants had a sort of sharecropping agreement, like those in the hacienda Las Cabezas who used to get one-third of the calves – some others, such as C. Ramos in Marta Magdalena, were entitled to pasture a fixed number of steers of their own.[20] Those with some capital had the opportunity to rent land. Furthermore, given the availability of *playones* and *baldíos*, the possibilities for grazing on communal land were still open in the 1940s, although conflicts over landownership were not uncommon. Thus owning cattle was often distinct from owning land, and cattle provided a living for a large number of people in the region, including some pastoral communities such as the Guajiro Indians and the San Basilio de Palenque.[21]

Production and trading in livestock involved an active market where cattle changed hands several times before reaching the final consumer. In general, in the Coast it required five years to produce a steer fit for

[18] Striffler, *El río San Jorge*, 97, and *El río Cesar*, 10. Similar cases of wild cattle could be traced in other Latin American countries. See V. M. Patiño, *Historia de la actividad agropecuaria en América equinoccial* (Cali, 1965), 364–5; H. Giberti, *Historia económica de la ganadería Argentina* (Buenos Aires, 1981), 22, 29; S. R. Duncan Baretta and J. Markoff, 'Civilization and Barbarism: Cattle Frontiers in Latin America', *Comparative Studies in Society and History* (1978), 591; G. Carvallo, *El hato Venezolano, 1900–1980* (Caracas, 1985), 18–19.

[19] Wylie, *The Agriculture of Colombia*, 119. A 1766 livestock census, which had been used to estimate the concentration of cattle ownership, left out those owners with less than 20 head of cattle, which seem to have been a considerable number. See H. Tovar Pinzón, *Grandes empresas agrícolas y ganaderas* (Bogotá, 1980), 102.

[20] 'Report on Las Cabezas', NAUS/ RG84, Consular general correspondence, Cartagena, 1921 (7); ASAS, 31 May 1914; L. Sawyer, 'Livestock in the Department of the Magdalena', Santa Marta, 23 July 1921, NAUS/ RG84: Santa Marta correspondence, 1921 (3).

[21] Dawe, *Account of a Journey*, 17, and N. Friedemann, *Ma ngombe: guerreros y ganaderos en Palenque* (Bogotá, 1979), 94, 97, 129.

TABLE 2.1 *Returns on Cattle Raising estimated by Amin Meluk, Cartagena, 1923 (Colombian pesos)*

Purchase of 3,000 2-year-old steers at $10 each	$30,000
To feed and care for the steers for 2 years	5,000
Maintenance of the estate	5,000
Interest (1% per month) on 2,400 ha of cultivated land ($50 per head)	28,000
Total for 2 years	68,000
Sale of 27,000 remaining after 2 years (10% dead/lost) at $30 each	81,100
Profit (30% of $40,000 investment)	12,200

Source: Amin Meluk, 'Memorandum', Cartagena, 12 Dec. 1923, NAUS/R84: American Consulate, general correspondence, Cartagena, 1923 (6).

beef. Although the pattern may have varied over time, cattle were usually bred by small ranchers who sold their steers at an early age – 1½ to 2 years – due to their lack of capital. Larger ranchers then raised the cattle to the age of about 4 years, before selling them to other ranchers who fattened the herds close to the centres of consumption. In these three stages of cattle production, the trader – who purchased and sold respectively from the breeder to the raiser, from the raiser to the fattener, and from the fattener to the final destination – played a significant role. After studying the conditions of the market, Oakley concluded that most cattle passed through at least six or even seven pairs of hands before reaching the retailer: 'breeder – to buyer – (and perhaps to another buyer) to raiser – to shipper – to fattener – to butcher'.[22]

Given the available information, it is virtually impossible to trace the fluctuations of cattle prices during the period. There were periods of low prices, such as the early 1870s, 1910s, and the 1930s. Periods of remarkably good prices for producers were usually related to export of live cattle: to Cuba in the 1880s and at the end of the century, and to Panama in 1916–19, 1922–5 and 1942–4.[23] Besides exports, other

[22] Oakley, 'Cattle Raising and Related Industries', 21. See also Boaz, 'Cattle Industry in Colombia', and Oakley, 'Observations Regarding Livestock Industry', 1, and E. C. Soule, 'Cattle Raising in Colombia', Cartagena, 22 Dec. 1920, NAUS/821.62221.

[23] *GB*, 20 Aug. 1871; Bank of London and South America, *Monthly Review*, London, 3/32, (July 1921), 126, and 7/79 (June 1925), 202; Bell, *Colombia*, 138; Boaz, 'Cattle Industry in Colombia', 10; F. Arias to B. Ospina, Bogotá, 30 July 1943, ASAS/C/25:148.

TABLE 2.2 *Percentages of Profits for Ten Cattle Ranches in Bolívar, Estimated by Kenneth Oakley, 1944*

Ranches	Acres	Profit (%)	Operating profit (%) [b]	Cost per head ($) [c]	Acres per head
Ranch 1 [a]	35,000	18.0	12.0	5.91	2.5
Ranch 2 [a]	19,760	13.0	7.5	8.12	3.0
Ranch 3 [a]	3,210	18.5	11.0	6.56	
Ranch 4	5,533	8.0	6.0	9.18	1.5
Ranch 5	122	6.0	4.2	7.36	
Ranch 6	928	7.8	7.4	7.64	2.5
Ranch 7	538	4.2	3.1	14.05	1.6
Ranch 8	1,215	9.0	7.0	7.07	1.2
Ranch 9 [a]	21,000	3.4	2.1	11.63	4.0
Ranch 10	1,212	7.0	5.0	18.62	4.0

[a] Included rented land.
[b] Not including changes in inventory value.
[c] Cost of producing calf to 1 year, or of grazing and caring for other animal 1 year.

Source: Oakley, 'Cattle Raising and Related Industries', 27.

factors influencing cattle prices were transportation facilities, production costs, population growth, the number of cattle available, which in turn was influenced by cattle-raising practices, weather conditions, disease and the like. The picture was a complex one and any attempt to analyse cattle prices has also to take into account regional variations, and the role of the different agents participating in the market.

It seems that returns from the cattle industry varied significantly according to the different stages of production and marketing. Larger-scale ranchers who could breed their steers and sell them at the age of 4 years were probably in a better position than cattle breeders and raisers since they were able to avoid the cost of intermediaries. In 1923 A. Meluk estimated that raising cattle could bring safe returns of 15 per cent a year (see Table 2.1), while D. M. Camargo, a large cattleman, calculated net returns of between 15 and 30 per cent.[24] According to

[24] *RNA* (May–June 1925), 317.

TABLE 2.3 *Prominent Cattle Dealers in Bolívar, 1928*

Name	Headquarters	Year of establishment	Annual business ($)	Employees
Oscar A. Gómez	Cartagena	1908	500,000	10
García y Samudio	Sincelejo	1912	250,000	
Joaquín P. García	Cereté	1918	65,000	5
Barguil y Caluma	Cereté	1925	100,000	5
Samuel Aduen y Cía	Ovejas	1927	75,000	6
Checri y Fayad	Lorica	1897	50,000	20
Arturo Samur G.	Sincelejo	1897	75,000	10
Diego Martínez y Cía		1862	510,000	
Lázaro María Pérez		1919	250,000	

Source: 'List of Prominent Cattle Dealers', Cartagena, 24 Mar.1928, NAUS / RG84, Consular-General correspondence, 1928 (5).

Oakley, however, not a single local rancher took full administrative costs into account when estimating their profits and losses. Oakley had the opportunity of surveying ten ranches of different sizes in 1944 (See Table 2.2), and reached the conclusion that, on average, cattle producers could only secure returns of 9.5 per cent. Profits were higher for larger ranches, involved in cattle breeding and fattening, where the value of land was low with poor outlets to markets. What motivated investment in cattle, however, was not so much higher but safer returns.

'Let the cattleman go bankrupt, while he sells his cattle so cheap!' The cry came from A. Percy, a cattle rancher from Bolívar, who complained about the lack of national support for the industry while the country demanded low prices for beef. According to Percy, intermediaries not cattle producers were to be blamed for the high prices of beef in the market – he identified intermediaries with *Antioqueño* traders.[25] However, as the cattle industry expanded, some merchants on the Coast also specialized in cattle trading (as illustrated in Table 2.3). Nevertheless, the Medellín fair was the most influential in fixing prices for livestock. Intermediaries – *Antioqueños* and *Costeños* alike – were keeping a significant proportion of the returns. 'Except for speculators,' Oakley observed, 'the only persons to receive

[25] *RNA* (July 1915), 450–1.

TABLE 2.4 *Distribution of Returns in the Price for Meat Paid by the Ultimate Consumer in the Interior, 1934 and 1943 (%)*

	1934	1943
Producer (breeder and raiser)	41.4	44
Transport to interior	14.4	12
Fattener in interior	15.2	23
Commission agents [a]	9.0	6
Butcher	20.0 [b]	9
Taxes		6

[a] Including local transport costs.
[b] Including taxes.

Source: Oakley, 'Cattle Raising and Related Industries', 32.

disproportionate shares of gross proceeds from cattle sales, probably are the transportation company owners and butchers'[26] (see Table 2.4). Percy's irritation against 'the *Antioqueño* trader' also reflected conflicting interests among cattle ranchers which were often highly localized. Similar clashes of interests can be identified in other cattle countries such as Argentina, where the livestock industry was also organized in various distinctive stages.[27] Since cattle raising largely took place in areas far away from the main centres of consumption, and since herds had to be transported long distances on the hoof thus losing weight, cattle were fattened in specialized ranches close to their final markets. There were areas on the Coast, such as San Juan del Cesar, Salamina, and Aguachica, mainly devoted to breeding and raising, while Southern Bolívar together with Northern Antioquia specialized in cattle fattening.

3. Beef in the Regional and National Diets

Cattle on the Coast was basically produced to meet the national demand for beef. 'The general use of beef,' the US Consul in Cartagena observed in 1924, 'either fresh or dried, as food for practically all classes of people doubtless has . . . been a factor in the

[26] Oakley, 'Cattle Raising and Related Industries', 31.
[27] See Giberti, *Historia económica de la ganadería Argentina*, 100–2, 165, 189, 202.

growth of the industry.' In Valledupar, according to Bolinder, 'dried meat played a big role in planning any menu'. Salted meat was often part of the *bogas*'s breakfast on the Magdalena river. With the introduction of steam navigation, the lower decks of the boats carried, next to the freight, 'live cattle for beef on the trip'.[28] There were variations in consumption patterns, among the different social classes, both in quantity and quality. *Jornaleros* in Marta Magdalena, for example, were given beef twice a week although 'the cattle that is given away for local consumption is worthless – without any commercial value'.[29] In 1944, salted meat was produced as a cottage industry throughout Bolívar, 'for the use of the poorer classes with no refrigeration facilities and for cowboys riding the range'.[30] All in all, the consumption of beef was nevertheless considerable. Expanding cities and towns in the region, such as Cartagena, Ciénaga, Aracataca and Barranquilla, were major centres of beef consumption. In the *matadero público* (abattoir) in Barranquilla, slaughtering increased at an annual rate of 4.3 per cent between 1872 and 1920 and at 4 per cent between 1920 and 1950 (see Table 2.5). On the whole, the proportion of head of cattle slaughtered to the number of inhabitants does not seem to have varied significantly between 1870 and 1919. During the following two decades, the population in Barranquilla grew more rapidly that the number of head of cattle being slaughtered, but the balance seems to have recovered during the late 1930s. By 1950, livestock slaughtered in the *matadero público* reached a new peak. Consumption of meat in Barranquilla fluctuated between 35 and 50 kg annually per capita during the period.

The region itself was a large consumer of beef, but the major markets for Coastal cattle were in the interior: 'Colombian people are meat-eaters and the consumption of beef, even among the poorest classes, is very high . . . beef cattle being the chief article of trade between one Department and another and one district and another'.[31] However, there were significant differences in consumption rates among the various provinces. Whereas departments such as Antioquia, Valle, Bolívar, Atlántico, and Tolima consumed between 35 and 50 kg of meat annually, others such as Boyacá, Cauca, and Nariño consumed

[28] Schnare, 'Cattle Raising', 1; Robinson, *A Flying Trip to the Tropics*, 49; Bolinder, *We Dared the Andes*, 93.

[29] Vallejo to Escobar, Marta Magdalena, 9 Nov. 1931, ASAS/C/118:83.

[30] Oakley, 'Cattle Raising and Related Industries', 26.

[31] Bell, *Colombia*, 143.

TABLE 2.5 *Stock Slaughtered in the* Matadero Público *in Barranquilla, 1870–1950 (selected years)*

Year	Cattle	Pigs	Sheep	Head of stock	Meat (000 kg)
1872 [a]				3,010	
1919 [b]	15,729	1,827		17,556	
1920	17,040	2,213		19,253	
1921	20,390	2,604		22,994	
1922	22,332	2,542		24,874	
1923	23,198	2,503		25,701	
1924 [c]				28,344	
1926 [d]				30,498	
1931 [e]	23,000	4,500	98	27,598	5,562
1932	23,000	4,900	147	28,047	5,383
1933	21,800	5,800	81	27,681	5,261
1934	23,500	7,700	107	31,307	5,512
1935 [f]	24,792	8,317	169	33,278	5,875
1950 [g]				72,734	

Sources: (a) F. Baena and F. Vergara, *Barranquilla* (Barranquilla, 1922), 421. (b) For 1919–23: *Informe que rinde la Comisión del Presupuesto al Concejo Municipal* (Barranquilla, 1924), Cuadros y Anexos. (c) M. Goenaga, *Acción Costeña* (Barranquilla, 1924), 80–1. (d) E. Rash-Isla (ed.), *Directorio comercial pro-Barranquilla* (Barranquilla, 1928), 191. (e) For 1931–4: Contraloría, *Geografía económica del Atlántico* (Bogotá, 1936), 123. (f) *BME*, Barranquilla, 28 Feb. 1936, 33. (g) J. R. Sojo, *Barranquilla, una economía en expansión* (Barranquilla, 1955), 130.

an average of just over 10 kg.[32] Livestock from the Coast supplied in large numbers the cattle markets in Antioquia, Caldas, Tolima, and Santander. In 1926 some 70,000 head of cattle left Bolívar for the Andean interior; in 1942 this figure was more than doubled. Between 1938 and 1943, 34 per cent of Bolívar cattle production was for domestic consumption, the rest was distributed in Antioquia (26%), Santander (17%), Tolima (16%), Cundinamarca (3%), Atlántico (2%), and other departments (2%).

The single largest market for cattle outside the region was Antioquia. Commercial links between Bolívar and Antioquia were strengthened in the mid-nineteenth century, after the opening of a track to Tarazá.[33] In 1874, an expanding trade motivated modest improvements in

[32] Contraloría, *Anuario General de Estadística* (Bogotá, 1934), 579; *Síntesis Estadística de Colombia* (Bogotá, 1944), 115; and *RNA* (1936), 492.

[33] *Mensaje del Gobernador* (Cartagena, 1852), 11.

communications: the *camino quinterín*, a bridle path, was built between Sahagún and Cáceres. Led by a local priest, cattlemen from Ayapel joined efforts to open a track towards the border with Antioquia.[34]

Concern about communications between the two departments was often expressed by their respective representatives in Congress. A railway project, linking Bolívar with Antioquia, raised high expectations in the region.[35] Work started, but the *Ferrocarril Central de Bolívar* was never completed. By the 1940s, two main routes were used in the transport of livestock to Antioquia. The first one included the movement of cattle on the hoof to the port of Yatí, near Magangué, in a trip that could last up to 12 days and during which the animals lost around 50 kg per head. In Yatí the herds were loaded on to special boats and taken to Puerto Berrío, from whence they were transported by rail to their final destination. Heavier weight losses, however, were incurred on the second route, an entirely overland drive from the Sinú to Medellín which lasted around 50 days, including stops for pasture along the way. Estimates of weight losses on this route, which could only be taken during the dry season, from December to April, varied from 80 to 140 kg per head.[36]

The city of Medellín played a significant role in the marketing of livestock. On the one hand, its consumption of meat, as shown in Table 2.6, was high: between 1929 and 1942, average meat consumption was over 47 kg per capita. Although pork in Medellín sold well, the demand for beef was also strong. The livestock fair in Medellín was so important that it conditioned cattle prices. Originally organized in 1888, the Medellín fair soon displaced that of Itaguí, which had previously dominated the market.[37] Table 2.7 illustrates the movement of stock from Bolívar in the Medellín fair between 1912 and 1950.

Antioqueño merchants became actively involved in the cattle industry. By 1891, T. Ospina had established a permanent link to buy

[34] *GB*, 17 Mar. and 26 Aug. 1874; 'Testimonio de P. Villegas al Presidente del Comité Ganadero', Montería, 6 Aug. 1928, ASAS/C/141: 87.

[35] *Anales del Senado* (4 Sept. 1919), 110, and (9 Nov. 1917), 317–18; *Anales de la Cámara de Representantes* (15 Dec. 1919), 432–3.

[36] See Hopkins, 'Annual Livestock Report', Bogotá, 25 Apr. 1945; R. N. Frankel, 'Plan for the Transportation of Fresh Meat', Medellín, 20 Sept. 1945, in NAUS/ RG166: NAR, Box 179, and Oakley, 'Cattle Raising and Related Industries', 22–3.

[37] See Empresas Varias de Medellín, *Ferias de ganados, 25 años* (Medellín, 1974), 5–6; Brew, *El desarrollo económico de Antioquia*, 213.

TABLE 2.6 *Livestock Slaughtering and Meat Consumption in Medellín, 1929–1950 (various years)*

Year	Cows/steers	Pigs	Meat per person (kg)
1929	26,114	15,921	48.04
1930	24,079	16,459	48.33
1931	23,347	13,007	45.98
1932	25,578	17,496	51.22
1933	26,732	18,615	50.67
1934	27,314	19,106	49.76
1935	28,292	17,816	49.22
1936	28,611	17,848	50.33
1937	27,550	19,618	43.61
1938	28,994	21,631	44.15
1939	28,996	20,678	41.65
1940	29,668	21,722	42.59
1941	31,653	24,384	45.07
1942	33,761	27,993	46.59
1943	37,798	29,651	
1946	43,078	30,592	
1947	47,271	30,244	
1948	47,499	25,731	
1949	49,715	27,316	
1950	53,378	31,834	

Source: *Anuario Estadístico de Medellín* (Medellín, 1938, 1942, 1943, 1950).

steers in Ayapel, Corozal and the Sinú with the purpose of selling them in Antioquia. In 1893, Ospina Hermanos and F. Vásquez set up a company to buy cattle in Bolívar, fatten them on their ranches, and sell them later in Medellín through the familiar arrangement of *ganado al partir*.[38] Several *Antioqueño* merchants bought land in Southern Bolívar for the purposes of livestock fattening. A look at the Hacienda Marta Magdalena serves to illustrate in more detail several aspects of the cattle industry as so far described.

38 Ospina to Mayans, Medellín, 14 Mar. 1891, Archivo Ospina Hermanos, Faes, Medellín, C/21:230.

TABLE 2.7 *Cattle from Bolívar Sold in the Medellín Fair, 1912–1950 (various years)*

Year	Head of cattle (000)	Value (000 pesos)
1912 [a]	21.8	859.9
1913	30.5	1,353.2
1914	17.6	731.1
1915	31.1	1,075.2
1916	28.0	1,033.8
1917	16.6	601.9
1918	17.1	654.8
1919	24.2	1,214.1
1920	17.7	654.8
1921	8.3	319.2
1922	15.7	537.8
1923	14.8	542.7
1924	25.3	1,092.2
1925	25.3	1,092.2
1926	27.2	2,138.7
1927	37.2	2,033.6
1928	38.2	2,378.9
1929	31.3	1,838.1
1937 [b]	30.2	2,761.2
1942	29.7	3,120.1
1943	35.6	4,197.2
1945	37.8	7,613.6
1949	41.8	16,449.2
1950	46.6	20,528.6

Sources: [a] 1912–30: 'Cuadros de movimientos de la feria de Medellín', ASAS. [b] 1937–50: *Anuario Estadístico de Medellín.*

4. Marta Magdalena, an Antioqueño Cattle Estate in Bolívar

In 1913, a group of entrepreneurs in Medellín founded the Sociedad Agrícola del Sinú with the aim of exploiting the land in Marta Magdalena, a hacienda near Montería. The new company had bought the estate from the Societé Française du Río Sinú, a Franco-Belgian venture which starting up in 1882 had taken possession of *baldío* land to extract timber, although plans had also been drawn up to fatten cattle and cultivate cacao. The Sociedad Agrícola del Sinú made clear its goals from the outset: to buy steers and fatten them for sale in the interior markets, particularly in Medellín and its surroundings.[39] Once established, the Sociedad Agrícola del Sinú faced two main tasks: to clarify land titles, and to get the fields into pasture.

The boundaries of the estate were not clearly marked. Deeds were inaccurate and neighbours made claims. In 1915, R. Salazar, administrator of Marta Magdalena, reported that A. Vega and A. Lacharme had moved their fencing onto the estate's property. Vega had taken possession of 203 *fanegas* claiming that he owned the plot after making an arrangement with the Franco-Belgian company. 'This is a difficult man who is causing us a lot of trouble', Salazar pointed out to his employer.[40] As laborious were the dealings with *colonos*. It seems that, in general, the hacienda managed to settle most of the disputes with original *colonos*, paying them for what was known as *las mejoras*, improvements made by the settler, and allowing them to stay for a fixed period of time on the plot under the condition that, at the end of the period, the *colono* would hand back the land sown with pasture. In 1914, Salazar came to an arrangement with eight settlers whereby he agreed 'to pay them for what they had already sown with pasture, at 7,000 pesos per *fanega* . . . while in addition some of the settlers would receive a few cattle for milking'.[41] Deals varied according to the quality of soil, the *mejoras*, and the individual involved. C. Ramos received 8,000 pesos. In addition, he was allowed to cultivate the plot for two further years with corn, plantains, yucca and *ñame*, and to graze up to fifteen head of his own cattle. Arrangements with the settler G. Martínez were given priority, due to his 'great influence over the majority of the local inhabitants'.[42] In some cases, where the land was considered worthless, the *colonos* were not disturbed.[43] Not all settlers were ready to accept the estate's offer. In 1917, twenty-six families of *colonos*, who had built houses, planted fruit trees, and sown the land with pasture, rejected any deal but

[39] 'Libros de actas y estatutos de la Sociedad Agrícola del Sinú', 20 Jan. 1913, ASAS.

[40] Administrator to Manager, 8 Jan. 1915, ASAS/C/106.

[41] Similar arrangements were made with several other settlers. See ASAS/C/49:53, ASAS/C/106:13 and 54.

[42] Administrator to Manager, 25 Apr. 1914, ASAS/C/44:53; 15 Jan. 1915, ASAS/C/106:13; and 22 Sept. 1914, ASAS/C/109:41.

[43] Administrator to Manager, 22 Mar. 1917, ASAS/C/107:89.

insisted on themselves buying the land from the Marta Magdalena, which they offered to pay for in labour.[44]

Thus the enclosure of the estate did not prevent problems of land ownership which seem to have become acute in the 1930s and were further aggravated by difficulties with squatters. According to the administrator in 1932, people's renewed enthusiasm for farming had motivated land invasions on neighbouring estates.[45] Squatters also started to move into Marta Magdalena, sometimes with the support and even at the instigation of the local authorities. In 1934, the Liberal *Corregidor* in Leticia set the squatters against one of the estate's foremen while he denigrated the owners of Marta Magdalena as Conservatives.[46] Amidst these problems, by 1932 boundaries in large parts of the estate had already been marked and fenced, although some plots were still open fields. Simultaneously with the process of enclosure and the clarification of boundaries, the administrator of the estate was active in *desmonte y siembra* – clearing the land for pasture. The periods 1914–18 and 1921–8 were mostly devoted to *desmonte y siembra.* In the 1920s, some 4,000 ha had been seeded with grass. The expansion of pasture was interrupted during the Depression but the estate managed to maintain the land already in use. By 1939, 9,000 ha out of the total 12,000 ha belonging to Marta Magdalena were seeded with artificial grass.[47] The expansion of herds often took place at a faster rate than the expansion of pasture land; thus the estate was obliged to rent neighbouring plots.[48] The expansion of herds in Marta Magdalena mostly took place between 1914 and 1921: the number of head of cattle grew from 4,760 to 10,567 during that period. From 1921 up to 1948, inventories registered figures of between 10,000 and 12,000 (see Table 2.8)

The Sociedad Agrícola del Sinú's main line of business was cattle fattening: to buy steers of between 1½ and 3½ years old with the aim at selling them later to the *Antioqueño* market. They regularly bought steers from *comisionistas* (middlemen) or directly from cattle breeders. In 1934, for example, they bought 1,005 head of cattle from C. Ruiz, a *comisionista* who in turn had acquired the herd in small lots – 13 to 200

[44] ASAS/C/107:90.

[45] Administrator to Manager, 6 Feb. 1932, ASAS/C/119:15.

[46] Administrator to Manager, 3 Nov. 1934, and Montería, 11 Dec. 1934, ASAS/C/75:13 and 158:23.

[47] Exbrayat, *Reminiscencias monterianas*, 87–90.

[48] Administrator to Manager, 8 and 15 Jan., and 13 Feb. 1915; and 19 May 1923, ASAS/C/106:3, 6, and 22, and 130:30.

head each – from other *comisionistas* or cattle breeders.[49] On several occasions, the Sociedad Agrícola del Sinú tried to avoid the use of intermediaries in order to maximize profits, although without much apparent success.[50]

TABLE 2.8 *Stock Owned by the Sociedad Agrícola del Sinú, 1914–1948 (Dec. figures)*

Year	Head of cattle	Pigs	Horses/ mules
1914	4,760	33	27
1916	6,029		
1918 (July)	8,157		
1921	10,567	395	63
1922	12,665	198	61
1924	10,789	140	94
1930 (June)	10,800		
1937	11,361	107	172
1940 (Apr.)	8,948	256	179
1943	12,031	171	204
1946	11,113	75	216
1947	11,962	83	
1948	10,682	198	

Sources: ASAS /C/117:31, 134:46, 83:17, and 'Libro de inventarios y balances', Dec. 1914 to Dec. 1948, ASAS/C/26.

Once the cattle had been fattened, they were taken to pasture-grounds owned by the Sociedad in Antioquia before being finally taken to Medellín. The herds were transported through the two routes described above: overland via Yarumal, or via Magangué. When transported overland, the herds took a variant of the old *camino padrero*. On the route, the herds – usually in groups of about 100 to 200 hundred head of cattle – stopped to pasture on rented land. Similar arrangements to feed the stock had to be made for the Marta Magdalena–Magangué route, which lasted 16 days: then the herds stopped in Montería, Cereté, Ciénaga de Oro, Sahagún, Chinú, Corozal, and La Gloria.

Besides pasture, land in Marta Magdalena was also used to cultivate crops to feed the resident labourers: plantains, coconuts, corn, yucca and *ñame*. Sometimes harvests produced a surplus for the local market,

[49] ASAS/C/75:68; C/40:110; C/126:73; C/127:17.

[50] 'Instrucciones para Emilio Cardona', ASAS/C/39:1–5.

as happened in 1927 and 1929 when corn from Marta Magdalena was sold in the region.[51] However, these were exceptional years. More often than not foodstuffs were supplied from elsewhere. Rice, a basic staple in the labourer's diet, was bought from Montería and from neighbouring farms.[52] From 1923 basic goods – coffee, sugar, soap, combs, and so on – were supplied in the shop opened by the administrator in Marta Magdalena. Most of this merchandise was bought from *Cartagenero* merchants, although there were also supplies from Montería, Barranquilla, and Medellín.[53] The existence of a shop in the estate did not keep away pedlars. Residents in Marta Magdalena also bought goods from a group of merchants that visited once a week. According to the administrator, who did not fear competition from these outsiders, those pedlars did 'very good deals, as they sell at inflated prices the goods that are not available at the shop'.[54]

The nature of Marta Magdalena's ownership as a joint stock company, with shares in the hands of Medellín merchants, determined to some extent the proprietors' absenteeism. While the estate's affairs were directly handled by an administrator who lived on the hacienda, the whole operation was supervised by a manager in Medellín, a shareowner in the Sociedad. The administrators were *Antioqueño* natives, and they usually developed a close relationship with members of the Sociedad. Apart from their salary, they were entitled to pasture their own cattle on the farm and often also to share a percentage of the calves born. It was common for the administrator to reside on the estate, where he lived a bachelor's life.[55]

Work on the estate varied. From the top position of *administrador* down to the domestic servants, there was a wide range of jobs for which different wages were paid: accountant, *capataz vaquero, vaquero, cuida cerdos, peón , capataz monte, ordeñador, cuida bestias, cuida praderas, patrón canoa, capataz hachero*, carpenter, shopkeeper, blacksmith, and so on.[56] To be a *vaquero*, in charge of driving the

[51] Administrator to Manager, 4 July 1916, ASAS/C/107:28 and 6 Jan. 1929, ASAS/C/116:1.

[52] Administrator to Manager, 12 May 1916, ASAS/C/107:35.

[53] ASAS/C/130:260 and 283.

[54] Administrator to Manager, 25 Feb. 1928, ASAS/C/129:18.

[55] Administrator to Manager, ASAS/C/127:8 and 9.

[56] See A. Palomino and others, 'Anteproyecto acerca de la reconstrucción de la racionalidad económica de la Sociedad Agrícola del Sinú', unpublished paper, Universidad de Antioquia, Medellín, 1985.

herds, was among the most sought-after jobs. It was not, however, a labour-intensive activity: it required a foreman and a dozen *vaqueros* to drive 100 head of cattle from Marta Magdalena to Magangué or Tarazá. Far more labour was employed in clearing the land for pasture, fencing the estate, and maintaining the pasture. Different types of labour were employed for these activities. Arrangements with tenants provided that, after a fixed period, the land should be handed back to the estate seeded with grass. Marta Magdalena also counted on a group of permanent labourers who lived on the hacienda and who were involved in jobs such as cooking, milking the cows, the upkeep of the herds, and the like. The majority of the labour employed in *desmonte y siembra* came from outside the estate. Sometimes the administrator tried to employ workers by paying on a piece-rate basis but without much success, due to the reluctance of people in the region to accept such an arrangement. The evidence suggests that in most cases wages were paid according to the number of days worked. Even in years of low activity during the Depression, Marta Magdalena on average employed between 100 and 200 *jornaleros* monthly to maintain the fields. In years of expansion such as 1938, the estate employed up to 400 *jornaleros*. Periodically, a foreman together with the administrator would recruit *jornaleros* from neighbouring towns. Scarcity of labour was a recurrent problem throughout the period. Besides the relatively low population density, the labour market became increasingly competitive: timber exploitation activities, oil exploration companies, public works, other cattle estates, and agricultural ventures in the region, all influenced the availability of labour for Marta Magdalena.[57] Thus wage rates, working conditions, and *anticipos* (payments in advance) played a significant role in the recruitment of *jornaleros*. In 1915, after some difficulties, the administrator managed to enlist a group of *jornaleros*, some for 60 days, some others for 40, at 0.25 pesos a day if paid in advance, otherwise at 0.30. Pressure for higher wages and *anticipos* was much in evidence.[58]

It is not possible to give a complete picture for wages in Marta Magdalena, although the evidence suggests that labour might have enjoyed relatively favourable conditions in the 1910s and most of the 1920s due to large demand for a scarce resource. This trend was reversed during the 1930s. By September 1929, the administrator was

[57] Administrator to Manager, 12 June 1915, 7 Sept. 1915, 6 Nov. 1919, 18 July 1925, ASAS/C/106:55 and 73, 108:42, and 126:58.

[58] Administrator to Manager, 7 Sept. and 8 Oct. 1915. ASAS/C/106:73 and 85.

under pressure to lower wages, but signs of an increasing labour supply soon disappeared after a recruitment campaign by the Army. At the end of 1929, however, he was able to lower wages, and was planning further reductions. By 1931 he again faced problems of labour supply. The newly established sugar *ingenio* at Berástegui was offering higher wages than the Marta Magdalena.[59]

The relatively strong position of labourers in the 1910s and the 1920s was also evident in their demands for *anticipos*. The available data suggests that advance payment was a demand of labour, and was regarded as a burden by the estate. Attempts by the administrator to abolish *anticipos* were in vain, as advance payment was a well-established custom.[60] Practically all employers paid *anticipos*, and this type of arrangement became competitive. Furthermore, it was often the case that once paid, labourers did not show up for work and it was difficult to coerce them. In 1921, the administrator reported a list of runaways with debts amounting to over 1,500 pesos, whose whereabouts were unknown.[61]

5. Livestock Exports

Between 1870 and 1950, the cattle industry experienced four periods of export prosperity: 1878–88 (with a brief interruption in 1884–85), 1898–1906, 1916–26 and 1941–4. During these years, first Cuba and later Panama were the main markets for a significant number of livestock shipped from Coastal ports.[62] Stock depletion in Cuba, as a consequence of the *Guerra de los Diez Años* (1869–78), together with the demand from the Panama canal works, had provided the demand for Colombian cattle exports during the first period of prosperity. It has been estimated that from Cartagena alone more than 50,000 head of cattle were shipped to Cuba between 1878 and 1881. According to the US Consul in Cartagena, trade with Cuba was becoming 'quite a large industry', to the extent that he warned 'our cattle men of Texas . . . otherwise they will find in the State of Bolívar a formidable

[59] See ASAS/C/116:67, and 86, 75:9, 76:151 and 128.

[60] Administrator to Manager, 8 Jan. 1915, ASAS/C/106:6. See also ASAS/C/106:73 and 78:9.

[61] Administrator to Manager, 3 Feb. 1921, ASAS/C/78:9.

[62] Ocampo, *Colombia y la economía mundial*, 369–75; Bell, *Colombia*, 138; Oakley, 'Exportation of Cattle' Cartagena, 7 Aug. 1943, NAUS/ FAR/ NR, 1942–5, Colombia, Livestock.

competitor'.[63] This market was, however, closed to Colombian cattle after import restrictions introduced by the Spanish government. Demand from Panama sustained high export levels until 1888. A combination of both domestic problems in Colombia and renewed demand from Cuba gave an impetus to exports at the end of the century. While Cuba wanted to restore her stock after the destruction of the war of independence, Colombian cattlemen found in the Cuban market the opportunity to avoid confiscation of their animals by the opposing armies in conflict during the *Guerra de los Mil Días*.[64] The government imposed an export duty of 20 pesos per head but cattle owners still made 'all possible efforts to ship their herds, preferring to pay the tax rather than to have their stock pass into the hands of the government'.[65] The trade induced cattle dealers from Bolívar to open branches of their firms in Havana.[66] Estimates vary, but it seems that at least 400,000 head of cattle were exported to Cuba between 1898 and 1906.[67] Pressures from cattlemen had originally forced the government to lower the export levy but it was raised again, causing protests in Bolívar. By 1907, discouraged by export restrictions and by Cuban recovery, cattle exports came to an end.[68]

Exports were revived by the demand for livestock from the Panamá Canal zone in the years during and immediately after the Great War. Between 1918 and 1922, about 93,000 head of cattle were shipped from Bolívar to Panama.[69] This route was again active in the 1940s, when F. P. Arias, a prominent Panamanian businessman and politician, managed to gain control of the trade. Through an agent in Cartagena, Arias purchased the stock from a few large-scale cattle owners. This policy was slightly amended as a consequence of pressures from small cattlemen and by 1943 Arias had arranged 'for a commission buyer from Corozal to visit the San Marcos–Ayapel region of Bolívar to

63 Cartagena, 22 Jan. 1882, NAUS/ RG84: Cartagena Consular records, despatches, C8.3 (5191). See also Torrenegro to Bolívar President, Cartagena 15 Apr. 1873, AGB, 1873.

64 It was estimated that in 1894 there were 2,485,000 head of cattle in Cuba. By 1904, after some stock had already been imported, the cattle population was 1,315,000; *Monthly Consular and Trade Reports* (Dec. 1905), 184.

65 *MCR*, 63/236 (May 1900), 16–17.

66 López, *Almanaque de los hechos colombianos*, 86.

67 Ocampo, *Colombia y la economía mundial*, 375; *Monthly Consular and Trade Reports* (Jan. 1905), 216.

68 *MCR*, 66/250 (July 1901), 447; *El Porvenir*, 13 Apr. 1904; *El Comercio*, 7 May 1910.

69 Oakley, 'Exportation of Cattle'.

make purchases from small ranchers'.[70] Besides Cuba and Panama, other markets were often reached by livestock exports from the Coast: Mexico, Peru, the Dutch Antilles, Costa Rica, Trinidad, and Venezuela. Cattle movement between Colombia and Venezuela usually worked in both directions, affecting the industry of the region.[71]

Although exports were not as important as the domestic demand for cattle, they did play a significant role in encouraging production by stimulating prices. As one group of cattle raisers from the Sinú, who were against the imposition of an export tax, observed to the Bolívar Governor in 1904:

> There is the firm belief in the Colombian interior that if cattle exports are not taxed, our herds will soon be diminished and therefore the price of this most important foodstuff (beef) will reach fabulous levels. . .What has happened in our cattle industry is no paradox: the more exports, the more cattle; the more land for pasture; and public wealth has been greatly increased . . .[72]

In cattle-producing circles, the external market was regarded as a blessing. 'With regard to the news about cattle exports', the Administrator of Marta Magdalena pointed out in 1915, 'one has to bear in mind that they express the wishes of cattlemen, and even of those not involved in the cattle industry, who believe that cattle exports mean gold in the Sinú'.[73] Meat consumers in the interior, together with intermediaries and cattle fatteners who supplied the Andean markets with Coastal stock, were strongly opposed to exports, and pressed the government to discourage them. This conflict of interests became more serious during periods of rising inflation, as in the 1940s, when exports for Panama were opposed by consumers and the Asociación Colombiana de Ganaderos – a lobby group representing cattle fatteners from the interior.[74] 'If exports to Panama were to be suspended', the President of the Federación de Ganaderos de Bolívar wrote to the Asociación Colombiana de Ganaderos, 'the most affected would be the

[70] Oakley, 'Exportation of Cattle'; Arias to Navarro, Panama, 14 June and 4 Aug. 1941, and Arias to Torres, 13 Jan. 1943, ASAS/C/25.

[71] See 'Economic Annual Report', Bogotá, 23 Mar. 1937, PRO, FO371/20624; Hijos de Arturo García to SAS, Sincelejo, 15 Feb. 1946 and 22 Oct. 1947, ASAS/C/64:268 and 65:151; and Bank of London and South America, *Fortnightly Review*, 12/269 (18 Jan. 1947), 12.

[72] *El Porvenir*, 13 Apr. 1904.

[73] Administrator to Manager, 12 June 1915, ASAS/C/106:54.

[74] Arias to Ospina, Bogotá, 30 July 1943, ASAS/C/25.

cattlemen from the Atlantic Coast, who thanks to this market alone, have been able to sell their cattle at a very good price'.[75]

6. The Failure of a Meat Packing Industry

Whenever prospects for exports improved, stock raisers hoped to benefit from an increased demand for their products. During the first two decades of this century, the world market for meat had experienced significant changes, due both to an increasing demand and improvements in technology, opening the field for newcomers. A congress of meat producers in the United States observed that while the world stock of bovines grew by 11 per cent between 1905 and 1913, the consumer population had increased by 25 per cent. Since the beginning of this century, the surplus of beef for export in the United States had been diminishing, thus motivating American export companies to search for new sources of supply. By 1913, the United States had become a beef importer. The world market was further influenced by the outbreak of the First World War, since the growing needs of European countries forced them to open up the trade hitherto restricted by tariffs and sanitary regulations, under the pressures from their own respective agricultural sectors.[76]

A few stock-raising countries benefited from the new conditions of the world market. Exports of Argentine frozen beef, which since 1900 had been replacing shipments of live cattle, were substantially increased: they rose from 276,000 to 1,554.000 carcasses between 1913 and 1918. During the same period, Argentine exports of canned meats rose from 13,000 to 191,000 tons.[77] Similarly, by 1914, exports of frozen beef had taken the place of salted beef in Uruguay, another country whose stock production was encouraged by the world market.[78] In view of the promising circumstances, stock raisers from Colombia –

[75] García to the President of the Asociación Colombiana de Ganaderos, Sincelejo, 10 Aug. 1943, ASAS/C/51:43

[76] International Institute of Agriculture, *International Trade in Meat* (Rome, 1936), 21; R. Perren, *The Meat Trade in Britain, 1840–1914* (London, 1978), 206–16; J. C. Crossley and R. Greenhill, 'The River Plate Beef Trade' in D. C. M. Platt, *Business Imperialism, 1840–1930* (Oxford, 1977), 293, 303–8; *Diplomatic and Consular Reports, Annual Series*, 5029, (London, 1912), 25–30; and *RNA* (Sept.–Oct. 1926), 354–5.

[77] Exports of Argentine chilled beef fell substantially during the same period; Crossley and Greenhill, 'The River Plate Beef Trade', 297–8.

[78] J. P. Barran and B. Nahum, 'Uruguayan Rural History', *HAHR*, 64/4 (1984), 655–73.

after all, the fourth largest bovine producer in Latin America – also sought a share in the expanding trade.[79] Visits from foreign envoys in the 1910s with a view to exploring the possibilities of Colombian cattle stimulated expectations. Officials from the United States and British governments, and representatives from meat packing companies toured the Coast, inspected the stock and met cattlemen to discuss plans for the development of the industry.[80] The enthusiasm expressed by cattle producers, though exaggerated, was thus not without foundation.[81]

However, legislation passed by the Colombian Congress between 1915 and 1919, apparently aimed to attract foreign capital, instead discouraged the development of an export-orientated meat-packing industry.[82] A 1915 law recognized some tax exemptions for future investments in this sector though only for a short period of time. In 1916, Congress approved the payment of interest on capital to potential investors but set limits to both the amount of money to be invested and the number of head of cattle to be slaughtered for export. According to a Senate Commission, the latter restriction 'was counter-productive, therefore nullifying the effects of the law'.[83] The cattlemen did not give up. In 1917, Congress was again discussing another bill which attempted to encourage the establishment of packing-houses on the Coast: interest premiums were higher than on those set up in 1916, and the total amount of capital which could be invested in the industry was also higher than in 1916. However, as an anti-monopoly measure, the government insisted on limiting the sum of money that any single meat-packing company was allowed to invest. Fears of foreign capital, in particular of the North American companies which had displaced the British ones from the Argentine beef trade, were expressed in the Senate. Congressmen such as Senator P. L. Mantilla opposed the project. Apart from their anti-imperialist feelings, they considered

[79] In 1915, the largest cattle population in South America was in Brazil, 31,000,000 head of cattle, Argentina, 29,000,000, Colombia, 10,000,000, and Uruguay, 8,000,000; *British and Latin American Trade Gazette* (7 May 1920), 168.

[80] See 'Porvenir de la ganadería en Colombia', and 'Informe sobre el Packing-house', *RNA* (July, 1915), 445, and (Jan–Feb., 1921), 323; 'Proposed Establishment of Packing-Houses', Cartagena, 10 June 1916, NAUS/ 821.6582/2.

[81] *La Unión Comercial,* 12 May 1916; *RCCB* (31 Oct. 1919), 7; *RNA* (165–6), (1917), 1499–1506, and 1530–7; Cunninghame Graham, *Cartagena and the Banks of the Sinú*, 176.

[82] At least four different laws were passed by Congress between 1915 and 1919. For a brief description of the contents of these laws see 'El packing-house de Coveñas y las petroleras de Infantas', *RNA* (Mar.–Apr. 1922), 328–34, and *Anales del Senado*, 19 Jan. 1920.

[83] *Anales del Senado*, 19 Nov. 1917.

governmental support excessive because a 'packing-house was a very profitable business'.[84] In the face of mounting difficulties, cattlemen from the Coast this time found an ally in the *Sociedad de Agricultores de Colombia* and it was decided to set up a commission to show to the members of the committees at both the Senate and the Lower Chamber the 'importance of immediate approval of the bill.'[85]

A compromise was finally reached, and at the end of 1917 the law was passed by Congress. The following year, the government awarded a contract to the Colombian Product Company – a joint venture formed by Ganadería Colombiana, Cartagena, and The International Products Co., New York, to establish a meat packing-house near the bay of Cispatá. While the government granted some tax benefits and subsidies, the company agreed to build the premises in less than two years, to slaughter for export at least 50,000 head of cattle a year, and to offer credits to regional cattlemen.[86] Work soon started, but not without further complications. 'I can confirm that there is no news, not even a recollection, of any attempt at building anything by the contractors' – a member of Congress, who claimed to have visited the region, fiercely accused the company in 1919.[87] A year later, however, different commissions from the Sociedad de Agricultores de Colombia, the Cámara de Representantes, and the central government witnessed progress: more than 600 workers were employed in building activities, including an aqueduct, housing, and a pier. By 1921, the company had spent $1,600,000 on construction materials, $1,100,000 on wages and $1,100,000 on stock.[88] None the less work progressed slowly. According to a Commission from the Cámara de Representantes, it was unfortunate that construction started 'in a period when the abnormal international situation impeded the prompt acquisition of materials we needed for this sort of work, and were usually only available from the external markets'.[89] Faced with all these obstacles, it was not until 1925 that the meat packing-house in Coveñas was ready for operation.

[84] *Anales del Senado*, 3 Aug. and 19 Nov. 1917

[85] 'Sesión de Noviembre 10 de 1917', Sociedad de Agricultores de Colombia, Actas, Bogotá, 1917–27, 43, 44, 107.

[86] Regional share-owners included C. and F. Vélez Daníez, and Diego Martínez y Cía; *RNA* (Jan.–Feb., 1921), 223–6; and 330–3, and *The Colombian Trade Review* (London, Mar. 1922), 22 .

[87] *Anales de la Cámara de Representantes*, 2 Oct. 1919.

[88] *RNA*, (Mar.–Apr., 1922), 379; 'Informe sobre el packing-house', 223–6.

[89] 'Informe sobre el packing-house', 223, and 'El packing-house de Coveñas y las petroleras de Infantas', 339.

Ten years after the first initiatives were taken, however, conditions in the world market had again modified. The cessation of hostilities after the War had been followed by a contraction in the demand for meat in Europe, where huge stocks of beef were then available. Between 1918 and 1922, Argentine exports of frozen beef had fallen by 27 per cent.[90] Under these circumstances, the obstacles faced by the Coveñas packing-house to conquer markets were multiple.[91] Undoubtedly, the quality of Colombian beef did not compare favourably with that of other countries such as the Argentine. A major disadvantage in the development of the meat packing-house in Coveñas was its high production costs. An Argentine Minister in Colombia gave a clear account of the problem to the Sociedad de Agricultores in 1925. According to the Minister, both the availability of stock and the production process determined a non-competitive price for Colombian beef on the world market. The consequences of backward technology were all too apparent: while an Argentine steer gave 325 kg of beef, a Colombian one only produced 180 kg. The disproportion in price was extremely discouraging: in Argentina, according to the Minister, one kg of beef cost $0.09; in Colombia, $0.75.[92]

The Coveñas packing-house was thus a doomed enterprise. In 1925, F. Vélez, one of the shareholders of the company, expressed his bitterness about the outcome: 'he told me without hesitation that it had been the worst venture in which he could have invested his capital'.[93] There were unsuccessful attempts to search for alternative markets in Mexico, Italy, and the United States. In the meantime, the company resorted to the export of live cattle. Two decades later, not one single head of cattle had been slaughtered. As Oakley observed, 'the factory never operated; the equipment long since has been sold or junked'.[94] Whether or not any opportunities were missed as a result of a hesitant Congress remains an issue for speculation. However, out of the political debate there emerged a clash of interests which partly reflected regional cleavages: middlemen from the interior were opposed to exports, fearing a scarcity of stock for the domestic market. Within the central government there was additional concern related to the influence of exports on the internal price for meat. Thus cattlemen

[90] Crossley and Greenhill, 'The River Plate Beef Trade', 297.

[91] 'El packing-house de Coveñas y las petroleras de Infantas', 339–40.

[92] *RNA* (Sept.–Oct. 1926), 352–77. A 1924 US Consular report reached similar conclusions. See Schnare, 'Cattle Raising'.

[93] Administrator to Manager, 16 Feb. 1925, ASAS/C/126:3.

[94] Oakley, 'Cattle Raising and Related Industries'.

from the Coast, who saw in the external sector a possible driving force for the development of the industry, had difficulties in finding support from business and political circles in the interior. When finally they did receive it, it was too late. None the less, the failure of the Coveñas meat packing-house served to expose some of the inefficiencies of cattle raising in the region and the need to improve stockbreeding, while it made cattlemen more aware of world market conditions.

This frustrating entrepreneurial experience might have deterred cattlemen from risking further capital in the development of a meat-packing industry. It did so for a while. Only two decades later, another serious attempt was made to sell chilled beef, but this time to the domestic market. In the mid-1940s, with the financial support of regional cattlemen and of *Antioqueño* capital, a Sociedad Abastecedora de Carnes was established with the aim of slaughtering cattle in Southern Bolívar and delivering chilled meat in carcasses to the interior markets.[95] By 1948 this company was slaughtering a mere nine steers a day to produce chilled beef for Medellín. According to J. J. García, unless that slim figure was increased to 200, the business could not be profitable.[96] Problems of transport, together with preference for fresh beef and market conditions – in which middlemen and butchers played a significant role, discouraged the development of a meat-packing industry for domestic consumption.[97]

7. Hides, Leather, and Dairy Products

Hides were always a valuable commodity. Within the generally poor performance of the Colombian external sector during the nineteenth century, hides were a constant export item. Although not impressive by world standards, the trade in hides grew steadily: from 1,050 tons in 1870 exports went up to 3,800 tons in 1898. Between 1906 and 1918, they averaged about 5,000 tons. In 1920 hides ranked third in importance among Colombian exports, after coffee and minerals, though they were soon overtaken by bananas and petroleum. Larger

95 García to P. N. Ospina and to B. Ospina, Sincelejo, 15 Feb. and 28 Dec. 1946, ASAS/C/64:268 and 2; Frankel, 'Plan for the Transportation of Fresh Meat'.

96 García to Ospina, Sincelejo, 22 Oct. 1947, and to *Abastecedora de Carnes*, Sincelejo, 10 July 1948, ASAS/C/65:154 and 182 respectively.

97 This pattern is very similar today. See Y. Castro, J. L. Londoño, et al., *Mercados y formación de precios* (Bogotá, 1982).

quantities of hides were exported during the inter-war years.[98] It is almost impossible to estimate regional participation in the hides trade, although given the importance of the cattle industry it is safe to assume that it was significant. A major portion of hides exported through Cartagena were produced in Bolívar. Similarly, most hides exported through Barranquilla, Santa Marta, and Ríohacha were of regional origin. Coastal merchants had good grasp of this commodity.[99]

The demand for hides in the domestic market was probably as significant, although again it is difficult to estimate this with any accuracy. By Oakley's time, large quantities of hides were still used on the ranches where the cattle were slaughtered for the manufacture of saddles, lassos, and even basic pieces of furniture.[100] Additionally, throughout the region, there were small tanneries that, in primitive fashion, processed two or three hides a day for the market. In the main urban areas, such as Barranquilla and Cartagena, larger tanneries were developed to supply leather for shoe factories. In 1899, there were at least five tanneries in Barranquilla producing sole leather for the ten well established shoe manufacturers. Founded in Cartagena in 1903, the Fábrica de Calzado de la Espriella Hermanos became one of the largest shoe factories in the region, with significant production levels and a wide market which included the Andean interior.[101] It should be borne in mind, however, that the demand for shoes was limited to the well-to-do and the main urban centres. In the countryside and rural towns of the coast, even among the better-off, the popular article of footwear was the *abarca*, or leather-soled sandals produced by local artesans. Tanneries, leather goods, and shoe factories played a leading role in the industrial development of Barranquilla and Cartagena. There were about 100 establishments manufacturing leather goods in Barranquilla in 1945. In terms of the number of jobs, the leather industry ranked fifth, after food processing, textiles, metallurgy, and timber works.[102]

[98] Ocampo, *Colombia y la economía mundial* 74; Wylie, *The Agriculture of Colombia*, 125–7; US Tariff Commission, *Agricultural, Pastoral, and Forest Industries in Colombia*, 36–8; Contraloría, *Síntesis estadística de Colombia, 1939–1943* (Bogotá, 1944), 39.

[99] Schnare, 'Cattle Raising', and Bell, *Colombia*, 147.

[100] Oakley, 'Cattle Raising and Related Industries', 40.

[101] *MCR*, 60/227 (Aug. 1899), 663–7; Grau, *La ciudad de Barranquilla*, 94; J. Urueta and E. G. de Piñeres, *Cartagena y sus cercanías* (Cartagena, 1912), 318.

[102] Contraloría General de la República, *Primer Censo Industrial* (Bogotá, 1947), 281, 307; Ospina Vásquez, *Industria y protección en Colombia*, 462, 475, 476, 603.

The commercial distribution of dairy products developed at a slower rate due basically to the lack of refrigeration facilities and to transport problems. However, the consumption of milk and cheese in the countryside was significant. In Ayapel, 'the poor who had no milking cows to produce cheese make use of those of their richer neighbours, who allow this sort of communism since milk here is of little value'.[103] On the large estates, the milk was often left to labourers and tenants, while small ranches counted on the milking of the calves to maximize production. However, without proper transportation facilities milk did not travel well, thus its commercial production was restricted to neighbouring markets. In 1917, milk in Cartagena was sold 'by peddlers who bring the milk from near-by ranches and carry it on mules or donkeys in tin receptacles which are not of the most hygienic sort . . . it naturally arrives in the city in a partly churned condition'. By then Diego Martínez and Co. was one of the few large cattle ranches manufacturing butter and powdered milk on a moderate scale.[104] Cheese could travel longer distances, besides being a basic staple of the regional diet. Cheese produced in Plato was distributed in Barranquilla, Magangué, Ciénaga, and Cartagena. In the 1940s, there were at least five important cheese-producing regions in Bolívar supplying the regional market: Montería, Cereté, San Jacinto, Zambrano, and Cartagena.

Besides direct links with the above industries, cattle also established links with other sectors of the regional economy. The largest sugar *Ingenios*, Sincerín and Berástegui, were founded by cattlemen. D. Martínez Camargo pioneered oil explorations on the Coast, financed urban development in Montería and established a bank in Cartagena. Cattle were a significant source of income for clients of banks in Barranquilla. *Barranquillero* cattle traders invested in urban development and in the emergent industrial sector of Barranquilla.

8. Conclusion: Pastoral versus Arable Agriculture?

In 1927, Alejandro López published his *Problemas colombianos*, a collection of essays where this *Antioqueño* engineer and Liberal

[103] Striffler, *El río San Jorge*, 152.

[104] American Consul to Sharpless Separator Co., Cartagena, 16 Mar. 1917; 'Packing of Milk and Butter', Cartagena, 18 Mar. 1921, NAUS/ RG84, Consular general correspondence, 1917 (5), and 1921(7).

ideologue identified the 'agrarian question' as the core issue of the country's development.[105] Drawing largely from his perception of the experience of coffee production in Antioquia, López attempted to set up a model for the future, based on the consolidation of an agrarian middle class produced by the division of land in smallholdings. López recognized that the two most important innovations made in Colombian agriculture since the second half of the nineteenth century had been coffee growing and the expansion of artificial pasture but, he added, they were 'quite different in character one from the other'.[106] While praising the natural virtues of coffee, López attacked cattle raising as an industry with negative effects on economic and social development. In the final analysis, what López condemned was the extensive nature of the cattle industry, although his fierce attack left little room for compromise. Unemployment, industrial underdevelopment, transport problems and inflation: all were aggravated by the way livestock were raised. The immense problems created by the cattle industry were damaging the whole country; thus López concluded 'these are not problems to be tackled by cattlemen but by statesmen'.[107] In addition, López complained that the best land was devoted to pasture instead of to arable farming. Furthermore, the expansion of artificial grasses had, in his opinion, curtailed agricultural growth. Although his initial analysis was related to the colonization of the Cauca Valley and Antioquia and its surroundings, he extended it to other parts of Colombia, including Bolívar. In Bolívar, apart from the general problems he had identified, he added the existence of debt-peonage as a means of enslaving rural labour.

The extent to which López's views on cattle prevailed among Colombian policy-makers at the time is difficult to assess. Some contemporary foreign observers had no praise for Colombian livestock production despite recognizing its importance. 'Cattle rearing as carried out in Colombia,' Pearse concluded, 'seems to appeal very much to the people on the Atlantic coast; it is evidently an occupation requiring very little hard work . . . It seems to be work for lazy people'.[108] Cattlemen certainly resented the way their activity and their own social status was undervalued: 'the view of our fellow compatriots,' A. Percy exclaimed, 'is that cattlemen are from an

[105] A. López, *Problemas colombianos* (Paris, 1927), later reprinted in Medellín in 1976.

[106] López, *Problemas colombianos* (Medellín, 1976), 45.

[107] Ibid., 47.

[108] Pearse, *Colombia, with Special Reference to Cotton*, 71.

inferior race, wear loincloths, and live in regions whose history has produced no heroes'.[109] Whatever the prevailing view, there is little doubt that López's work had a considerable impact on his own generation and in the years to come. Although it was not explicitly acknowledged, his ideas about the irrational use of land were later shared by the 1950 IBRD Mission headed by Lauchlin Currie, whose report was highly influential in further analyses of Colombian development. 'The cattle fatten on the plains while the people often have to struggle for a bare existence in the hills': this was one of the Mission's conclusions in identifying the problems of the rural sector.[110] In 1957, H. Toro Agudelo, later to become Colombian Minister of Agriculture, echoed López's ideas, condemning the cattle industry as both 'dangerous' for the national economy and socially unjust.[111]

The history of livestock in Colombia has been a neglected field among scholars, but the few references to it have tended to support Alejandro López's impressions.[112] Fals Borda stressed the contradiction between the expansion of the cattle hacienda and the local peasant economies, using as evidence the history of hacienda Berástegui, from its expansion after the mid-nineteenth century until its final dismantling in the 1930s. His portrayal of the cattle hacienda followed closely the traditional view of the semi-feudal estate of colonial origins, although he was quick to note the rapid incursion of the Coastal hacienda in capitalist ventures. None the less Fals Borda argues that the expansion of the cattle hacienda took place through the use of coercive and exploitative labour arrangements of a pre-capitalist nature, such as *concierto*, *arriendo por pastos*, *avances*, debt-peonage and *matrícula*.[113] Following closely López and Fals Borda, Salomón

[109] *RNA* (June 1913), 450.

[110] *The Basis of a Development Program for Colombia* (Baltimore, 1950), 63; see also 61–2.

[111] H. Toro Agudelo, *El problema social agrario en Colombia* (Bogotá, 1985), 44–50. Carlos Lleras Restrepo, President of the republic 1966–70, an outstanding figure in the Liberal party and in 20th-century Colombian politics, acknowledged Alejandro López's influences on his agrarian policies. See C. Lleras Restrepo, *Crónica de mi propia vida* (Bogotá, 1983), i. 82.

[112] For the influence of López on agrarian historians see Bejarano, 'Orígenes del problema agrario', and D. Mesa, 'El problema agrario en Colombia, 1920–1960', in *La agricultura colombiana en el siglo XX* (Bogotá, 1978), 30–67, 84–93.

[113] His *Capitalismo, hacienda y poblamiento en la Costa Atlántica* and his later series, *Historia doble de la Costa Atlántica*, constitute one of the few systematic approaches to the subject. Taken as a whole, however, his work presents a more complex picture than the one given by its later interpretations, where the contradiction between the cattle hacienda and the peasant economy tends to dominate the analysis.

Kalmanowitz also strongly condemned the expansion of livestock as a 'historical calamity' for national development.[114] According to Kalmanowitz, cattle took the best land away from peasants, cattlemen used the land irrationally and imposed coercive and extra-economic controls on the rural population. To sum up, the view that seems to have prevailed since the years of Alejandro López regards the history of cattle – Coastal cattle in particular – as a hindrance to development because it impeded the expansion of arable agriculture, widened social inequalities by displacing peasants from the land, and imposed an archaic structure of social relations. This interpretation, backed by scant empirical evidence, is based on several other related assumptions, among them, that land could have been better used in agriculture, that cattle were exclusively both a large-scale operation and a landowner venture, that land enclosures had expanded rapidly after the introduction of barbed wire fencing in the 1870s, and finally that cattle haciendas were able to overcome the recurrent problems of labour shortages by accumulating land.

The evidence so far presented in the last two chapters offers a somewhat different view of the history of cattle in Colombia and the role it played on the Coast during the period under study. The existence of a contradiction between cattle and agriculture, as suggested by traditional interpretations, is a misleading one. It is true that, within the municipalities, there were often clashes around the use that was given to communal land. However, in the long term the shift to pasture was the rational answer to frustrated experiences in agriculture. As shown in Chapter 1, plagues, floods, and droughts, lack of transport, and shortages of labour, successively discouraged agriculture. Furthermore, it is not clear that the best land in the Coast was devoted to cattle. Large investments in drainage, irrigation, and transport were required to put land into cultivation.[115] Since livestock can be taken to the market on the hoof, problems of transport could be overcome. Thus given the conditions of land, capital, and labour, together with the expectations of safer and higher returns, it seems that for many in the region it was more attractive to invest in cattle rather than risking the uncertainties of agriculture.[116]

[114] S. Kalmanowitz, *El desarrollo de la agricultura en Colombia* (Bogotá, 1982), 111.

[115] For an exceptional observation on the poor quality of the soil in the Atlantic plains, see Ospina Vásquez, *El plan agrario*, 17, 19.

[116] 'It no longer pays to plough and it pays to graze', the London *Times* pointed out in 1880 when cultivating wheat in England had ceased being profitable, while the

Traditional interpretations of Colombian agrarian history have also overlooked the crucial distinction between cattle ownership and landownership. Investing in livestock was often a different business from investing in land: land could be rented; cattle could be held in a share agreement; tenants could have grazing rights; herds could be pastured on public or communal land. Although there was significant overlap, at times owning cattle was more important than owning land. This was particularly the case during most of the nineteenth century and the beginning of the twentieth, while land was relatively easily accessible. One of the conflictual issues once land enclosures expanded was precisely that of previous grazing rights. Furthermore, stock raising was not exclusively a large-scale operation. As suggested in this chapter, there developed a localized specialization of labour, determined by the different stages of cattle production in relation to its final market. Further research might shed more light on the working conditions of cattle owners in relation to the size of their holdings, their relationship with landowners, their links with agriculture and obviously their links with other cattlemen, among them the middlemen who enjoyed a leading role in the expansion of the industry. This chapter has also offered an alternative view of social relations within the cattle industry, although it is still hard to offer any definite conclusions. All the evidence, however, points to a situation of acute shortages of labour and relative accessibility of land. Traditional interpretations have argued that in conditions of labour shortage, landlords resorted to both accumulating land and immobilizing labourers by debt.[117] As noted here, the information offered by the archives of the Sociedad Agrícola del Sinú suggests otherwise, and coincides with previous findings on the subject of peonage, summarized earlier by Arnold J. Bauer and more recently by Simon Miller, 'that the system of indebtness . . . often

journal of the Royal Agricultural Society of England, the *Agricultural Gazette*, advised that farmers should lay some of their arable fields to pasture. Between the 1870s and the 1890s, some 4 million acres were additionally incorporated to pasture in England. There was another movement to increase pastured land during the 1920s. See J. Brown, *Agriculture in England: A Survey on Farming, 1870–1947* (Manchester, 1987), 33–6, 87. Pounds has shown how in continental Europe, during the early years of the 20th-century, there was 'a growing tendency for agriculture to concentrate on animal products in areas which were best suited to their production', see N. J. G. Pounds, *An Historical Geography of Europe, 1800–1914* (Cambridge, 1985), 247.

[117] E. Domar, 'The Causes of Slavery or Serfdom: A Hypothesis', *JEH* 30, (1970), 18–32.

reflected the power of labour to negotiate significant advances or access to land'.[118]

Overall, this chapter has stressed the importance of the cattle industry, not only for the region but for the national economy as well. Stock raising was a widespread activity, one in national hands that involved a significant number of people. It supplied Colombians with a basic source of food. It provided raw materials for an emergent industrial sector. Though less so than in some other South American countries, it also provided exports of hides and cattle on the hoof. When moved from the ranches to the market, cattle were a visible and subsequently a taxable commodity, and thus became a main source of local public finances during most of the period. Finally, it guaranteed safe returns which were sometimes transferred to other sectors of the regional economy. It was an industry whose importance was tied to the very conditions of the country. Its development was not without obstacles, as was demonstrated by the failure to extend its links to external markets by investment in meat–packing. Improvements in technology were slow to arrive, other countries proved to be more competitive, and returns were limited. None the less, these shortcomings should not detract from the significance of cattle. In Colombia's fragmented territory, with acute problems of transport, livestock at least integrated the sparse and scarcely populated Coast with the national market, while providing a basic source of exchange for the region.

[118] S. Miller, 'Mexican Junkers and Capitalist Haciendas, 1810–1910: The Arable Estate and the Transition to Capitalism between the Insurgency and the Revolution', *JLAS*, 22/2 (May 1990), 251, and A. J. Bauer, 'Rural Workers in Spanish America: Problems of Peonage and Oppression', *HAHR*, 59/1 (1979), 34–63.

3
Town and Countryside

1. Introduction

Rural life in the region did not revolve only around crops and livestock. In 1874, artesans and merchants, state officials and school teachers, priests, physicians, and even artists already had a place in the growing cattle districts of Sincelejo, Corozal, and Sabanalarga.[1] Though small in numbers, their importance was greater relative to the dimensions of their society.

The pace of change in rural areas was as varied as the number of settlements. When the British geographer Simmons visited the region in 1878, Patillal, which was expanding due to a large trade in cheese and cattle, was 'only a collection of farms, but they are fast closing into a town'. Corral de Piedra, a former cattle farm, was 'now a small village'. Some places also suffered stagnation. Valledupar, 'once a large town of fine houses with balconies . . . has through the revolutions . . . fallen step by step . . . and is one mass of ruins'.[2] Valledupar recovered, though gradually and in the spartan fashion which characterised the cattle country. Bolinder, who first visited Valledupar in 1915, described the simplicity of the lifestyle of the town, whose environment was still more rural than urban: 'it often happened that the peace was disturbed by a whole herd of cattle being driven through'. Bolinder returned to Valledupar in 1920 and again in 1936 when he found that 'modernization had made big inroads in the old town'.[3] A salient feature of rural towns was their individuality. 'All of them are enviously different from each other', Cunninghame Graham observed during his journey in Southern Bolívar. The niceties of city life, and its darker side too, were generally absent from this rustic world. In Sincelejo, Cunninghame Graham pointed out, 'there are no drinking-bars, such as are to be found in nearly every town of Argentina; no cinemas; no hooligans; no poor; few rich, and . . . life rolls along pleasantly enough'.[4] However, some improvements raised hopes of real and effective progress: the construction of the

1 *GB*, 8 Jan., 12 Mar., and 10 Sept., 1871, 17 Mar. 1874.

2 Simmons, 'On the Sierra Nevada', 691, 708.

3 Bolinder, *We Dared the Andes*, 91–100 and 129–31.

4 Cunninghame Graham, *Cartagena and the Banks of the Sinú*, 222, 223.

Palacio Municipal, an electricity supply company, two plants producing soda water, a brick factory, two regular newspapers, a motor car service, were all signs of change in the 'curious little town' of Sincelejo in 1914.[5] While in distant inland towns the rhythm of growth was constrained by poor communications, some places in Northern Magdalena experienced sudden changes as a consequence of the banana export boom. Aracataca was a typical 'shock town' for casual observers. Growing up after the expansion of the banana plantations, Aracataca was soon also the centre of an active trade: 'all the houses have become canteens and bars . . . or a combination of these as well as general stores'.[6]

TABLE 3.1 *Number of Municipios by Population Size in the Coast, 1870–1950*

Year	– 2,000	2,000–5,000	5,000–20,000	20,000–100,000	Over 100,000
1870	63	44	15	0	0
1905	27	40	24	2	0
1918	5	45	50	4	0
1928	0	40	55	10	1
1950	0	15	81	15	2

Sources: *Anuario Estadístico de Colombia* (Bogotá, 1875), 30-1, 39-40; *Anuario General de Estadística* (Bogotá, 1934), 105, 106, 112; Colombia, *Censo de Población* (Bogotá, 1951).

Settlements were scattered throughout the region. In 1870, the majority of the Coastal population lived in *municipios* of under 5,000 inhabitants and there was a large number of small settlements with no more than 2,000 (see Table 3.1). By 1905, there were only two *municipios* of over 20,000. During the second and third decades of this century, Coastal *municipios* expanded rapidly but they hardly exceeded 20,000. Although by 1950, 20 per cent of the population lived in Barranquilla and Cartagena, about 50 per cent were spread out between 81 *municipios* of between 5,000 and 20,000. Alongside an overwhelmingly rural picture – where farms were gradually turning into villages and villages into towns – river- and seaports on the Coast,

[5] *Memoria que presenta el Secretario de Gobierno* (Cartagena, 1914), 269–71.
[6] Peña, *Del Avila al Monserrate* (Bogotá, 11913), 197.

the main outlets for Colombian trade during the period, began to see major urban developments. These commercial towns were centres of regional integration; some of them also linked the region with the country and the country with the world economy: Cartagena, Santa Marta, and Ríohacha on the Caribbean Sea; Lorica and Montería on the Sinú River; Magangué, Mompox, and Barranquilla on the Magdalena River.

This chapter explores the extent to which Coastal cities were affected by regional development. The major focus of attention is Barranquilla, which from being a tiny village at the time of independence became the most important Colombian port during the second half of the nineteenth century. The following sections attempt to identify the regional scope of Barranquilla's commercial and industrial activities by looking at the routes of trade; the origins of *Barranquillero* merchants, their activities, and their links with the region; the impact that Barranquilla's development may have had in encouraging Coastal agriculture through a growing demand for both food and raw materials for the industrial sector. This is followed by a similar though less detailed analysis for other major towns such as Cartagena. In a concluding section, I discuss some of the prevailing views on the role played by secondary cities in regional development.

2. Barranquilla: From Port to Regional Centre

'If you were to drop a plummet line 2,000 miles due south from the Statue of Liberty,' Kathleen Romoli opened her account on Colombia in 1941, 'it would strike Barranquilla, a gleaming busy city sprawling in hot sunlight . . . where the Río Magdalena empties into the sea. Barranquilla is the front door to Colombia'.[7] This had not always been the case. 'Barranquilla is entirely a product of modern times', F. Loraine Petre had pointed out in 1906.[8] What was striking for the visitor, foreign and national alike, was the commercial nature of the

[7] K. Romoli, *Colombia: A Gateway to South America* (New York, 1941), 1.

[8] Petre, *The Republic of Colombia*, 165. The origins of Barranquilla are a matter of historical debate. Most historians agree, however, that the emergence of Barranquilla did not follow the traditional pattern of foundations of Spanish colonial towns. See J. A. Blanco Barros, *El norte de tierradentro y los orígenes de Barranquilla* (Bogotá, 1987); N. Madrid Malo, *Barranquilla, el alba de una ciudad* (Bogotá, 1986); F. Baena and J. R. Vergara, *Barranquilla* (Barranquilla, 1922).

city, for Barranquilla had neither the colonial attractions of neighbouring Santa Marta and Cartagena nor their enchanting surroundings. 'For the traveller,' Blair Niles observed in 1924, 'Barranquilla exists solely as a place from which he proceeds somewhere else.' Niles was obliged to stay and had the chance to see Barranquilla 'as something more than a starting point': 'We found it a stirring ambitious place, with factories for the making of bricks and soaps, candles and shoes, matches and chocolates, and with important textile mills and tanneries'.[9] These impressions of industrious activity were combined with the dismal face of the town: offensive smells around the river; the intolerable heat; appalling sanitary arrangements; the unprepossessing architecture; pigs and donkeys rolling freely about the sandy streets; food 'certainly (did) not recall the Carlton', and hotels not on the same level 'as even sixth rate European hotels'.[10] Observers all the same rarely failed to notice the signs of progress. Reclus in the mid-nineteenth century, Scruggs in 1905, Niles in 1924, Romoli in 1941, all had to acknowledge the remarkable transformation of Barranquilla from a humble village to a prosperous place, and each of them related this transformation to changes that had taken place in the previous two or three decades prior to their respective visits.[11]

Gradual changes, however, had been taking place since the early republican period. In 1836, exports from Sabanilla – a small fishing hamlet on the Caribbean Sea – already tripled those of the traditional port of Cartagena. Sabanilla, 'the meanest town' that Holton saw in New Granada during his visit in 1854, was in fact the seaport of Barranquilla.[12] Ten miles distant from Sabanilla on the left bank of the Magdalena River, Barranquilla was in a privileged geographical position: next both to the sea and to the main artery of Colombian trade. Thus Barranquilla's growth during the nineteenth century followed the pace of exports and imports through Sabanilla, and was conditioned in turn by the efficiency of communications between the

[9] B. Niles, *Colombia, Land of Miracles* (New York and London, 1924), 176–8.

[10] Petre, *The Republic of Colombia*, 165–7

[11] E. Reclus, *Mis exploraciones en América* (Valencia, 1910), 52–8; W. Scruggs, *The Colombian and Venezuelan Republics* (Boston, 1905), 31–5; Niles, *Colombia, Land of Miracles*, 176–8; Romoli, *Colombia: A Gateway to South America*, 231–7.

[12] I. Holton, *New Granada: Twenty Months in the Andes* (London, 1957), 7.

river- and the seaports.[13] Up to 1871, Sabanilla and Barranquilla were linked by means of the Canal de la Piña, through which goods and passengers were transported in small boats or *bongos* like the one taken by Reclus, 'a sort of lighter made out of ill fitted planks'.[14] In 1871, the completion of a railway between Barranquilla and Sabanilla gave considerable impetus to foreign trade, as can be appreciated from Table 3.2. Four years after the railway started operations, exports and imports through Santa Marta had shrunk dramatically, while Sabanilla – that is to say, Barranquilla, took the lead among Colombian ports.

TABLE 3.2 *Comparison of Imports and Exports through Santa Marta and Sabanilla, 1870–1874 (value in $US)*

Year	Imports		Exports	
	Santa Marta	Sabanilla	Santa Marta	Sabanilla
1870	4,084,250	392,135	3,603,299	2,378,854
1871	3,932,827	655,731	4,449,629	1,550,895
1872	3,973,512	2,433,834	2,820,409	2,852,966
1873	2,135,543	7,012,631	823,902	7,104,859
1874	1,036,037	8,350,000	292,860	8,764,786

Source: *Accts.* and *Papers*. 35, *Commercial Repts*, LXXVI (London, 1875), 363.

Sabanilla, however, did not possess an appropriate harbour. '[It is] in reality little more than a roadstead . . . [and] so bad a one,' a British Consul remarked in 1873, 'in consequence of its exposure to the weather, and its want of depth of water, which obliges vessels of any size to anchor 3.5 miles form the shore, causing thereby great inconvenience and loss of time in loading and unloading'.[15] The railway was thus extended to neighbouring harbours, first to Salgar and later to Puerto Colombia, where a 4,000 ft. pier was built in 1893 to overcome the lack of a proper harbour (see Map 4.) These improvements enabled Barranquilla to remain the most important Colombian port. By 1906, about 60 per cent of the country's foreign

[13] T. Nichols, 'The Rise of Barranquilla', *HAHR*, 34/2 (May 1954). By the same author, *Tres puertos*, ch. 9, 12. See also E. Posada-Carbó, *Una invitación a la historia de Barranquilla* (Bogotá, 1987), 17–22; L. E. Nieto Arteta, *Economía y cultura en la historia de Colombia* (Bogotá, 1962), 264–5; and his *El café en la sociedad colombiana* (Medellín, 1971), 18–19, 62, and 67.

[14] Quoted in Baena and Vergara, *Barranquilla*, 158.

[15] *PP*, 27, LXV (1873), 48.

trade took the Barranquilla–Puerto Colombia route. However, it was by then evident that the future of Barranquilla as a port depended on the opening of the mouth of the Magdalena to allow ocean-going steamers to reach its river docks directly. Though of impressive length, the pier did not solve Puerto Colombia's shortcomings.

In 1906, the *Barranquillero* merchant community launched a campaign to open Bocas de Ceniza, the sand bar which impeded the full navigation of steamers through the mouth of the river. The project – which will be analysed in detail in the following chapter – became not only a matter of civic pride but one of survival, particularly after the opening of the Panama Canal when the Pacific port of Buenaventura threatened Barranquilla's supremacy. Linked to the main coffee-producing regions through an expanding railway network, Buenaventura soon captured a significant proportion of the coffee trade, thus displacing Barranquilla as the main port for Colombian exports.[16] The opening of Bocas de Ceniza in 1936 gave Barranquilla the double condition of river- and seaport, though the advantage was diminished by the problems of navigations in the Magdalena River.

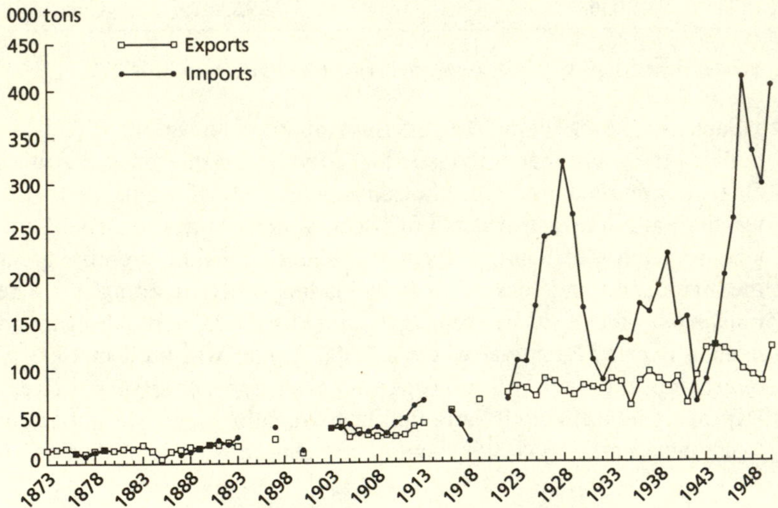

FIG. 3.1 Barranquilla Port: Exports and Imports, 1873–1950
Sources: See Appendix I

[16] See Ch. 4.

A large proportion of Colombian imports still entered though Barranquilla and by 1950 the port remained the most prominent on the Colombian Caribbean. Its future was then once again in jeopardy. (Fig. 3.1 illustrates the movement of exports and imports through Barranquilla between 1873 and 1950).

Between 1870 and 1950, Barranquilla thus served as a major centre from where Colombian products were shipped overseas and from where imports were distributed throughout the country. From its early years, the port attracted a growing population which soon became involved in a wide range of economic activities. Population grew steadily: 11,000 inhabitants in 1870; 40,000 in 1905; 64,000 in 1918; 152,000 in 1938, and 279,000 in 1950. Between 1905 and 1938, Barranquilla had the fastest-growing population among the major Colombian departmental capitals. Subsequently its pace of growth slowed in comparison with Cali, Bogotá, Medellín, and Bucaramanga, although it remained the largest city in the region.[17]

The bulk of this growth was due to migratory movements from other Coastal areas, although Barranquilla also received a large number of immigrants from the Andean interior and a significant group of foreigners. During the first half of the nineteenth century, the town grew at the expense of Cartagena and Santa Marta. Merchants from these and other centres in the region moved their headquarters to Barranquilla. Fergusson, Noguera & Co. were established in Santa Marta in 1855; forty years later their main offices were in Barranquilla, as were those of other *Samario* merchant houses, such as Evaristo Obregón and Joaquín de Mier. Antonio Volpe & Co., who had settled in El Carmen in 1896, moved to Barranquilla in 1911. Paccini & Paccini from Magangué, V. Dugand & Hijos from Ríohacha, A. Clavería from Ciénaga, all moved their headquarters to Barranquilla.[18] A growing urban economy together with the attractions of a more modern way of life encouraged further movements of people from the Coast to Barranquilla. Rural hardship, sometimes the result of natural disasters, also motivated migration. In 1916 hundreds of people from Calamar moved to Barranquilla after serious floods.[19]

[17] J. R. Sojo, *Barranquilla, una economía en expansión* (Barranquilla, 1955), 134.

[18] *RCCB* (18 Feb 1928), 2–11; M. Goenaga (ed.), *Acción costeña* (Barranquilla, 1926); Banco Dugand, *Informe de la Junta Administradora a la Asamblea General de Accionistas* (Barranquilla, 1920).

[19] *La Nación*, 17 Nov. 1916; *El Pequeño Diario*, 21 Aug. 1918; P. M. Revollo, 'Las inundaciones del Río Magdalena', *Revista Geográfica* 1/1 (1952), 29–35.

MAP 4. *Transport and Communications*

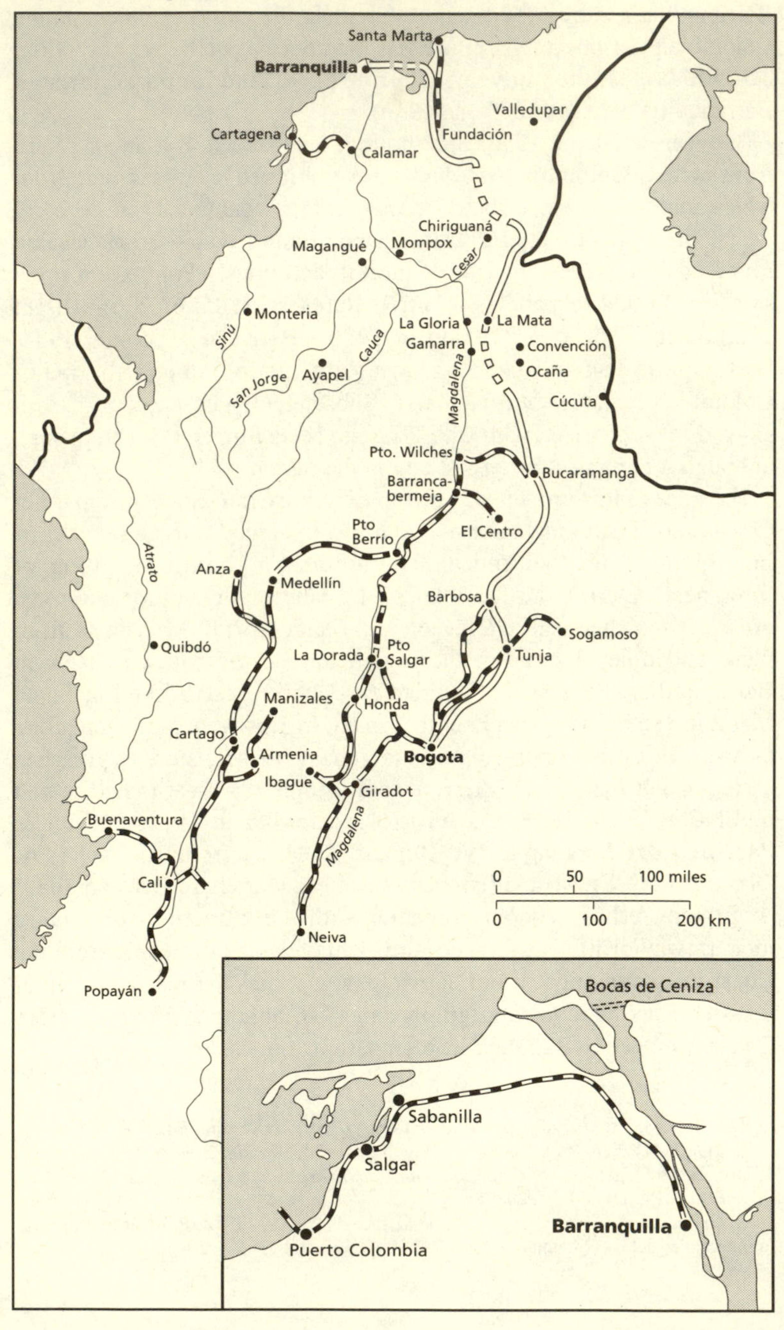

TABLE 3.3 *Rate of Growth of Barranquilla compared with that of Coastal Departments, 1870–1950*

	1870	1905	1918	1928	1938	1950
Barranquilla	100	245	456	1,107	1,214	2,311
Atlántico	100	106	168	379	434	746
Bolívar	100	57	139	236	300	418
Magdalena	100	44	174	293	n.d.	498

Sources: see Table P. 1.

Political factors also influenced decisions to move. The example of Pedro María Revollo's family, who settled in Barranquilla in 1876, illustrates how political turmoil during the nineteenth century could encourage migration. After the death of General Juan José Nieto in 1866, Revollo's father, a member of the Nieto faction which had been hitherto in power, left Cartagena fearing political prosecution. He moved with his family first to Santa Marta and later to Ciénaga. In Ciénaga, however, the continuous hostility of the villagers towards Nieto's followers forced them to move again.[20] They finally settled in Barranquilla where they mixed socially with fellow *Cartagenero* immigrants. Were the Revollos a typical family? Probably not, but their example does suggest a degree of politically motivated migration. J. H. Palacio recalled how, as a consequence of political events in 1885, several Liberal families from Cartagena moved to Barranquilla.[21] Why was Barranquilla a refuge for political emigrants? Barranquilla developed a self-assertive civic pride based on its tolerance and its open nature, a city of immigrants.[22] In 1949, when the country once again suffered intense political violence, Barranquilla was regarded as a peaceful city, a haven for refugees.[23]

Politics, however, were not the main reason for settling in Barranquilla. What the city offered were economic opportunities and the prospects of a better life. As Barranquilla gained in importance, it became one of the most attractive centres for migration in the country.

20 Revollo, *Memorias*, 2, 13, 35–6.

21 J. H. Palacio, *Historia de mi vida* (Bogotá, 1942), 69.

22 *Informe del Secretario de Gobierno* (Barranquilla, 1933), 3.

23 From American Consul, Barranquilla, 6 and 14 Dec. 1949, NAUS/RG84, Barranquilla Consulate, Segregated Records, 1939–40, Box No. 2.

Unfortunately, it is impossible to give an accurate picture of these movements throughout the period but, as Table 3.3 suggests, between 1870 and 1950 Barranquilla grew at the expense of the rest of the Coast. The 1951 census gives an appreciation of the significance of regional immigrants in the city's population. According to this census, 74 per cent of the 103,184 immigrants who were then settled in Barranquilla had been born either in Bolívar or in Magdalena.[24] As a city of immigrants, both national and foreign, Barranquilla was regarded as a land of opportunities. 'This place welcomes with great ease anything that favours its well-being', A. J. Márquez noted in 1913, praising Barranquilla's openness.[25] Márquez, a physician, was writing with the benefit of his father's experience. Born in 1799, of a Spanish father and a *Barranquillera* mother, Esteban Márquez had become the wealthiest man in town by the 1870s, having been a pedlar during his youth. 'He is a common man and barely knows how to write and read', the US Consul described him in 1882.[26] Márquez made his fortune in foreign trade, from where he moved into real estate and banking. He was prominently involved in the development of nineteenth century Barranquilla.[27] If living on the Plaza de San Nicolás had any social status, Márquez owned two houses of the eastern side of the main square. Symbolically, his family house on the *Plaza*, inherited by his children, was later bought by a Palestinian immigrant, E. Muvdi, who in 1916 was already a successful merchant.[28] Self-made men, whether second generation *Barranquilleros* such as Márquez or foreign immigrants as was Muvdi, were integrated into a relatively fluid social élite, where they shared with more 'traditional' families their enthusiasm for progress. The degree of openness of Barranquilla society may have changed over the years. However, there is little doubt that it was precisely Barranquilla's readiness to receive newcomers that attracted immigrants while it provided the town with a stimulating environment for business activities.

[24] Sojo, *Barranquilla, una economía en expansión*, 136–8; E. Havens and E. Usandizaga, *Tres barrios de invasión* (Bogotá, 1966), 20.

[25] A. J. Márquez, *Saludo a Barranquilla* (Barranquilla, 1913), 15–25.

[26] US Despatches from US Consuls in Sabanilla, 1878–84, NAUS, film T426/5.

[27] Goenaga, *Lecturas locales*, 253, 416–21; Baena and Vergara, *Barranquilla*, 314, 318–9.

[28] Rebollo, *Memorias*, 135.

3. Commerce, Banking, and Industry

As a major port, Barranquilla's trade consisted largely in the transshipment, forwarding, and distribution of merchandise. Most of the river steamship companies had their headquarters in Barranquilla and the city also had agencies for the ocean lines calling at its harbour: Elder & Fyffes & Co. Ltd., Frederick Leyland & Co. Ltd., Pacific Steam Navigation Co. Ltd., among others, were calling regularly at Puerto Colombia in 1929.[29] Important Colombian merchant houses had branches in Barranquilla but *Barranquilleros* themselves directed the city's business. In 1895, there existed some twenty-five or thirty commercial houses, 'all of them well equipped, commanding large resources, and enjoying first-rate credit,' and many of them acting as 'commission agents for houses in the interior'.[30] With their headquarters in Barranquilla, for many of these houses the Coast was their main commercial district.

Some of those who had moved to Barranquilla kept a branch in their town of origin: Fergusson, Noguera & Co., in Santa Marta; Antonio Volpe & Co., in El Carmen; Paccini & Puccini in Magangué; A. Clavería in Ciénaga.[31] The opening of new branches or the distribution of their merchandise through forwarding agencies in the region gives an idea of the scope of their market. Volpe opened branches in San Jacinto, Plato and Chalán; D. Marino & Lacoraza, who established in Barranquilla in 1913, had branches in Santa Marta and Magangué by 1928; Alejandro A. Correa & Co. also operated in Mompox and Magangué; Aepli, Eberbach & Co., distributors of *Singer* sewing machines, had outlets in Bolívar, Magdalena, and Santander as did Paccini & Puccini with their Italian merchandise. In 1895, it was estimated that of the total value of imports which annually entered through Barranquilla, two-thirds were destined for the Andean interior, and the remaining third was distributed in Barranquilla and in the departments of Bolívar, Magdalena, and part of Santander.[32]

29 J. Garnett Lomax, *Republic of Colombia: Commercial Review and Handbook* (London, 1930), 98.

30 *PP*, 37, LXXXV (1896), 442.

31 The activities of these merchant houses and their markets are documented in A. Martínez Aparicio and R. Niebles (eds.), *Directorio Anuario de Barranquilla* (Barranquilla, 1892); Goenaga, *Acción Costeña;* E. Rash-Isla (ed.), *Directorio Comercial Pro-Barranquilla* (Barranquilla, 1928); A. L. Carbonell (ed.), *Anuario Comercial Pro-Barranquilla* (Barranquilla, 1936).

32 *PP*, 37, LXXXV (1896), 468.

Many of these merchants also traded in regional products, in particular, tobacco, cotton, salt, cattle, and hides. Santo Domingo & Co., D. J. Senior, and Paccini & Puccini, for example, traded in cattle; Lascano y Cía and Antonio Volpe & Co. in hides; the Compañía Agrícola and the Empresa Algodonera e Industrial, in cotton. The majority of these firms did not specialize in a particular product but they dealt instead in a variety of goods, some as exporters, others as importers, often as both. At the same time, some were also commissioning agents, money-lenders, and even agricultural entrepreneurs. *Barranquillero* merchants developed further links with the agricultural sector on the Coast by financing crops, buying and selling land, or even becoming directly involved in agricultural production. Advances made throughout the year on prospective crops was a 'recognized system'.[33] This practice was common in the tobacco region of El Carmen and in the cotton districts of Atlántico and Magdalena. The Cámara de Comercio in Barranquilla followed closely the prices of agricultural products and cattle.[34] During the 1890s and the first two decades of this century, there was an active group of merchants buying and selling land in Remolino, Sitionuevo, and Ciénaga. The banana boom also attracted the attention of Barranquilla's commercial sector. A few merchants, as noted previously, established their own plantations. Despite the dominant presence of the United Fruit Company, they also managed to have a share not only in the production of bananas but also in the trading activities throughout the banana zone.

Senior, de Sola & Co. exemplified the wide range of activities of *Barranquillero* merchants at the end of the nineteenth century. They operated mainly as an export–import house; on the *Plaza del Mercado* they kept one of their two general stores, while their headquarters were in Calle del Comercio where they also acted as agents for the Transatlántica de Barcelona and the Northern Fire-life Assurance Co.; they were founding shareholders of the Banco de Barranquilla, and in 1890 they established El Impulso, a modern cotton-gin. In addition, the Seniors had considerable investments in real estate and eventually became involved in banana production.[35]

33 *PP*, 49, XCIX (1899), 34.

34 *RCCB* (3 Jun. 1934), 4, and (15 Mar. 1944), 3.

35 Martínez Aparicio and Niebles, *Directorio Anuario*, 122, 149, 282, 350–1, 390; *MCR* (May–Aug. 1895), 47; Banco de Barranquilla, *Informes y Balance General* (Barranquilla, 1889), 7; Colombia, *Misión de Rafael Reyes*, 48; 'Indice de la Notaría Primera de Ciénaga'; 'Informe No. 3', 24–5, 30, and 'Informe No. 5', 17, MDC.

An important element in the regional market was the travelling salesman, a virtual 'wheel of commerce' in the scattered and poorly communicated towns of the Coast. Their written records are scarce but many may have followed the routes taken by Jacinto Sarasúa. In the 1920s, Sarasúa used to take a boat from Barranquilla to Mompox, where he spent the first two days of his usual commercial tour around Bolívar. From Mompox he took a barge to Magangué, 'where our friend Pedro Bacci provided us with a white horse, a pack-mule, and a guide who knew his way to Sincé and Sincelejo'. Equipped thus with horse and pack-mule, Sarasúa continued his business in Corozal, Ovejas, San Jacinto, San Juan de Nepomuceno, and Calamar. From Calamar he went to Cartagena and back by train and then boarded the first ship back to Barranquilla. 'After travelling for a month,' Sarasúa recalled,' . . . one felt, as a large advertisement in La Gloria stated: "here you suffer but you also enjoy yourself", as we arrived there happily ready to sit on our behind before taking orders from our clients'.[36] On different occasions, Sarasúa toured Magdalena and Santander, visiting clients as in Bolívar, taking orders, and expanding the commercial network of his company.

While commercial travellers were opening and strengthening markets in Coastal towns for what Barranquilla had to offer, the city, in turn, was a recipient of large quantities of foodstuffs from the region. Barranquilla's immediate surroundings were so arid that they did not produce 'any vegetation other than dwarf cacti and brambles'.[37] The public market was located on a side canal of the Magdalena, 'an obligatory site, since all the merchandise sold here is brought by water and not by land as it happens elsewhere'.[38] When Robinson visited the market in 1892, the water's edge 'was crowded with canoes, all dug out of single logs, and some of surprising size'. In the market, he noticed 'a great variety of fruits', 'immense heaps of dried fish' and 'great piles of dried shrimps'.[39] Basic foodstuffs – plantains, fish, *panela*, rice, lard, yucca, cheese, and cattle for beef consumption – came from neighbouring provinces, via the Magdalena river. Plantains were a popular product in this regional trade; so was fish. In the 1940s, the entire population of Aracataca Viejo lived from fishing, 'carrying the

[36] Sarasúa, *Recuerdos*, 25–6. For the regional scope of travelling salesmen, see Martínez and Niebles, *Directorio Anuario*, 299. For a description of the activities of a travelling salesman in Venezuela, see O. Gerstl, *Memorias e historias* (Caracas, 1974).

[37] Scruggs, *Colombian and Venezuelan Republics*, 31.

[38] Grau, La *ciudad de Barranquilla*, 35.

[39] Robinson, *A Flying Trip to the Tropics*, 38, 39.

catch nine hours by canoe to Barranquilla, where they deliver it, believe it or not, on ice. After unloading the fish, they refill their canoes with ice and start back'.[40] Shortages of food, basically of rice due to the locust plagues, were met by imports, although during the 1930s and 1940s Barranquilla was one of the main markets for the growing rice production of San Jorge, Sinú, and other areas in Bolívar.[41] Imports of wheat for flour production were also significant. Wheat from the interior uplands could not compete on the Coast.

The growing activities of the port led to the establishment of the first banks. In 1873 prominent members of the merchant community from Barranquilla and from other Coastal towns founded the Banco de Barranquilla as a joint stock company. The bulk of the founding members were *Barranquillero* residents but the new venture also attracted some capital from Santa Marta, Cartagena, Mompox, Tubará, and Ocaña.[42] The bank's business included 'discounting of commercial paper, effecting loans on collateral securities and selling bills of exchange on Europe and the United States'. Shortly after its operations started, the bank opened agencies in Magangué and in the tobacco-producing centre of El Carmen.[43] Its business was concentrated in Barranquilla, although linked to the regional economy. Cattle exports to Cuba in the 1890s, for example, were of great benefit to the bank. The Banco de Barranquilla managed to survive several upheavals but finally closed in 1904, as a consequence of the disastrous effects of the *Guerra de los Mil Días*.[44] Nevertheless, its closure was immediately followed by the establishment of the Banco Comercial de Barranquilla, practically a continuation of the former bank, as can be seen by looking at the members of the Board of Directors. Most of the shareholders of the Banco Comercial had also previously invested in the Banco de Barranquilla.[45] The new institution started operations in 1905 under difficult conditions due to failures in the coffee and cotton crops, and a drop in the cattle trade as a consequence of a prolonged drought. By 1910, the bank could inform its shareholders of a remarkable increase

[40] Romoli, *Colombia: A Gateway to South America*, 252.

[41] *RCCB* (15 Sept. 1934), 2; IET, 4th Trimester, 1946.

[42] de Mier to the *Secretario General del Estado de Bolívar*, Barranquilla, 23 Mar. 1873, AGB; and *Boletín Industrial*, 30 Mar. 1873.

[43] *GB*, 25 Oct. 1873, 7 May 1874.

[44] Banco de Barranquilla, *Informes y balance general presentados por la Junta Directiva a la Junta General de Accionistas* (Barranquilla, 1889). See also similar reports dated Jan. 1890 and July 1899.

[45] Baena and Vergara, *Barranquilla*, 500; and *Banco Comercial de Barranquilla, 1905–1955* (Barranquilla, 1955), 5–13.

in deposits, and in 1919, despite unfavourable conditions as a consequence of the war, the Board prided itself on the achievements of the bank in terms of prestige, number of clients, and amount of business.[46] Good management, stable administration, and conservative policies – as Kemmerer had recognized – allowed the Banco Comercial to overcome troubled times and, by 1950, it was the only surviving local bank.[47]

Besides the Banco de Barranquilla and the Banco Comercial, five other banks were established with local capital, though they had a much shorter life: Banco Márquez (1883–93), Banco Americano (1883–1904), Banco del Atlántico (1901–04), Banco de Crédito Mercantil (1914–25), and Banco Dugand (1917–25).[48] In contrast to the Banco de Barranquilla and the Banco Comercial, most of these institutions were recognized as family businesses rather than joint ventures.[49] The Banco Dugand was founded by V. Dugand & Hijo, a merchant house established by a French immigrant who first settled in Ríohacha, moving to Barranquilla in 1902. Despite the fact that the family was in control of the bank, the Dugands did manage to attract local capitalists to subscribe bank shares, including a significant number of Syrian immigrants.[50] The Banco Dugand experienced remarkable growth during its first three years of operations, probably due to the flourishing coffee exports that were still being shipped through Barranquilla. In 1920 it had opened agencies in Cartagena, Ciénaga, Magangué, Ríohacha, and Santa Marta, besides those in the Andean interior. In that year the 150 bank shareholders received a 14 per cent interest on their investments.[51] This apparently solid

[46] *Banco Comercial*, 16–27.

[47] 'Memorandum of conversation with Mr. Van Dusen on Mar. 20, 1923', Princeton University, Edwin Kemmerer Papers (I wish to thank Adolfo Meisel for allowing me to see this document).

[48] *RB*, 10 Oct. 1889; *RCCB* (3 June 1920), 13–15; Baena and Vergara, *Barranquilla*, 499–508; *Libro Azul de Colombia* (New York, 1918), 261–7. It should be born in mind, however, that local capital was not exclusively channelled through these institutions. Several merchants were often ready to lend money in an informal financial market hitherto unexplored. In the 1930s, for example, banana planters such as J. F. Riascos & Co., and José Noguera Gnecco, had contracted mortgage liabilities with Elias M. Muvdi; see Santa Marta manager to Barranquilla branch, 4. Jan. 1932, Bolsa/A21/3.

[49] See A. Meisel and E. Posada, 'Los bancos de la Costa Caribe, 1873–1925' in F. Sánchez, ed., *Ensayos de historia monetaria y bancaria de Colombia* (Bogotá, 1994), 229–66.

[50] Banco Dugand, *Informe de la Junta Administrativa a la Asamblea General de Accionistas* (Barranquilla, 120); and Baena y Vergara, *Barranquilla*, 508.

[51] In 1920 interest rates in Barranquilla were 10 per cent; Meisel and Posada, 'Los bancos de la Costa Caribe', 254.

organization, however, plummeted a few years later. By the end of 1921, the bank had already felt the consequences of the recession and in 1925, it was taken over by the Banco de Colombia.[52]

'The commercial public is well catered for in the way of banking facilities', the British Consul in Barranquilla had reported in 1923.[53] (Table 3.4 illustrates the movement of banks in Barranquilla between 1872 and 1936). In addition to some national banks, which had started to establish branches during the nineteenth century, foreign banks also developed business in Barranquilla with the growth of the city in the 1910s and the 1920s: the Banco Mercantil Americano, the Commercial Bank of Spanish America, the National City Bank, The Royal Bank of Canada, the Anglo-South American Bank, were among the most prominent. By the 1950s, there were seventeen banking institutions, foreign and national alike, operating in Barranquilla. Their original involvement in Barranquilla was clearly linked to the port. In 1926, the manager of the Bank of London and South America described his business as 'especially . . . handling . . . documents relating to goods consigned to the Bank's clients in the interior, payments of custom duties . . .' and so on. 'Fixed term deposits in Barranquilla,' the manager pointed out a year later, 'appear to be comparatively scarce'.[54] By the early 1930s when Barranquilla was reported 'to develop in a remarkable manner', 'in spite of the sever times through which Colombia [was] passing', some of these banks had strengthened their links with other business interests besides exporters and importers. The bulk of the Bank of London and South America's clients were 'dependent for income on rent from properties, cattle and local industries'. Important textile and saw-mills, cigarette factories, urban developers, and, obviously, prominent merchant houses were dealing with the Anglo-South American Bank and the Bank of London and South America.[55]

Nevertheless, as a financial centre, Barranquilla was lagging behind Bogotá, Medellín, Cali, and Manizales by the 1950s.[56] While some of

[52] C. C. A. Lee, *Report on the Economic Conditions in the Republic of Colombia (London, 1924),* 22–3; and W. J. Sullivan, *Report on the Commercial and Economic Situation in the Republic of Colombia* (London, 1925), 50.

[53] Lee, *Report*, 22.

[54] Barranquilla Branch to the Head Office, Barranquilla, 12 Apr. 1926, and 13 Apr. 1927, Bolsa/B1/49 and 85.

[55] Barranquilla Branch to the Head Office, 24 Apr. 1930; to Chairman and Directors, 17 July 1930; and to Bogotá Office, 21 Jan. 1931, Bolsa/B1/368, 429, 432, 550. See also 'Barranquilla inspection letter', 11 Sept. 1931, Bolsa/A19/5.

[56] Sojo, *Barranquilla, una economía*, 45–58.

their banks started to adopt a regional and even a national outlook, the few *Barranquillero* banks were liquidated and the only survivor – Banco Comercial – kept a low profile, restricting its operations to Barranquilla. Yet the influence of local banks in the development of the city was significant, particularly before the 1920s. Around them, a group of merchants was actively involved in improving the conditions of the port, bettering public services, and encouraging new industries.

When Alejandro López visited Barranquilla in 1938, he was impressed by its industrial growth.[57] His first visit in 1905 had left little impression. López was now so overwhelmed as to believe that, given its geographical position – which allowed the city quick access to raw materials – Barranquilla was set not only to supply the national market but also to become an industrial entrepôt for the Caribbean. López's enthusiasm was a reaction to obvious signs of progress. With the exception of boatbuilding and rum distilleries, soap production seems to have pioneered industrial development in Barranquilla: La Industria, established in 1877, El Porvenir in 1878, La Cubana in 1883 – which by 1896 was expanding its market throughout the region.[58] Other industries were also developing, some of them using imported steam-powered machinery: tanneries, brick and tile production, saddleries, cotton-gins, shoe manufacturing, and saw-mills. Established by the river canal that reached the centre of Barranquilla, many of these factories received their raw materials from neighbouring districts. Cotton, divi-divi, mangrove, salt, timber, hides, were all products that linked Barranquilla with the region during this early phase of industrialization. In turn, manufactured goods reached Coastal towns. Attempts to ship even ice to interior points on the river, and to Ciénaga and Santa Marta, at the risk of losing a large proportion, show the search for a market beyond the city limits.[59]

Again local merchants played an important role in encouraging industrial development as they diversified their business. Barranquilla was also a place of small workshops, originally developed around ship-building activities. In 1892, the *Directorio Anuario* included significant numbers of blacksmiths, brassworkers, carpenters, bakers, silversmiths, shoemakers, and tailors. Soon industry was adopted as

[57] *El Heraldo*, 4 and 5 Jan. 1938.

[58] See Grau, *Barranquilla en 1986*, 90–105; Martínez and Niebles, *Directorio Anuario*, 95–6; E. Pellet, 'Veinte años en Barranquilla 1866–86', in *RCCB* (15 Dec. 1936), 12. See also S. Solano and J. Conde, *Elite empresarial y desarrollo industrial de Barranquilla, 1875–1930* (Barranquilla, 1993), 37–58.

[59] *MCR* (July 1900), 238, 272–5.

TABLE 3.4 *Banks Established in Barranquilla, 1873–1936*

Year	Name of bank	Year of establishment	Origin of the capital
1873	Bogotá	1872	National
	Barranquilla	1872/3	Local
1883	Barranquilla	1872/3	Local
	Nacional	1882	National
	Americano	1883	Local
	Márquez	1883	Local
1919	Comercial de Barranquilla	1904	Local
	Crédito Mercantil	1913	Local
	Dugand	1917	Local
	Mercantil Americano	1918	Foreign
	Banco López	1919	National
1922	Comercial de Barranquilla	1904	Local
	Dugand	1917	Local
	Commercial Bank of Spanish America	1920	Foreign
	National City	1920	Foreign
	Alemán Antioqueño	1920	National
1928	Comercial de Barranquilla	1904	Local
	Colombia		National
	Alemán Antioqueño		National
	The Anglo South American Bank		Foreign
	London and South America		Foreign
	Royal Bank of Canada	1925	Foreign
1936	Comercial de Barranquilla	1904	Local
	Colombia		National
	Bogotá		National
	The Anglo South American		Foreign
	Francés e Italiano		Foreign
	Royal Bank of Canada		Foreign
	Alemán Antioqueño	1920	National
	Central Hipotecario		National
	Hipotecario de Colombia		National
	Caja Colombiana de Ahorros		National
	Caja de Crédito Agrario		National

Sources: Bell, *Colombia: A Commercial and Industrial Handbook* (Washington, 1922); F. Baena and J. R. Vergara, *Barranquilla, homenaje del Banco Dugand* (Barranquilla, 1922); E. Rash-Isla (ed.), *Directorio comercial pro-Barranquilla* (Barranquilla, 1928); E. Grau, *La ciudad de Barranquilla en 1896* (Barranquilla, 1896); T. Nichols, *Tres puertos de Colombia* (Bogotá, 1973); A. L. Carbonell (ed.), *Anuario comercial pro-Barranquilla* (Barranquilla, 1936).

part of a civic ethos: 'it is the great means through which to achieve happiness for humankind', Márquez wrote in his *Saludo a Barranquilla* in 1913, and he added: 'industry awakens intelligence . . . thanks to it people gain respect everywhere . . . industry is a mysterious gift that transforms humble peoples into great nations, full of monuments and respectable sages'.[60]

Industry had a long way to go to reach this stage but it continued growing, first, encouraged by protectionist measures taken by the Reyes Administration (1904–9) and later mainly by external influences: the Depression and the two World Wars. Throughout these years, new industries were developed, mostly textile and flour mills, beverage and food-processing factories, and chemical plants. The first systematic attempt to describe the industrial structure of Barranquilla was made in 1945, when the *Contraloría General de la República* carried out the First Industrial Census of Colombia. According to these censuses, among the most prominent lines of manufacture, there were 99 establishments involved in the production of leather goods, 98 in foodstuffs, 88 in clothing, 74 processing timber, 53 in metallurgy, 22 in textiles, and 14 in beverages. The size and importance of these industries varied: 39.1 per cent of industrial capital in Barranquilla was invested in textiles, 15.5 in metallurgy, 13.9 in food-processing, 10.8 in beverages, 4.4 in the processing of timber, 4.4 in chemicals, 2.9 in clothing, and 2.5 in leather goods, among the eight most important sectors.[61]

'The protection of these Coastal flour-mills works even against common sense.' The attack came from the Minister of Hacienda in 1912, when he labelled as 'exotic' those industries that were developed using imported raw materials, particularly candle and match factories, flour and textile-mills.[62] By 1934, 126 industrial establishments in Barranquilla consumed 6,957,999 Colombian pesos in raw materials, out of which just 25 per cent were spent on national products, the remainder on imports. A decade later, however, the proportion of national raw materials used by *Barranquillero* industries had increased to almost 50 per cent. As shown in Table 3.5, among the most

[60] Márquez, *Saludo a Barranquilla* , 10.

[61] Contraloría, *Primer censo industrial de Colombia, 1945: Departamento del Atlántico* (Bogotá, 1947), 15. Industrial production from Barranquilla contributed significantly to national production in the following sectors: metallurgy (26.2%), chemicals (23.9%), timber (18.5%), textiles (17.4%), leather goods (13.7%), clothing (12.8%), and beverages (9.6%). See Ospina Vásquez, *Industria y protección* , 602–3.

[62] *Informe del Ministro de Hacienda* (Bogotá, 1912), 28–39.

important sectors that were spending larger amounts on national raw materials in 1945 were food-processing, textiles, clothing, leather production, and timber.

TABLE 3.5 *Value of Raw Materials Consumed by Barranquillero Industries according to their Origins, 1945 (pesos)*

Sector	National	Imported
Food industry	7,711,646	4,868,653
Paper production	16,427	305,056
Graphic arts	11,681	478,694
Rubber products	65,948	18,201
Beverages	1,763,869	1,280,021
Leather goods	2,160,560	375,859
Tools	80,446	7,769
Timber	1,824,799	124,772
Metallurgy	154,214	2,864,855
Mineral products	185,326	201,513
Tobacco	314,444	212,273
Textiles	4,788,653	4,304,654
Clothing	2,241,666	1,133,041
Other	91,189	184,936

Source: Contraloría, *Primer censo industrial*, 327-8.

It is impossible to calculate what proprotion of the national raw materials consumed by the *Barranquillero* industries was produced in the region (Table 3.5). Nevertheless, it seems valid to assume that in the cases of textiles, timber and food-processing, and leather goods, a significant percentage of raw materials originated from the Coast. In turn, manufactured goods from Barranquilla found a ready market in neighbouring Coastal towns. La Industria, established originally in 1877 and later to become the largest saw-mill in Colombia, produced lumber for construction, boxes, windows, doors, and furniture. It received its raw materials from Coastal timber zones and sold its products, aside from Barranquilla, in Santa Marta, Ciénaga, and all the towns along the Magdalena River up to Girardot.[63] Regardless of the origin of the raw material, the Coast was the immediate market for *Barranquillero* industrial products: shoes from Fábrica de Pinedo

[63] 'To the Shareholders of the Compañía Nacional de Maderas La Industria', Barranquilla, 18 July 1930, APF.

Hermanos, matches from Shemel, nails from Colombia Industrial, beer from Cervecería Aguila: all relied on the expanding market of the neighbouring region.[64] Yet the relationship between city and region – the latter as both a supplier of raw materials and a market for industrial products, was fraught with difficulties. A glance at the development of the textile industry gives an appreciation of the limitations of this relationship, as well as some of the problems faced by industrial development as a whole.

Several cotton-ginning companies had been developed during the last decades of the nineteenth century but the modern textile industry did not take off in Barranquilla until 1910, when the Fábrica de Tejidos Obregón was founded. In turn, prices offered by the Barranquilla, together with the Medellín mills, stimulated cotton-growing in the region during the second decade of this century. By 1929, the chief industry in Barranquilla was the manufacture of cotton goods: there were seven main plants with a total of 20,000 spindles and 1,000 looms. During the 1930s and 1940s, the expansion of the industry largely occurred through the processing of other fibres: silk, rayon and wool. Yet nine out of the twenty-three textiles plants in production in 1945 were weaving cotton, although as shown in Chapter 1, cotton growing had not kept pace with the development of the textile industry.[65]

In 1910 Tejidos Obregón started to manufacture cotton drills with 72 looms. Established by the merchant house Evaristo Obregón and Co., the new textile venture was then jointly managed by two members of the Obregón family who had received technical training in England.[66] The plant grew steadily, with 200 looms by 1914, 300 by 1916, 400 by 1924, when it was considered the single largest cotton textile factory in Colombia. By 1943, it was still the most important cotton mill in Barranquilla, though much of the machinery was by then obsolete. The plant's future was further hampered by labour problems: it was reported that the installation of new looms had been disappointing 'due

64 López, *Almanaque de los hechos*, 59, 256.

65 Garnett Lomax, *Republic of Colombia*, 98; Carbonell (ed.), *Anuario industrial*, 67–71; and Contraloría, *Primer Censo Industrial*, 327.

66 *Daily Consular and Trade Reports*, Washington, 12 Dec. 1910 (136), 967. For descriptions of the Obregóns and their business activities, see 'Anglo–Colombian Relations: Disturbing Incidents', Bogotá, 20 Dec. 1943, PRO, FO371/38041; Department of Overseas Trade, *Report on the Finance, Industry and Trade of the Republic of Colombia* (London, 1922), 14; and Solano and Conde, *Elite empresarial y desarrollo industrial*, 79–101.

to lack of technical skill on the part of the workmen and their opposition to . . . automatic machinery'.[67]

TABLE 3.6 *Main Textile Industries in Barranquilla, 1944*

Company	Year organized	Capital invested ($000)	Origin of capital	No. of employees
T. Obregón	1910	1,714	Local	916
Jaar & Co.	1943	205	Local	83
Marysol	1943	850	Foreign	350
Indurayon	1936	2,856	n.d.	409
Filta	1934	1,428	Local	100
Celta	1934	142	Local	206
Alfa	1936	142	Local	167
T. Atlántico	1937	457	n.d.	405

Source: Vice-Consul Wardlaw, 'Barranquilla Textile Industry'.

Besides developing their own 1,000 ha plantation in Remolino, the Obregóns had encouraged cotton growing in Atlántico and Magdalena by distributing free seed and advancing money against future crops. In 1932, their mill alone consumed about 30 per cent of the raw cotton produced in the Coast. Between 1921 and 1934, Tejidos Obregón had only rarely imported raw cotton, being supplied for most of those years by regional plantations.[68] During the following decade, however, the mill had to resort to imports. The Obregóns even turned against protectionist measures to promote national cotton growing. In 1941, Rafael Obregón publicly attacked a bill in Congress which attempted to increase the tariff on duties for the importation of raw cotton. According to him, cotton cultivation in Colombia was seriously hindered by the lack of technology, and tariff protection on its own would only benefit foreign textile industries.[69] Some years later, the

[67] Vice Consul Wardlaw, 'Barranquilla textile industry'. NAUS/ RG166/ FAR, NR, 1942–45, Colombia, Box 180. M. Archila has suggested that the radicalism of labour demands in Barranquilla gave an additional advantage to the development of the textile industry in Antioquia, largely based on women's labour. See his *Barranquilla y el río: una historia social de sus trabajadores* (Bogotá, 1987), 30–1.

[68] See Ospina Vásquez, *Industria y protección*, 475; 'Cotton Production and Consumption in the Barranquilla Consular District', Barranquilla, 13 Dec. 1933, NAUS, RG166/ FAR/ Colombia, General Information, Box 132; Contraloría, *Geografía económica del Atlántico*, 158.

[69] *La Prensa*, 25 Nov. 1941.

plant was closed down. Apart from labour problems, Tejidos Obregón – like many *Barranquillero* industries – faced the restrictions of a relatively limited market, and were further constrained by the difficulties of transport.

Concern about the shortcomings of Coastal industries *vis à vis* those from the interior was expressed by members of the Cámara de Comercio as early as 1924. Asked to give an account of the state of local industry, the Cámara de Comercio's Commission pointed out that Coastal manufacturing benefited from some obvious advantages, mainly its position by the sea, being closer therefore to the external market and to the sources of raw materials. Unfortunately, the Commission added, set against this natural advantage there were some serious drawbacks: high freights and river taxes which impeded Coastal manufactured goods from competing favourably in the most populated markets of the interior; higher salaries than those of the interior; higher electricity costs, since the interior had access to cheaper sources of energy; more exposure to foreign competition, as industries in the interior were naturally protected by distance and costly communications.[70]

A variety of obstacles thus stood in the way of the development of industry, but despite their shortcomings not all factories suffered the fate of Tejidos Obregón. As previously shown, Barranquilla's industry did expand during the 1930s and 1940s, though the earlier dynamism which had made her the third largest Colombian industrial centre had significantly ebbed by 1950.[71] Distant from the wealthier and more populated coffee regions, Barranquilla was now lagging behind Bogotá, Medellín, and Cali. Access to national markets was hampered by poor transport. Under these circumstances, it became evident that Barranquilla's industrial future depended on the economic growth of its neighbouring region. As one contemporary analyst put it: 'this was a powerful reason for *Barranquilleros* to spread progress and wealth throughout the Atlantic Coast'.[72]

70 *RCCB*, 15 Sept. 1924, 16–17.

71 See essay by Meisel in Meisel and Posada, *Por qué se disipó el dinamismo industrial*, 1–40.

72 Sojo, *Barranquilla, una economía*, 186.

4. Employment, Housing, and Services

The largest concentration of labour in Barranquilla was initially gathered around port activities although, as the city expanded, construction and services and also industry offered new opportunities for employment. According to the 1918 census, there were 5,167 people employed in 'arts and craft, and industry'. More elaborate figures were given by the first industrial census in 1945, according to which there were approximately 14,000 people directly employed by industry: in textiles, metallurgy, food-processing, timber works, and in leather goods production, among others. However, a large number of independent labourers were also employed in crafts. According to a 1935 official publication, there were 10,000 artesans in Barranquilla.[73] A glance at the names of labour unions which were recognized by the state between 1920 and 1937 indicates the predominance of port activities and of the local craft industry.[74] The active presence of artesans influenced by anarchist ideas was, in the opinion of Ignacio Torres Giraldo, a principal obstacle to the organization of the labour movement.[75] Despite the difficulties he encountered, union membership in Barranquilla reached higher levels than in the rest of the country. According to a 1948 publication, 70 per cent of the Barranquilla labour force belonged to a union, compared to 14 per cent in Bogotá, 21 per cent in Medellín, and 61 per cent in the river port of Honda.[76]

Occasional employment, particularly in construction work and obviously in the docks, was the usual condition of a significant proportion of Barranquilla labourers. Falls in trade hit the city hard and brought social unrest. In 1918, work stoppages by dockers developed into a general strike when 'the city was practically in the possession of a mob totalling about 5,000 people'. Petty thievery was increasing in 1929, when it was 'conservatively estimated that there [were] unemployed in Barranquilla and its immediate vicinity 5,000 workers'.[77] Numerous unemployed demonstrators joined in the 1931 general strike organized by a civic movement in support of the Bocas

[73] Contraloría, *Geografía económica del Atlántico*, 161.

[74] Torres Giraldo, *Los inconformes*, iv. 184–8 and 253–61, v. 67, 95–8, 135–40, 188.

[75] Torres Giraldo, *Los inconformes*, iv. 62.

[76] R. Bernal Salamanca, *Las condiciones económico-sociales y el costo de la vida de la clase obrera en la ciudad de Barranquilla* (Bogotá, 1948), 30.

[77] American Consul to Secretary of State, Barranquilla, 5 Jan. and 16 Mar. 1918, 17 Sept. 1929, NAUS/ 821.5045/5; 821.50 and 50/7; Bell, *Colombia*, 199.

de Ceniza project. Again in 1942, unemployment had risen significantly: the majority of construction workers were reported to be without jobs, and stevedores 'who formerly were employed full-time at the Maritime Terminal now consider themselves fortunate to obtain work for one or two days each week'.[78]

Periods of high unemployment notwithstanding, it was the growth of Barranquilla, and the job opportunities it offered which made the place attractive in the long run for new settlers. As early as 1897 new shanty districts made their appearance. Years later, Kathleen Romoli was quick to notice these neighbourhoods, often the product of sudden growth: 'Any taxi driver in Barranquilla will show you a whole quarter that grew up by concerted action in a single night of feverish shanty building on the private grounds of a Colombian gentleman, and which has taken on triumphant permanence'.[79] Not all growth was unplanned nor did it all result in such informal extensions of the city.

Between 1920 and 1936, the urban shell in Barranquilla expanded from 590 to 1,541 ha. In 1928 on average there were two houses built daily. Eight years later, in 1936, Barranquilla ranked second among Colombian cities in terms of levels of construction activity. In 1930, there were 18,050 buildings; by 1951, this number had almost doubled.[80] Fig. 3.2 illustrates the construction movement in Barranquilla between 1928 and 1947. As shown, the effect of the Depression was disastrous for the sector. It slightly recovered in 1936/38 and again after 1943 but by 1946 it had still not reached 1929 levels. Nevertheless, growth had been impressive. 'Capital in concrete', was the expression Romoli used to describe Barranquilla.[81]

Patterns of urban settlement changed with economic growth. At the end of the nineteenth century, the better-off had already moved to a new residential area 'on a gentle slope', where they built villas, 'many of them . . . pretty, surrounded by gardens and covered with luxuriant creepers'.[82] The ubiquitous plaza as a symbol of power and social prestige, which characterized traditional Spanish-American cities, was absent from Barranquilla. Here the emergent wealthy were ready to settle in new suburbs. Developed in the 1920s by the American

[78] Vice Consul Wardlaw, 'Annual Economic Report', Barranquilla, 20 Nov. 1942, NAUS, RG166: NR, 1942–5, Box 174.

[79] Romoli, *Colombia*, 34.

[80] See *BME*, Barranquilla, 8 Apr. 1932; Report from the US Commercial Attaché in Colombia, Bogotá, Jan. 1937, NAUS, RG151/Bureau of Foreign and Domestic Commerce, Bogotá, 1938; Sojo, *Barranquilla, una economia en expansión*, 147.

[81] Romoli, *Colombia*, 231.

[82] Petre, *The Republic of Colombia*, 165.

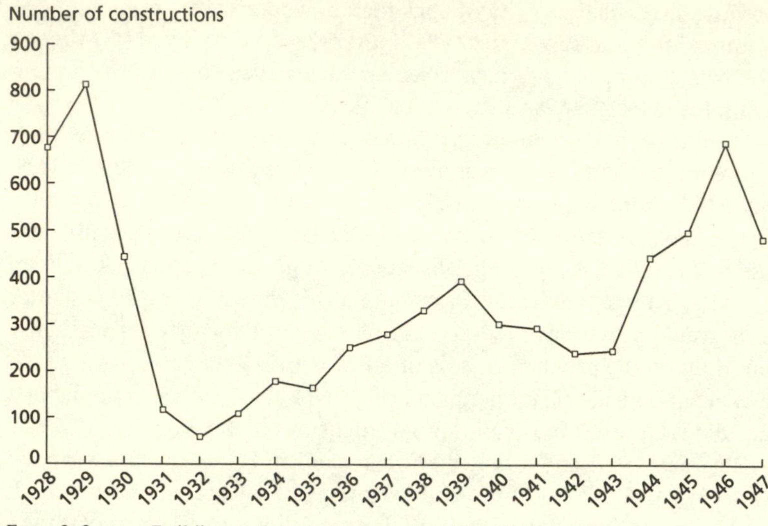

FIG. 3.2 Building Activity in Barranquilla, 1928–1947
Sources: APF

immigrant Karl C. Parrish, El Prado, a residential site on the outskirts of the city which some visitors compared to El Vedado in Havana, identified prosperity in Barranquilla with its modern aqueduct and its planned and paved boulevards. There were 'several splendid mansions' but for the most part, as Eleanor Early observed, 'wholesome little houses, essentially domestic and liveable'.[83] The success of El Prado served as model for other neighbourhoods that were springing up to accommodate a middle class. In addition, there were some official attempts to plan the development of quarters for the urban poor.[84]

Improvements in public services followed although not always at the same pace as urban growth. In 1880, an aqueduct was built in an attempt to replace the dozens of mules that hitherto used to distribute from door to door the muddy water from the Magdalena River. An electric light plant was installed by 1896, serving just over 300 houses out of a total of 4,000. The telephone was an obvious novelty, 'it is used for all purposes, even to greet each other in the mornings'; but it

[83] E. Early, *Ports of the Sun* (Boston, 1937), 211.
[84] R. Borelly, *Informe del alcalde de Barranquilla* (Barranquilla, 1945), 46.

also served business, 'since, as the consequence of the climate, everyone tries to be out in the street as little as possible, the telephone is constantly used for all sorts of transactions'.[85]

The changes of the 1880s and the 1890s were a prelude to the transformation that Barranquilla would experience during the 1920s with the establishment of the Empresas Públicas Municipales. The city, through an American loan, was able to invest in the modernization of public facilities, including the water supply and sewage systems, pavement of the streets and new buildings in the public market. In 1931, a report from the Bank of London and South America gave an account of the city's achievements, where it concluded that 'undoubtedly it is far ahead in many respects [of] other towns of the country'.[86] There was still much left to be desired. While population grew steadily, efforts to increase the capacity of the aqueduct to meet an expanding demand failed because of financial constraints. The manager of the Empresas Públicas faced great obstacles in raising rates; some local politicians and factory owners opposed the installation of water-meters.[87] Moreover, the achievements, such as they were, were soon overshadowed by rapid population growth. The inauguration of the aqueduct in 1929 was followed by its expansion in 1936, when its capacity was doubled. By 1945 the city was again short of water. In 1948 a commission backed by the *Alcalde* and the *Concejo Municipal* looked in vain for an American loan to back a plan for further city development.

No other city in the region – and few in the rest of the country – paralleled Barranquilla in the improvement of public services in the 1920s and 1930s. The city thus became a major attraction for those in search of urban comfort. Additionally, Barranquilla offered some medical, leisure, and education facilities, although a university was not established until 1945. Even cultural activities were springing up in a place that hitherto had been considered a mere *ciudad fenicia*. In 1950, when Gabriel García Márquez moved to work in Barranquilla, he found a literary circle that had formed during the 1940s around Ramón Vinyes and José Félix Fuenmayor, whose influence on his achievements the Nobel prizewinner would later acknowledge.[88]

[85] Grau, *La ciudad de Barranquilla,* 107, 44–55, 28–30.

[86] 'Monthly Review', 27 Feb. 1931, Bolsa/B1/585.

[87] See section on public finances in Ch. 6.

[88] García Márquez, who had received here part of his secondary education, worked as a journalist in Barranquilla in 1950–4. See J. Gilard (ed.), *Gabriel García Márquez:*

From being a 'humble village', Barranquilla became the most important port both on the Caribbean and on the Magdalena River, and a regional centre for the development of the Atlantic Coast: it attracted migrants from rural areas and from other Coastal towns; it established significant links with the agricultural sector of the region, both as a consumer of raw materials and foodstuffs and as a supplier of manufactured goods; and it provided the region with a variety of services.

For all its commercial predominance, however, the seat of the Church on the Coast was not Barranquilla but Cartagena, a port which preserved some political ascendancy over regional affairs and remained the main Coastal centre for higher education throughout the period.

5. Challenges to Supremacy

In contrast to Barranquilla, Cartagena was often portrayed as the symbol of urban stagnation. 'Belonging entirely to the past,' as A. S. Forest described it in 1913, Cartagena 'has escaped unharmed the vandal hand of progress.' Forest compared the town to 'an old painting by a master hand, mellow and sedate', but he considered it 'one of the most backward of the cities on the southern continent' where business was doomed to failure.[89] Overwhelmed by San Felipe de Barajas, the largest single fortress built by the Spaniards, and the colonial architecture behind the city walls, foreign visitors were bound to be enchanted by 'the atmosphere of bygone centuries'. True, Cartagena had suffered decline after independence as a result of the greater facilities offered to trade by its rival ports, to where even some *Cartagenero* merchants moved their headquarters. 'Once so important a city', a British Consul lamented in 1860, Cartagena 'has now . . . dwindled away almost to nothing'.[90] Some signs of reawakening were in evidence in the late 1860s, although the bases for long term recovery were not laid until Rafael Núñez took over as head of the State of

Textos costeños (Barcelona, 1981), 8–56; id., 'El grupo de Barranquilla', *Revista Iberoamericana*, 128–9 (July–Dec. 1984), 905–35.

[89] A. S. Forest, *A Tour through South America* (London, 1913), 119–25.

[90] *PP*, LXV (1860), 503. The decline of Cartagena after independence and the subsequent rise of Santa Marta is described in *PP*, LXVII (1873), 909–14. A history of the rivalry among Cartagena, Barranquilla, and Santa Marta is found in Nichols, *Tres puertos del Caribe*.

Bolívar between 1873 and 1876.[91] In 1874 the Banco de Bolívar was established, the city erected a clock tower, installed gas lighting of the streets, and constructed a promenade outside the walls. Overall, the most significant undertaking was the recuperation of the Canal del Dique, a waterway communicating Cartagena with the Magdalena river that had been abandoned since the wars of independence and which was finally reopened in 1881. (Table 3.7 illustrates the gradual recovery of the port in Cartagena between 1879 and 1886.) The advantages of Cartagena as a port were further enhanced with the completion of a railway that linked the city with the river port of Calamar.

A revival in foreign trade encouraged urban growth and the development of local industries. In 1891, an electricity plant was set up and in 1905 a new aqueduct replaced the old and unhealthy system of cisterns. By 1907, cotton mills, mosaic, soap, candle, and shoe factories – the latter 'enjoying a good name in the interior of the Republic' – were successfully established.[92] Construction and remodelling of buildings followed. Old houses were converted into dwellings and offices: La Merced church became a Municipal Theatre and the Convent of Santa Teresa de Jesús the headquarters of the police. It was outside the city walls that progress was most prominent: factories, docks, and residential suburbs expanded Cartagena beyond its traditional frontiers. By 1930, when it had a population of about 70,000, Cartagena ranked fifth among Colombia's cities. However, during the 1930s Cartagena went through another period of stagnation due to the opening of the Bocas de Ceniza in Barranquilla. Only after improvements in local communications could Cartagena regain its former advantages. Cartagena played a similar role in the region to that of Barranquilla but on a smaller scale. As the port developed, Cartagena became another centre of attraction for regional entrepreneurs who joined local merchants and foreign immigrants in their search for new business opportunities in an expanding town. Diego Martínez Camargo and Carlos Vélez Daníes were among the

[91] *PP*, 35, LXXVI (1875), 361–2, and J. W. Park, 'Preludio a la presidencia: Rafael Núñez, gobernador de Bolívar, 1876–1879', *Boletín de Historia y Antiguedades*, 63 (Oct.–Dec. 1876), 519–35.

[92] *PP*, 42, LXXXVIII (1907), 639; J. P. Urueta and E. G. de Piñeres, *Cartagena y sus cercanías* (Cartagena, 1912), 300–22; D. Bossa Herazo, *Cartagena Independiente: Tradición y desarrollo* (Bogotá, 1967), 159–66; E. Lemaitre, *Historia general de Cartagena* (Bogotá, 1983), iv. 455–505.

TABLE 3.7 *Exports and Imports through Cartagena, 1876–1886 ($)*

Year	Imports	Exports
1876	196,408	747,669
1877	420,552	666,390
1878	597,391	996,735
1879	752,728	832,224
1880	735,624	1,154,795
1881	1,002,363	1,264,639
1882	811,070	1,362,228
1883	1,022,631	1,677,071
1884	912,230	1,774,282
1885	1,002,631	1,165,010
1886	1,593,423	2,463,765

Source: *PP*, 36, LXXIII (1883), 474, and 35, LXXXIII (1887), 618.

most successful examples. Born in Montería in 1869, Martínez Camargo established his trading firm Diego Martínez & Co. in Lorica in 1893 and later moved to Cartagena where he had studied law. From his new headquarters, Martínez Camargo continued to oversee his cattle business while launching new ventures: a public transport company in 1902, the Cartagena Oil Refining Co. in 1908, a butter factory in 1910, the Colombian Steamboat Co. in 1914.[93] Carlos Vélez Daníes was born in Ríohacha in 1859, although his father was originally from Cartagena, where he eventually settled when the port recovered. Vélez Daníes was one of the largest livestock traders in the region and one of the main supporters of the meat packing-house in Coveñas. His success in the cattle industry allowed him to invest in sugar production and in banking: he established the Ingenio Central Sincerín in 1905 and contributed to the foundation of the Banco de Bolívar in 1907 and the Banco Industrial in 1913.[94] Some other *Cartagenero* merchants and entrepreneurs reached the regional market, but Cartagena's sphere of interests was severely restricted by problems of communication. Through the Sinú and Atrato Rivers, by means of coasting trade, Cartagena reached markets in Southern Bolívar and the

[93] López, *Almanaque de los hechos*, 38, 86, 226, 326; *Libro azul*, 287; Bossa Herazo, *Cartagena independiente*, 141–52.

[94] *Libro azul*, 277–8; López, *Almanaque de los hechos*, 355; J. J. Ortega Torres (ed.), *Marco Fidel Suárez: Obras* (Bogotá, 1966), 873.

Chocó. However, difficulties in establishing links with the Magdalena River impeded Cartagena from reaching a wider regional market: the Canal del Dique required permanent dredging and the railway to Calamar was too costly to compete with river navigation down to Barranquilla. Thus while Cartagena managed to expand its commercial interests to the Sinú and Atrato regions, Barranquilla was in a better position to establish its influence in the rest of the Coast through the Magdalena river and its tributaries.

Despite Barranquilla's economic prominence, Cartagena remained as the main educational and political centre in the region. Established in 1828 under the name of Universidad del Magdalena e Istmo, the Universidad de Cartagena – as it was later called – was the most important institution of higher education on the Coast, practically the only one until 1945, when the Instituto de Tecnología was founded in Barranquilla. It monopolized the study of the professions in the region – medicine, law, veterinary science, and philosophy.[95] Similarly, Cartagena was the centre of regional politics. During the second half of the nineteenth century, the influence of Cartagena in Colombian national life rose with the role of Rafael Núñez. In 1905, under President Reyes, Barranquilla was made the capital of Atlántico, a small department segregated from Bolívar, thus officially recognizing its political importance. Nevertheless, Cartagena was still the capital of a larger and more populous territory. Moreover, until 1930 the three Coastal departments formed one constituency for the election of Senators, and there Cartagena exercised a determining power. In spite of its economic success, Barranquilla had still to challenge the traditional supremacy that Cartagena enjoyed over the region.

To be sure, Barranquilla was not the only emergent city following the gradual process of economic growth that took place in Colombia from the mid-nineteenth century. As the capital of a large department, Cartagena was also challenged by other southern towns of growing importance which would eventually demand political independence from the old city. Similar challenges were faced by Santa Marta in Magdalena. These emerging towns represented new economic and social values in opposition to traditional centres of power: Barranquilla versus Cartagena and Santa Marta, Montería and Sincelejo versus

[95] Urueta and Piñeres, *Cartagena y sus cercanías*, 235–65. In 1894, the Bolívar Governor stressed the importance of the University for the Atlantic Coast; Román, *Mensaje del Gobernador*, 18.

Cartagena, Magangué versus Mompox, Ciénaga and Valledupar versus Santa Marta.

Soon after the wars of independence foreign trade through Santa Marta had surpassed that of Cartagena, and the former city enjoyed a period of modest growth as a transit point before receiving a severe blow in 1871 with the inauguration of the Barranquilla–Sabanilla railway. However, the economic opportunities of Santa Marta as a commercial port had been limited, since most operations were handled from Barranquilla.[96] Other towns in Magdalena were growing faster than Santa Marta. 'Far from a centre of activity, it looks like a leisure camp', Reclus had observed in the mid-nineteenth century. His visit to Ciénaga, in contrast, left a different impression: 'Ciénaga does not disappoint the visitor . . . The new buildings everywhere are signs of material progress . . . Most of its population consists of Indians and mestizos who owe their prosperity to hard work'.[97] Situated between Santa Marta and Barranquilla and in a rich agricultural zone, Ciénaga had gained commercial importance by 1850, by when its population was already larger than that of Santa Marta. Revollo recalled how the place had attracted immigrants from coastal towns, from the Andean departments of Tolima and Antioquia, and even from the Dutch Antilles.[98] Between 1870 and 1905 Ciénaga was one of the fastest-growing towns in the Coast. To the modest gains already achieved at the end of the century was added the new wealth brought by the banana boom. Santa Marta also benefited from this trade but Ciénaga continued to grow at a faster pace. 'In proportion to its size,' a report from the Anglo-South American Bank noted in 1926, 'Ciénaga is reputed to be the richest town in the country'.[99] What was notable about Ciénaga was its condition as a place in the making, where new opportunities were offered to entrepreneurs and adventurers, until its rhythm of growth came to a halt with the 1943 banana crisis. In 1950 Ciénaga was still a larger town than Santa Marta.

Near the junction of the Magdalena, Cauca, and San Jorge rivers, Magangué also became an important commercial centre which, like Ciénaga, was an emerging town rivalling the old river city of Mompox. Changes in the main canal of the Magdalena river in the early 1860s had isolated Mompox while benefiting Magangué, but

[96] *PP*, 29, LXV (1871), 217, and 35, LXXVI (1875), 372; Nichols, *Tres puertos*, 151–66.

[97] Reclus, *Viaje a la Sierra Nevada*, 50–1.

[98] Rebollo, *Memorias*, 2–5.

[99] 'Inspector's inspection letter', 15 Dec. 1926, Bolsa F4/4.

before that in the 1840s the Magangué fairs had already made the place well known to merchants from all over the country. Magangué became another focus of regional growth, developing faster than most other Coastal towns between 1870 and 1905. Its growth continued steadily from 1905 onwards, conditioned by the trade movement on the Magdalena river. Small-scale industries were developed to provide basic local needs: straw mats, sandals, saddles, tinware, Panama hats, soap and cigarette factories.[100] In general, however, manufactured goods in Magangué and its surrounding district were supplied by Barranquilla.

6. Conclusions: The Region and its Secondary Cities

In his stimulating comparative history of Salta, Mendoza, and Corrientes in Argentina, the late James Scobie advanced some hypotheses about the growth of secondary cities in Latin America and their role in regional development.[101] First, secondary cities were 'oases of modernity' for their own regions: they benefited from the inroads of progress, without transmitting them to their hinterlands. Second, the growth of these cities was mainly the result of external influences, which conditioned their dependent position. Finally, city growth produced few changes in urban ecology or social structure. Although the Argentine urban system developed on a different pattern from the Colombian – the former being characterized as a 'high-primacy' urban structure in contrast to 'low-primacy' in the latter[102] – it is worth exploring Scobie's hypotheses in the light of the evidence given in this chapter.

[100] *Memoria que presenta el Secretario de Gobierno* (Cartagena, 1914), 233; 'Magangué: Location and Description', APF.

[101] J. R. Scobie, *Secondary Cities of Argentina* (Stanford, 1988). He defined secondary cities as centres 'possessing the characteristics of present-day cities of at least 20,000 inhabitants and yet not included among the country's major cities'. Between 1850 and 1910, when his analysis takes place, this concept thus embraces 'most of the provincial or state capitals in Latin America, as well as several ports, but excludes the national capital and the country's second-ranked city of the eight largest Latin American countries', ibid. 4. According to Scobie's definition, Barranquilla, which by 1900 had over 30,000 inhabitants, classifies as a typical secondary city.

[102] J. R. Scobie, 'The Growth of Cities', in L. Bethell (ed.), *Latin America: Economy and Society, 1870–1930* (Cambridge, 1989), 164. See also R. Morse, 'Trends and Patterns of Latin American Urbanization, 1750–1920', *Comparative Studies in Society and History*, 4, (1974), 427; B. Roberts, *Cities of Peasants* (London, 1978), 47–9.

The emphasis on 'the parasitic and monopolistic rather than the generative and relay functions' of Latin American cities has been part of the 'dependency' approach towards development. In this sense, large urban centres are regarded as 'outposts of foreign politic economic control which in turn dominates, exploits, and depresses its own nation or regional hinterland'.[103] The experience of Coastal cities, as shown in this chapter, does not support this view. Barranquilla's growth since the mid-nineteenth century was in the hands of an active group of local merchants which included regional, national, and foreign immigrants. It was the depression of neighbouring centres which might have induced migration to Barranquilla, as this port flourished due to its advantages over the traditional rival towns. It is true that originally Barranquilla grew as a result of external influences. After all, its primary and natural function as a port was the handling of imports and exports. This is not, however, an explanation for growth exclusive to Latin American cities. As the geographer Dickinson has shown for the case of Western Europe, the size of cities had depended 'upon both the productivity and access of its hinterland, as well as on its contacts with the wider world by river and sea communications'.[104] Furthermore, with the development of the port, other activities linked to the regional economy followed. *Barranquillero* merchants were ready to invest in industries which in their infancy were largely dependent on regional raw materials such as cotton, hides, salt, and divi-divi. Since Barranquilla's immediate surroundings were not fertile, the growth of the city motivated the production of foodstuffs and raw materials elsewhere in the region, although undoubtedly Barranquilla also consumed significant quantities of foreign imported goods. Manufactured goods from Barranquilla, either locally produced or imported by its merchants, reached a regional market. Economic growth also brought changes in Barranquilla's 'urban ecology'. At the end of the nineteenth century, the better-off – a *mélange* of newcomers and old names – were already living in the suburbs. During the rapid development of the 1920s, once again new residential settlements became the symbol of social status and wealth.

It is hard to see why *Barranquillero* entrepreneurs should have had an interest in insulating their hinterland from the changing character of the city. Given the opportunity, they were ready to invest in regional

[103] Morse, 'Trends and Patterns', 427.

[104] R. Dickinson, *The City-Region in Western Europe* (London, 1967), 19. See Pounds, *An Historical Geography*, 185,

ventures. Moreover, Barranquilla was far from being the only expanding town in the region. Just over a hundred miles distant from Barranquilla, Cartagena was struggling to preserve its traditional supremacy and by 1900 signs of recovery were evident particularly outside the old city walls. True, the involvement of the United Fruit Company in the banana trade partly explains the sudden growth of the Northern Magdalena region. Yet Ciénaga was already flourishing by the 1870s, strongly linked to Barranquilla. Several towns were thus also expanding, some at a faster rate than others, and some prospering at the expense of former old colonial settlements. The result was a 'hierarchy of regional centers', in which Barranquilla played the role of 'natural capital', a city which in Dickinson's words, 'grows to importance without the intervention of high authority, by virtue of its favourable geographical position, and the enterprise of its people'.[105] This picture is in sharp contrast to Salta, Mendoza, and Corrientes as described by Scobie, where no other secondary cities existed within their respective provinces.

Traditional rivalries among towns on the Coast and provincial loyalties were also part of this history. Nichols has shown the importance of these rivalries in understanding the development of Cartagena, Barranquilla, and Santa Marta.[106] However, from a regional perspective, it is possible to appreciate the different, though not always mutually exclusive functions that these towns and cities were serving. Given the slow development of transport and the dependence on river navigation, it was naturally easier for Cartagena to reach markets on the Sinú. This was an area distant from Barranquilla, although its commerce often managed to reach this market. Barranquilla's economic supremacy was undoubtedly due to its position by the Magdalena River, a main artery of trade that brought the city constantly in contact with a vast area of the Coast. A similar role was played by Magangué, a river-port whose fairs encouraged further integration of regional and national markets.

This close relationship between city and region explains not only the potentials for Barranquilla's development but more importantly its limitations. The coastal market was small in size and widely dispersed. As a British report pointed out in 1930, 'in connection with the markets of the coast . . . the vast majority of the people have a relatively low standard of living, a taste for cheap goods and a limited purchasing

105 Dickinson, *The City-Region*, 6, 11.

106 Nichols, *Tres puertos*.

power'.[107] Fully aware of these problems, the obsession of local merchants and industrialists was to reach the Andean markets. They had therefore to overcome the barrier of transport – an obstacle that will be analysed in the following pages.

[107] Garnett Lomax, *Republic of Colombia*, 102.

4
Transport

1. Introduction

In 1888 the Secretary of Government in Bolívar attributed the economic stagnation of the *departamento* to its poor communications. It was commonly believed that development of transport meant progress. Yet it was also considered that the region could exploit the great advantages offered by the several rivers which formed a vast hydrographic system. 'Fortunately for us,' the President of Magdalena pointed out in 1869, '. . . communication is facilitated by the fact that most of the population lives by the sea coast or by navigable rivers, making unnecessary costly works to improve transport'.[1] For inland towns and villages it was a different story. Sincelejo, Corozal, and Chinú all resented their isolation. During the rainy seasons the few mule tracks were impassable. Moreover, in spite of the President's optimism, most of the rivers were not navigable for long periods during the year, and resources were often not available to maintain the canals free from obstructions. Steam navigation on the Coast was thus reduced to the main rivers, basically the Magdalena and the Sinú, but there were obstacles to be overcome.

The Magdalena river and its tributaries provided the region with a natural means of communication and, in turn, 'integrated' the Coast with the Andean interior. Exports, first tobacco and *quina*, and then coffee, had consequently stimulated traffic on the river. Barranquilla, Cartagena, and Santa Marta together with inland river-ports such as Calamar and Magangué experienced significant growth. For these ports, easy access to the river and communications between the river and the sea were fundamental concerns. The removal of Bocas de Ceniza and the maintenance of the Canal del Dique became public priorities for Barranquilla and Cartagena respectively. The region saw its future in terms of improvement of navigation in the Magdalena. However, alternative routes and new means of communication altered the prospects. As early as 1874, Robert Bunch, British Minister at

[1] *Memoria del Secretario de Gobierno* (Cartagena, 1888), 117; and M. A. Vengochea, *Mensaje* (Santa Marta, 1869), 9.

Bogotá, suggested the abandonment of the Magdalena in favour of other means of transport as the only way out for the isolated Colombian interior.[2] After the opening of the Panama Canal in 1914, the discussion about transport became a struggle over routes. Though formerly railway construction was orientated towards the Magdalena river as the main artery of trade, thenceforth railways started to look towards the Pacific. This trend was consolidated after 1930 when the programme of public works was centred on building roads almost exclusively in the interior. Up to 1950 no railway or highway communicated the Andean interior with the Coast. Communication between the north of Colombia and the interior depended on the vagaries of the Magdalena river, and the achievements of Scadta, the successful commercial airline that was established in Barranquilla in 1919.

This chapter analyses the problems of transport in the Colombian Caribbean. The first section looks in some detail at developments in the Magdalena river: if river navigation was originally a natural means of 'integrating' the region with the Andean interior, as time went on it became an increasingly inadequate means of communication between the centre and the north of the country. The second section describes the rise of the Pacific route, while showing that the gradual displacement of the Magdalena river as the main artery of Colombian trade went hand in hand with the development of other means of transport, in an atmosphere of regional rivalries. The third section is a study of the *Bocas de Ceniza* project to open the mouth of the Magdalena river. This serves to show not only the problems in implementing a work of this nature, but also the importance that *Costeño* entrepreneurs and politicians continued to attach to water transport. The fourth section briefly analyses the lack of progress regarding railway and road development on the Coast, in striking contrast to air transport – the focus of the final section. In the conclusion, I discuss the impact of transport problems for both regional economic development and national integration.

[2] *PP*, LXXIV (1874), 572.

2. The Magdalena River

Water transport formed the backbone of Coastal communications, and the economic development of the region hinged around the Magdalena river.[3] *Champanes*, like the one used by Felipe Pérez during his trip in 1864, and *bongos*, 'great barges built out of trunks which could carry between 60 and 70 tons in merchandise', together with different types of small canoes were popular means of transportation even after the consolidation of steam navigation.[4] In Jegua, Cunninghame Graham had no trouble in obtaining transport to Magangué, for 'canoes were plentiful and paddlers easy to be found, as all the population was, as it were, amphibious and born to the canoe'; later, on the Magdalena, 'great barges, known as bongos, crept along the banks'. During the second decade of the twentieth century, as A. S. Forest observed, much of the merchandise was 'carried still in large canoes about thirty feet long'.[5]

Since 1823, efforts were made to introduce steam navigation on the hazardous Magdalena river. It was a perilous process of trial and error, and the progress made during the second half of the nineteenth century was short of achieving final solutions to the many problems of river transport.[6] The growing number of steamers navigating the main river artery and its tributaries illustrates the development of transport in the Magdalena after 1870: there were 10 steamers in 1873, 23 in 1887, 30 in 1896, 38 in 1913, and 133 in 1928. In 1936 the number of steamers had fallen to 71. Between 1870 and 1950 at least 50 steamship companies were established to navigate the Magdalena river and its tributaries.[7] Changes in ownership, bankruptcies, mergers, confiscations, and the emergence of new competitors were frequent in the complicated history of river transport.

[3] R. Gómez Picón, *Magdalena, el río de Colombia* (Bogotá, 1945).

[4] F. Pérez, *Episodios de un viaje* (1864–5) (Bogotá, 1946), 33; Saffray, *Viaje por la Nueva Granada*, 54–5.

[5] Cunninghame Graham, *Cartagena and the Banks of the Sinú*, 240, 246; Forest, *A Tour through South America*, 124.

[6] R. L. Gilmore and J. P. Harrison, 'Juan Bernardo Elbers and the Introduction of Steam Navigation in the Magdalena River', *HAHR* (Aug. 1948), 325–59; Nichols, *Tres puertos*, 45–9; R. C. Beyer, 'Transportation and the Coffee Industry in Colombia', *Inter-American Economic Affairs*, 2/3, (1948), 17–30; F. Zambrano, 'La navegación a vapor por el Río Magdalena', *ACoHSC*, 9 (1979), 63–75.

[7] *PP*, 27, LXV (1873), 45; CII (1888), 394; 37, LXXXV (1896), 469; 28, LXVIII (1913), 557; Contraloría, *Geografía económica del Atlántico*, 186–7; and J. Acosta, *Manual del navegante* (Barranquilla, 1945), 9–47.

TABLE 4.1 *Steamship Companies in the Magdalena River and Tributaries, 1870–1950*

Name of company	Years	Owners/Shareholders
Cía. Internacional	1870-86	Hoyer Hermanos, D. López Penha
A. Weckbecker	1873	A. Wechbecker
F. J. Cisneros	1877-1866	F. J. Cisneros
Cía. Col. de Transportes	1886-1902	Alemana, Internacional, Cisneros
B. Martínez Bossio	1886	
F. Pérez Rosa	1887-91	F. Pérez Rosa
Gieseken & Held	1887	Gieseken & Held
Vapores F. Pérez Rosa	1890-1909	F. Pérez Rosa
N/ción por el Dique	1891	P. Vélez, Cía. Inglesa de Vapores
Fluvial de Cartagena	1896-1914	
M. River Steamboat Co.	1898-1914	
Santa Marta Wharf Co.	1898	
Cía. Antioqueña	1899-1909	
Alemana de N. Fluvial	1900-09	L. Gieseken
Hanseática de Vapores	1900-09	
Cortes Blanco & Co.	1905	Cortes Blanco & Co.
Antioqueña de Transportes	1909-31	
Alianza de T. Fluviales	1909-14	Alemana, Hanseática, Pérez Rosa
F. Pérez Rosa	1911	F. Pérez Rosa
Vapores Genaro Pérez	1912	
Col. Rwy. & Nav. Co.	1914-31	
Vapores Lindemeyer	1918-41	
Naviera Colombiana	1919	
Vapores N. Salzedo Ramón	1923	N. Salzedo Ramón
E. Fluvial de Ciénaga	1924	
Vapores J. Montes	1925	J. Montes
Vapores del Dique	1925	D. Vélez, J. Montes, L. del Valle
Tolima de Navegación	1927	
Fluvial de M. Betancur		
E. Navegación Santander	1927	
Cía. Transporte Fluviales	1928	
Cía. Nacional de Transportes		
Nacional sin Transbordo	1929-34	
Zuluaga & Reyes	1929-33	
Empresa Nardo	1934-40	
E. Unidas del Dique	1934	
Empresa Marvasquez	1942	M. Vásquez
Vapores Armando		
Cía. Fluvial del Magdalena		

Sources: J. Acosta, *Manual del Navegante* (Bogotá, 1945), 9-31; E. Rash Isla (ed.), *Directorio Comercial Pro-Barranquilla* (Barranquilla, 1928), 237, 247, 52.

Five major periods can be identified in the development of the river transport business: 1870–86; 1886–1902; 1902–14; 1914–31; 1931–50. Each period marked the rise of certain companies and the decline of others. Between 1870 and 1886 the Compañía Unida – a merger of the three most important companies dating from 1857 – took the lead against the competition of a dozen other companies. In 1886 F. J. Cisneros joined his own efforts with the Cía. Alemana and the Cía. Internacional to found the Cía. Colombiana de Transportes, which became the largest navigation enterprise, strengthened by its takeover of the Compañía Unida in 1890. Some other companies emerged after 1886, but the Cía. Colombiana de Transportes remained the most important until its liquidation at the turn of the century.[8] Between 1902 and 1914, two major concerns, L. Gieseken and the Magdalena River Steamboat Co. disputed control of the river. In 1914, the Magdalena River Steamboat Co. was reorganized as The Colombian Railway and Navigation Co., which remained the largest single company until 1931, when it too disappeared.[9] The period 1931–50 saw a relative decline in freight and a reduction in the number of boats and companies. A few companies had survived the 1930 crisis, and some others emerged. In 1941 the government tried to create a Compañía Fluvial Unica but faced the resistance of smaller companies owned by *Costeño* families, who argued that the project would only benefit the largest companies in the hands of *Antioqueño* capital.[10] By then however, the future of river transport on the Magdalena looked bleak. Scepticism about the river, failure to organize an efficient system and labour conflicts had all contributed to the gradual abandonment of the Magdalena route in favour of railways and roads towards the Pacific port of Buenaventura. Table 4.1 is an attempt to summarize the history of the main river companies during the period. The list is not exhaustive but illustrates the intensity of entrepreneurial activity in the Magdalena. An examination of the Compañía Colombiana de Transportes, one of the most important ventures during the second half of the nineteenth

[8] See Nichols, *Tres puertos*, 59–60; Baena and Vergara, *Barranquilla*, 281–95; Martínez Aparicio and Niebles, *Directorio anuario*, 25–55, 80–90; *Board of Trade Journal*, London, 26 (Feb. 1899), 168–70.

[9] 'Colombia Railways and Navigation Co.', London, 28 Sept. 1918, PRO, FO135/412; Martínez Aparicio and Niebles, *Directorio anuario*, 90–1; P. F. Martin, 'Trade-Travel in Colombia. Pleasures and Perils of the Magdalena', *British and Latin American Trade Gazette* (7 Oct. 1920), 346, 348, and The Colombian Railways and Navigation Co., *Visit Colombia* (London, 1930).

[10] *La Prensa*, 5 Dec. 1941.

century, further illustrates the nature and scope of these enterprises. Established in Barranquilla in 1886, the Compañía Colombiana was originally a merger of three companies, as already mentioned: Alemana, Internacional and Cisneros's firm. A Cuban engineer involved in the construction of Colombian railways, Francisco Javier Cisneros was the entrepreneur behind the new venture. Cisneros was backed by local capital and *Barranquillero* entrepreneurs, who shared with him the board of directors. J. Cortissoz, a *Barranquillero* merchant, was together with Cisneros the manager of the company. The Compañía Colombiana de Transportes had 16 steamers in 1892, its own warehouses and shipyard in Barranquilla, and agencies in Cartagena, Santa Marta, Magangué, Pueblo Viejo, Calamar, Puerto Berrío, Ocaña, Bucaramanga, Girardot, Medellín, Honda, and Bogotá.[11]

Some foreign capital, in partnership with national entrepreneurs, was involved in river transport, as in the case of the Compañía Colombiana de Transportes and the Colombian Railways & Navigation Co. *Antioqueño* capital was also significant. The Naviera Colombiana, established in 1919 and one of the most important companies during the 1930s and 1940s, was controlled by Medellín shareholders.[12] Regional capital was also considerable, not only from Barranquilla, Cartagena, and Santa Marta, but also from smaller ports such as Ciénaga and Calamar. A well-established group of immigrant entrepreneurs, integrated into the regional economy and society, had a leading role in the transport business.

Since the successful experience of the Compañía Unida, the majority of the largest companies had their headquarters in Barranquilla, where they also built shipyards, warehouses, and wharves.[13] With their network of related activities at the river-ports along the Magdalena, their contribution to the creation of employment – loading and unloading cargo, building and repairing steamers, crewing on the boats – was highly significant to the economy of the Coast. An early proliferation of smiths and carpenters in Barranquilla was also linked to the development of river transport.[14] After Barranquilla, Magangué

[11] Martínez Aparicio and Niebles, *Directorio Anuario,* 80–90; Grau, *La ciudad de Barranquilla*, 103–4; PP, 37, LXXXV, (1896), 469.

[12] For the Naviera Colombiana see Rash(ed.), *Directorio comercial*, 112; Contraloría, *Geografía del Atlántico*, 189.

[13] During the early Republic, Barranquilla had already become an important centre of river transport. See Bonney (ed.), *A Legacy of Historical Gleanings*, 447, and Nieto, 'Geografía histórica, estadística y local de la provincia de Cartagena', 35.

[14] *PP*, LXXXV (1896), 469.

was the other Coastal town that benefited most from river traffic in the period under study. During the first half of the nineteenth century, Mompox had been the most important trading centre on the Magdalena river. However, when Felipe Pérez travelled on the Magdalena in 1864, he did not visit Mompox 'nor the pretty island of Margarita, since we went down the river through the Brazo de Loba, more convenient for navigation'. Pérez instead visited Magangué, 'famous for its fairs and notable for its beautiful and picturesque hamlet'.[15] Magangué fairs were already important in the mid-nineteenth century but the diversion of river traffic from Mompox to Magangué in the early 1860s evidently strengthened the latter's development.[16] By 1873, these fairs had become thrice-yearly events when, 'the large sums of capital in circulation convey a positive view of the wealth of the country and a flattering prospect for the future'.[17] Of greater significance was Magangué's commercial position as the gateway to the Bolívar savannahs and the adjacent valleys of the San Jorge, the Lower Cauca, and the Nechí. All steamers passing up and down stopped at Magangué, from where freight was distributed by small boats, canoes, and mules throughout an extensive hinterland. In turn, Magangué was a main outlet for cattle raised in Southern Bolívar, as well as for rice, tobacco, corn, and sugar. In the 1920s it was estimated that over 50,000 head of cattle passed annually through Magangué, then considered to be 'the principal food supply center on the Magdalena'.[18]

Although lacking the intensity of traffic of Barranquilla and Magangué, many other Coastal towns depended on the river. In 1895, Robinson observed that 'we also stopped a few times each day at little mud and thatch villages to take on or put off freight . . . the crew and passengers have gone off to make purchases or to trade'. Years earlier, Rosa Carnegie-Williams had noted down the typical trade in these riverside markets: eggs, pineapples, chickens, water-melons, *totumes*, *dulces*, *losa* bottles for water, and even 'some pretty yellow birds'.[19]

15 Pérez, *Episodios de un viaje*, 41.

16 On the significance of Magangué's fairs during the 19th century see e.g. A. Parra, *Memorias* (Bogotá, 1912), 61, 68, 70; Striffler, *El río Cesar*, 12; *PP*, 35, LXXVI (1875), 355; Rothlisberger, *El Dorado*, 27.

17 *GB* , 25 Oct. 1873.

18 'Magangué: Location and description of Magangué and adjacent territory served by the Cía. Colombiana de Servicios Públicos of Magangué, Colombia, SA', n. d., possibly 1928, APF. See also *The Board of Trade Journal,* 24 (Feb. 1898), 167; *Informe del Ministro de Obras Públicas: Documentos* (Bogotá, 1919), 326.

19 Robinson, *A Flying Trip to the Tropics*, 55; Rosa Carnegie-Williams, *A Year in the Andes or a Lady's Adventure in Bogotá* (London, 1882), 236, 240.

By 1928, the steamers of The Colombian Railway and Navigation Company were calling at more than thirty river-ports between Barranquilla and La Dorada.[20] An important occupation along the river was cutting the wood used to fuel the steamers. The boats stopped three or four times a day to take on wood, 'piled up along the shore at convenient places and sold to the steamers by the owners'.[21]

Basic to the development of river transport were the export commodities of tobacco, *quina*, and coffee. For a long time most imports also entered through the Magdalena and were distributed from its various ports to the main centres of consumption. Internal trade within the region was largely carried out by means of water transport. Livestock was of particular importance. Some companies, such as the Empresa Fluvial de M. Betancourt and the Vapores de N. Salzedo Ramón built special barges for the transport of cattle, apparently their main line of business.[22] As shown, Magangué became the most important livestock distribution centre, whence cattle was shipped to Barranquilla, Puerto Berrío, Puerto Wilches, and La Dorada. Between 1940 and 1944, some 107,000 head of cattle were transported yearly on the Magdalena river.[23] Undoubtedly, coffee was the most important single cargo in the Magdalena from the late nineteenth century to the 1930s and the diversion of coffee exports to Buenaventura, as will be shown, entailed the relative decline of the river.[24]

Its physical conditions had always been a major problem. As the British Minister observed in 1874,

> The whole river is subject to alternate floods and falls, which seriously interfere with navigation. During the rainy season the steamers can scarcely stem the current, whilst during the long droughts communication with the coast is practically suspended. It is a most inconvenient and disagreeable means of travel. So long as it is, as now, the only one, Colombia can never emerge from her isolation.[25]

Navigation, as Robinson pointed out in 1896, took place without 'charts, lighthouses, or buoys . . . yet the channel is continually

[20] Rash Isla (ed.), *Directorio comercial*, 241.

[21] See Pérez, *Episodios*, 44; Soêur Marie Saint Gautier, *Voyage en Colombie* (Paris, 1893), 31; Martínez Aparicio and Niebles, *Directorio Anuario*, 89.

[22] Rash (ed.), *Directorio comercial*, 246; Acosta, *Manual del navegante*, 30–1, 44.

[23] *Anuario General de Estadística* (Bogotá, 1944), 196.

[24] In 1897 coffee was already 54.5% of the total cargo in the river but hides represented a significant share: 33.5%; see Zambrano, 'La navegación a vapor', 73; Horna, 'Transportation modernization', 35–6.

[25] Bunch, 'General Report', 572.

changing and the pilot can tell at a glance when to cross from one side to the other'.[26] Similarly, river-port facilities remained primitive. In 1929 an American report observed how there were no docks or cargo jetties along the river between Barranquilla and Girardot. Even the heavy freight was carried by dockers, 'rolled into the river and pulled out with chains'. There were no derricks, except in Barranquilla and Girardot, nor shelter for the freight, except for the most perishable articles. Years later the writer Christopher Isherwood could still observe the absence of docks: 'the steamer simply pushes the bows of the barge up against the bank, a plank is thrown across and a cable made fast to a tree'.[27] Under these conditions, cargo was condemned to long delays and high costs.

By and large the physical conditions of the Magdalena hindered further transport development on the river. Navigation was particularly difficult between Calamar and La Dorada during the dry seasons, in general the early months of the year. Rothlisberger described the hazards on his journey in 1882:

> The river is very low and we make little progress; the boat has to move weighing up its course. It steams at a very low speed along the canal, while a sailor at the stern continuously inserts a pole in the water to measure the depth. 'Seven feet' – shouts he – 'five', 'four', 'five', until suddenly we hear: 'three' (just three feet). The boat stops and has to start retreating in search of a new route. At five in the afternoon we have to interrupt the journey and moor our boat mid-river on a grass-covered island. Around us, not a sign of human life . . . We are on the Magdalena completely isolated. There is no other option . . . That ordeal lasted for four eternally long days.[28]

Rothlisberger's frustration was less important than that suffered by trade. As pointed out in a British report in 1913, 'the long delays involved in getting goods from the coast prevent . . . a rapid turn-over of capital . . . This added to high freights and high customs duties, results in high prices, with the consequent restriction of commerce'.[29] In February 1924, 'some 60 boats, or practically the entire river fleet',

[26] Robinson, *A Flying Trip*, 54.

[27] See 'Water Transportation', 24 June 1929, NAUS/ 821.811/9; and C. Isherwood, *The Condor and the Cows* (London 1949), 25; Robinson, *A Flying Trip*, 54.

[28] Rothlisberger, *El Dorado*, 32. Fifty-four years later, W. E. Dunn wrote down in his travel notes, ' . . . It takes very skilful navigation to avoid the shallow sand banks, and endless manoeuvring is often necessary to get around the sharp bends and shallow places': 'Travel Notes: Trip from Bogotá to Barranquilla and Cartagena via Rail and the Magdalena River', Bogotá, 20 Sept. 1944, NAUS/ RG166, NR, 1942–5, Box 170.

[29] 'Report on the Condition and Prospects of British Trade', *PP*, 28, LXVIII (1913), 557.

were reported 'fast in the mud and the remaining vessels wisely kept in port'. Both importers and exporters had suffered from the delay and, as a result of the conditions of the river, 'an increasing amount of produce is being shipped through the port of Buenaventura'.[30] Total paralysis of traffic between November and May, owing to the shallows of the river, was a recurring problem. In January 1926 navigation came to a halt: the steamboat companies refused to sell tickets for any destination on the Magdalena; in turn the insurance companies refused 'to insure steamboats plying on the river . . . and the steamboat companies have publicly announced that they will not be responsible for any freight lost, broken or stolen'.[31] Coffee producers and traders were particularly affected by such adverse conditions. In January 1921 it was calculated that 'some 50,000 bags of coffee are stored away in warehouses, awaiting shipment, and in these circumstances it is very difficult to foretell what price this coffee will fetch on reaching the exterior'. In March 1928 it was reported that 'very few wholesale houses are placing orders abroad, most of them holding very large stocks' and 'the suspension of navigation on the Magdalena brought a decline in producing markets dependent on that river'.[32]

From the establishment of the Junta de Canalización del Río in 1878, the idea of channelling the river became a subject of regional speculation. The government imposed a tax on river transport with a view to financing the undertaking but little was achieved. Inefficiently invested, the sum collected was small in relation to the task.[33] Apart from distributing the tax among a variety of works connected with the Magdalena, the national government occasionally used the money for other purposes, causing regional resentment. In 1919, a decision to invest resources from the canalization tax in the Ferrocarril del Tolima motivated the organization of the Liga Costeña, a regionalist movement strongly backed by the private sector and local politicians, which generated momentary concern about national unity in Bogotá circles. To guarantee the proper investment of the river tax, Coastal interests demanded the establishment of an autonomous body in charge of

[30] American Legation to the Department of State, Bogotá, 25 Feb. 1924, NAUS/ 821.811/4.

[31] Id., Jan. 1926, NAUS/ 821.811/6.

[32] London and River Plate Bank, *Monthly Review*, 3/29 (Jan. 1921), 82; and 10/112 (Mar. 1928), 142. See also 9/97 (Dec. 1926), 30, and 11/125 (Apr. 1929), 197.

[33] See *PP* 49, XCVIII (1904), 617; 'Report on the Conditions and Prospects', 557; *Informe del Ministro de Obras* (Bogotá, 1919), 147; *Anales del Senado*, 3 Dec. 1918, 427; American report, undecipherable date, probably 1944, NAUS/ RG226, Records of the Office of Strategic Services, file 3984.

Magdalena affairs. It met with the opposition of the central government. Moreover, the river tax was seen as a further burden adding to the disadvantages of the Magdalena over other routes. In 1941 a project to extend the tax to all customs-houses was defeated in Congress due to 'the tenacious lobby of congressmen from Western Colombia'. The gradual reduction of the tax was finally agreed.[34]

Little canalization was carried out. In 1881 the government employed the services of a German engineer who, after a brief survey, concluded that the country lacked the resources to undertake the required work and sent in a plan merely for the dredging of sand bars and removal of driftwood. Later contracts led to further disappointments.[35] In 1913, a British report accepted that 'canalization works on an extensive scale might prove beyond the country's resources', but, the report went on, 'a loan, secured on the revenue derived from the tax and expended by responsible foreign engineers and contractors, might greatly improve existing conditions'. However, no thorough investigation of the problem had been made, and thus no systematic work to improve the conditions of the river had been carried out. Some expectations were raised in 1920 when the government signed a contract with the German firm Julius Berger Konsortium to study the river. As a result, six years later, Berger was assigned a further contract of 6,000,000 pesos to work on the canalization of the Magdalena but nothing was achieved. In 1928, the contract was cancelled because 'the building contractor, which had already received the sum of 4,527,164 pesos had only carried out a small fraction of the planned work'.[36] Two years later, the government announced that even these minor achievements would be wasted.

Scepticism invariably prevailed in the face of the problems of the river. To the American Minister in 1924, the general attitude was 'an incomprehensible lethargy', and 'even the President, when petitioned by the coffee growers to take measures to alleviate the hardship, opened himself to local humorists by stating that he would like to do something but that the matter was in the hands of the heavenly

[34] D. S. Barnhart, 'Colombian Transport and the Reforms of 1931: An Evaluation', *HAHR* (Feb. 1958), 21. See also *RCCB* (31 Jan. 1945), 47–50, and *La Prensa*, 17 Dec. 1940 and 15 May 1941. For the Liga Costeña, see Ch. 6.

[35] Nichols, *Tres puertos*, 63, and Baena and Vergara, *Barranquilla*, 297.

[36] *Memoria del Ministro de Obras Públicas* (Bogotá, 1930), 78–9; Julius Berger Konsortium, *Memoria detallada de los estudios del Río Magdalena, obras proyectadas para su arreglo y resumen del presupuesto* (Bogotá, 1926); *El Tiempo*, 5 Dec. 1920; and 'Colombia: Annual Report, 1929', Bogotá, 16 Jan. 1930, PRO, FO371/14221.

powers'.[37] According to President Suárez the canalization of the river was unthinkable, 'as hard as building the great wall of China'. Such was the opinion of influential journals such as the *Revista Nacional de Agricultura* and *El Tiempo*.[38] If there were any doubts about the size of the task, the Berger experience provided more arguments to the opponents of the river. By 1931, the government had ruled out any canalization project. According to the Minister of Public Works, financial constraints meant that future investment in the river would be limited to dredging.[39] River transport interests and Coastal public opinion thought otherwise. According to the *Gerente* of Naviera Colombiana,'. . . the river, save a few isolated and unsatisfactory efforts, has remained in its natural state. We have been led to believe that to make the Magdalena navigable would require resources beyond our economic capacities. This view is overly pessimistic'.[40]

Labour unrest along the river added more difficulties to the Magdalena route. The first significant strike at the docks took place in Barranquilla in 1910. In January 1918 a work stoppage at the docks evolved into a general strike. During the 1920s and 1930s a succession of strikes characterized industrial relations on the river, while a variety of unions were established in practically every river port along the Magdalena.[41] The labour leader Ignacio Torres Giraldo recalls some thirty labour organizations along the river which were recognized by the government between 1920 and 1937. Most of them joined Fedenal in 1937, when one of the most significant strikes of the period took place, 'the greatest and best organized struggle of the Magdalena river' as he described it.[42] One achievement of the 1937 movement was that

[37] American Minister to the Department of State, Bogotá, 25 Feb. 1924, NAUS/ 821.811/4.

[38] Ortega, *Marco Fidel Suárez*, 982; *El Tiempo,* 1 Jan. 1919; *RNA* (May–June, 1919), 1954.

[39] *Memoria del Ministro de Obras Públicas* (Bogotá, 1931), 25–6. Sir Alexander Gibbs was also of the opinion that the traffic was not sufficient to invest in canalization, see Sir A. Gibbs, 'Informe sobre el río Magdalena', in Ministerio de Obras, *Compilación de estudios: Conceptos e informes por el Consejo de Vías de Comunicación y la Comisión de tarifas ferroviarias y ferrocarriles* (Bogotá, 1932), 294.

[40] *La Prensa,* 15 May 1941, and 26 Jan. 1942.

[41] Torres Giraldo, *Los inconformes*, iv. 3, 39, 61–2, 88, 264–7, 270–1, v. 42, and Archila, 'Barranquilla y el río', 45–58. The manager of Empresas Unidas del Dique gave a description of the state of affairs in 1938: he 'stated that in the navigation business . . . troubles had been particularly aggravated: refusal to work at night, refusal to work more than eight hours a day, refusal to handle . . . That in the navigation business they have to deal with ten or more syndicates', British Vice-Consul to HM Minister in Bogotá, Cartagena, 6 Jan. 1938, PRO, F0371/21444.

[42] Torres Giraldo, *Los inconformes*, v. 126.

the union acquired the right to select members of the crews, a concession which would remain a source of conflict between Fedenal and the shipping companies in the years to come.[43] Overemployment, lack of discipline, opposition to the introduction of new technology, and subsequently high labour costs were often quoted as among the main problems of the Magdalena. 'The boats in the Magdalena have the largest crews of any fleet in the world', a group of small shipping companies observed in 1941, while they also blamed government intervention in the industry and the strength of the unions for the failure to mechanize loading and unloading operations.[44] A communist-led organization, Fedenal was the strongest labour union in Colombia up to 1945, when the bitterness of the confrontation was highlighted in a speech by President Alberto Lleras: 'I cannot allow, without causing a scandal and without letting authority be reduced to wretchedness, two governments in the republic: one in the river, and another in the rest of the country'.[45]

3. The Pacific Route

Under such circumstances – hazardous navigation, inefficient shipping conditions, and labour unrest – the search for new routes and means of transport were made all the more necessary. The advice of the American Consul in 1928, 'to recognize the fact that the Magdalena river must be abandoned as the main artery of transportation', was certainly shared by many Colombians, particularly coffee exporters and producers from the western provinces.[46]

By 1912, as shown in Table 4.2, Colombian foreign trade was mostly handled through the Caribbean ports of Barranquilla and Cartagena and, to a lesser extent, Santa Marta. However, with the opening of the Panama Canal in 1914, the Pacific port of Buenaventura came to rival

[43] Ibid. See also M. Urrutia, *The Development of the Colombian Labour Movement* (New Haven and London, 1969), 179.

[44] *La Prensa*, 5 Dec. 1941.

[45] A. Lleras, *Un año de gobierno, 1945–6* (Bogotá, 1946), 136.

[46] 'Opinion Regarding Projected Barranquilla–Cartagena Railroad', Barranquilla, 8 Oct. 1928, NAUS/ RG84, Barranquilla, political reports, 1928. In 1927, the geographer G. T. Renner concluded that 'the Magdalena is an exceedingly poor highway to serve any country as a national trunk line', G. T. Renner, 'Colombia's Internal Development', *Economic Geography*, 3 (1927), 261.

TABLE 4.2 *Import and Export Trade of Main Colombian Ports, 1911–1912 (£)*

	Imports		Exports	
Ports	1911	1912	1911	1912
Barranquilla	1,922,710	2,489,106	1,648,898	2,446,322
Cartagena	867,161	1,016,861	1,185,432	1,333,032
Santa Marta	75,750	88,807	460,645	490,726
Buenaventura	370,707	767,954	356,148	268,593
Tumaco	210,499	234,275	314,668	283,431
Cúcuta	138,596	153,694	417,531	598,584

Source: 'Report on the Trade of the Consular District of Bogotá for the Years 1909-13', 24.

the Magdalena route and the Caribbean ports. In January 1915 the Pacific Railway from Buenaventura reached Cali; in May 1917 it reached Palmira. In 1926 the Minister of Public Works informed Congress that '. . . the government has directed the largest resources to this task'. By 1930 the Pacific Railway was integrated into the Caldas Railways and plans were made to cross the mountain ranges to join the line to the Tolima Railway. By then the Pacific and Caldas Railways, together with the Antioquia Railway, formed a western network which linked Buenaventura with the most important coffee-producing areas. Buenaventura gained additional advantages with the completion of a highway to the sea in 1945.[47]

As shown in Table 4.3, the diversion of coffee exports through Buenaventura followed the opening of the Panamá Canal. In 1916 the bulk of coffee exports was still shipped from the Caribbean ports of Barranquilla and Cartagena, to where it had been transported from the producing areas via the Magdalena river. By 1926, exports from Buenaventura had multiplied more than fivefold while those from

[47] J. A. Ocampo, 'El desarrollo económico de Cali en el siglo XX', in J. A. Ocampo and S. Montenegro, *Crisis mundial, protección e industrialización* (Bogotá, 1984), 370–2; D. Monsalve, *Colombia cafetera* (Barcelona, 1927), 851–5; A. Ortega, *Ferrocarriles colombianos* (Bogotá, 1923), 451–514; *Memoria del Ministro de Obras Públicas al Congreso* (Bogotá, 1926), 29; R. P. Platt, 'Railroad Progress in Colombia', *Geographical Review*, 16 (1926), 87. In 1931, a British report considered that British interests in Colombia were better served by 'facile ingress and egress via an Atlantic port . . . as opposed to a Pacific port which would endure American predominance', Dickson to Foreign Office, Bogotá, 31 Aug. 1931, PRO, FO135/430.

TABLE 4.3 *Ports in Colombian Coffee Exports, 1916–1926 (tons)*

Year	B/quilla	B/ventura	C/gena	Cúcuta	Sta. Marta
1916	44,948	8,697	9,178	9,282	375
1917	32,439	11,087	12,283	6,275	555
1918	41,384	10,408	11,303	5,375	364
1919	50,574	14,758	18,825	15,249	1,444
1920	31,852	27,137	18,037	9,014	501
1921	68,897	37,552	21,493	11,321	1,372
1922	66,370	20,892	5,217	12,954	373
1923	71,766	31,061	10,438	9,966	355
1924	69,550	33,774	16,542	12,486	495
1925	58,180	34,227	15,667	8,321	448
1926	73,841	47,396	15,446	10,304	131

Source: D. Monsalve, *Colombia cafetera* (Barcelona, 1927), 626

Barranquilla or Cartagena had not even doubled. In 1944 Buenaventura was handling nearly 60 per cent of coffee exports. Cali, a city a hundred odd miles away from Buenaventura, now became the headquarters of the most important coffee exporters.[48] The growing movement of coffee through Buenaventura was also reflected in the general level of exports. Total exports from Buenaventura exceeded exports from Barranquilla for the first time in 1931. From 1934 Buenaventura became the leading export port of Colombia (See Fig. 4.1). Imports were also moving through the Pacific port in large quantities, although Barranquilla remained the point of entry for approximately 40 per cent of Colombian imports until the end of the period.

The rise of the Pacific route created much concern and regional bitterness on the Coast. In a speech in the *Teatro Cisneros* in 1928, M. Rash-Isla warned of the rise of Buenaventura and appealed for the need to 'defend the interests of Barranquilla against "dangerous forces"'. A leading article in *La Nación* went further: 'there is no parallel to the war that the Western region of Colombia, especially the Cauca Valley, is waging against the Atlantic Coast'.[49] Moreover, what started as a

[48] Ocampo, 'El desarrollo económico de Cali', 373–6; M. Palacios, *El café en Colombia* (Bogotá, 1979), 223, 261, 281, 309; Monsalve, *Colombia cafetera*, 262; Mac Greevey, *An Economic History*, 258.

[49] Rash, *Directorio comercial*, 305–12; *La Nación*, 26 Oct. 1931.

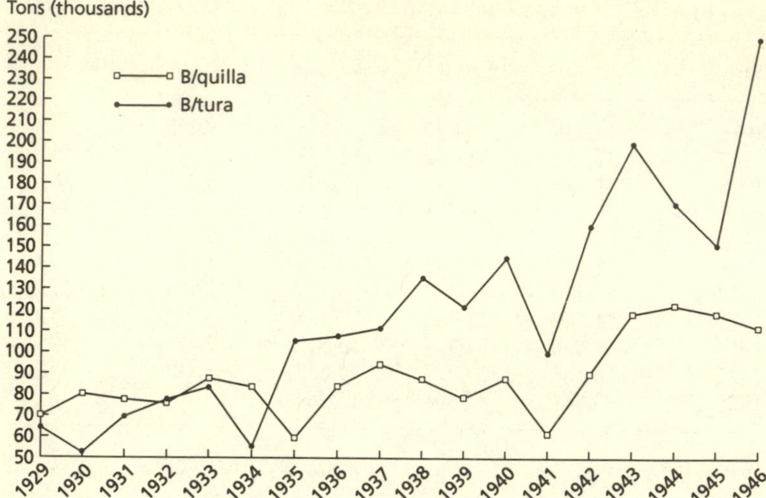

FIG. 4.1 Barranquilla and Buenaventura Exports, 1929–1946
Sources: APF

struggle between two routes became a struggle between the Pacific Railway and the Magdalena river. Strong regional feelings in favour of investing in the river were made explicit, as already mentioned, in the establishment of the Liga Costeña in 1919. Debates in Congress about the river took the form of regional confrontations, although congressmen from the Coast tried to make the issue a national one.[50] Public criticism of the river was rebutted as part of an orchestrated campaign by the Pacific Railway's interests, which were unfairly benefiting from state support. According to *La Prensa*, 'powerful interests from Western Colombia had valuable access to official circles ... in diverting the coffee trade from the Magdalena river route to Buenaventura'. One particular advertisement issued by the Consejo de Ferrocarriles criticizing the river caused an outrage in Barranquilla. 'It is beyond belief that such a campaign has originated from an official body', *La Prensa* complained, while Rafael Obregón blamed the Consejo de Ferrocarriles for establishing subsidized tariffs 'with the explicit purpose of giving official support to the Pacific route'.[51]

[50] *Anales de la Cámara de Representantes*, 14 Oct. 1919 and 3 Feb. 1923; *Anales del Senado*, 18 Sept. 1919.

[51] *La Prensa*, 14 Feb. 1941.

The development of a non-river transport system was already taking place during the 1920s. Between 1923 and 1930, for example, over 110 million pesos were spent on railways. After 1930, following a report by the Consejo de Vías de Comunicación, new emphasis was given to road construction; by then it was evident that investment in the Magdalena river was not on the government's agenda.[52] While coffee producers, political leaders, local officials, and public opinion from the interior pressed for the improvement of roads and railways, the Coast remained obstinately attached to the idea of developing the Magdalena river. In Barranquilla, priority was given to the opening of the river mouth, Bocas de Ceniza, while in Cartagena public concern was centred on the Canal del Dique. The significance of these projects, particularly Bocas de Ceniza, merits further consideration.

4. Bocas de Ceniza

Bocas de Ceniza was the general name given to the principal mouth of the Magdalena river, some 10 miles from Barranquilla. There, a shifting and unstable sand bar impeded ocean vessels from reaching the city (see Map 4). However, the removal of this obstruction by natural currents during the 1870s and 1880s raised hopes for the consolidation of Barranquilla as both a river- and sea-port. Between 1877 and 1886, 107 steamers and 459 vessels passed through Bocas de Ceniza on their way to Barranquilla. 'I do not know any other river with such an easy entry', the commodore of the French ship *Burdonnais* declared after having explored its conditions in 1878.[53] His enthusiasm, shared by local merchants, did not last long. In 1887 the sand bar again made it impossible for ocean ships of large draught to enter the Magdalena, but the short period in which it had temporarily disappeared stimulated public interest in the opening of Bocas de Ceniza, as a substitute for the railway and pier at Puerto Colombia. It was not an obviously easy task. 'Whether this can be done or not,' the British Consul wrote, 'and, if done, whether the financial results of such an expenditure would be productive, is a matter for speculation'.[54]

[52] See Ministerio de Obras, *Compilación de estudios*, and Barnhart, 'Colombian Transport and the Reforms of 1931', 1–24.

[53] 'Estadísticas de los buques marítimos que han entrado a Barranquilla por Bocas de Ceniza', Barranquilla, 29 May 1935, in APF; and *RCCB* (30 Apr. 1929), 2–3.

[54] *PP*, LXXXV (1896), 281–2.

In 1906, local merchants met in Barranquilla to discuss ways of funding a scientific study of the river mouth. Two years later, financed by the merchants themselves, the American engineer Lewis Haupt produced his 'Report Regarding the Proposed Canalization of the Bocas de Ceniza', which was sent to the national government.[55] As a result of further pressures, the government decided in 1914 to contract another study, this time with the German firm Julius Berger Konsortium, but the project was halted by the outbreak of First World War. In 1919, public concern in Barranquilla about the stagnation of the project led to the establishment of the Compañía Colombiana de Bocas de Ceniza, a joint stock venture financed by the Barranquilla business community, with the aim of pressing the government to support the opening of Bocas de Ceniza.[56] Objections to both Haupt and Berger's projects had been raised in a Pan-American Scientific Congress in 1916, so the Compañía Colombiana decided to contract a third study. At their request, in 1921 the American engineers Black, McKenney & Stewart embarked on a project to dredge the bar at the mouth of the river and erect breakwaters at an estimated cost of $6,000,000 in American gold.[57] However, on account of the expense, the government decided to limit works to a mere dredging operation, which by 1923 – when the project was reported to be 'practically at a standstill' – had proved to be insufficient to keep Bocas de Ceniza open.[58] Additional problems arose when the German Berger company claimed preferential rights to take over the works, in accordance with its 1914 contract with the government.

While the Compañía Colombiana favoured the American project, officials within the Ministry of Public Works were inclined towards Berger. By 1925 delays in signing a contract to carry on the Black, McKenney & Stewart project had exacerbated public opinion in

[55] L. Haupt, 'Report Regarding the Proposed Canalization of the Bocas de Ceniza', Philadelphia, 15 Feb. 1908, in APF.

[56] The company was organized by leading merchants and bankers of Barranquilla, with a capital of $1,000,000; 10% of it 'was subscribed in a few minutes at the first general meeting called'; American Consul to State Department, Barranquilla, 5 June 1919, USNA/ 821.812/69. See *RCCB* (31 May 1919), 17–23, and (30 Apr. 1929), 3–22.

[57] Black, McKenney, & Stewart, *The Bocas de Ceniza and Magdalena River to Barranquilla, Colombia* (Washington 1921); Nichols, *Tres Puertos*, 213; 'Letter-agreement between Compañía Colombiana de las Bocas de Ceniza and Black, McKenney, & Stewart', Washington, 19 Apr. 1919, in NAUS/ 821.812/127.

[58] 'Developments Projects in Barranquilla', Barranquilla, 31 Oct. 1921; Black, McKenney, & Stewart to the Secretary of State, New York, 27 July 1925, NAUS/ 821.812/100 and 129.

Barranquilla: 'Mass demonstrations last night were impressive, unprecedented. An atmosphere of deep discontent, restlessness and aggravation prevails here'.[59] The Barranquilla Chamber of Commerce commissioned three outstanding community leaders to press the national government for a prompt decision. An agreement was finally reached in July 1925 when the government signed a contract with Ulen & Co. to develop a modified version of Black, McKenney & Stewart's project at a total cost of 3,200,000 pesos.[60] Considering its goal achieved after six years of lobbying, the Compañía Colombiana dissolved itself.

Further and even more intense regional pressure was exerted before the works were concluded. In 1929 a campaign initiated by a new Minister of Public Works, backed by the Bogotá press and the Sociedad Colombiana de Ingenieros, led to the cancellation of the contract with Ulen & Co. The American company was accused of mismanagement of funds and failure to fulfil its commitments: not only had the works not been completed within the agreed period but the company had also spent almost twice the original estimated budget.[61] In turn, Ulen & Co. argued that the delays and increased costs were due to *force majeure* and to the government's dilatoriness and obstruction: 'delays in authorizing purchases and failure to authorize important items'; 'failure to furnish funds'; 'changes of plans'; 'delay in approving salaries of employees and laborers'; 'hostile attitude of government representatives'.[62] In Bogotá the debate took on a nationalist tone, while in Barranquilla the issue at stake was the role of the central government in the development of the project.[63] In a letter to the Minister of Public Works, the President of the Chamber of Commerce backed the American company and reminded the Minister how, in several instances, *Barranquillero* merchants had themselves

[59] President of the Chamber of Commerce to Roncallo, Carbonell, and Pumarejo, Barranquilla, 7 May 1925, in *RCCB* (30 Apr. 1929).

[60] *Diario oficial,* 10 July 1925; Nichols, *Tres puertos*, 214.

[61] By Feb. 1929, more than $6,000,000 had been spent on the project. See *El Nuevo Tiempo*, 3 Feb. 1929, and *El Espectador*, 14 Feb. 1929. For the arguments of the Minister, see *El Tiempo*, 9 Mar. 1929. According to an American official in Bogotá, the Minister was a politician who was trying to gain prestige by exploiting the Bocas de Ceniza issue, NAUS/821.812/198. 'Picaroons' was the expression used by a British report in reference to the American company; see 'Colombia: Annual report', Bogotá, 16 Jan. 1930, PRO, FO371/14221.

[62] Ulen & Co. to the Secretary of State, New York, 7 Mar. 1929, NAUS/ 821.812/194.

[63] See e. g. *Mundo al Dia*, 7 Feb. 1929; *El Tiempo,* 13 Feb. 1929; *El Espectador*, 13 Feb. 1929; *El Diario Nacional,* 14 Feb. 1929.

provided funds when government delays threatened the paralysis of the works. Local newspapers shared the Chamber of Commerce's views; so did political leaders such as Pedro Juan Navarro who, in a speech in the Teatro Municipal in Bogotá stressed 'the importance of opposing a pushy Minister who threatens to close Bocas de Ceniza'. In May 1929, faced with the government's decision, leading members of the Barranquilla community set up the Committee for the Defence of Bocas de Ceniza. A commission was sent to talk with the Minister in Bogotá. Its efforts were in vain; by June 1929 Ulen & Co. had left the country.

Now temporarily in charge of the works and pressed by public opinion in Barranquilla, the government started to look for alternatives. In July 1929, a new Minister of Public Works was appointed. He approached the Parrish brothers, successful urban developers in Barranquilla, and suggested that the government would consider a *concesión* project to finish Bocas de Ceniza and build an additional modern port.[64] The Parrish brothers started to search for a formula with financial assistence from the United States: Harris, Forbes, & Co., Electric Bond & Share Co., Stone Webster & Blodget Co., First National Corporation, Raymond Concrete Pile & Co., even Ulen & Co., all were included in the original proposal, being persuaded by the Parrishes about the potential profitability of Barranquilla as a port and the possibilities of its position next to the unexploited Magdalena Valley.[65] *Concesiones*, however, were not held in high esteem in Bogotá.[66] Furthermore, the usual delays in Congress, where the project had to be approved, oncoming presidential elections, and finally the Depression again postponed any decision.

In 1930 a new government came to power. With it a new Minister of Public Works was appointed and fresh negotiations were initiated. In September 1930 Conservative and Liberal leaders from Barranquilla sent a joint message to Coastal senators asking for their support for Bocas de Ceniza. A new *concesión* project had been introduced into Congress and was received by further criticisms and delays. Public opinion in Barranquilla was enraged.[67] The situation was aggravated by the effects of the Depression: the crisis had severely hit the

[64] For the role of the Parrish family in the development of the region, see Ch. 5.

[65] Harris, Forbes & Co. to R. Parrish, New York, 13 Aug. 1929; K. C. Parrish to: Berge, New York, 14 Aug. 1929, Head, Deerfield, 15 Aug. 1929; and to R. Parrish, New York, 10 Aug. 1929; 'Memorandum with Reference to the Barranquilla Port and Terminal Work', n. d. (possibly 1931), in APF.

[66] *El Nuevo Tiempo*, 29 Sept. 1929.

[67] *La Prensa*, 9 Sept. and 17 Oct. 1930.

construction and industrial sectors, thus exacerbating a serious problem of unemployment. Social unrest followed: on 22 October 1931 'the mobs had forced all business houses, banks, and bus transportation companies to shut down . . . demonstrators carried Colombian flags, placards and signs with skulls and cross bones bearing among other legends: "down with the public enemies of Barranquilla"'. According to the American Consul, 'the demonstrations . . . have been systematically organized by some of the most prominent people in Barranquilla in protest of the procrastination exhibited by the authorities in Bogotá in connection with the approval of a contract for the opening up of the Bocas de Ceniza'.[68] The protest became violent and continued until the following day when the Army intervened. In his report to the President, the Governor of Atlántico did not hide his sympathies for the cause of the demonstrators.[69]

In the face of demonstrations – the Parrishes were warned – the government would not negotiate. Accused of being behind the movement, the Parrishes tried to distance themselves from the 'civic strike'. On 23 October, R. Parrish wrote to the President to 'assure you emphatically the wishes that our project be considered by the government only for its merits and not under the pressure of an over-enthusiastic regionalism'.[70] In November 1931 the government reached an agreement with the Parrish interests, but the original *concesión* idea was abandoned. A different project was outlined and it was not until 1933 that the government finally signed a contract with R. Parrish – on behalf of the Compañía del Puerto y Terminal de Barranquilla, Raymond Concrete Pile Co. and Winston Brothers – to open Bocas de Ceniza and build additional port facilities at Barranquilla. In December 1936 the Bocas de Ceniza were officially declared open, giving a new impetus to the development of the port.

The works did not provide, however, a final solution for the problems posed by the river mouth. Lack of maintenance and dredging, inadequate design, the formation of new shoals and bars, were all identified as causes for the problems that had again emerged in the 1940s and 1950s. Sir Alexander Gibbs, who had supervised the works in the 1930s, advocated 'a gradual execution of the works so as to

68 American Consul to Secretary of State, Barranquilla, 23 Oct. 1931, NAUS/ RG84, Political reports, Barranquilla, 1931.

69 Atlántico Governor to Olaya Herrera, Barranquilla, 24 Oct. 1931, in AEOH, section 1/23, Gobernaciones, Atlántico.

70 R. Parrish to Olaya Herrera, Bogotá, 23 Oct. 1931, APF.

allow the results to be closely studied and thus ensure that the natural forces set up are under control'.[71] Such technical considerations, however, go beyond the scope of this book. What is important to stress here is, first, the amount of attention and effort expended by Barranquilla's leaders and public opinion in opening the mouth of the river and, secondly, the achievements of the regional movement in terms of influencing the direction of public investment.

The importance attached to Bocas de Ceniza by *Barranquilleros* has to be understood in the context of the development of the Magdalena river. 'The opening of Bocas de Ceniza will bring all the benefits we are hoping from it, if we complement this work with the improvement of navigation conditions in the Magdalena river', T. S. Salcedo pointed out in 1919.[72] K. C. Parrish had in mind an export-led development of the Magdalena Valley:

> the largest area of rich agricultural uncultivated land in Colombia that could be worked by machinery is the lower Magdalena River Valley and its tributaries.
>
> It is the first 300 miles from the Atlantic Coast where the great opportunities for development are. The Bocas de Ceniza would open this vast territory to ocean transportation. This would furnish an outlet to the ocean for the products that go into Magangué, the St. Louis of Colombia. . .
>
> All products of the Magdalena, Lower Cauca, San Jorge, Cesar and other rivers would be furnished with cheap water transportation to all foreign ports.[73]

However, by focusing regional pressures almost exclusively on water transport, the Coast was left behind in the new development of roads and railways that was taking place in the Andean interior. Furthermore, by relying on the Magdalena as practically the only means of communication with the interior, the Coast lost further advantages to the Pacific route – the latter identified with the more secure investment in roads and railways.

5. Railways and Roads

The development of railways followed the same pattern that originally characterized their development nationwide. As Huckin observed in

[71] Sir A. Gibbs, 'Problems Connected with the Bocas de Ceniza', 20 Mar. 1945, PRO, FO135/481.

[72] *RCCB* (31 May 1919), 18–19.

[73] K. C. Parrish, 'Bocas de Ceniza', n. d. (possibly 1929), in APF.

1910, 'railway construction in Colombia has confined itself to short lengths of line, each intended to overcome some special difficulty or supply some local need'.[74] Thus, the Barranquilla Railway was built to connect Barranquilla with a point on the coast, in view of the difficulties that impeded ocean vessels from entering the Magdalena river mouth. The Cartagena and Santa Marta Railways were laid to link these ports with the Magdalena, although the latter never reached the river, ending in the banana zone. In 1910, the three lines together had an extension of 226 km. out of a national total of 900 km. In 1926, when the country's network totalled 2,360 km., the Coast had only increased its track by 102 km.: 65 km. on the Santa Marta Railway and 37 km. on the failed Central Bolívar Railway. Nevertheless, many of the new lines in the Andean interior had been 'constructed with a view to finding an outlet to the River Magdalena'.[75] By 1943 Colombia had 3,467 km. of railways; of these just 370 km. were located on the Coast, including 44 and 88 km. of private railways in Sincerín and the banana zone respectively. With the exception to the extension in the Santa Marta line and the failed attempt to build a track between Cartagena and Medellín, by 1950 local railway development had scarcely progressed beyond its nineteenth century origins. (See Table 4.4, and Map 4.)

However, the coastal lines were important. The first track to be completed was the 10-km. railway from Barranquilla to Salgar in 1872 – the Ferrocarril de Bolívar – built by a German concern. After a short interval when it was taken over by the government, the railway was managed by F. J. Cisneros. His interests were in turn transferred to the Barranquilla Railway & Pier Co. of London in 1888. That same year the line was extended 5 km. to Puerto Colombia due to the shallowness of the bay at Salgar, and in 1892 the company opened its 4,000-ft.-long pier, a great improvement. According to Huckin in 1910, 'no railway in Colombia has played a more necessary part than the Barranquilla line'.[76] The track was not only of great benefit to Barranquilla as the main Colombian port of the time, but also proved in itself to be a profitable enterprise.[77] By 1928, however, complaints over service and high freight rates were frequent. Moreover, with the opening of Bocas

[74] V. Huckin, 'Report on the Railways of Colombia', *PP*, 38, XCV (1910), 6.

[75] Pearse, *Colombia, with Special Reference to Cotton*, 35.

[76] Huckin, 'Report on the Railways', 13. See also Nichols, *Tres Puertos*, 111–20; and A. Ortega Díaz, *Ferrocarriles colombianos* (Bogotá, 1923), 296–332.

[77] *The Barranquilla Railway and Pier Company, Limited* (London, 1928), 2; and Huckin, 'Report on Railways', 13.

TABLE 4.4 *Railway Development in Colombia, 1883–1944 (km)*

Railway	1881	1910	1923	1944
Barranquilla	24	27	28	0
Cartagena	0	105	105	110
Santa Marta	35	94	159	216
Central Bolívar	0	0	37	0
Sincerín	0	0	0	37
Girardot	30	157	217	398
Narino	0	0	30	114
Northeast	0	0	61	285
North (Section 1)	0	62	95	128
North (Section 2 and South)	18	69	210	254
Pacifico	16	94	610	875
Western Trunk	0	0	12	38
Antioquia	37	102	258	382
Caldas	0	0	117	125
Cundinamarca	0	0	76	223
Tolima	0	0	76	69
Cucuta	53	71	102	68
La Dorada	24	119	111	111
Barrancabereja	0	0	28	27
Carare	0	0	15	0
Lobitos Oil Company	0	0	13	0
TOTAL	237	900	2,360	3,460

Sources: 1888: *PP*, 32, LXXVIII (1889), 593; 1910: V. Huckin, 'Report on the Railways of Colombia', *PP*, 38, XCV (1910), 49; 1923: Pearse, *Colombia, with Special Reference to Cotton*, 35-6; 1944: Contraloría General de la República, *Síntesis estadística de Colombia, 1939-1943* (Bogotá, 1944), 60–1.

de Ceniza under way, the future of the railway was already in question. The company was acquired by the national government in 1933 and by 1940 the railway had been practically abandoned.[78]

Like the Ferrocarril de Bolívar, the Cartagena Railway was built during the nineteenth century: in 1894, a track of 105 km. linked Cartagena with the Magdalena river at the port of Calamar. Unlike the Ferrocarril de Bolívar, the Cartagena Railway was not a successful business, although trade in Cartagena did improve as a result of better communications with the river.[79] The line suffered from 'the result of cheap construction' and the primitive arrangements 'for transferring goods to and from the river steamers at Calamar', so, Huckin

[78] Horna, 'Transportation Modernization', 42; Nichols, *Tres puertos*, 224–5; Contraloría, *Síntesis estadística de Colombia*, 60; A. Ortega Díaz, *Ferrocarriles colombianos: Legislación ferroviaria* (Bogotá, 1949), 27.

[79] *MCR* (Jan.–Apr. 1890), 153.

concluded, 'the lot of the Cartagena has not been altogether a fortunate one'.[80] Originally built by an American concessionaire, the railway was sold in 1906 to a British concern, the Cartagena Railway Co., later to become the Colombia Railways & Navigation Co. As shown, during the second and third decades of the twentieth century, this company was the largest transport company in the Magdalena, with a strong interest in navigation in the Canal del Dique, which ran parallel to the railway. From the 1920s attempts were made by the government to acquire it, which it finally did in 1939. During the 1940s, the railway was running at a heavy loss and it was closed down in 1950.

Thus at the end of our period, the only working line on the Coast was the Santa Marta railway. Originally designed to link Santa Marta with the Magdalena river, the track reached Ciénaga in 1887, was extended to Río Frío in 1890 and to Fundación in 1906, a total of 96 km.[81] From 1891, when the railway transported its first 73,693 bunches of bananas, it became dependent on the fruit trade. By 1906, the United Fruit Company purchased a controlling interest in the railway, although nominally it remained a British concern. The main line was never extended beyond Fundación, but the Fruit Company built a large network of branch tracks in the banana zone. Initial plans to continue the railway down to Plato, on the Magdalena river, were never accomplished, opening the way for a long legal dispute which involved the national and local governments, the Santa Marta Railway, and the United Fruit companies.[82] The dispute was finally settled in 1932, when a double agreement was reached: the government acquired the line but the Santa Marta Railway, under the financial control of the United Fruit, leased it for thirty years. After the banana crisis in 1947 the contract was cancelled and the national government took formal control of the railway. By 1950, however, the Ferrocarril Nacional del Magdalena, as it was then called, had still not been extended beyond Fundación.

Road development also failed to challenge the supremacy of the waterway. In 1917, as the Governor of Bolívar pointed out, 'what we call here royal roads are the same routes used by the indigenous people in ancient times . . . they are only accessible to people on foot or

80 Huckin, 'Report on the Railways', 17.

81 See Ortega Díaz, *Ferrocarriles colombianos: Legislación ferroviaria,* 44–54; *Documentos relacionados con el Ferrocarril de Santa Marta* (Bogotá, 1923), 38–48.

82 Ferrocarril de Santa Marta, *Exposición que al honorable Congreso de 1915 hace el gerente de la compañía* (Bogotá, 1919); *Documentos relacionados con el ferrocarril,* 42–69.

horseback, but not to wheeled vehicles . . . except during the driest seasons and for relatively short journeys'.[83] A few improvements were made but in 1949 there was still no proper road between Barranquilla and Cartagena, as noted by Christopher Isherwood who experienced the difficulties of the journey.[84] By and large, transportation between inland points remained confined to animal traction – horses, mules, and donkeys – where no waterway served.[85] Exceptionally, some concern was shown over road conditions to the interior, mere cattle trackways which linked the Coast with Antioquia and Santander.

Pressure to build roads came mostly from inland towns, such as Carmen, Corozal, and Sincelejo, which suffered isolation during rainy seasons and sought better outlets for their agricultural products. A road linking Sincelejo with the port of Tolú was, for example, a longstanding demand of this province. In 1871, shortly after having been cleared, the track became impassable because of heavy rains. Two years later, an effort to improve the road was failed through the lack of funds. New hopes for improvement were raised in 1882, when the government signed a contract to build a road but nothing was done, and in 1914 a new contract with the same purpose was signed with another firm. In 1933, from June to December, there was no traffic between Sincelejo and Tolú as a consequence of a 'hard winter'.[86] Some other inland towns faced similar problems. Despite its location on the river Cesar, Valledupar, for example, sought to improve its communications by building a road either to Ríohacha or to Santa Marta in order to overcome its isolation.[87]

There was little money available. In 1917 the Governor of Bolívar described the causes of slow road development: income from the three available sources – *contribución de caminos*, *auxilios departamentales*, and *auxilios nacionales* – was insignificant, and additionally 'it often

[83] *Mensajes e informes del Gobernador* (Cartagena, 1917), 7–8; 'Roads in and around Barranquilla', Barranquilla, 29 Feb. 1928, USNA/ RG84, Barranquilla, correspondence, 1928.

[84] Isherwood, *The Condor and the Cows*, 16.

[85] Schnare, 'Facilities of Transportation and Communication in the Cartagena Consular District', 2.

[86] Santo Domingo Vila, *Informe del Presidente constitucional*, 66; *Mensaje del Presidente constitucional* (Cartagena, 1883), 41–6; *El Heraldo*, 15 Apr. 1883; Zubiría to the Bolívar Governor, Cartagena, 15 Dec. 1887, AGB, 1887; *Memoria del Secretario de Gobierno* (Cartagena, 1888), 123; *Memoria que presenta el Secretario de Gobierno* (Cartagena, 1914), 89–90; and Obregón, *Memoria de Gobierno*, 230–1.

[87] M. A. Vengochea, *Mensaje que el Presidente del Estado del Magdalena dirije a la Asamblea Lejislativa* (Santa Marta, 1869), 10; *Informe del Secretario de Hacienda* (Santa Marta, 1920), 102–9.

disappears into the pockets of unscrupulous tax collectors'. A report by the *Ingeniero de Caminos* was more explicit: the distances to be covered in the department were too great and the population too sparse; the tax system was inefficient, and the management of public roads lacked central direction.[88] In 1914, for example, the local road tax in Atlántico produced only 2,000 pesos; with this, in addition to a monthly *auxilio departamental* of 600 pesos, all the government could achieve was the improvement of some tracks and 1.5 km. of a new road. The distribution of meagre *auxilios departamentales* among fifty-six *municipios* in Bolívar, as the Governor pointed out in 1935, led to scattered effort and no practical result.[89] Aid and direct investment in roads by the national government were rare. Between 1926 and 1931, while Antioquia received 3,208,045 pesos for departmental road construction, Atlántico was allotted 40,000 pesos. During the Abadía administration, when the national government directly invested a total of 26,123,541 pesos in roads, just over 700,000 pesos were received by the Coast, and that was to be distributed among several projects.[90] As late as 1950, no proper highway linked the Coast with the interior, though plans were at last being made to build one. (Map 4 illustrates the plan to complete the Carretera Troncal Oriental, which would link Barranquilla with Bogotá).

6. Air Transport

In remarkable contrast with the slow progress of roads and railways was the development of air transport. Established in Barranquilla in 1919, the Sociedad Colombo-Alemana de Transportes Aéreos, Scadta, was the first successful commercial airline in South America. Scadta was originally organized as a German-Colombian joint stock company, controlled by L. Gieseken. In 1922, an Austrian industrialist, Peter von Bauer, bought Gieseken's interests and became Director. Von Bauer pursued a diplomatic policy of giving Scadta a Colombian appearance.[91]

[88] *Mensajes e informes del Gobernador* (Cartagena, 1917), 8.

[89] C. Del Castillo, *Mensaje e Informes del Gobernador* (Cartagena, 1917), 8.

[90] *Mensaje del Gobernador* (Cartagena, 1935), 10.

[91] Major Bradley to Secretary of State, Canal Zone, 17 Aug. 1925, NAUS/ 821.706 SCA 2/34. See also See H. Boy, *Una historia con alas* (Madrid, 1955), 57; 'Memorandum on Scadta', 11 May 1939, USNA/ 821.796 SCA 2/444; R. R. G. Davies, *Airlines of Latin America since 1919* (London 1984), 207, 211, 215.

Scadta experienced steady growth during the 1920s. After regularizing a round flight once a week from Barranquilla to Girardot, and Girardot to Neiva, the company opened a service between Barranquilla and Cartagena. The achievements were significant. 'The service which has been offered to the Colombian public by this company during the past year and a half', an American report commented in 1922, 'has proved not only the most impressive but the most popular and practical foreign undertaking during that period'.[92] In 1925, after a successful trial flight in the Caribbean region, Scadta attempted to expand its commercial services to cover the area, a pioneer experiment at first frustrated by the American refusal to grant permission to Scadta to land in the Panamá Canal zone.[93] By 1933 Scadta was covering, among other national routes, Barranquilla–Bogotá and Barranquilla–Ciénaga–Santa Marta six times weekly; Barranquilla–Cartagena, and Barranquilla–Puerto Berrío–Medellín four times weekly. Its international connections included Kingston, Havana, Miami, Cristóbal in the Canal Zone, and Maracaibo.[94]

From its origins, Scadta's headquarters were established in Barranquilla, which was also the residence of most of its directors and of some of its stockholders. As the main centre of operations of what was the virtual monopoly of air transport in Colombia, Barranquilla became an airport of great importance, 'one of the best equipped airports in South America'.[95] Through Scadta Barranquilla strengthened links with Coastal towns, Cartagena, Ciénaga, Santa Marta, Montería, Magangué, El Banco, San Marcos, and Ayapel, and also shortened the distance from the Andean interior. The strong relationship that developed between Scadta and the *Barranquillero* community is shown by Scadta's defence of the Magdalena route; by the involvement of local shareholders in the nationalization process of the company in 1938–40; finally, in the riots that took place in 1942, when the President of Avianca – as the company was then renamed – decided to move its headquarters to Bogotá.

[92] Bogotá, 27 Feb. 1922, NAUS/ 821.796 SCA 2/23.

[93] 'Experimental Flight of Colombian Commercial Aviation through Central America', Guatemala, 28 Aug. 1925, NAUS/ 821.796 SCA 2/33. See W. P. Newton, 'International Aviation Rivalry in Latin America, 1919–1927', *JIASWA* 7 (July 1965), 345–56.

[94] Consul E. W. Magnuson, 'Air Transportation in Colombia, South America', Barranquilla, 2 Aug. 1933, NAUS/ 821.796 SCA 2/347. For a financial history of the company, see M. del Corral, 'Análisis de la vida financiera de la Scadta desde el año de 1939 para atrás . . .', Bogotá, 25 Oct. 1940, NAUS, RG59: file number missing.

[95] Magnuson, 'Air Transportation in Colombia', 4.

During the 1920s, Scadta's route followed the Magdalena, its fleet consisting mainly of hydroplanes. Given Scadta's success there, Pan-American thought that the best way to compete in Colombia was to concentrate on the Bogotá–Buenaventura route. A plan, outlined by Pan-American officials, argued for this route instead of the Magdalena.[96] Scadta protested in vain when the government approved of a Pan American trial flight between Bogotá and Buenaventura in 1929. Leading members of the Barranquilla business community expressed concern to von Bauer over the prospects of the Bogotá–Buenaventura line, and asked him to improve the service between Barranquilla and Bogotá. Von Bauer did not think, however, that the organization of a regular trans-Andean line between Buenaventura and Bogotá was such an easy task as supposed by Pan-American, and promised that once the economic situation had improved, 'we shall not lose a moment to establish through-traffic between Barranquilla and Bogotá'.[97] Faced with the threat of competition, and taking advantage of Pan-American's delay in establishing its Colombian service, Scadta also initiated plans to cover the Bogotá–Buenaventura route. Nevertheless, by 1929 Scadta had reached an agreement with Pan American over the Pacific route. In 1931 Pan-American bought a controlling share package of Scadta, although von Bauer remained director of the company and the deal was not made public until 1939, during the nationalization process.[98]

In the 1920s Scadta had managed to develop a close relationship with the national government. Soon after its establishment, the company received government permission to handle an aerial postal service and was allowed to produce its own postage stamps. In 1924 Congress approved a national *auxilio* of 65,000 pesos for the company. In turn, Scadta agreed to establish a flying school, to train military pilots, and to help the government in the event of war. During the trial flight to Central America and the Caribbean in 1925, a letter of introduction carried by von Bauer and signed by President Ospina gave the journey

[96] Willcox to Trippe, New York, 23 May 1929, NAUS/ 821.796/41. For the competition between Scadta and Pan-American see S. J. Randall, 'Colombia, the United States and Inter-American Aviation Rivalry, 1927–1940', *JIASWA*, 14/3 (1972), 297–324.

[97] P. von Bauer to R. Parrish, Barranquilla, 19 May 1930, APF.

[98] Randall, 'Colombia, the United States and Inter-American Aviation Rivalry', 313; Davies, *Airlines of Latin America*, 224; American Minister to Secretary of State, Bogotá, 4 Feb. 1930, and 27 Feb. 1934, NAUS/ 821.796 SCA 2/301 and 353.

an 'official character'.[99] After the short war with Peru in 1932, there was, however, much dissatisfaction in the government with Scadta due to the company's reluctance to train army pilots.[100] The government did not become directly hostile to Scadta, but now encouraged the development of other airline companies. In June 1933, *Antioqueño* capital backed the organization of Saco, an airline operating daily flights between Medellín and Bogotá. By early 1935, Saco's operations were at a standstill due to lack of funds. Saco increased its capital and tried to convince the *Antioqueño* government to subscribe to company shares. A further attempt to rescue the company was made in 1937, when the national government invested 200,000 pesos in Saco's shares.[101] Thus when it was decided to nationalize Scadta in 1938, the government already had a strong interest in Saco. As a consequence of the war, negotiations to nationalize Scadta became further mixed up with the question of German nationals and enterprises, involving the US State Department and Pan-American interests.[102] After complex dealings, an arrangement was finally worked out whereby Scadta incorporated Saco, with Pan-American retaining a majority of the new company's shares, and the government acquiring 20 per cent, while the remainder was distributed among the minority *Barranquillero* group of Scadta's shareholders and other national investors.[103]

The initial administration of Avianca illustrates the conflicting interests in the struggle over the company: the *Barranquillero* group of J. M. Santodomingo, J. A. Blanco, and J. Montes enjoyed significant participation together with the government on the board of directors, while a former Saco director, M. del Corral, was appointed as president of the company backed by Pan-American.[104] The *Barranquillero* group

99 American Legation to Secretary of State, Bogotá, 23 May 1924, NAUS/821.796 SCA 2/27; *Diario Oficial*, 15 Nov. 1924.

100 American Legation to Secretary of State, Bogotá, 2 June and 12 Nov. 1933, NAUS/ 821.796 SCA 2/345 and 351.

101 Commercial Attaché to Secretary of State, Bogotá, 24 July 1939, NAUS/ 821.796/108. See also 'Memorandum of conversation between James H. Wright, from the American Embassy, Bogotá, and Evan Young, Vice President Pan Air', 26 July 1939, NAUS/ 821.796 SCA 2/460.

102 See Randall, 'Colombia, the United States and Inter-American Rivalry'; D. Bushnell, *Eduardo Santos y la política del buen vecino* (Bogotá, 1984), 29–36. The negotiations are well documented in NAUS, RG59: State Decimal File, Colombia, 1940–9. See also Boy, *Una historia con alas*, 243–8.

103 Braden to Secretary of State, Bogotá, 30 Oct. 1939, NAUS/ 821.796 Avianca/6; and Division of the American Republics, 'Avianca', Washington, 14 Jan. 1943, NAUS/821.796 SCA 2/460.

104 *El Liberal,* 9 June 1940.

– linked, it appears, to von Bauer – had tried to retain control of the reorganized Avianca and had opposed the appointment of del Corral.[105] Tension between the opposing interests reached a peak in October 1942 when it became known in Barranquilla that del Corral had decided to transfer Avianca headquarters from Barranquilla to Bogotá. A bitter press and radio campaign was followed 'by mass demonstrations . . . during three days and general strike'. A campaign was carried on to raise funds to purchase Avianca shares owned by Pan-American, while some observers reported 'that there is a tendency to speak in Barranquilla of the "good old Scadta days"'. Politicians in the city council did not miss the opportunity to take advantage of popular fervour: it was agreed that if the transfer of Avianca's headquarters to Bogotá took place, the council 'would declare a total strike of the commercial, industrial and air river and land transportation activities of the city . . . in addition closing the shops, factories and public and private offices'.[106] However, a compromise between the vice-president of Pan-American and the Barranquilla group was reached on 29 October: 'the headquarters of Avianca will remain in Barranquilla but the office of the President of the company will be established in Bogotá and the meetings of the board of directors will be held in Barranquilla or Bogotá as the board itself may decide'.[107]

7. Conclusion: Transport, Colombia's 'Ancient Enemy'

'The achievement of greater production', a British survey observed in 1950, 'is always in danger of neutralisation by Colombia's ancient enemy – the problem of transport'.[108] Thus transport was still an acute national problem in the mid-twentieth century, despite the significant improvements that the country had been undergoing in her means of communication. These new developments – with the exception of air transport – mostly took place outside the Coast. As roads and railways gradually displaced the Magdalena river as the traditional artery of Colombia's trade, an east–west orientation towards the Pacific – instead of a south–north orientation that had formerly prevailed –

105 Braden to Secretary of State, Bogotá, 4 Dec. 1939, NAUS/ 821.796 Avianca/17.

106 Lane to Secretary of State, Bogotá, 19 and 20 Oct. 1942, NAUS/ 821.796 Avianca/278 and 280.

107 Ibid, 821.796 Avianca/281.

108 Scopes, *Overseas Economic Surveys, Colombia*, 26.

conditioned a different pattern of national integration, further weakening the links between the Coast and the Andean interior.

Time and again, local officials showed concern about the limitations that transport difficulties posed for economic growth. In 1935, the Bolívar Governor Carlos del Castillo toured the Southern provinces of his *Departamento*. He had made the same journey some thirty years earlier, so he could draw some comparisons: among all the towns visited, Governor del Castillo witnessed progress only in Lorica, Cereté, Montería, and Sincelejo. The remainder were as he found them three decades earlier. He looked for an explanation: 'What is the cause of these different developments? Without any doubt, the absolute lack of communication'.[109] Even cattle, which could be taken on the hoof to market, faced difficulties during rainy seasons. For officials such as the Bolívar Governor in 1917, the problem was a vicious circle: 'businesses languish and public finances do not improve as a consequence of poor communications; and these in turn do not improve because trade does not prosper and because the treasury lacks the means'.[110] One way out was to resort to the central government for financial help. But national public investment in transport was as influenced by regional pressures as by technical considerations. As a 1926 British Annual Report pointed out, 'in its endeavour to reconcile conflicting regional interests the Colombian government has committed itself to a number of schemes . . . money being indifferently expended upon them all'.[111] While regional pressure in the Pacific was directed to the need to invest in railways and roads which linked the east with the west of the country, the Coast remained attached to water transport, isolating itself from the new currents of national development.

The concern of the Coast, however, was a natural one. Since not only the most important but the majority of towns were developed by a waterway of one sort of another, and since a significant proportion of the population depended on river navigation, pressure from the Coast was centred on the need to improve conditions of rivers and canals. To what extent the country had the capacity to develop a river such as the Magdalena is difficult to assess and beyond the scope of this book. The fact remains however that investment in the Magdalena was small and far from systematic. An inefficient service and labour unrest, in addition to the difficult conditions of navigation, discouraged any

109 C. Del Castillo, *Mensaje del Gobernador* (Cartagena, 1935).

110 *Mensajes e informes del Gobernador* (Cartagena, 1917), 8.

111 Bogotá, 25 Feb. 1926, PRO, FO 371/11132.

serious attempt to invest in the river. By banking its future almost entirely on water transport, the Coast was losing out: the displacement of the river by roads and railways inevitably resulted in the development of the alternative route towards the Pacific. Regional pressures were relatively more successful in attracting the central government's attention to the problems of the Dique Canal and Bocas de Ceniza. Both required major engineering works which were never properly accomplished. Whatever the achievements, they were preceded by long, obstinate campaigns which, as the case of Bocas de Ceniza shows, illustrate the way public works of such dimensions were developed in Colombia. They all had to overcome shortages of public funds, regional jealousies, frequent changes in ministers and subsequent changes of policies, lack of technological skills, corruption, and inefficiency. Furthermore, as originally conceived, the advantages of Bocas de Ceniza lay in the development of river transport, so its future was inextricably linked to the fate of the Magdalena river. Amidst the frustrations of river navigation and the slow development of roads and railways, the achievements of air transport were all the more remarkable. Although Scadta was a German-financed venture, it was enthusiastically backed by the Barranquilla commercial élite. This enthusiasm was not only the expression of a town open to foreign capital and immigration but also showed the urgency felt about improving communications with the Andean interior. Both as a port and as an emergent industrial centre, Barranquilla was increasingly concerned about reaching the wealthier and larger Andean markets.

Despite the access of air transport, communications between the Coast and the interior remained largely dependent on the Magdalena river. As new means of transport were developed in the interior, the region lost its advantages: coffee exports gradually abandoned the Caribbean ports, and regional products had to meet increasing transport costs to reach the Andes. Paradoxical as it may sound, with the defective transport system of the nineteenth century, the Coast managed to develop closer links with the interior than during the first half of the twentieth century. For Alejandro López, this increasing isolation became a problem of national sovereignty since the Coast was left 'at the mercy of foreign influences'.[112]

[112] López, *Problemas colombianos*, 293.

5
External Influences

1. Introduction

When Rothlisberger visited Barranquilla in the 1880s, he remarked on the significant influence of foreign immigrants in the development of the town.[1] In a country where the influx of international migration was small compared to Argentina or Brazil, the presence of foreign immigrants and capital on the Coast is worthy of attention. Barranquilla had a cosmopolitan flavour. Other Coastal areas besides Barranquilla were also influenced by the transnational movement of people and capital. At the turn of the century, the United Fruit Company took over a French venture involved in growing bananas, while a group of Syrians, Palestinians, and Lebanese had already become successful traders scattered throughout the region.

To what extent then can Coastal development between 1870 and 1950 be related to foreign influence? In exploring this question, this chapter aims to illustrate the features of a region relatively open to the outside world compared to the rest of the country. Since the Syrians constituted the largest group of immigrants to settle on the Coast, one section is devoted to their particular experience. This is followed by an analysis of foreign migration to Barranquilla which, as a successful port, attracted the most immigrants. A detailed study of an American entrepreneur, Karl C. Parrish, who moved to Barranquilla at the beginning of the twentieth century, serves to show not only the influence that immigrants had on the development of the city but also the way they were integrated into the local community. Finally, I look at the impact that foreign capital, the activities of the United Fruit Company in particular, had on the region. In the conclusions, I challenge the predominant view of the banana industry as an enclave, a foreign outpost without significant links with the national economy. I argue that, in spite of the hegemonic presence of the United Fruit Company, developments in the banana zone in Northern Magdalena encouraged regional trade, fostered internal migration and therefore a labour market, and brought agricultural and even industrial growth in the region. But before moving into the subject proper, it is worth

[1] Rothlisberger, *El Dorado*, 14.

looking at the way Colombia tackled the issue of foreign migration in general.

2. 'Colombia for the Colombians'

The bulk of the migration that went to Latin America between 1824 and 1924 – around 91 per cent out of a total of 11 million persons – settled in Argentina and Brazil, and to a lesser extent in Uruguay.[2] The remainder was spread over the continent. Some countries – Cuba, Mexico, Chile, and Peru – received a significant number of immigrants. Colombia was certainly one of the countries that attracted few. Up to 1939, foreign-born inhabitants in Colombia never exceeded 0.34 per cent of the total national population.[3] Several attempts were made by the Colombian Congress to encourage immigration and laws to this end were passed in 1884, 1894, 1920, 1926, and 1928. In 1894, Congress allocated a sum of 150,000 pesos to be spent annually on immigration policies; in 1926 a special bureau was organized to deal with immigration and colonization, and in 1947 a Dirección General de Inmigración was set up as an adjunct to the Ministry of Foreign Affairs.[4] However, laws in themselves did not necessarily mean effective encouragement of immigration nor did they reflect national attitudes. The number of laws and the different policies adopted could even be interpreted as ways of discouraging instead of encouraging immigration. As the head of the Bureau of Immigration and Colonization rightly said in 1929: 'There are some excellent written laws about colonization, but the ministry has no money and such resources as are available are not sufficient'.[5]

Some foreigners did not feel welcome. 'Tous est pour l'étranger obstacle, difficulté, tracasserie', Candelier complained after his arrival to Colombia in the late 1880s. According to Pearse, politicians and other influential people objected to the offer of houses and financial

[2] M. Mörner, *Adventurers and Proletarians. The Story of Migrants in Latin America* (Paris, 1985), 47.

[3] F. Bastos de Avila, *Immigration in Latin America* (Washington, 1964).

[4] Policía Nacional, *Codificación de leyes y decretos ejecutivos sobre extranjeros* (Bogotá, 1928), 273; J. M. Goenaga, *Colonización de la Sierra Nevada de Santa Marta* (Bogotá, 1911), 9; *El Agricultor*, 6 (1894), 272–3; Bank of London and South America, *Fortnightly Review*, 12/278 (24 May 1947), 81.

[5] Albarracín to Montalvo, Bogotá, 24 July 1929, ANC, Sección República, Ministerio de Industria, Baldíos, vol. 21, 62.

assistance to immigrants, which gave rise to the slogan 'Colombia for the Colombians'.[6] Moreover, there were official restrictions against particular groups of immigrants and the government did not always favour their participation in certain economic activities.[7] Even in the most favourable conditions, the British Minister was of the opinion that 'British settlers would be well advised to direct their attention to British colonies where they will not have to face a strange language and completely un-English conditions'; and he concluded, 'this is not a place for small, and presumably innocent, capitalists or settlers'.[8] The result in Colombia with regard to immigration was, as Bastos de Avila observed, an 'abundant legislation from a historical point of view while very little was actually achieved'.[9]

Given the acute labour shortage, and the fact that Bolívar and Magdalena showed the lowest population density among Colombian departments, Coastal politicians and entrepreneurs were often keen to encourage immigration. As President of Bolívar in 1870, R. Santodomingo Vila introduced some measures to attract immigrants. In 1884, the Magdalena Senator J. M. Goenaga put forward a project in Congress to establish a colony of immigrants in the Sierra Nevada. Years later, however, he complained that nothing had been done; regarding immigration, he pointed out, 'public opinion has not awakened in the highlands as it has in Mexico, Chile and Argentina'.[10] More practical steps had been taken in 1871, when a group of entrepreneurs from Santa Marta set up a Compañía Anónima de Inmigración i Fomento, with the aim of encouraging immigration for agricultural development. In 1892, an Italian C. Vedovelli-Breguzzo published a programme to establish a Societa per Azioni to colonize the Sierra Nevada.[11] There is no evidence of any results of these ventures. Nevertheless, some Italians did settle in Magdalena where they were involved in growing tobacco, cacao, and bananas. Individual farmers

[6] Candelier, *Río–Hacha et les Indiens*, 21; and Pearse, *Colombia, with Special Reference to Cotton*, 99.

[7] Restrictions were imposed on Chinese, gypsies, Syrians, Greeks, Hindus, and North Africans. *La Epoca*, 26 Nov. 1913; W. H. Koebel (ed.), *Anglo-South American Handbook* (London, 1921), 275.

[8] British Legation, Bogotá, 2 Apr. 1925, PRO, FO371/10616.

[9] Bastos de Avila, *Immigration in Latin America*, 5.

[10] *GB*, 6 November 1870; Goenaga, *Colonización de la Sierra*, 13.

[11] *GB*, 4 June 1871; Alarcón, *Compendio de historia*, 261; C. Vedovelli–Braguzzo, *Programma di una societa per azioni per la colonizzazione di 2,000,000 di pert met di terreni concessi del governo colombiano nella Sierra Nevada di Santa Marta* (Milano, 1892).

who were short of labour sometimes recruited immigrants, although on a small scale. Several attempts were made to bring labourers from the West Indies but they were 'mostly confined to service . . . in British and American interests'. Language was a barrier and in 1905 the few trials were reported to have proved 'unsatisfactory and costly'.[12] The main influx of labour during the twentieth century, however, did come from the West Indies, basically workers employed in the banana plantations. In 1916, the United Fruit Company employed just over a hundred British West Indians. During the 1920s the number of immigrants from the West Indies grew, but 'this labour is floating in character and the men do not, as a rule, become permanent residents'.[13] Overall, the bulk of the labour force in the banana zone, unlike in parts of Central America, remained Colombian.

Time and again Coastal entrepreneurs showed their concern over the need for immigration. In 1919, M. Dávila Pumarejo – a pioneer in banana exports – suggested that the Colombian Minister in Italy take advantage of the post-war situation, foreseeing that unemployment might encourage Italian migration to Colombia. Dávila Pumarejo stressed the lack of population, gave examples of economic failures in the region due to labour shortages, and called attention to the successful experiences of the immigration policies carried out by Argentina, Brazil, and the United States.[14]

Thus there is evidence that some regional forces made genuine efforts to promote immigration. Yet these were far from systematic and, for a variety of reasons, they often failed. Mass European immigration was discouraged by climatic and economic conditions, and immigration of labour from non-European countries only took place on a small scale and proved uneconomic.[15] Early failures, such as the French colony established by J. E. Gouget during the 1870s, did not encourage further movements.[16] A few adventurers arrived in the region after escaping from their misfortunes elsewhere, such as one Frenchman who, after speculating with an immigrant company in Venezuela, tried his luck in Cartagena with an oil factory during

[12] *PP*, 35, LXXVI (1875), 361; 59, CXXIII, p. 742, and 47, XCI, p. 296.

[13] Bell, *Colombia*, 361. See also 'List of British West Indians employed by the United Fruit Company', 1916, PRO, FO135/395.

[14] *RNA*, (June 1919), 4–7, 9–13.

[15] *PP*, LXXIV (1874), 367. See also W. H. Hirst, *A Guide to South America* (London, 1915), 186; and *MCR* (July–Sept. 1888), 542.

[16] H. W. Bates, *Central America, the West Indies and South America* (London, 1878), 221.

the mid-nineteenth century.[17] A number of immigrants first arrived as employees of foreign companies, or as commercial travellers, and decided to settle in the country after surveying the possibilities of establishing their own businesses: Rameu, a French engineer, around whom the French colony in Ríohacha congregated daily when Reclus visited the town, was originally employed by a merchant from Le Havre to build wells in Guajira; Lacharme, Dereix, and Crump came to the Sinú as employees of mining, cacao, and timber exploitation companies respectively; R. Glasser and F. Eckardt were part of the staff of the German firm Aepli & Eberbach; the American K. C. Parrish came as a mining engineer to explore Southern Bolívar before settling in Barranquilla.[18] In addition, some immigrants arrived in Colombia as exiles from their home countries.

The number of foreigners who settled in the Coast were small. According to the figures available in the censuses, in 1912 there were 2,664 foreigners living in Atlántico and Bolívar; in 1918 the number of foreigners in Atlántico had risen to 4,580; and in 1938 there were 7,281 foreigners in the Coastal departments. Of the total of foreigners then living in Colombia 33.7 per cent were found on the Coast.[19] Moreover, in spite of their small numbers, foreigners played a most significant role in the regional economy. With their skills, their knowledge of the international market, and their abilities to attract capital from overseas, foreigners were prominent in a variety of economic activities: Gieseken & Held and Volpe & Co, for example, were important tobacco and coffee traders during the nineteenth century; R. Joy, F. J. Cisneros and Hoenisberg & Wessels played at different times a significant role in river transport; A. Dereix founded the first bank in the Sinú in 1906; Senior, de Sola, & Co. established the largest cotton cleaning factory in Barranquilla in 1890; Bichara, Jassir & Co. were large wholesale traders in Barranquilla. Their names also illustrate the diversity of their national origins: German, Italian, French, Jews from the Dutch Antilles, British, American, and Syrian. The influence of the

[17] Striffler, *El Río Cesar*, 285–9.

[18] Reclus, *Viaje a la Sierra*, 75–6; Candelier, *Río–Hacha et les Indiens*, 54; Exbrayat, *Reminiscencias monterianas*, 25–7, 81; Berrocal Hoyos, *La colonización antioqueña*, 52–67.

[19] The 1912 census does not give figures for Magdalena, and the 1918 census does not give figures either for Magdalena or Bolívar. See *Censo General de la República de Colombia levantado el 1 de marzo de 1912* (Bogotá, 1912); *Censo de Población de la República de Colombia levantado el 14 de octubre de 1918* (Bogotá, 1923); 'Annual Economic Survey of Latin America', *Commercial Pan American* (Washington, 1942), i. 108.

immigrants extended beyond the economy. Their presence was also felt in education, in religion, and even in social movements. The Catholic Church was in the hands of foreign-born bishops: two Italians, E. Biffi and A. Brioschi were the Archbishops of Cartagena between 1881 and 1910. The frequent presence of a Spanish or Italian priest, and 'sometimes a Syrian', did not escape the attention of Cunninghame Graham during his trip in the Sinú. From the 1880s a Capuchino mission, mostly Spanish and Italian members of the order, was devoted to education in the Guajira.[20]

3. The Syrians

In terms of their numbers and the role they played in the regional economy, Syrians deserve further attention. Syrians, Lebanese, and Palestinians, generally known as *turcos*, were among the largest group of immigrants during the period. Cunninghame Graham noticed their presence in Sincelejo, Jegua, Palmito, and Lorica, where 'nothing is more common than to hear Arabic spoken'.[21] They settled in practically every town where there were opportunities for business, particularly in Cartagena, Cereté, Montería, Ciénaga, Aracataca, Ayapel, Fundación, and of course Barranquilla, where their exotic dress was reported in the local press.[22] Driven from their homeland for a variety of reasons, Syrians started to arrive in Colombia during the 1880s and there was a growing influx of Syrian immigrants which had reached its peak by the 1920s. Between 5,000 and 10,000 Syrians entered Colombia during the period 1900–30.[23]

20 J. J. Ortega Torres (ed.), *Marco Fidel Suárez: Obras* (Bogotá, 1966), ii. 34, 1270; Cunninghame Graham, *Cartagena and the Banks of the Sinú*, 6; J. A. de Barranquilla, *Así es la Guajira* (Bogotá, 1953), 158–88.

21 Cunninghame Graham, *Cartagena and the Banks of the Sinú*, 7, 195, 222, 241. (For practical purposes, Syrians, Lebanese, and Palestinians will be referred to generally as Syrians.)

22 *República*, 15 Jan. 1919. The presence of Syrians was widespread throughout Colombia. In 1945, Ahmed Mattar identified Syrians living in 72 different Colombian towns. See A. Mattar, *Guía social de la colonia de habla árabe en Colombia* (Barranquilla, 1982); and L. L'Estrange-Fawcett, 'Lebanese, Palestinians, and Syrians in Colombia', in A. Hourani and N. Shehadi (eds.), *The Lebanese in the World* (London, 1992), 361–78.

23 Fawcett, 'Lebanese, Syrians and Palestinians', 366. An analysis of 'push' factors of Lebanese emigration in C. Issawi, 'The Historical Background of Lebanese Emigration, 1800–1914', in Hourani and Shehadi (eds.), *The Lebanese*, 13–32.

By 1921 Syrians formed 'possibly the most numerous and important element in the trade and commercial life of the coast centers'.[24] In Barranquilla, they rapidly integrated into the business community: in 1916, Syrian houses were active members of the newly formed Chamber of Commerce, and by 1930 a large proportion of storekeepers were said to be 'born with the early sun in the Levant'.[25] In 1927 the manager of the Bank of London and South America in Cartagena reported that 'during the last few years there has been an enormous increase in the number of Syrian traders in this city and in the volume of business they do . . . They appear to be rapidly overhauling their native competitors'.[26] Their emergence and consolidation in trade was even more prominent in smaller towns such as Lorica.[27]

Many Syrian merchants specialized in trading cotton-print goods, both wholesale and retail. However, they also traded in a wide range of articles. J. Abisambra in Ayapel was typical: he advertised merchandise of all sorts, including hardware, stationery, drugs, cattle, rice, lard, and timber.[28] A few Syrians were also involved in exploiting the land. As early as 1899, S. Abuchar took possession of *baldíos* in the Atrato region, where he planted rubber, cacao, and pasture, and established a saw-mill. By 1906, Abuchar, who had his headquarters in Cartagena, was one of the main rubber exporters in the Chocó together with another Syrian firm, A. & T. Meluk.[29] In 1919 he entered into an agreement with the Meluks to establish the Compañía Azucarera de Sautatá.[30] A. & T. Meluk had been established in 1894 by two Syrian brothers with branches both in Cartagena and Quibdó. The Meluks, whose annual business was estimated at about $500,000 in 1926, imported cotton goods, hardware, and foodstuffs, and exported platinum, gold, rubber, and ipecacuana; in addition, they also traded in cattle, forest products, and land.[31] Like Abuchar and the Meluks, other

[24] Bell, *Colombia*, 36.

[25] 'Report on Barranquilla Consulate', Barranquilla, 10 Jan. 1930, PRO, FO369/2129/K2129.

[26] Inspection Letter, Cartagena, 3 Feb. 1927, BOLSA/A22/1.

[27] *Memoria del Secretario de Gobierno* (Cartagena, 1914), 229.

[28] *Alef*, 8–10 (Jan.–Mar. 1939), 12.

[29] Abuchar to the Minister of Public Works, Cartagena, 9 Jan. 1905, in ANC, Ministerio de Industrias, Baldíos, XXIII, 6–8. H. C. Pearson, *What I Saw in the Tropics* (New York, 1906), 258.

[30] Inspection Letter, Cartagena, 6 June 1927, BOLSA/A22/1; and US Consul report, Cartagena, 5 May 1933, NAUS/ RG84, Cartagena Consulate. Correspondence, 1933 (3).

[31] See *Libro Azul de Colombia*, 290; 'List of Exporters of Forest Products', Cartagena, 20 July 1926, NAUS/ 821.6171/1; 'List of Possible Sellers of Land',

successful Syrian firms were involved in a wide range of business activities, establishing commercial links throughout the region and with the interior. Some successful merchants invested their profits in industry: paper bags, leather goods, textiles, clothes, and soap were among the several products that Syrians were already manufacturing in Barranquilla, Cartagena, and Ciénaga during the 1930s and 1940s.[32]

Syrian immigration provided overall a remarkable example of integration. True, at times regulations were passed that restricted their entry into the country, although they do not seem to have been very effectively applied. Certain sectors of the population did not show much liking for this wave of immigrants. *Turco* could have a pejorative sense and occasionally minor disturbances developed into demonstrations against Syrian shops.[33] Such obstacles probably provided encouragement for the establishment of centres such as the Sociedad Siria de Beneficiencia de El Banco, whose main goal was to offer 'mutual protection to its members and the defense of Syrian honour and prestige'.[34] A sense of loyalty towards the motherland was kept up through publications such as *Alef* or radio programs such as La hora Arabe – yet the editor of *Alef* was a Colombian and Colombians supported the journal with advertisements. Even traditional Colombian newspapers such as *El Porvenir* sometimes supported Syrian interests. An awareness of Syrian identity did not prevent assimilation. Religion was not a barrier and language problems were easily overcome. If intermarriage was not the general rule, it was certainly not the exception: 113 out of a total of 617 heads of family identified by a study conducted in 1945 were married either to Colombians or women with one Colombian parent.[35] Above all, business was the most conspicuous means of integration. It is difficult to identify to what extent joint firms between Colombians and Syrians, such as Mendoza, Lajud & Co. established in 1903, were a common practice.[36] Nevertheless, by trading in remote provinces, they opened up

Cartagena, 22 Mar. 1926, NAUS, RG84: American Consulate, general correspondence. Cartagena, 1926 (5).

32 See various advertisements in *Alef,* Jan.–Mar. 1939; and Mattar, *Guía social,* 11, 14, 19, 20, 22, 46, 49, 51, 54.

33 'Riotous Meetings in Cartagena', Cartagena, 16 Dec. 1910, NAUS/ 821,00/362.

34 'Estatutos de la Sociedad Siria de Beneficiencia', ANC, República, Ministerio de Gobierno, Sección 4a, Justicia (17), 1929, 243.

35 Mattar, *Guía social.*

36 *RB* , 30 June 1903.

unexplored markets; by investing their surplus in other activities in the region, they were regarded as a progressive force in the economy.

As the Syrian example has shown, foreigners could be found scattered throughout the region, although they naturally tended to be concentrated in the ports and centres where greater commercial opportunities were offered. The largest concentration was in Barranquilla. Their activities in this port illustrates the extent of their influence in Coastal development.

4. Barranquilla: a Cosmopolitan Port?

In 1872 the Colombian Miguel Samper was impressed by the number of foreigners he came across in Barranquilla and by how often the English language was spoken 'in offices, the port, the railway and on the steamers'. For Samper, the commercial activities of Barranquilla stood in clear contrast to 'the stillness of the Andean cities'.[37] It was to the influence of a merchant community, largely formed by foreigners, that contemporary observers attributed Barranquilla's development: 'they have kept this city, since thirty or forty years ago,' P. J. Eder pointed out in 1913, 'in the van of progress in Colombia'.[38] Barranquilla was often referred to as a cosmopolitan place.

Its cosmopolitanism was clearly related to its outstanding condition as a Colombian port: sixteen countries had consular representatives in Barranquilla in 1892. Shops in the Plaza San Nicolás, such as Baena Hermanos, advertised at their doors, 'English spoken, on parle Français, si parla Italiano'. With similar pretensions, the *Boletín Municipal de Estadística* sometimes published articles and advertisements in foreign languages. In 1872, E. Pellet founded *The Shipping List*, an influential commercial newspaper published in English. The head of the Colegio Ribón, the leading *Barranquillero* school at the turn of the century, was a German, and sixty girls attended the Protestant Colegio Americano.[39] There was a Protestant Church,

[37] In J. L. Romero, *Latinoamérica: las ciudades y las ideas* (Mexico, 1976), 220.

[38] P. J. Eder, *Colombia* (London, 1913), 187. See also E. Reclus, *Mis exploraciones en América* (Valencia, 1910), 58; N. Góngora Echenique, *Lo que he visto en Colombia* (Madrid, 1932), 176; and M. Rodríguez and J. Restrepo, 'Los empresarios extranjeros de Barranquilla, 1880–1900', *Desarollo y Sociedad* (Bogotá, May 1982).

[39] See Grau, *La ciudad de Barranquilla*, 26–30, 32, 114; Martínez Aparicio and Niebles, *Directorio Anuario*, 73–7, 114; Goenaga, *Lecturas locales*, 73; *BME*, Barranquilla, 6 (30 Oct. 1931).

and a Protestant cemetery, next to the Jewish and Catholic cemeteries, later united as the Cementerio Universal, so named because 'Barranquilla is bound to be the common fatherland of families from different nationalities and religions', and the city should offer them the appropriate place for their 'eternal rest'.[40] By 1933, Barranquilla had at least ten social clubs, among them one Anglo-American, a German, an Italian, two Spanish, and one Chinese.[41]

A look at the statistics, however, suggests that the picture of Barranquilla as a cosmopolitan place needs some qualification. In 1875, there were only just over 300 foreigners living in Barranquilla, or 1.9 per cent of its total population. Their numbers had gone up to 862 by 1912. During the following years, they increased further: 1,595 in 1918, 4,379 in 1928, and 5,379 in 1951.[42] The records are not systematic and they reveal the official number of foreigners living in Barranquilla in given years, so it is not possible to estimate how many foreigners in total settled in the town during the period, although they do illustrate the small scale of immigration into Barranquilla. Nevertheless, the figures become more significant if they are applied to the active working population. Half of the foreign males who arrived in Barranquilla during the first three months of 1931 were registered as merchants; a few were bankers, industrialists, engineers, electricians, tailors, smiths, bakers, but there were also artists, photographers, schoolteachers, and bullfighters.[43] In 1938, foreigners accounted for 4.5 per cent of Atlántico's active population. More than half of them were engaged in the service sector – transport, banking, hotel-keeping, commerce, utilities, representing some 12 per cent of those employed in this sector overall. Their participation in the professions was higher, 21 per cent, but in the industrial sector lower, 5.4 per cent.[44] Since the majority – over 90 per cent – of foreigners in Atlántico lived in Barranquilla their significance to Barranquilla's economy was evidently larger.

40 'Cementerio Universal', Barranquilla, 9 Mar. 1869, in Baena and Vergara, *Barranquilla*, 408–9.

41 E. Carbonell Insignares, 'Apuntes sobre la colonia China en Barranquilla', Barranquilla, 8 July 1979, unpublished article.

42 Restrepo and Rodríguez, 'Empresarios extranjeros', 94; *Censo general. . .1912*; *Censo de población . . . de 1918; BME*, Barranquilla (20 Nov. 1930), 14; Sojo, *Barranquilla, una economía en expansión*, 138.

43 *BME*, Barranquilla (20 May 1931), 6.

44 *Anales de Economía y Estadística* (Bogotá, 1938), iii. 50.

TABLE 5.1 *Foreigners Living in Barranquilla according to Nationality of Origin, 1875, 1928, and 1951*

Country of origin	1875	1928	1951
Netherlands	67	n.d.	88
Venezuela	46	385	351
Cuba	36	121	119
Great Britain	33	153	169
United States	31	161	441
France	31	109	179
Germany	26	236	350
Italy	23	748	460
Denmark	5	n.d.	n.d.
China	n.d.	192	115
Syria	n.d.	680	560
Spain	n.d.	791	607
Panama	n.d.	124	222
Poland	n.d.	n.d.	173
Others	5	659	244

Note: n.d. = no data.
Sources: Restrepo and Rodríguez, 'Empresarios extranjeros', *Desarrollo y Sociedad* (Bogotá, 1982), 94; *BME*, Barranquilla, 20 Nov. 1930, 14; Sojo, *Barranquilla* (Barranquilla, 1955), 138.

Table 5.1 shows the nationality of foreigners who came to Barranquilla during the period. In 1875 the largest group came from the Dutch Antilles, more precisely from Curaçao, followed by Venezuelans, Cubans, British, Americans, French, Germans, and Italians. Spanish, Syrians, Americans, and Chinese, among many others, joined the foreign community during the following years. At least forty-two different nationalities registered in the Barranquilla a*lcaldía* in 1931. More often than not, however, business was carried out regardless of nationality. Sometimes, merchants might have originally arrived as representatives of particular national interests but soon they were involved in local life, dealing with people, goods, and companies from different countries. O. Berne, for example, Belgian Consul and French Vice-Consul in 1892, imported merchandise from Great Britain, France, Germany, Spain, and the United States, and was also a representative for German transport and insurance companies. Joint ventures of different nationalities, such as Champan & Martínez or Danouile & Wessels, were not exceptional. The most interesting example during the nineteenth century was the establishment of the Banco de Barranquilla. Organized as a joint stock company in 1873, the bank was the result of combined efforts of Colombian merchants together with Jews from the Dutch Antilles, Germans, French, and Venezuelans, among others.[45]

Some nationalities were more prominent than others. From the mid-nineteenth century, a group of Jewish merchants from Curaçao had been prominent in the Barranquilla business community. From trading, they expanded their interests to banking, real estate, and industry. With the Germans, they formed the largest taxpaying group among the foreign population in the early 1870s.[46] In turn, Germans were often given credit for Barranquilla's progress from the importance of their merchant houses and their original involvement in the construction of the railway that linked the town to the seaport of Sabanilla.[47] Germans were practically commanding the trade of Barranquilla at the end of the century, 'since not only do they extend their operations to the various towns in our immediate vicinity, but are, at the same time, agents for business houses in the interior. They give the lead to the export trade in cotton and tobacco, and some other native products'.[48] During the pre-war years, German houses still led in number and importance among foreign business firms. Their interests were diverse: river transport, wholesale and retail trading, coffee and tobacco exports, cattle production, commission business, and forwarding agencies, among others. After the First World War, Germans managed to re-establish their favourable position in Colombia due to 'a succession of representatives of remarkably high calibre'.[49] In Barranquilla, the most important German venture during the inter-war years was Scadta, the airline founded in 1919 in collaboration with *Barranquillero* entrepreneurs.

The example of L. Gieseken illustrates German involvement in Barranquilla's economy and society. Gieseken came to Barranquilla in

[45] *Boletín Industrial*, 30 Mar. 1873; Banco de Barranquilla, *Informes y balance general* (Barranquilla, 1889).

[46] *GB*, 9 Apr. 1871; I. Croitoru Rotbaum, *De Sefarad al Neosefardismo* (Bogotá, 1977), i. 168–72.

[47] *PP*, 29, LXVII (1873), 917. See also Bates, *Central America, the West Indies and South America*, 321; and *Revista de Colombia*, 28 Nov. 1873.

[48] *PP*, 49, XCIX (1899), 34.

[49] 'Colombia. Report for Year Ending June 1928', Bogotá, 12 Apr. 1929, PRO, F0 371/ 13479. See also *PP*, 28, LXVIII (1913), 559.

the 1880s and with A. Held founded Gieseken & Held as partners of a Bremen firm H. Schutte, Gieseken & Co. By 1892, Gieseken & Held were exporting hides, coffee, and tobacco, among other products, serving as agents for German and British insurance companies, were owners of a river steamship company and the local newspaper *El Anunciador*, and *concesionarios* of the Lotería de Bolívar. Their general store in Calle San Roque sold textiles, foodstuffs, hardware, glass, and pharmaceutical products.[50] From his early years in Colombia, Gieseken had been interested in river transport. In 1887 he founded his first steamship company which at the end of the century was transporting 10 per cent of the freight carried on the Magdalena river. In 1900 he founded the Empresa Alemana de Navegación Fluvial and in 1908 he led the merger of all the smaller river companies to compete with the Magdalena River Steamship Co.[51] In addition, Gieseken owned land in Barranquilla, Puerto Salgar, El Carmen, and Honda; and, when Scadta was established in 1919, Gieseken was its most important financial backer. He settled permanently in Barranquilla where he soon became part of the social élite: in 1888 he contributed to the foundation of the Club Barranquilla.[52]

Besides Germans, other European immigrants were also prominent in Barranquilla. Larger in numbers, Italians and Spanish were spread throughout the social ladder as workers or employees but also commonly as small entrepreneurs, although some firms were leading members of the business community. British migration to Barranquilla was negligible, but there was a Pensión Inglesa, the rendezvous of those 'unfortunate English' who had decided to settle in this 'uninteresting', 'third-rate city'.[53] However, British capital, labour, and management were involved in the completion and running of the railway to Puerto Colombia which played a significant role in Barranquilla's development until the opening of Bocas de Ceniza. By 1930, British interests consisted 'chiefly of the Barranquilla Pier and Railway Co. . . . and branches of . . . three British Banks'.[54] French interests were less significant, although in 1905 a French immigrant

[50] Martínez and Niebles, *Directorio Anuario*, 253, 429, 357, 328–31.

[51] Restrepo and Rodríguez, 'Los extranjeros de Barranquilla', 101; Acosta, *Manual de Navegante*, 21, 25, 30; *Board of Trade Journal*, London, 26 (Feb. 1899), 168.

[52] Texas Petroleum Co., Land Department, Bogotá, Indice Notaría Primera de Barranquilla, 25, 27; Indice Notaría Segunda de Barranquilla, 48–60, MDC; and J. F. Sojo, *El Club Barranquilla* (Barranquilla, 1942), 7.

[53] C. Cameron, *A Woman's Winter in South America* (London, 1910), 242

[54] 'Report on Barranquilla', 10 Jan. 1930, PRO, FO369/ 2129.

established the firm V. Dugand & Hijo which became later the Banco Dugand.

5. Karl C. Parrish, an American Entrepreneur

'Since holding this post', a US Consul pointed out in 1883, 'I have met with but one representative of an American commercial house.'[55] In contrast, four decades later, a British report observed the progress of American capitalists, who 'continue to show great activity in this country, and numbers of Agents are constantly travelling through the various departments, personally investigating opportunities for profitable investment'.[56] American influence in Barranquilla was prominent after the First World War. 'Outside Havana and Panama,' a 1928 Pan-American Union publication pointed out, 'perhaps no Caribbean city offers a better illustration of coordination and cooperation between North Americans and South Americans in municipal upbuilding than does Barranquilla.'[57] During the 1920s, Barranquilla received a significant influx of American capital and entrepreneurship, a development largely fostered by the activities of Karl C. Parrish.

A mining engineer, Parrish came to Colombia for the first time in 1904, as an employee of the Andes Mining Development Co., to work in their mines at Guamaco, a distant town in the interior of Bolívar.[58] Having surveyed the possibilities of the mining industry in the country, he went back to the United States in search of finance; in association with Chicago capitalists he founded a new company to exploit the Champane Mine in the Department of Bolívar. Years later he established his residence first in Cartagena and finally in Barranquilla, where he became involved in real estate. He was originally interested in the development of both towns but objected to Cartagena because 'the wealth there has been and is more concentrated than in Barranquilla. Also many of the better class of people have already

[55] *MCR* (July–October 1883), 48.

[56] Lord H. Hervey to Earl Curzon, Bogotá, 27 Feb. 1920, PRO, F0371/ 4458.

[57] 'The New Barranquilla', *The American City Series*, 5B (Washington, 1928), 11.

[58] See 'Iowans Invade Latin America', *Los Angeles Times*, 3 Nov. 1930, newspaper clipping in the APF. In 1930, the US Minister in Bogotá described Parrish as a 'very shrewd and successful businessman and contractor' who was associated with several American banks and a number of prominent American companies; Caffery to the Secretary of State, Bogotá, 6 Mar. 1930, NAUS/ 821.812/250.

built good houses.'[59] In contrast, Parrish showed enthusiasm over the development of Barranquilla. 'Barranquilla,' he wrote to a businessman in Pennsylvania in 1920, 'is getting to be a real boom town . . . Everything is overflowing and it looks as if [it] was going to be the largest commercial city in northern South America'.[60] Ten years later, he prided himself on the influence he had had over Barranquilla's development: 'Barranquilla is often mentioned as having had the only sane and sound management in all northern South America and thereby, the city, and Parrish and Co. are receiving quite a little fame'.[61]

In association with Manuel and Enrique de la Rosa – members of an old *Barranquillero* family – and with other US citizens, Parrish founded the Compañía Urbanizadora El Prado in 1920, with an initial capital of $300,000. The immediate goal of the company was to build a modern neighbourhood on the outskirts of the city, along the lines of a North American suburb: big avenues, plenty of green areas, spacious houses surrounded by gardens, sports facilities, and a country club.[62] The size of the enterprise and its rapid growth promoted the company's direct involvement in practically every single step of Barranquilla's urban development: the paving of its sandy streets, the organization of public services, the construction of its aqueduct and its sewage system. The sale of the plots was a success from the start and soon the neighbours of the traditional Calle Obando moved their residences up to the more pleasant area of El Prado, nearer to the sea. Some of the new owners seemed over-enthusiastic. 'The tendency is to build too expensively,' Parrish's father wrote, 'The trouble is to hold these fellows down to what they can afford.'[63] Despite these fears, the company collected its payments satisfactorily. In 1928, El Prado had 260 *mutuarios*; among them only sixteen had difficulties in paying. To

[59] Parrish to Manning, Barranquilla, 18 Apr. 1920, APF.

[60] Parrish to Robinson, Barranquilla, 28 May 1920, APF.

[61] Parrish to Guyant, Barranquilla, 10 May 1920, and to Higgings, New York, 2 Oct. 1929, APF.

[62] *Escrituras y estatutos de la Compañía Urbanizadora El Prado* (Barranquilla, 1920).

[63] R. L. Parrish to Harvey, Barranquilla, 30 Jan. 1921, APF. R. L. Parrish, Parrish's father, worked as a lawyer in Des Moines. He visited Barranquilla on several occasions, when he took the opportunity to check the company's books and review its financial condition. He published several articles on Colombia in an Iowan newspaper where he spoke of the country's prospects for development and observed the possibilities for foreign investment. The articles were later published in a pamphlet, *An Iowan's View of Colombia, South America* (n. p. 1921).

the modern neighbourhood were added a country club and a first-class hotel, run in association with members of the Obregón family.[64] Besides El Prado, with its spacious and sometimes luxurious houses, the company also planned the construction of 'small but well-built houses, for which there is large demand'.[65] The Compañía Urbanizadora El Prado was one of the most profitable ventures that Parrish undertook. It was through El Prado that he managed to accumulate land and capital which in turn gave him the security from which to launch future business. Following the success of El Prado, he integrated his real-estate business with other ventures, a brick-factory and a saw-mill, the biggest on the Colombian Coast.[66]

However, El Prado was confronted by the municipality's restricted capacity to expand its public services in keeping with the rate of growth of the town. The dimensions of the new Barranquilla had overwhelmed its nineteenth-century infrastructure, so Parrish decided to promote several public work projects. For this purpose, he negotiated a loan with the Central Trust Co. of Illinois for $5,000,000 which was contracted by the municipality in 1925.[67] Parrish & Co. would undertake the construction works: an aqueduct, a sewage system, the paving of the streets, and the rebuilding of the public market. The Central Trust loan redefined the management of public finances in Barranquilla over a period of several years by the creation of the Empresas Públicas Municipales under the administration of a *Junta Autónoma*, a body independent from the city council. To ensure the collection of the loan, a North American citizen, Samuel Hollopeter, was placed in charge of the new public utilities; he was to manage them for the next twenty years. The conditions of the loan were the origin of struggles between the North American administration and certain local politicians; having being excluded from the arrangement, the latter resented not having control over the municipal company. In 1929, several members of the city council were seeking the negotiation of another foreign loan with the advice of the Foundation Company, a North American firm interested in taking over

[64] El Prado's style marked a new period of architecture in Barranquilla, resembling the architecture of modern Havana. See *Historia Gráfica de la Urbanización de El Prado* (Barranquilla, 1945).

[65] Parrish to Foy, Barranquilla 15 Oct. 1930, APF.

[66] 'Notes for Mr. F. H. Baker regarding properties under Compañía Colombiana de Inversiones', memorandum by K. C. Parrish, Barranquilla, 13 March 1931; 'To the shareholders of the Compañía Nacional de Maderas La industria', 18 July 1930, APF.

[67] See Ch. 6.

the public works of the town and displacing Parrish & Co. 'I feel it my duty to advise Washington,' Parrish wrote in 1929, 'that American interests are endeavouring to destroy the only successful manager form of government set up in South America . . . The businessmen are very much incensed, but the bad politicians are in power.'[68] Not all the politicians were against the loan. Parrish enjoyed cordial relations with several public figures such as A. Pumarejo, a liberal leader of the Department of Atlántico, also a businessman. E. de la Rosa, shareholder of El Prado, and M. T. Mendoza Amarís, their legal adviser, were members of the leading body of the local Liberal Party.[69] With the support of their political friends, the Chamber of Commerce, and most of the private sector, Parrish managed to control, in common agreement with the Chicago banking interests, the Empresas Públicas Municipales for several years. During Enrique Olaya Herrera's government, Parrish and his brother, who by now had joined the family business, received invitations to organize public utilities in other Colombian towns, following the Barranquilla model.

Parrish's enthusiasm for the development of Barranquilla was linked to its potential as a Caribbean port. Thus he became a leading advocate of the Bocas de Ceniza project, believing that the opening of the mouth of the river would also mean better opportunities for the development of the Magdalena Valley, creating sound conditions for large-scale investment in the agricultural sector. Parrish's interests were directly involved in Bocas de Ceniza first in 1929, when the national government, through the Minister of Public Works, asked him to put forward a proposal to secure the rapid completion of works after the cancellation of the contract with Ulen & Co.[70] The original project was halted by the Depression and by the change of government; but in May 1933 the government signed a contract with R. Parrish, on behalf of the Compañía del Puerto y Terminal de Barranquilla, Raymond Concrete Pile Co., and Winston Brothers Co., aimed at the opening of the Bocas de Ceniza and the construction of the docks in Barranquilla, a project which encouraged a new period of commercial prosperity.[71]

[68] Parrish to Head, Deerfield, Ill., 20 Aug. 1929, APF.

[69] *La Prensa*, 8 Jan. 1934.

[70] 'Memorandum on Bocas de Ceniza project', Barranquilla, 11 Oct. 1929, NAUS/RG84, Barranquilla Consulate, Security Segregated Records, 1929–49, Box 1.

[71] Harris, Forbes & Co. to R. Parrish, New York, 13 Aug. 1929; Parrish to: Berge, New York, 14 Aug. 1929; Head, Deerfield, 15 Aug. 1929; and R. Parrish, New York, 10 Aug. 1929; 'Memorandum with reference to the Barranquilla Port and Terminal Works', n. d., APF.

Apart from their close involvement in Barranquilla's development, the Parrish brothers also had wide-ranging interests in several other Coastal towns and in the Andean interior. In Cartagena, their activities did not fare so well as in Barranquilla, although in 1931 they were approached several times with requests for collaboration in reorganizing Cartagena's public services. Responding to these demands, the Parrish brothers tried to negotiate an arrangement for Cartagena with the Electric Bond and Share Co., but their efforts were frustrated by the lack of co-operation from the *Cartageneros*: 'They have never learned the secret of doing business with big companies . . . that the management of a city is like any other business.'[72] In Santa Marta, the Parrish brothers managed to control 2,000 out of the 6,000 shares of Cervecería del Magdalena, representing a capital sum of $200,000. In 1930, this company covered a wide market comprising Santa Marta, Ciénaga, the banana zone, and towns along the Magdalena River and Bucaramanga. During these years, the Cervecería del Magdalena was facing fierce competition from the breweries of Barranquilla owned by the Osorio family. Parrish tried to consolidate both interests to avoid what he considered a noxious rivalry. There were long negotiations with the main shareholder of Cervecería de Barranquilla, but these were fruitless. The failure of these negotiations, the consequences of the price war between the breweries, and the effects of the Depression, compelled Parrish to sell his interests in the Magdalena brewery to Cervecería Bavaria of Bogotá.[73] The Parrishes' failure as brewers in Santa Marta and their frustrated involvement in Cartagena's development was counterbalanced by their interests in public utilities and their investments in other regions of Colombia.[74] In addition to their various interests in the Coast, the Parrishes continued to invest in mining operations in the Andean interior, while they were also interested in real estate developments in Cali, Medellín, and Bogotá.[75]

While investing in Colombia, where he settled as a permanent resident with his family, Parrish preserved his links with the United

[72] K. C. Parrish to R. Parrish, Barranquilla, 22 Aug. 1931, APF.

[73] R. Parrish to Davies, Barranquilla, 26 July 1929; Cornelissen to Parrish, Barranquilla, 29 July 1930, APF.

[74] 'Location and description of Magangué'; Parrish to Head, Barranquilla, 23 Apr. 1931, and to Foy, Barranquilla, 15 Oct. 1930.

[75] R. Parrish to Vice-President of Colombian Steamship Line, Barranquilla, 10 July 1928; 'Memo para la Junta Directiva de la Compañía Urbanizadora El Prado'. n. d., APF.

States. The success of his ventures reinforced his connections with business circles in his native country. Up to 1931 Parrish maintained an office in New York, where he was a frequent visitor in search of financial backing, partners for his new enterprises, and contact with foreign firms interested in expanding their businesses in South America.[76] Parrish represented the interests of Griffith Bros., General Motors, Fairbank Morse, Electric Bond and Share Co., among other firms in Colombia. His renown abroad and the connections he managed to establish through his entrepreneurial activities made him an important contact for those companies interested in investing in Colombia. But his own close relations with investors and firms in the United States did not prevent conflicts with other North American companies or with American officials. The bitterest confrontation was with the Foundation Company, described previously, when the latter tried to take over the public works that Parrish & Co. had secured in Barranquilla. Nor was the relationship between Parrish and the American banks established in Colombia cordial. Parrish criticized the role that American banks were playing in the country; he preferred to do business with English bankers.[77] He also sought English support for his Bocas de Ceniza project, believing that an international group, instead of the exclusive presence of North American capital, was more acceptable to Colombian public opinion. This attitude earned him the hostility of certain American diplomats, who also accused Parrish of being unpatriotic for his pro-Scadta stand in the conflict between the German airline and Pan-American.[78]

6. Foreign Capital and the United Fruit Company

The involvement of the United Fruit Company in the Coastal economy and society poses questions of a different nature. In contrast with the individuals or the family firms, the United fruit Company represented the centralized multinational corporations which began to reshape the world economy after the turn of the century.[79] A distinctive feature of

[76] Caffery to the Secretary of State, Bogotá, 8 May 1930, NAUS/ 821.812/255.

[77] Parrish to Foy, Barranquilla, 26 Nov. 1930, APF.

[78] US Minister to the Secretary of State, Bogotá, 30 Jan. 1930, NAUS/821.812/245.

[79] For the United Fruit Company, see Ch. 1. For the rise of 'Big Business' in the United States, N. Lamoreaux, *The Great Merger Movement in American Business, 1895–1904* (Cambridge, 1985). See also M. Witkins, *The Maturing of Multinational Enterprise: American Business Abroad from 1914–1970* (1974), 2 vols.

this successful venture was the scale of its operation. In Colombia, as in other countries where it operated, United Fruit achieved 'an admirable economic organization', which integrated production of bananas with their transport, loading, shipping, and marketing.[80] The Colombian experience was however particular in, first, the higher degree of participation of local cultivators in banana production; second, the national character of the vast majority of the labour force; and third, the smaller significance of banana exports to Colombian economy as a whole.[81] All the same, though banana exports and United Fruit were not so significant to the national economy, their overall impact on the Coast was overwhelming.

The development of banana plantations by the United Fruit Company was often portrayed as an American crusade to master the tropics, a crusade organized by 'men who believed that it was possible to convert the miasmic swamps and jungles . . . into vast plantations of nodding bananas'. Some contemporaries even tried to outline the 'philosophy' of a 'new empire' which rested 'on refusing to accept the status quo as something ordained by the Almighty', consequently committed to 'the creation and exchange of wealth and the cure and prevention of disease'.[82] In contrast to this vision of a benevolent empire, early interpretations of economic imperialism blamed the United Fruit Company – and foreign capital in general – for hindering development.[83] More recently, the concept of enclave has been used to describe an export venture with few links with the domestic economy. By monopolizing the factors of production and the trading of the fruit,

[80] C. F. Jones, 'Agricultural Regions of South America', *Economic Geography*, 5 (1929), 409.

[81] For the features of banana production in Central American countries, see Ellis, *Las transnacionales del banano*, 31–74; Bulmer-Thomas, *The Political Economy of Central America*, 1-43; and J. C. Gaspar, *Limón, 1880–1940: Un estudio de la industria bananera en Costa Rica* (San José, 1979). At their peak (1910–14), banana exports represented 9% of Colombian total exports; 1915–34, a mere 6%, the trend now being one of steady decline. In 1913, about 50% of export earnings in Costa Rica came from bananas. In 1929, banana exports represented 25.2% of total exports in Costa Rica, 12.9% in Guatemala, 84.9% in Honduras and 18.3% in Nicaragua. See McGreevey, *An Economic History of Colombia*, 207, and Bulmer-Thomas, *The Political Economy of Central America*, 8, 34.

[82] Adams, *Conquest of the Tropics*, 53; Crowther, *The Romance and Rise of the American Tropics*, 10–12, 199, 315, 354–5. The view of a 'benevolent empire' conquering the tropics was commonly conveyed in the North American press; see 'The Green Gold of the Tropics', *Outlook* (Sept.–Dec., 1922), 186–8; 'Empire Builder', *The Nation* (3 July 1929), 5–6.

[83] F. Rippy, *The Capitalist and Colombia* (New York, 1931); Kepner and Soothill, *The Banana Empire*.

the American company impeded competition. By establishing the practice of the company store – where labourers were paid in *vales*, which in turn were exchanged for subsidized imported products – the fruit company discouraged local industries and the development of the local commercial economy. According to this view, the United Fruit Company isolated the *zona bananera* from the rest of the country.[84] A review of the conditions under which the banana industry developed in Colombia up to 1945, and its effects on the region, suggests a more complex picture.

There is, of course, no doubt that United Fruit managed to acquire a dominant position by establishing control of the international marketing of bananas, a latecomer to the world market. Before this company was founded at the turn of the century, the marketing of bananas in the US was a more competitive business.[85] Colombians, who had been successful in trading with coffee abroad, failed with bananas. Some Colombians, such as S. Pérez Triana, did attempt to export the fruit but failed to establish themselves in the business. The product could not be stored for long, nor in ordinary warehouses. The need to dispose of the fruit quickly required an efficient system of transport and distribution.[86] In Central America, as Victor Bulmer-Thomas has suggested, the banana industry fell under foreign control because of the lack of national interest in the unhealthy Atlantic Coast, therefore opening the way for the companies which 'offered to build the infrastructure and provide the labour in an area where the opportunity cost of land appeared to be zero'.[87] This was not the Colombian case where, since the 1880s, nationals had been producing and shipping bananas to external markets, using national labour. Nevertheless, by being displaced from the trading of the fruit, under the growing monopolistic conditions of the market, Colombians lost control of the local industry. Meanwhile, the consolidation of United Fruit went hand in hand with its achievements in overcoming the problems of marketing bananas: a fleet of ships specially conditioned for the cargo, development of a sophisticated system of communications for handling the fruit with expediency, an efficient organization for the loading and unloading of bananas, and a vast

[84] White, *Historia de una ignominia*, 26; Botero and Guzmán Barney, 'El enclave agrícola', 371; Bejarano, *El régimen agrario*, 148; and D. Fajardo, *Haciendas, campesinos y políticas agrarias en Colombia, 1920–1980* (Bogotá, 1980), 35–8.

[85] Crowther, *The Romance and Rise of the American Tropics*, 173.

[86] See Pérez Triana's perceptive comments in *RNA* (30 Oct. 1908), 264–5.

[87] Bulmer-Thomas, *The Political Economy*, 15-16.

network of wholesalers in its final markets.[88] Additionally, by developing several sources of supply far apart from each other the American company was able to overcome recurrent losses from 'devastating floods, droughts, "blow-downs", and diseases'.[89]

The successful development of the banana industry required the large capital investment provided by the United Fruit Company, in physical infrastructure, communications, and health.[90] Investments in infrastructure included irrigation canals, drainage, tramways, housing, and sewage systems. Given the levels of rainfall, irrigation was needed in the Colombian Banana Zone for at least seven months a year.[91] United Fruit built some irrigation works and claimed that the company furnished water from its canals to local growers at a lower rate than the one charged by the municipality of Ciénaga.[92] However, the concentration of canals in the hands of the company also meant that it controlled access to water, causing further resentment among cultivators. Similarly, though some investment was made in expanding communications, this was done to the exclusive benefit of the banana industry. The control of the railway by United Fruit, in conjunction with the company's handling of the marketing of bananas, was a source of recurrent and bitter conflict.

Health, on the contrary, was one sector where the ideal of a benevolent empire might have some reality. Pneumonia, malaria, nephritis, and pulmonary tuberculosis were among the common local diseases. Research on tropical disease received significant support from the company, hospitals were built in its different divisions, and its

88 E. S. Gregg. 'Trading with the Tropics', *Economic Geography,* 1 (Oct. 1925), 397, and UFC, *A Short History of the Banana* (Boston, 1904).

89 J. T. Palmer, 'The Banana in the Caribbean Trade', *Economic Geography*, 8 (1931), 267.

90 Available figures differ about the company's investments in the region: while Crowther estimated $US15,000,000, an American Vice-Consul calculated 70,000,000 pesos ($US=1 peso) in 1928; according to Kepner and Soothill, the holdings of the company were estimated at $US30,000,000 in 1932; in Kepner and Soothill, *The Banana Empire*, 287. See also Crowther, *The Romance and Rise of the American Tropics,* 284, and J. White, 'The United Fruit Company in the Santa Marta Banana Zone, Colombia: Conflicts of the 1920s', (B.Phil., Oxford, June 1971), 19–20.

91 Fawcett, *The Banana,* 235; Jones, 'Agricultural Regions of South America', 407–8.

92 L. Sawyer, 'The Banana Industry', Santa Marta, 9 May 1920, NAUS/821.6156/44. See also Kepner and Soothill, *The Banana Empire*, 290; 'Memorandum on Water', Bogotá, 28 Sept. 1931, NAUS/ RG84: General correspondence, US Embassy, 1931 (16); and 'Concepto que el Gobernador del Magdalena, a solicitud del señor Ministro de Industrias rinde sobre el problema de las aguas en la zona bananera', Bogotá, 14 July 132, AEOH, s. 4/22, Gobernaciones, Magdalena.

medical department kept rigorous statistics, published in an annual report also devoted to medical investigation.[93] In Magdalena, the company built a $US100,000 hospital and some outlying medical centres. By 1919 hospital admissions in Santa Marta were over 4,500 and a laboratory was studying local malaria.[94] Widening the scope of the service was a recurrent demand on the company, whose employees also resented the levy of 2 per cent on their wages for medical attention.[95] United Fruit was obviously no charity organization and controlling tropical diseases was regarded as part of their business, but it did build and run its hospital, in a region where neither the state nor any private organization had developed any sort of health service.[96]

The way United Fruit controlled communications within the banana zone, and the international marketing of the fruit, may serve to reinforce the enclave view, while the company's investments in health may be interpreted as one of the achievements of a 'benevolent empire'. What also needs to be re-examined is the overall impact that the banana trade had on local planters and labour, and how the income received from a growing export was transferred to other areas of the regional economy. From its entry into Colombia, the United Fruit Company faced modest but relatively widespread competition from local cultivators in the production of bananas. Earlier unsuccessful experiences with tobacco, sugar, and cacao in northern Magdalena had motivated a growing interest in bananas given the new opportunities offered by the world economy. As a consequence, there was an active land market in Magdalena. In 1912, for example, there were at least 138 purchases of farms in the Ciénaga district. Just five of them were bought by the United Fruit company, totalling an area of about 160 ha; the rest were transactions among individual cultivators or landowners, the majority of plots having sizes of between 1 and 10 ha.[97] As shown in Chapter 1, during the following years, United Fruit gained control over more land through direct purchases and mortgages against loans, and expanded its plantations. However, the company never produced

[93] United Fruit Company (Medical Department), *Thirteenth and Fourteenth Annual Reports* (Cambridge, Mass., 1924, 1925), 7 and 10 respectively. See also Wilson, *Empire in Green and Gold,* 189.

[94] *Eighteenth Annual Report,* 289, 361.

[95] Rippy, *The Capitalists and Colombia,* 181.

[96] This was acknowledged by a parliamentary report in 1935: *Informes que rindió a la honorable Cámara de Representantes la Comisión*, 13.

[97] Texas Petroleum Company, Land Department, Bogotá, 'Magdalena: Indice Notaría la. de Ciénaga', 1827-1941, MDC.

more than 50 per cent of Colombian bananas for export, and by 1937 about 80 per cent of banana exports were produced by local cultivators. Given their significance, both in numbers and in their involvement in the production stage of the industry, this group of banana cultivators has to be taken into account: their social and geographical origins, their relationship with the United Fruit Company, the level of profitability of their ventures, their behaviour as entrepreneurs, and their links with other sectors of Coastal economy and society.

For one thing, this group of banana growers was far from being a static one. Their numbers increased over the years: about 280 in 1908, 350 in 1927, 480 in 1837, 600 in the early 1940s. Throughout this period, some of them went out of business, while there were newcomers, although many of them, and their descendants, remained attached to the banana culture. Fifty-seven of the family names that were cultivating bananas in 1908 were absent from the group of prominent cultivators in 1927. By then more than 90 new family names had been added to the group classified by Diego Monsalve as *propietarios colombianos de bananeras* in Ciénaga and Santa Marta.[98] With the exception of a small number of foreign immigrants at the beginning of the century, the bulk of banana growers were Colombians. Most of them were natives of the Magdalena department, although they also came from Atlántico, Tolima, Santander, Antioquia, and Cundinamarca. Merchants from Barranquilla, such as Evaristo Obregón & Co. and Senior & Wolf, figured among the largest planters in 1908. The Bordas, from Bogotá, were neighbours of the banana farm Colombia, owned by a *Santandereano* of national prestige, General Benjamín Herrera.[99] Some of them, such as Obregón, Senior, and Herrera himself, were absentee investors and, in turn, some *Magdalenenses* decided to establish their residence in Barranquilla looking for urban comfort as they became better-off. However, most banana planters were permanently settled in Magdalena, either in Santa Marta or in the growing town of Ciénaga, or in the emergent populations of Aracataca, Ríofrío, and Fundación. What seems to have characterized the *zona bananera* was its high degree of mobility of both people and resources.

[98] D. Monsalve, *Colombia cafetera* (Barcelona, 1927), 738-742; and *Misión de Rafael Reyes*, 45-9.

[99] Notary records give evidence of *Barranquillero* involvement in the banana zone; Indice Notaría Primera de Ciénaga, 1912, and Indice Notaría Primera de Santa Marta, 1857–1905, MDC. Involvement by entrepreneurs from the Andean interior in bananas is illustrated in Luna Cárdenas, *Un año y otros días*.

Notwithstanding the constraints imposed by the dominant position of the American corporation in the industry, local cultivators benefited from United Fruit by having access to credit. The company provided growers with working capital, much needed when storms destroyed large proportion of plantations. Similarly planters had a guaranteed market for their crop. Although conditions varied over the period, and the purchasing price was often a source of friction,[100] the company paid out large sums in fruit purchases. Moreover, as Bulmer-Thomas has suggested for the case of Central American countries, since the price paid by United Fruit was a fixed price, this meant that cultivators at least avoided to some extent price instability, while the company carried the risks of market fluctuations. Average retail prices of bananas in the United States decreased steadily from 1920 to 1940.[101]

The point to be stressed here is that the spectacular growth of the banana trade after the turn of the century, led by United Fruit, led to the expansion of production by local cultivators. Profitable opportunities were opened up. Some banana planters spent their returns 'on the luxuries of life, without thinking about the morrow',[102] but many others kept strictly to business. In turn, income received by growers was paid out in wages, taxes, and consumption expenditures, or invested in further banana ventures, real estate, or other economic activities. Some of them invested in industry. Banana planters – Dávilas, De Miers, and Salzedos, among others – 'all of whom enjoy excellent reputation and standing', were the main shareholders of Cervecería del Magdalena, a brewery 'very well installed by German experts' in 1928.[103] The Salzedos, in addition, invested in river transport. A. Correa, a large banana planter, was also involved in commerce, cattle, and banking. The picture is far from complete, but the evidence does suggest that the traditional assumption that local banana planters, 'once they earned an extraordinary income, left the Magdalena' should be reconsidered. there were significant examples of efficient banana planters who diversified their profits into other sectors of the regional economy.

[100] The differences between cultivators and the Fruit Company regarding the important question of price is discussed in White, *Historia de una ignominia*, and LeGrand, 'El conflicto de las bananeras'. See also Ch. 1, s. 6 above.

[101] Bulmer-Thomas, *The Political Economy of Central America*, 15; and US Department of Commerce, *Statistical Abstract of the United States* (Washington, 1943), 381.

[102] Magdalena Governor to President Olaya, Santa Marta, 12 May 1931, AEOH, s. 3/76.

[103] Inspector's Inspection Letter, 18 July 1928, BOLSA/F4/3.

Bananas also meant employment. High wages attracted many migrants to Magdalena, not only from neighbouring Coastal departments but also from inland. The number of workers, and the conditions of employment in the United Fruit's own operations varied during the period, but there is little doubt that wages were higher there than in other regions and sectors of the economy.[104] The monetary impact of wages on the domestic economy has often been overlooked because United Fruit paid a proportion of them in scrip to be exchanged for goods in its own stores. Scrips, however, were often quickly monetized. As Rippy observed, 'a group of unscrupulous money-changers sprang up who . . . bought the scrip at a discount of 25 per cent just as they do in some southern cotton mill towns in the United States'.[105] On pay days, every other week, labourers congregated at the farms, where 'merchants arrived to sell clothes and rum'; in the evenings they were attracted by the temptations of night life in town: 'they visited the canteens, tried their luck with the lottery and cards, and went to the brothels owned by Italians, Syrians and creoles', while they were always threatened by thieves, ready to steal from them a few pesos.[106] Gambling, brothels, and thieves may not be healthy signs of development but they do indicate circulation of cash. Given the migrant origin of much labour in the banana zone, how many of them settled permanently in the area and how many were just temporarily employed?[107] From a different angle, what proportion of wages were remitted back home? Besides drinking and gambling, what else were wages spent on? How did inflation affect wages? These questions remain open, and they are not intended to suggest that living conditions in the banana zone were not generally deplorable. Together with the evidence previously offered, they do draw the attention to the existence of a larger monetary economy in the banana zone whose links with the domestic economy have been hitherto neglected.

Besides planters and labour, other sectors of the local and regional economy also benefited from the banana boom. Between 1900 and 1950, the department of Magdalena experienced one of the most

104 *Informes que rindió a la honorable Cámara*, 13-14, 33-4.

105 Rippy, *The Capitalists and Colombia*, 181.

106 Testimony by A. Rojas Rojano, in Arango, *Sobrevivientes de la bananeras*, 41-2.

107 Very little is known about internal seasonal migration; but according to a British report in 1924, the expansion of banana plantations by the American company 'gave rise to a considerable amount of employment of a temporary nature. This was supplied by workers from other departments, who have now returned'; Sullivan, *Report on the Commercial and Economic Situation in the Republic of Colombia*, 58.

dynamic population growth-rates in the country. This was mostly centred in the towns in the banana belt: Santa Marta, Ciénaga, Foundación, and Aracataca. A growing population encouraged the cultivation of other crops besides bananas: corn, manioc, rice, and sugar for domestic consumption were all locally produced by smallholders, some of them recently settled in the zone.[108] Large quantities of regional fish and beef were consumed in the banana zone. The cattle industry in Southern Magdalena was certainly encouraged by the growing demand for beef. Although they often resented the competition from the United Fruit Company's stores, which offered goods at subsidized prices, local traders also had a share in the benefits of a growing economy. Some of them, such as G. M. Daníes, an importer of groceries in Santa Marta, enjoyed an 'excellent reputation and standing'.[109] Services also followed: lawyers, physicians, drug stores, cinemas, and newspapers were all signs of development in the region. In addition, during the second decade of the century, a few factories were springing up in Santa Marta and Ciénaga: household furniture, bricks, beer, cigarettes, tiles, cement pipes, soap, and pasta were produced locally as internal demand was growing. Factories in Santa Marta were described as 'solidly built, without extravagance . . . the machinery . . . the best of its kind'.[110]

The economic growth motivated by the banana trade was not confined to Northern Magdalena. The link between the banana zone and the southern cattle regions of the department has already been noted. Seasonal labour migration probably meant that part of the wages earned in the banana zone was spent in other Colombian regions. Outside the banana zone, Barranquilla was the city that most benefited from the growing trade in the fruit. The link between the expansion of banana exports during the period and the growth of Barranquilla – which by the 1920s was not only the most important Colombian port but the third largest Colombian industrial centre, has been largely ignored by historians. Contemporaries, however, were well aware of a close economic relation: 'what most encouraged business activities in Barranquilla,' Sarasúa the travelling salesman

[108] Bell, *Colombia*, 187. LeGrand has emphasized the presence of an active peasantry involved in the production of foodstuffs besides bananas and plantains; 'Campesinos y asalariados en la zona bananera', 185.

[109] Santa Marta Manager to New York Office, 15 May 1928, BOLSA A21/2. For the activities of an important merchant house in Ciénaga, Agapito Clavería, see Sarasúa, *Recuerdos de Barranquilla*, 120–30.

[110] Inspection letter, Santa Marta, 15 Dec. 1926, BOLSA/F4/4.

recalled, 'was the daily movement of ships and barges to Ciénaga and neighbouring ports'.[111] There was certainly an active movement of goods and people in a 'well organized' daily river service covering the 100 miles of distance between Barranquilla and Ciénaga.[112] *Barranquillero* entrepreneurs, as already observed, had themselves a significant stake in the banana zone. Some of them invested in plantations. Some of their firms, such as the Banco Dugand and the Banco Comercial, had agencies in Santa Marta and Ciénaga. Businessmen from Santa Marta and Ciénaga also contracted loans from *Barranquillero* money-lenders, such as Elías M. Muvdi.[113] Wholesale traders in Barranquilla were suppliers of general merchandise in the banana zone. A significant proportion of the stocks in cotton print goods and dry goods, for example, were 'imported through Barranquilla by the large Syrian houses'.[114] Soap manufacturers in Santa Marta got part of their raw materials from Barranquilla. Manufactured goods from Barranquilla, such as Cerveza Aguila and those produced by La Industria, found a ready market in the banana zone.[115] In turn, foodstuffs produced in the banana zone reached the *Barranquillero* market.[116] As a newspaper pointed out in 1911, events in Magdalena were followed closely in the neighbouring department because 'many Barranquilleros had significant interests at stake in the banana zone'.[117]

7. Conclusions: The Impact of External Influences

At first sight, the general picture presented above appears to be a familiar one in the field of foreign influence on Latin America. From the last decades of the nineteenth century up to the 1930s, there was a significant influx of foreigners and foreign capital to the region, setting the pace of economic growth through the promotion of exports. Foreigners from different nationalities settled in Latin America and

111 Sarasúa, *Recuerdos de Barranquilla*, 22.

112 Sullivan, *Report on the Commercial and Economic Situation in the Republic of Colombia*, 58.

113 Santa Marta Manager to Barranquilla Branch, 4 Jan. 1932, BOLSA/A21/3.

114 Bell, *Colombia*, 187–90.

115 Santa Marta Manager to Barranquilla Branch, 11 July 1932, BOLSA/A21/3; Luna Cárdenas, *Un año y otros días*, 169; Sarasúa, *Recuerdos*, 24.

116 LeGrand, 'Campesinos y asalariados en la zona bananera', 185.

117 *Ferrocarril de Santa Marta: Escritos de la prensa del país* (Barranquilla, 1911), 28.

became involved in practically all aspects of economic life. After the First World War the predominantly European influence gave way to the American presence. Though it is difficult to trace an accurate picture, and the situation varied from country to country, their impact went beyond the economy, being felt at almost all levels of Latin American society.[118] At a closer look, some particular features emerge from the Colombian experience.

The first obvious difference was its scale: there was no mass foreign immigration, nor was the influx of foreign capital as significant as in many other Latin American countries. Yet compared to the national trend, the presence of foreigners and foreign capital in the Colombian Caribbean was relatively significant. Immigrants such as A. López-Penha – novelist, bookseller, and pharmacist – acknowledged that they found in the region a more open intellectual atmosphere than in the Andean interior.[119] Although foreigners settled throughout the Coast, their presence was more prominent in Barranquilla, whose commercial elite resembled what C. A. Jones has labelled a 'cosmopolitan bourgeoisie', to describe the merchant community of mixed nationalities which emerged in such major ports as Buenos Aires during the second half of the nineteenth century.[120] Traditionally, the impact of foreign immigration in Latin American has been analysed within the framework of the centre–periphery relationship, focusing attention on the European dominance during the nineteenth century and its later displacement by North American capital. The importance here of Syrian immigration – in terms of numbers and in its contribution to entrepreneurial activities – suggests the need to take sometimes a different approach to appreciate the real contribution of the outside world to Latin American economies and societies.

The extent to which foreign immigrants and companies managed to exercise power and control over the region also deserves more detailed consideration. This question is raised by Parrish's involvement in the development of Barranquilla as well as by the United Fruit Company in the banana industry. Parrish's control of Barranquilla's public utilities, following the appointment of S. Hollopeter as manager of Empresas

[118] Mörner, *Adventurers and Proletarians*, 35–85; N. Sánchez Albornoz, 'Population', in L. Bethell (ed.), *Latin America, Economy and Society, 1870-1930* (Cambridge, 1989), 88-101.

[119] R. I. Bacca, 'El modernismo en Barranquilla', *Boletín Cultural y Bibliográfico*, 30/33 (1944), 84.

[120] C. A. Jones, *International Business in the Nineteenth Century: The Rise and Fall of a Cosmopolitan Bourgeoisie* (Brighton, 1987), 66–93.

Públicas Municipales in 1925, might be pictured as the local government relinquishing its power in the face of American interests. However, Parrish's business did not follow the American flag. His joint ventures with nationals and his economic interests identified him intimately with the *Barranquillero* business community. There is little doubt that the deal with the American bank was regarded as of much benefit to urban development. The history of the Empresas Públicas Municipales was not devoid of political friction, as often happened with other public utilities under foreign control in Latin America.[121] Yet in contrast to the manager of the Barranquilla Railway in 1930, for whom there was little sympathy, Hollopeter was generally held in high esteem by public opinion both for his diplomatic abilities and for the Empresas Públicas's achievements. As a British report observed,

> the very first essential for any foreign company carrying on exploitation work in Colombia, and more especially in any enterprise of public utility, is that they must have the right type of manager who must, before everything else be a diplomatist. That he have the technical qualifications is a secondary matter . . . If the chief local representatives . . . have the tact – the knack of getting on the right side not only of the authorities but of the people among whom he is working, all will go smoothly, while if he has not got these essential qualities, no matter how able he is from a technical and business point of view, he and his enterprise will become unpopular and he will find spokes in his wheels at every turn.[122]

The United Fruit Company does not appear to have displayed the features of the diplomatist. The company was the focus of attention by early studies on American 'economic imperialism', where control, as in other types of imperial relations, rather than negotiation, is the key defining element.[123] According to Kepner and Soothill, this corporation not only had the power to throttle competitors and ruin planters but also

[121] See L. and C. Jones and R. Greenhill, 'Public Utility Companies', in Platt, *Business Imperialism*, 77-118.

[122] British Legation to Craigie, Bogotá, 19 Dec. 1930, PRO, FO135/429.

[123] The literature in this field is vast. For a review of the dependency debate, see C. Abel and C. Lewis, *Latin America, Economic Imperialism and the State* (London and Dover, 1985). For early studies in economic imperialism in relation to the United Fruit Company, see Rippy, *The Capitalists and Colombia* and Kepner and H. Soothill, *The Banana Empire*. A critique of anti-imperialist views about the United Fruit Company is in S. Lebergott, 'The Return to US Imperialism, 1890-1929', *Journal of Economic History* 60/2 (June 1980), 229–52. For a review of the different approaches of imperialism from a general perspective, see M. Doyle, *Empires* (Ithaca, NY, and London, 1986), 19–47. See also W. Mommsen and J. Osterhammel (eds.) *Imperialism and After* (London, 1986).

to 'dominate governments'.[124] Subsequent studies of the United Fruit Company in Colombia have echoed this view in a more radical fashion: here the company is sometimes portrayed as having established an almost absolute control over local and even national government. This interpretation often fails to take into account the circumstances under which the development of bananas took place. Similarly, it too readily assumes that all politicians were bribed and manipulated whenever convenient, and that policies towards the industry were imposed by the foreign company on a government which paid little attention to local demands. But above all it overlooks the limits that even powerful companies such as United Fruit faced in their dealings with Colombian politics.

From the outset, the involvement of United Fruit in this country took place against decidedly mixed feelings about the role of the United States in Latin America, a consequence of Theodore Roosevelt's intervention in the secession of Panamá from Colombia in 1903. Though the company was granted some facilities to operate at the beginning of the century, as a result of Reyes's general policy of encouraging exports, it faced the opposition of other influential national circles. In any case, circumstances changed at the end of the second decade of this century. Pressed by public opinion, the Colombian government showed some disposition to oppose United Fruit, but without disregarding the economic interests that were already at stake in the region. Since the Colombian economy did not rely at all exclusively on the exports of bananas, the national government was in a better position to deal with the American corporation than its counterparts in Central America.

In the 1920s, the government decided to nationalize the Santa Marta railway, which involved a long suit in the Colombian courts. In 1924, the President was said to be 'exerting pressure on the Supreme Court . . . in order to influence a decision in favour of the government' in the case of the railway.[125] In 1929, the national government rejected a petition from the American company to import 10,000 labourers from the West Indies.[126] Relations between the central government and United Fruit seriously deteriorated in the 1930s, particularly during the first López Pumarejo administration (1934–8), which favoured the

[124] Kepner and Soothill, *The Banana Empire*, 336.

[125] Norton, Rose & Co. to Under-Secretary of State, London, Jan. 1924, FO371/9592.

[126] Torres Giraldo, *Los inconformes,* iv. 115.

unions during labour conflicts and pursued a more active policy of state intervention in the banana industry.[127]

The prevailing mood in the Coast towards foreign capital may have been slightly different, conditioned by a higher degree of openness towards the outside world. Early anti-American feelings were counterbalanced by the sudden growth of the banana trade, and its effects on the regional economy. In addition, local politicians were probably more prone to be influenced by the American corporation, either because they themselves had a stake in the industry, or through bribery. Nevertheless, local hostility towards United Fruit also developed. The Magdalena governor during Concha's administration (1914–18), showed his dislike for the American company. Prestigious local politicians, such as Manuel Dávila Flórez and Pedro Juan Navarro, publicly campaigned against United Fruit. Accusations of corruption, of conflicts of interest, involving governors and deputies in Magdalena, were commonplace. Even attacks against the company by politicians and local officials were often seen as pressure to force United Fruit to accept a deal of one sort or another.[128]

The bribed, however, easily turned against the company when circumstances changed. Furthermore, occasional bribery of officials and politicians could hardly have had a longstanding effect, with recurrent changes in government and successive elections. Public opinion counted. And a hostile press, both local and national, including 'anonymous hand bills' whose language 'not infrequently borders on licence', fostered suspicion and emnity towards United Fruit. Judges were influenced by this atmosphere: 'It is impossible not to realize the odium to which the judge would be exposed as the result of a decision in favour of the foreign company'.[129]

Other sectors of Colombian society were also ill-disposed towards United Fruit. Merchants, both from the zone and from Barranquilla, resented competition from company stores. Local growers often saw their position hampered by United Fruit's control of the market. Labour dissatisfaction was encouraged by the company's reluctance to enlarge its payroll instead of relying on arrangements on a piecework basis. Labour demands were mixed with those of a growing influx of

[127] A. Tirado Mejía, *Aspectos políticos del primer gobierno de Alfonso López Pumarejo, 1934–38* (Bogotá, 1981), 223-5, 278-87.

[128] Valdeblánquez to Ospina, Santa Marta, 19 June 1923; Royero to Ospina, Santa Marta, 11 June 1923, AGPNO, in-correspondence, 1923.

[129] British Legation to Foreign Office, Bogotá, 25 Mar. 1924, PRO, FO.371/9592.

immigrants and squatters who settled on both state and United Fruit land. A combination of the above elements together with the undiplomatic behaviour of United Fruit and political agitation in the region at times produced acute social unrest and serious strikes against the company.[130]

In the long term, however, hostility was generally counterbalanced by an accommodation of interests. There were times of prosperity, such as the first two decades of this century, and times of crisis. By abandoning the enclave model it would be possible to appreciate with more accuracy the effect the banana trade had on the regional economy. This impact has hitherto been simplified. Similarly, analyses of United Fruit in Colombia based too exclusively on simple theories of economic imperialism have failed to appreciate any of the complexities in the relationship that existed between the company and the politics of the country. The tradition is not a new one. As a British report pointed out in 1930, 'the local authorities and politicians, notwithstanding the immense public benefits derived from the enterprise of the United Fruit Co. and its subsidiaries, appear to regard them as a public enemy, and seldom lose an opportunity of making their position difficult'.[131]

130 See Ch. 1, s. 6 above.

131 'Colombia, Annual report', Bogotá, 16 Jan. 1930, PRO, FO14221/1930.

6
Politics, the Region, and the State

1. Introduction

Addressing the *Consejo de Delegados* which gathered in Bogotá in 1885 to reform the Colombian constitution, President Rafael Núñez made a famous appeal: 'that enervating sectionalism must be replaced by a vigorous universality'.[1] Núñez, a *Cartagenero* who had once claimed that Colombia was not a single nationality but a group of nationalities, who had unsuccessfully campaigned for the Presidency on a *Costeño* regionalist ticket in 1875, became the main force behind the centralization of the Colombian state. His experience in power – as President of Bolívar, Minister and President of the Union – led him to his final belief in the need for strengthening the national government to reverse what he saw as a fatal trend from 'unity' to 'fragmentation'.[2] The subsequent centralizing reforms introduced by Núñez, embodied in the 1886 constitution, were a turning–point in the history of Colombian politics. They did not prevent further internal conflict. Political turmoil at the turn of the century, three years of civil war, resulted in the secession of Panamá. But the outcome of the War of Thousand Days, which favoured the ruling Conservative party, inaugurated a new period of political stability. Although there were incidents when voices on the Coast called for secession during the first decades of this century, they did not constitute any serious threat to the national state. Nevertheless, the process of national consolidation was always faced with regional opposition and criticism, and went forward amidst enormous difficulties.

By looking at the relationship between the Coast and the central state, and at the ways local politics fitted into the national picture, this chapter aims to identify the extent to which the region showed distinct political behaviour. Three major questions guide the analysis: how did the Coast react to the centralizing tendencies of the Colombian state, particularly after 1886?; did *Costeño* regionalism pose any real threat to national unity?; what was the nature of *Costeño* politics? The

1 R. Núñez, *La reforma política* (Bogotá, 1945), ii. 432.
2 Ibid. 436.

chapter opens with a section that explores the problems of local government– and how these conditioned its increasing though limited dependence on the central state. The second section analyses the degree of control that the national executive exercised over local politics, and the circumstances under which that control could be effective. This is followed by two brief sections that further illustrate the difficulties in consolidating the national state on the Coast: the avoidance of conscription and the widespread presence of contraband. The fifth section looks at some of the regionalist movements that emerged during the period – their objectives and their general impact on the relationship between the region and the central state. The final section shows how the partisan struggle integrated the Coast into national politics, although the region developed a politically distinct behaviour and power remained fragmented overall.

2. The Tasks and Problems of Local Government

In 1888 the Prefect of Barranquilla made an official tour of the province. At Campo de la Cruz he 'miraculously' met the *Alcalde* – the rest of the district's employees were involved at the time in their own agricultural activities, so he could hardly review fully the affairs of the town. His final assessment left few doubts: public administration in Campo de la Cruz was neglected, due to 'unsuitable personnel'. Although the Prefect did not regard the situation in Galapa to be as serious, he thought that, as in Campo de la Cruz, a school should be established, otherwise these towns would be left at the mercy of 'an ignorant people'. The account of his official visit is a vivid description of the poverty of government throughout the province. Few of the towns he visited owned the buildings where public functions were carried out; the district schools were without books, maps, and blackboards; salaries for public employees were miserable. Under these circumstances, the government was often powerless: Ponedera and Tubará, despite being tiny villages, were 'ungovernable'; their inhabitants displayed a complete lack of regard for the authorities.[3]

Two basic problems, among many lesser ones, were faced by those who governed: the recruitment of personnel and the establishment of state authority. The organization of a bureaucracy, particularly outside

[3] *Memoria del Secretario de Gobierno* (Cartagena, 1888), CXX, CXXII, CXXIV, and CXXVI; 'Relación de la visita del Alcalde', 2 Dec. 1888, AGB.

the provincial capitals, was hindered notably by the poverty of the state but also by a reluctance to accept public duties. Top officials were often concerned about their isolation, and public posts 'were regarded with horror by suitable people (*personas idóneas*). To convince anyone to take on any public post, one has to resort to ties of friendship; the eventual acceptance is regarded as a great sacrifice'.[4] According to the Prefect of Corozal in 1888, very few people were willing to accept the responsibility of the post of *Alcalde*, judge, or municipal treasurer. The difficulties were more acute in the smaller towns where the number of suitable candidates was limited, and any eventual selection was constrained by the intense personal rivalries present in parochial life. Since government officials were badly paid, and consequently difficult to recruit among the better-off, the relationship between rulers and collaborators was often based on personal ties which, in turn, conditioned the nature of government. According to the Prefect in Lorica, he had no choice but to be lenient with regard to the way his agents carried out their duties.[5] In addition, those who governed could not count on the support of an efficient police force to support their authority. Given the problems of public order, more often than not the task of government was accompanied by a feeling of impotence. After popular uprisings against land enclosures in Arjona in 1884, the *Alcalde*'s response was to resign: 'the situation here is too fragile as the authorities do not enjoy the prestige they had in the past; people have no respect for officialdom or the law. What is required is an iron hand that I do not possess.'[6]

The organization of a bureaucracy and the establishment of state authority had to overcome further obstacles such as those posed by partisan rivalries, corruption, and elections. The problems of public administration in Bolívar were vividly described by the Secretario de Gobierno in 1936:

> It would be pointless to pretend that there does not exist a morbid atmosphere surrounding the administration: the City council against the *Alcalde*, because he wants to have a free hand in appointing the members of his cabinet; the *Alcalde* against the Treasurer because the latter refuses to pay his salary; a judge removed from his post with no regard for his constitutional rights . . . shameless cases of entrenched nepotism.[7]

[4] *GB*, 23 June 1873.

[5] *Memoria del Secretario de Gobierno,* CXX.

[6] *Primer Suplente de la Alcaldía* to the Governor, Arjona, 24 Apr. 1884, AGB.

[7] *Memoria del Secretario de Gobierno* (Cartagena, 1936), IV.

In the midst of this 'morbid atmosphere', some officials resigned in despair. 'I am tired of so much intrigue, of those vociferous press campaigns, full of lies', said R. de Armas, explaining the difficulties of government in Magdalena to President Concha as he begged to be replaced.[8]

At the heart of these problems lay the question of public finances. 'The government is not strong,' E. Baena pointed out in taking the oath as President of the Estado Soberano de Bolívar in 1873, 'not because the institutions are weak but because the state lacks the resources to meet even the most basic necessities.'[9] The fiscal problems of nineteenth-century Colombia identified by Malcolm Deas were even more prominent when looked at from the departmental and municipal perspective and, generally, they remained a serious constraint to state action throughout the period under study.[10] Most of the *municipios* faced acute fiscal penury. The finances of the *departamentos* could hardly support public administration in the *municipios* and the several smaller entities spread across the region. If *municipios* tended to depend financially on *departamentos*, these, in turn had to rely on the national budget.

Weak finances do not make for strong governments and those who governed were well aware of their debility. 'A poor government like ours, which cannot pay for an Army to support it, has to rely on public opinion': the Magdalena President's statement was not only a recognition of evident poverty but also a warning against further taxation.[11] Despite their weaknesses, it would be wrong to underestimate the political sensitivity of the tax systems, both in *municipios* and *departamentos*. Their analysis could reveal, besides the poverty of the regional economy, the intensity of the struggle to control the few resources of the state. As Table 6.1 illustrates, two basic *rentas* – the tax on *aguardiente* (sugar-based alcohol) and the *consumo de ganado mayor* (slaughter duty) – remained the most important revenues throughout the period; three others – income tax, tobacco duty, and *salinas* (salt monopoly) – gained or lost importance according to changing circumstances; the rest, besides the ubiquitous

[8] Magdalena Governor to Concha, Santa Marta, 10 Mar. 1917, AJVC.

[9] *GB*, 26 Oct. 1873.

[10] Deas, 'Los problemas fiscales en Colombia durante el siglo XIX', in his *Del poder y la gramática* (Bogotá, 1993), 61–120.

[11] M. A. Vengochea, *Mensaje (del) Presidente del Estado S. del Magdalena* (Santa Marta, 1869).

auxilios (subsidies) from the national budget, were a collection of minor revenues.

Attempts to establish a direct form of taxation were pursued by the Bolívar government during the 1870s. In the face of growing hostility, the tax had been abandoned by 1883 and it was not reintroduced until 1918, this time as a national levy by the central government.[12] The most prominent taxes were those on consumption: alcohol, beef, tobacco, salt, among others. Since cattle production was the major economic activity of the region, it was one of the main sources of public revenue. Taxing livestock producers would have been physically impossible and resorting to a slaughter tax was the easiest way to collect the levy. Nevertheless there were still ways to avoid its payment. In 1873, the Governor of Mompós observed how from the neighbouring state of Magdalena salted beef was smuggled into Bolívar.[13] Furthermore, as in many other cases in nineteenth-century Colombia, the cost of collecting the tax was a heavy burden and the government often thought that it was a better deal to auction it. Problems varied according to the different nature of the various *rentas*, but they all tested the power of the state to impose an efficient system. The *renta del tabaco*, established as a departmental levy in 1909, soon developed into a state monopoly resembling its colonial precursor. Despite the original intention of taxing just the consumption of tobacco, the authorities became involved in controlling practically all stages of the market. It was an undertaking whose success required an extensive policing operation for which the *departamentos* had not the means. The results could have been predicted: discouragement of production, smuggling, corruption. The salt monopoly posed problems related to conflicts between the region and the central government. A common difficulty in all taxes was the organization of their collection: recurrent changes from direct administration to tax-farming through public auctions, *remates*, also revealed political issues at stake. The case of the *renta de licores* in Atlántico serves to illustrate this point.

In 1914 Abel Carbonell, then Director of Public Education in Atlántico, denounced the *renta de licores* to President Concha, declaring that it had become a source of excessive political power

12 Protests against income tax are well documented in AGB, 1874.

13 *GB*, 23 June 1873.

TABLE 6.1 *Income of the State/Department of Bolívar, 1871–1916 (Colombian pesos)*

Sources	1871	1877	1886	1898/9	1917
License to produce local alcohol	15,882	12,000	57,718	580,000	273,028
Income tax	39,025	100,000			
Slaughtering tax	47,574	90,000	80,158	276,000	160,135
Register	3,123	6,000	5,288	9,600	12,222
Flour consumption tax	8,967	10,000	83,709		
Postage	991	1,600	1,483	1,600	
Saltworks compensation		20,000		96,000	39,400
Dique toll	247	300	140		
Railway grants		6,000	6,000	12,000	
Additional 10%		18,000	12,630		
Departmental assets		2,000	1,180	1,000	
Lazar house grant		2,400		3,000	2,952
Real estate				45,000	
Inheritance tax		800		4,000	
Official publications	121	800	45	200	
Hospital grants				6,000	
Stamped paper	63	9,000	11,082		
Electricty				24,000	
Other grants					14,200
Tobacco					68,037

Sources: *GB*, 22 Oct. 1871, *DB*, 29 Nov. 1876; *Infome del Secretario de Hacienda de la Gobernación del Departamento de Bolívar* (Cartagena, 1988), 121; *Registro de Bolívar*, 29 Dec. 1898; *Mensaje e informes del Gobernador del Departamento de Bolívar* (Cartagena, 1917), 63.

in the Department.[14] J. F. Insignares, a leading member of the Conservative party, was manipulating the local Conservative Directory to influence the selection of *Diputados* to the *Asamblea*, so that a friendly majority in this body could provide a favourable deal for the *renta de licores* under his control. The power of this *renta* was omnipotent, influencing even the judiciary. In September 1915 Carbonell was appointed Atlántico Governor and launched a campaign against the *renta*. His efforts were fruitless. In January 1917 he recognized that the *renta* had a larger and better-paid workforce than

[14] A. Carbonell to Concha, P. Carbonell to Concha, and Rozo to Concha, Barranquilla, 10, 17 and 23 Dec. 1914, in AJVC, Boxes 1 and 13.

the government.[15] His strongest attack was probably contained in his 1918 message to the *Asamblea*, where he opposed the auctioning of the *rentas* as a practice of government. He also showed concern for the need to repress rather than to encourage the consumption of alcohol. Carbonell was entirely opposed to the *renta de licores*, its power in the electoral process, its depressing influence on sugar-cane production in the Department, and its corrupting elements. His conclusion was definite: the *Empresa de Licores* was an ever expanding power, threatening the very existence of government.[16] Carbonell's attempt to regain state control over the *renta* were a failure, and Insignares's power was enhanced when, after the 1918 Presidential elections, he replaced Carbonell as Governor of Atlántico, although he only remained in the post for two months. The *Asamblea* was still an Insignares stronghold. In 1923 the *renta* tried to extend its power to neighbouring Magdalena to the concern of that department's Governor. Pressure mounted to persuade President Ospina to intervene against the *renta*.[17] In April 1927 the *departamento* reassumed direct administration of the *renta de licores*.[18]

Similar problems to those raised by the *renta de licores* could be traced in analysing the different ways the state attempted to secure revenues. What emerges, overall, is the palpable weakness of the state at the level of *departamentos* and *municipios*, the latter's general lack of financial autonomy combined with intense political rivalries and instability. Significant improvements were sometimes achieved, and the *departamentos* together with a few *municipios* managed gradually to develop other sources of revenue. In 1937 the Atlántico Governor praised the recent achievements of the administration: income was on the increase and was more efficiently managed.[19] The gains were, however, modest: a few miles of new roads; the construction of buildings for local administration and schools, which had hitherto used rented properties; proper uniforms for the Police. Needs were pressing and local governments had to cope directly with problems of health, crime, housing, and unemployment. But local revenues could not cope with the growing demands on public expenditure.

[15] A. Carbonell to Concha, Barranquilla, 28 Jan. 1917, AJVC, Box 1.

[16] A. Carbonell, *Mensaje que el Gobernador del Atlántico presenta a la Asamblea* (Barranquilla, 1918), 6–13, 14–15.

[17] Magdalena Governor to Ospina, Santa Marta, 14 Aug. 1923, AGPNO.

[18] E. González, *Mensaje del Gobernador del Atlántico* (Barranquilla, 1928), 14–15.

[19] R. Blanco de la Rosa, *Mensaje del Gobernador* (Barranquilla, 1938), 14.

While *departamentos* struggled to survive with budgets that tended to remain stationary, a growing gap was developing between the revenues of those *municipios* with an industrial or commercial base whose populations were increasing, and those in the rural areas whose agrarian economy resisted taxation.[20] This was particularly the case for Barranquilla and Cartagena, and to a lesser extent for Santa Marta, although some improvements were achieved in towns such as Ciénaga and Montería. During the second decade of this century, Barranquilla's revenues had been growing steadily although at a modest rate.[21] By the mid-1920s, the fiscal condition of the municipality had improved significantly. In 1924, the City Council introduced some technical innovations to the structure of the budget with the aim of catching up with new developments. By then, local taxes were contributing 21.5 per cent of Barranquilla's revenues. A major proportion of the *municipio's* income came from the proceeds of municipal assets – basically the public market, the slaughterhouse, and the returns of a few investments in service companies. Despite the improvements, the commission set up by the Council to study the budget considered that revenues were still low in relation to Barranquilla's industrial and commercial activities.[22]

Nevertheless, it was the sound fiscal situation of the municipality that, in 1925, allowed Barranquilla to contract a loan of $5,000,000 with the Central Trust Company of Illinois, to be invested in a modern aqueduct, a sewage system, street paving, and the extension of the market place. Subsequently, public services experienced significant improvement. According to a 1931 British report, Barranquilla was 'perhaps the only town in Colombia . . . which serves as an example of competent administration'.[23] Conflicts between the Empresas Públicas Municipales – the company in charge of the utilities – and the City

[20] For a general illustration on this point, see G. Ardant, 'Financial Policy and Economic Infrastructure of Modern States and Nations', in C. Tilly, (ed.), *The Formation of National States in Western Europe* (Princeton, 1975), 166, 174, 180–1, 193–6.

[21] *Informe que rinde la Comisión de Presupuesto al Concejo Municipal* (Barranquilla, 1924), 34; Rash-Isla (ed.), *Directorio Comercial Pro-Barranquilla*, 175; *BME*, Barranquilla, 67 (31 Oct. 1938), 5.

[22] *Informe que rinde la Comisión*, 7–10, 19.

[23] Explanatory Comments on the Presidential Message to Congress of July 1931', in PRO, FO.371/1931. When in 1931 the Colombian government prohibited remittances of dollars for repayment of external debts, Barranquilla deposited in Colombian currency the loan service in the official depository banks in Barranquilla to the order of the US trustee bank, and continued to do so until the ban was lifted in 1939; Parrish Jr. to Schwarzenbach, Lowell, Mass., 10 Sept. 1948, APF.

Council, whose members constantly pressed for the reduction of rates and higher levels of public expenditure, were recurrent, particularly during times of economic crisis. The Depression severely hit the economy of the city and during the following decades Barranquilla's finances could hardly cope with the new demands of a growing population. By 1936, the aqueduct was already working to its maximum capacity. In 1948, when a City Commission appealed in vain to the US bond market for a similar loan to that of 1925, the picture was a desperate one: the water supply system was insufficient for the needs of the population; only 10 per cent of Barranquilla had proper sewerage, and only 20 per cent of its streets were paved; the public market and the slaughter house were both in appalling condition.[24] However limited the achievements were, there is little doubt that the gap between Barranquilla's public finances and those of the rest of Coastal towns – with the exceptions mentioned above – was very wide.[25]

In a situation of general penury, *municipios* and state/*departamentos* alike depended on the national budget. During the federalist period, 1863–85, this lack of financial autonomy contradicted the basic principles of the political system. As the *Secretario de Hacienda de la Unión* observed in 1884, 'if [the states] continue to resort to the Federal Treasury to satisfy their local necessities – to found or support a hospital, to build an aqueduct, to open a new road . . . to increase ninefold central government expenditure . . . then the federation loses its rationale'.[26]

The abandonment of federalism two years later was far from an immediate remedy. In 1897, the Minister of Hacienda complained that 'no Senator or Representative believes that he has fulfilled his duties until he obtains from the national Treasury some financial contribution for the department or province that elected him'.[27] Members of Congress jealously preserved their right not only to oversee how public money was spent, but above all to intervene in the decisions about where the money should go. In 1912 the Minister of Hacienda made an unsuccessful appeal to congressmen to curtail their demands in order to

24 See Empresas Públicas Municipales, *Informe de la Junta Administradora* (Barranquilla, 1936); *La Prensa*, 2 May 1940; K. C. Parrish Jr., S. Hollopeter, and J. Gerlein to W. Bauer, Harwichport, Cape Cod, 17 Aug. 1948, APF.

25 See Contraloría, *Geografía Económica del Atlántico*, 237.

26 *Memoria del Secretario de Hacienda* (Bogotá, 1884), 148.

27 *Informe presentado al Congreso de la República en sus sesiones ordinarias de 1898 por el Ministro de Hacienda* (Bogotá, 1898), XIV.

rationalize public expenditure.[28] It was a vain effort. Conditioned by the weakness of their *departamento* and *municipio* finances, power over the national budget was a resort of major political importance which congressmen were not prepared to relinquish. Gradually, the executive managed to strengthen its position, but in 1949 the central government was still trying to implement reforms that would avoid 'that pitiful sight, which we have witnessed so many times, where the funds from the Treasury have been dispersed, fragmented into a thousand little budgets without any results for the country'.[29] Thus financial dependence on the central state did not necessarily mean political dependence – congressmen, regionally rooted, could not be ignored by the national executive. Even after the political centralization of 1886, local politics were far from being easily controlled from the centre.

3. The Pitfalls of Political Centralization

Political centralization was a major goal of the 1886 constitutional reforms. Appointed by the President, governors were placed at the head of each *departamento*. *Alcaldes* in command of each *municipio* were, in turn, appointed by these governors. In theory, presidents and governors alike had the right to appoint and replace their dependants at will. In practice, however, they could not ignore the political considerations which governed their relations with the elected bodies, the national *Senado* and *Cámara*, the departmental *asambleas* and the municipal *concejo*s. Moreover, the governors and their *alcaldes* had to share administrative functions with the *asambleas* and *concejos*; their power was conditioned by their relations with those involved in the electoral process. As heads of the *departamentos*, governors were expected to implement presidential policies, guarantee public order, preserve the balance of power, and keep the national government informed about regional affairs. Presidents never had absolute control over *departamentos*' s affairs. But with care they did manage to exercise influence, at times successfully, although often against a background of intense political conflict.

President Suárez's correspondence shows his concern about departmental matters and a degree of interference. It also shows that

[28] *Informe del Ministro de Hacienda* (Bogotá, 1912), XIV.

[29] *Memoria de Hacienda* (Bogotá, 1951), 75.

governing was a delicate business. Suárez was fastidious in his observations about the distribution of posts, as can be observed by the instructions he sent to the Atlántico Governor in 1918:

> It is not appropriate that the Governor be linked to any of the two Conservative wings . . .; 3) It is very appropriate that the Secretary be a Liberal, this being the political affiliation of the vast majority of the population in Barranquilla . . . 4) It is appropriate that the appointments do not go to passionate politicians; 5) Given the current state of affairs it is not appropriate to introduce any substantial changes [in the cabinet]; 6) when the situation permits, it would be appropriate to replace Pumarejo and Carbonell with more moderate elements from their respective circles.[30]

In this particular case, Suárez was trying to dissuade the Governor from resigning, while he made clear the central government's position in relation to the various factions that were competing for power in Atlántico. His instructions to the Governor included advice on how to govern amid conflicting interests:

> I beg you again to keep calm and cultivate friendly relations with all parties, without any appearing a favorite . . . Given the great esteem in which I hold you, and my own obligation to ensure that peace reigns in the department, I hope that you will be able to display those qualities of prudence and sacrifice that are crucial in situations like this. I imagine myself being Saint Sebastian, tied to the oak tree and receiving a hail of arrows.[31]

If Suárez's instructions to the Atlántico Governor had on this occasion a compromising tone, he sometimes issued peremptory orders as in 1918, when he asked the Governor of Magdalena to replace with 'friends' the *alcaldes* in Ciénaga and Aracataca, or in July 1919 when he disapproved of the appointment of the *prefecto* in Ríohacha.[32]

Conditions obviously changed according to the different political circumstances surrounding presidents and governors, their respective personalities, and the nature of their relationship. Presidents could exercise some degree of control over governors and, through them, over the *departamentos*. Governors often consulted presidents about the suitability of candidates for *alcaldías*. If governors did not abide by their instructions, they could be and were replaced.[33] However,

30 Suárez to Atlántico Governor, Bogotá, 16 Nov. 1918, Copiador, Libro Segundo, AMFS. 31 Ibid.

32 Suárez to Magdalena Governor, Bogotá, 2 and 24 Dec. 1918, 15 Oct. 1919, AMFS.

33 See e. g. Restrepo to Teran, Bogotá, 21 Jan. 1911, ACER, Correspondence, Jan.–Apr. 1911.

presidents could not ignore regional politics when appointing governors.

Moreover, once appointed, the main concerns of governors were related rather to local politics where their relations with the *asambleas* were of the first importance. As quasi-administrative bodies, the *asambleas* shared with governors the handling of a *departamento*'s affairs: they intervened, for example, in the organization of the bureaucracy, and they had the power to decide over public expenditure. As elected bodies, they enjoyed an autonomy which was denied to governors, though their power and room for manoeuvre was limited by frequently fragile political alliances. Since *asambleas* were major instruments of electoral power, their role in regional politics was of considerable significance. To govern without the *asamblea's* support could be an impracticable task. The example of the *renta de licores* offered above, illustrated how the *asamblea* in Atlántico had more power than the governor to decide on departmental fiscal policies. Attempts by the governor to curtail the *asamblea's* might were met with measures against his administration.[34] Carbonell singled out his main opponent, the dominant force behind the *asamblea's* decisions: 'Dr. Insignares . . . is here another governor, but stronger and unaccountable.'[35] Similar problems to those confronting Carbonell were faced by other governors throughout the period.[36] Against the hostility from *asambleas*, governors might resort to the judiciary, and they also looked for the support of public opinion.

The central government followed such conflicts closely. To some extent they determined presidential decisions. Occasionally, the combination of both a regional political base and support from the President coincided in the appointment of a governor who could exercise an unusual degree of power. Eparquio González started his political career during the nineteenth-century civil wars, in which he achieved the rank of general. By 1909, when he was appointed the local *Administrador de la Hacienda Nacional*, González was climbing up the political ladder under the shadow of J. F. Insignares. In 1914, he was appointed *Alcalde* of Barranquilla and, in 1919, *Secretario General* of the department. His power was strengthened when he was elected President of the Atlántico *Asamblea*. In 1921 González was

[34] Carbonell to Concha, Barranquilla, 5 May 1916, AJVC, Box 1.

[35] Carbonell to Concha, Barranquilla, 5 May 1916, Ibid.

[36] Magdalena Governor to Olaya, Santa Marta, 4 July 1933, AEOH, s. 5, 21, *Gobernaciones*: Magdalena/Santander Norte.

handling the *Consejo Electoral* from which position he engineered his election to the Senate. After the 1922 elections when General Ospina became President, González organized a successful campaign to press for his own appointment as Atlántico Governor. González exercised an exceptional degree of personal power: besides counting on presidential support, he controlled the *asamblea* and the electoral machinery. He was later reappointed by the next president, and his administration lasted for six years (1922–28).[37]

This was, however, an exceptional case. Instability was the rule. Between 1908 and 1922, and 1928 and 1940, Atlántico experienced twenty-one changes in the governorship. Sixty different heads of government ruled Bolívar during ninety different administrations between 1870 and 1950. The turnover in Magdalena was even higher: during the same period, there were seventy-nine different heads of government during 106 different administrations (see Appendix 2). Changes of *alcaldes*, *secretarios*, and low-ranking civil servants were probably even more frequent. Even the largest towns such as Barranquilla did not escape instability: between 1890 and 1940, Barranquilla had fifty-five different *alcaldes* in seventy-nine different administrations. With the exception of the periods 1895–99 and 1923–28, on average *alcaldes* in Barranquilla barely stayed in power for more than a year.

So far, this chapter has dealt with the state at the regional level in trying to appreciate its dimensions as well as the problems it faced. It is true that *departamentos* and *municipios* – which for the purpose of this analysis have been identified as the two levels of the nation-state in the region – had been incorporated in a centralized organization after 1886. However, this process of national integration was hampered by the degree of power which still resided in Congress, in the *asambleas* and *concejos*, which implied an effective political decentralization. Thus, if, on the one hand, the weak *departamentos* and *municipios* seemed to demand a stronger role of central government in regional life, on the other hand, the nature of political power in the region limited the central government's autonomy of action. Under these contradictory conditions, the result was a generally weak state:

[37] See Sánchez to Ospina and García to Ospina, Barranquilla, 8 Aug. 1922, in AGPNO. During his long administration, González was recurrently accused of arbitrary acts and abusing his power for his own interests. See Dávila, Escorcia and Padilla to Ospina, Barranquilla, 5 May 1923, Sept. 1923, and Sabanalarga 26 June 1923, respectively, in AGPNO, correspondence, 1923; *La Nación*, 3 Mar. 1923.

departamentos and *municipios* were constrained by poor finances, dependence on the central government, and fragmented political power; but the control exercised by the central government over these administrative jurisdictions was, in turn, limited by pervasive regional politics. A further demonstration of the weakness of the nation-state on the Coast can be found in the general avoidance of conscription, and in the scale of contraband trade throughout the region, a discussion of which follows.

4. Resistance to the Nation-State: The Avoidance of Conscription

Travelling in the San Jorge region, Striffler observed how the inhabitants 'go to a lot of trouble to allow the obstacles to better communication to remain as they are. There is an eternal panic among these people over conscription, and men live startled like real savages.'[38] *Costeños* were probably no more eager to avoid the Army than the majority of Colombians, and ways of recruiting people in the nineteenth century, and resistance to being recruited, perhaps did not differ much from the practices followed elsewhere in the country.[39] However, as the Minister of War pointed out in 1911, 'while some regions such as Antioquia, Caldas, Cundimarca, Santander, supply their respective volunteer contingents, some others, like the Atlantic Coast, do not supply a single solider'.[40] After the reorganization of the National Army in 1886, and later attempts to modernize it, the Coast always proved to be one of the most difficult regions to enforce conscription, and military service was effectively avoided by a large proportion of the population. In 1917, remarking on 'the sparsity of military spirit', Governor Carbonell explained to President Concha: 'It is very difficult here to get people willing to go to the battlefield to defend their own party, and impossible to get them to fight the opposition; so Coastal garrisons are permanently recruited from the interior'.[41] The reverse was rarely the case. Sometimes, even with

[38] Striffler, *El Río San Jorge*, 85.

[39] Some towns from the interior, however, were proud of their contribution to the Army. See M. Deas, 'La presencia de politica nacional en la vida provinciana', 157. For the lack of collaboration of *Costeños* to partisan armies during the 19th-century civil wars, see J. H. Palacio, *La guerra de 85* (Bogotá, 1936), 202, 204, 205.

[40] *Informes del Ministro de Guerra al Congreso* (Bogotá, 1911), XLI. See also General Sicard Briceño, *Goegrafía Militar de Colombia* (Bogotá, 1922), 68, 69.

[41] Carbonell to Concha, Barranquilla, 26 May 1917, AJVC, Box 1.

reinforcements from the interior, the barracks were undermanned. Presidential envoys, specially sent to inspect the barracks, were alarmed by the failure of recruitment. Even powerful Governors such as General González had to admit their inability to enforce military service.[42]

Recruitment was difficult in a sparsely populated region with poor communications. In rural areas, characterized by a relatively independent existence, there was a long tradition of resistance to authority. In urban centres, professional mediators provided means of avoiding conscription.[43] The small size of the Colombian Army determined a selective process and *Costeños*, given their proven hostility to the service, did not make suitable candidates.[44] Could the avoidance of conscription be interpreted as resistance to the nation-state? In other words, did it have any political meaning? Since both regional and national authorities faced similar difficulties in recruitment, was resistance attached to political partisanship? During the so-called *Hegemonía Conservadora*, the government did show concern about Liberal sympathies among the Coastal population, but this only encouraged further selective recruiting. Moreover, Coastal Liberals were no less reluctant to join a Liberal army than a Conservative one. Although there were some towns with an active history of participation in civil wars, these were exceptions. Avoidance of conscription was thus more related to traditional ways of life and values rather than politics. However, the idea – shared, among others, by T. Rueda Vargas – that the army would help to consolidate national integration was hampered on the Coast by the effective resistance to military service.[45]

[42] Vengochea to Ospina, 25 Apr. 1923, AGPNO; *Acción Costeña*, 52; and Urdaneta to Ospina, Santa Marta, 8 Feb. 1924, AGPNO.

[43] *La Nación*, 29 July 1916.

[44] In 1924 the Army had a force of 6,000 men: 'The physique of the troops is on the whole good, the smallness of the annual contingent of recruits making it easy to select the best', in 'Colombia. Annual report, 1924', Bogotá, 20 Jan. 1925, PRO, FO371/10616.

[45] T. Rueda Vargas, *El Ejército Nacional* (Bogotá, 1944), 148. For perceptive though brief observations on the nationalizing effects of Armies in Europe, see Harvie, *The Rise of Regional Europe*, 24–7.

5. Resistance to the Nation-State: Contraband

Smuggling as an activity with significant impact on the regional economy had been carried out in the Coast since Colonial times. By the end of the eighteenth century, Jamaica – later replaced by the Dutch Antilles – had become one of the main centres from where goods were smuggled into New Granada through many small Caribbean bays into which vessels could enter without much official impediment.[46] 'There is no doubt,' the British Minister pointed out in 1874, 'that a great quantity of foreign merchandise is smuggled into Colombia'; but he also noted, ' it is easier to state this fact than to find a remedy for it'.[47] It is impossible to estimate the extent of the contraband trade on the Coast but Ministers of Hacienda, naturally concerned about custom revenues, were quite aware of its sizeable dimensions.[48]

Prominent among the isolated bays suitable for smuggling were several points in the Guajira, which helped give the peninsula an outlaw character. Goods were smuggled into the Guajira and thence distributed to Santa Marta, Barranquilla, and Cartagena. 'It is virtually true that Ríohacha and Guajira live from contraband,' a US consular report observed in 1941, while it noted that contraband stocked 'every store in Ríohacha and Guajira, and perhaps every store from Ríohacha to Fundación', and they were also carried to Barranquilla. The conclusions of the US report left little doubt about contraband in the region:

> The freedom of movement of merchandise and people (of all nationalities) along this coast with practically no interference by the Colombian Government officials is typical of the general lawlessness of the region, and it is indicative of the fact that potentially anything can happen out here without the Colombian Government's knowing about it or without that government's doing anything about it.[49]

[46] See J. I. de Pombo, *Comercio y contrabando en Cartagena de Indias* (1800), (Bogotá, 1986); and Fals Borda, *Mompox y Loba.*

[47] *PP*, LXVI (1874), 48.

[48] *Informe del Ministro de Hacienda* (Bogotá, 1916), XC.

[49] M. Alvarez Jiménez, 'Informe del administrador de la Aduana de Ríohacha', 12 Apr. 1919, in *Informe del Ministro de Hacienda* (Bogotá, 1919), 77; 'Contraband: Port Captain and Customs Administration', Ríohacha, 9 Oct. 1941, NAUS, ref. incomplete.

The Dutch Antilles and Venezuela were the main sources of contraband.[50] In 1941 this include 'Japanese silks, Scotch whisky, American cigarettes, American canned foods, and American guns and ammunition'. In turn, divi-divi, hides, pearls, and cattle were the main items of contraband export.[51] As the British Minister had observed, it was easier to state the facts than to find remedies for them. A long coastline, with a large number of small bays and creeks poorly guarded by underequipped customs officers, made the task of effective patrolling practically impossible. Customs tariffs were often set too high. Underpaid officers were exposed to bribery. Contraband was not considered a serious criminal offence.[52] In 1919 the *Administrador de la Aduana* in Ríohacha described the conditions under which he was supposed to prevent contraband. Undermanned and ill-equipped there was little his thirty-five officers could do: 'instead of prosecuting smugglers, they are on the defensive, locked inside the customs buildings, fearing an assault'.[53] In 1941 conditions seemed to have deteriorated even further. Ministers of Hacienda were dismayed in the face of what looked like a phenomenon that had moved beyond the control of the state. The generalization of contraband, its social acceptability, and the conditions under which it was established, exceeded national government's powers.[54]

6. Regionalism: a Challenge to the Nation-State?

In 1874 a Society of Representatives from the Atlantic Coast was organized to promote the candidacy of Rafael Núñez for the Colombian Presidency.[55] Delegates from the States of Bolívar, Magdalena, and

50 Alvarez Jiménez, 'Informe del Administrador de la Aduana', 78. Also see his 1920 report in *Informe del Ministro de Hacienda* (Bogotá, 1920), 70; and Sanders, 'Contraband: Port Captain and Customs Administration'.

51 See T. Sanders, 'Guajira Peninsula', Ríohacha, 1 Mar. 1941, NAUS, re. incomplete, and de Castro to the *Administrador Tesorero de la Aduana*, Santa Marta, 20 June 1923, AGPNO.

52 See *Anales de la Cámara de representantes*, 17 Nov. 1992, and Mendoza, *Informe del Ministro de Hacienda*, LCII.

53 Alvarez Jiménez, 'Informe del administrador de la Aduana', 78. See also de Castro to the *Administrador Tesorero de la Aduana*, Santa Marta, 24 June 1923, AGPNO; L. J. Pacheco, 'Informe del administrador de la Aduana de Santa Marta', *Informe del Ministro de Hacienda* (Bogotá, 1921), 79.

54 *De Tomás Eastman al Consejo de Ministros* (Bogotá, Jan. 1911), 12.

55 Born in Cartagena in 1825, Núñez had served in both local and national governments during an intense political career. Between 1863 and 1874, however,

Panama met in a convention in Barranquilla, where the Núñez campaign was launched amid regionalist rhetoric in support of 'the rights of the Coast', despite the existence of a Liberal wing in Magdalena strongly opposed to Núñez. The presidential campaign, which has been analysed at length elsewhere, posed a serious challenge to the dominant Radical wing of the Liberal party, and was accompanied by acrimony and violence.[56] What is interesting to observe, for the purpose of this chapter, is the emergence of a *Costeño* regionalism, hitherto dormant, as an electoral issue. Whatever meaning was given to the 'rights of the Coast', they certainly meant regional demands for a larger share in national resources and power, including access to the Presidency.[57] Núñez, however, lost the election to Aquileo Parra. He would later recall the bitterness of the campaign, as well as the resentment it had left in the region as a consequence of attacks by the Radical press against *Costeño* race, morals, and working habits.[58] After this defeat Núñez was elected President of Bolívar for the period 1876–9, during which time he also attended the Senate and served as Minister of Finance. From these positions he skilfully built up a solid nationwide political base.[59] Thus Núñez was elected Colombian President in 1880, was re-elected in 1884, and after the 1885 civil war transformed the political system from federalist to centralist. There is no need here to go into details about this controversial statesman, the most powerful Colombian politician during the second half of the nineteenth century. Suffice it to say that while Núñez was in power – and he remained an influential figure until his death in 1894 – *Costeño* interests were carefully looked after.

Núñez had lived abroad, including Le Havre and Liverpool, where he served as Colombian consul. The standard biography of Núñez is I. Liévano Aguirre, *Rafael Núñez (Lima, 1944)*. For his rise to power, J. W. Park, *Rafael Núñez and the Politics of Colombian Regionalism, 1863–1886 (Baton Rouge, La.*, 1985). The historiography of Núñez is dicussed in H. Delpar, 'Renegade or Regenerator? Rafael Núñez as Seen by Colombian Historians', *JARH* 35 (1985), 25–37.

56 J. W. Park, 'Regionalism as a Factor in Colombia's 1875 Election', *The Americas*, 42/4 (1986), 453–72; H. Delpar, *Red Against Blue: The Liberal Party in Colombian Politics, 1863–1899* (Alabama, 1981), 110–17; and E. Posada-Carbó 'Elections and Civil Wars in Nineteenth-century Colombia: The 1875 Presidential Campaign', *JLAS*, 26/3 (1994), 621–50.

57 For the *Costeño* programme, see *Panama Star and Herald*, 8 Mar. 1875, in CFBC, Films 1411, vol. 2, file 158.

58 Núñez, *La reforma política*, i. 69; Park, *Rafael Núñez*, 300.

59 J. W. Park, 'Preludio a la Presidencia: Rafael Núñez, Gobernador de Bolívar, 1876–1879', *Boletín de Historia y Antiguedades*, 63, (Oct.–Dec. 1976), 519–35.

Despite the nationalization of the *renta de salinas*, Núñez ensured that the Coastal departments received an indemnity. The central government supported the Dique project and the Cartagena–Calamar railway, which improved communications between Cartagena and the Magdalena River. Núñez's natural sympathies for Cartagena were balanced by his support for the opening of Bocas de Ceniza and both the Bolívar and Santa Marta Railways. Above all, Núñez showed concern for the improvement of conditions in the Caribbean ports and strengthening of transport between the Coast and the interior. *Costeños* gained access to positions in the national bureaucracy, to the extent of provoking jealousies in Bogotá.[60] *Costeño* regionalism, which in 1875 had been defined by its attempts to strengthen links with the centre in order to share national power, disappeared, its demands being partially fulfilled. As long as Núñez was in power, regional, and national interests did not appear to conflict.

By 1910, however, regionalism was back in the air, this time giving rise to fears of secession, a consequence of the loss of Panama. In Cartagena, after some *Antioqueño* appointments in the customs house, a mass rally, originally organized in protest against Archbishop Brioschi, developed into violent riots against the central government. Shops were sacked. Leaflets calling for secession were distributed among angry demonstrators. Anti-Church feelings, together with political resentment against the Restrepo administration, were expressed in an upsurge of regionalism. President Restrepo reacted promptly by replacing the Bolívar Governor to secure the department's loyalty to the national government and to restore public order.[61] Secession was never a real threat. However, the mere fact that it was seriously considered as such by the authorities revealed not only their sense of the fragility of their authority but also how, given its possible popular appeal, the mention of secession could be an effective political tool. During the second decade of the twentieth century, calls for secession were heard repeatedly in public demonstrations; newspaper articles played with the idea.[62] Ill-feeling against the interior and the national authorities had increased.

60 De Rafael Núñez a los ciudadanos diputados, Cartagena, 1878, AGB, 1878; R. Núñez, *Mensaje del Presidente constitucional* (Bogotá, 1882), and his *Mensaje del Presidente constitucional* (Bogotá, 1888); also by Núñez, *La reforma política*, i. 16, 137.

61 Restrepo to Segovia and to Terán, Bogotá, 17 and 21 Jan. 1911; Martínez Camargo to Ragonessi, Cartagena, 17 Jan. 1911, ACER. See *El Porvenir*, 22 Dec. 1910.

62 Restrepo to Reyes, Bogotá, 30 Nov. 1911, in Restrepo, *Orientación Republicana*, i. 380, ii. 276–7; Restrepo to Segovia, Bogotá, 17 Jan. 1911, ACER; Rodríguez Diago to

Nevertheless, as in 1875, regionalist demands were directed towards greater participation at the national level rather than political autonomy. In the 1910s, there was a growing feeling in the region that national interests were being redefined to the detriment of the Coast. The distribution of posts in the national bureaucracy was a major concern for local politicians. So was the management of national finances. The *renta de salinas*, in particular, was the source of bitter controversy. Delays in remitting the indemnity, and even reluctance to accept constitutional Coastal rights over the exploitation of salt, were a recurrent cause of regional complaints. Furthermore, there was growing suspicion that the organization of the salt monopoly favoured the mines in Zipaquirá over *Costeño* saltworks. A fierce debate in Congress in 1918, when Senator Dávila Florez warned of secession, revealed the bitterness of regional feelings over the salt issue.[63] Private interests further encouraged regional cleavages. Criticism in Bogotá of oil contracts between the government and Coastal entrepreneurs was met with regionalist arguments. Opposition to the establishment of meat packing-houses offended Coastal cattlemen. Described as 'exotic', Coastal industrial developments were criticized by the Minister of Finance.[64] Yet what motivated the strongest regional reaction was the transport issue, an issue contentious enough to mobilize public opinion. As already described in a previous chapter, Coastal interests in the Magdalena river and Caribbean ports felt threatened by new developments in national transport. In 1918 a decision by the central government to divert funds from the *impuesto de canalización* – a river levy – to the Tolima Railway caused regional outrage. Prominent leaders from Coastal ports, backed by the local press, launched the Liga Costeña, a regional movement above party alliances which had a short but significant life.[65]

Concha, 3 Dec. 1914, and 5 Apr. 1916, AJVC, Box 13; *El Porvenir*, 22 Dec. 1910; *Anales de la Cámara de Representantes*, 28 Jan. 1919; and *La Nación*, 4 Sept. 1916.

63 *Informe del Secretario de Hacienda* (Santa Marta, 1919), 11–16; A. L. Armenta, *La renta de salinas marítimas: Sus defectos y el modo de corregirlos* (Barranquilla, 1914); *El Día*, 9 Dec. 1918; *El Universal*, Barranquilla, 18 Jan. 1919; *Heraldo de la Costa*, 15 and 16 Jan. 1919; *Anales del Senado*, 8 Aug. 1917.

64 *Informe del Ministro de Hacienda* (Bogotá, 1912), pp. XXVIII–XXXIX; Ospina Vásquez, *Industria y protección*, 446–8; Burgos Puche, *El General Burgos*, 275, 285–6.

65 See E. Posada-Carbó, 'La Liga Costeña de 1919, una expresión de poder regional', *Boletín Cultural y Bibliográfico del Banco de la República*, Bogotá, 22(3) (1985), 34–46.

On 18 January 1919, the former Minister of Finance, T. Surí Salcedo, opened the First Assembly of the Liga Costeña in Barranquilla, describing the sensitive issue of river transport as a principal regional concern and a major cause of grievance against the central authorities. Far from being a radical cry, Surí's was at once a balanced account of Coastal needs and an appeal for more attention from the national government. Demands went beyond the problems of transport to cover a wide range of economic, political, and social matters. They included the establishment of an autonomous body to administer the Magdalena river; the improvement of Caribbean ports; the denationalization of the *salinas marítimas*; the construction of railways to promote the development of the cattle industry; the encouragement of foreign immigration; the reduction of customs duties on flour and wheat imports; constitutional reform to increase the number of Coastal senators.[66] In Bogotá, news of the Liga Costeña was received with great concern. The press classified the movement as either a secessionist or a political conspiracy. Fearing a revolution, President Suárez instructed his governors to control any movement of arms, and decided to tour the Coast himself during the same week that the Liga was officially inaugurated.[67] His visit flattered the Liga, enhancing its political significance, but it did not satisfy regional aspirations. Suárez himself did not turn out to be a popular figure. In Barranquilla he alienated public opinion by being 'prominently identified . . . with the clergy, the fact that his own private priest and confessor accompanies him, has caused much unfavorable comment'.[68]

Whatever the impression left by the President's visit, the regionalist issue had mobilized the central government and forced it to pay greater attention to Coastal concerns. Later Liga assemblies were held in Cartagena and Santa Marta, but the fears of a secessionist movement proved to be unfounded. During its existence, the Liga served as a pressure group for Coastal interests in central government circles. Coastal demands were seriously considered by the Cabinet, they were discussed at length by the press while senators and representatives, a

[66] 'Memorial del Presidente de la Liga Costeña al Presidente de la Cámara de Representantes', Cartagena, 14 Aug. 1919, in Archivo del Congreso de la República, Cámara de Representantes: Memoriales y Solicitudes, Bogotá, V, 1919.

[67] Suárez to Magdalena and Atlántico Governors, Bogotá, 2 Dec. 1918, AMFS, Copiador, 12, 13; *El Tiempo*, 11, 12, 21 Jan. 1919, respectively.

[68] American Consul to the Secretary of State, Barranquilla, 23 Jan. 1919, NAUS/ 821.00/435.

few of them members of the Liga, raised them in Congress.[69] As the 1922 presidential election approached – with Liberals challenging Conservatives in the ballot box for the first time in many years – the regional alliance was dismantled to give way to partisan realignment. Moreover, both the candidates, Pedro Nel Ospina and Benjamín Herrera, had strong links in the region which guaranteed local loyalties and sympathies.

Though the Liga Costeña disappeared as an independent group, manifestations of regionalism as an ideology capable of mobilizing public opinion persisted throughout the period. Mass demonstrations in 1930 in support of Bocas de Ceniza were to some extent motivated by regionalist feelings. In 1934, an *Asamblea Inter-departamental de la Costa*, organized by *diputados* from Bolívar, Magdalena, and Atlántico, met in Cartagena to discuss issues similar to those raised by the Liga Costeña.[70] The anti-Avianca mass rallies of the 1940s had a regionalist motivation. Throughout the period, regionalist issues were constantly raised by the press.

It would be wrong to assume that regionalism was a mere tool used by politicians, journalists, and businessmen for their own purposes. If they posed as regionalists it was precisely because regionalism had historical roots and some popular appeal. There were certainly clear expressions of a *Costeño* culture and, perhaps more to the point, conscious efforts to recapture its distinctiveness. The expression *Costa Atlántica*, the title of a newspaper published in Barranquilla in the 1880s, already had a particular connotation by the mid–nineteenth century. Some authors, such as Raymond L. Williams, trace the origins of these attempts to rationalize a particular regional identity back to the publication of J. J. Nieto's novel, *Ingermina* (1844).[71] Early literary manifestations of belonging to a reality which was neither the nation nor the native town, the *Costa*, were , for example, present in the literature of the *Cartagenero* Manuel María Madiedo. His *Nuestro siglo XIX* (1868), in the tradition of the literary genre dealing with local customs, *costumbrismo*, offered several portrayals of a *Costeño* identity.[72] There was no parallel to the Victorian regional novel, but Williams for one has identified a specifically *Costeño* narrative

[69] Goenaga, *Lecturas locales*, 195–210; *Heraldo de la Costa*, 28 July, 2 Aug. 1919; *La Nación*, 24 July, 1 Aug. 1919; *El Imparcial*, 2 Aug. 1919; *Anales del Senado*, 11 Feb. 1920.

[70] *El Estado*, 12, 14, 16 Apr. 1934.

[71] R. L. Williams, *Novela y poder en Colombia, 1844-1987* (Bogotá, 1991), 131.

[72] M. M. Madiedo, *Nuestro siglo XIX* (Bogotá, 1868), 168–9, 347–8.

tradition, which reaches its peak with Gabriel García Márquez's *One Hundred Years of Solitude* (1967).[73] In a political sense, *Costeño* regionalism was obviously strengthened by Núñez's campaign of 1875. Decades later, as a result of the Liga Costeña, a *Costeño* rhetoric re-emerged with strength, with economic and cultural as well as political undertones. A *Vocabulario Costeño* was published in 1922. *Acción Costeña*, a commercial directory of the region, followed in 1926, while a *Diario de la Costa* and *Heraldo de la Costa* were edited in Cartagena and Barranquilla respectively.[74]

Notwithstanding such developments, the different manifestations of *Costeño* identity were far from being the expressions of an homogeneous reality. Within the region, traditional loyalties to cities sometimes clashed with *Costeño* feelings. There is a history of rivalry among the ports, Barranquilla, Cartagena, and Santa Marta. Furthermore partisan and class loyalties should also be considered when pondering the nature of Coastal regionalism.

6. National Partisanship and Regional Factionalism

Deep-rooted local and regional feelings overlapped with other loyalties. Identification with party politics encouraged *Costeño* involvement in a political nation that had developed since the early days of the republic, through the struggle for power between Liberals and Conservatives.[75] Paradoxically, while polarizing the Colombian population often to the extreme of civil war, partisan identification also served to integrate the

[73] Williams, *Novela y poder*, 119–64. García Márquez has been variously refer to as 'lyrical historian of his region'; and as 'a child of the Caribbean who has chosen to write about the Caribbean from more cosmopolitan centres'; G. H. Bell-Villada, *García Márquez: The Man and his Work* (Chapel Hill and London, 1990), 42; and S. Minta, *García Márquez: Writer of Colombia* (New York, 1987), 4, 134. Whether or not García Márquez's masterpiece, *One Hundred Years of Solitude*, can be classified as a 'regional novel', is a matter open to debate. For a brief but useful introduction to the regional novel in England and Wales in the general context of regional historiography, see R. A. Butlin, 'Regions in England and Wales, *c.*1600–1914', in R. A. Dodgshon and R. A. Butlin, *An Historical Geography of England and Wales* (London, 1990), 223–54.

[74] A. Sundheim, *Vocabulario costeño o lexicografía de la región septentrional de la República de Colombia* (Paris, 1922); M. Goenaga, *Acción Costeña* (Barranquilla, 1926).

[75] For the politics of this period, see D. Bushnell, *A Modern History of Colombia* (Stanford, Calif., 1993); Delpar, *Red Against Blue;* Deas, *Del poder y la gramática*; C. Abel, *Política, iglesia y partidos en Colombia* (Bogotá, 1987); and C. Bergquist, *Coffee and Conflict in Colombia, 1886–1910*, (Durham, 1978).

country by creating nationwide allegiances. Electoral campaigns brought together, politically though not physically, Colombians from distant and often isolated areas of the national territory. As the country experienced an intense electoral calendar, presidential campaigns in particular created a nationally aware electorate. Newspapers, often published just for electoral purposes, discussed national issues. As the Atlántico Governor acknowledged in 1914, the population was generally indifferent towards public affairs except during electoral times, when the partisan spirit was raised.[76]

To what extent did regional politics coincide with national trends? In other words, were there any characteristics distinctive to *Costeño* politics? Helen Delpar has identified the Coast as a typical Liberal stronghold during the nineteenth century, mainly due to its relatively large number of black and mulatto inhabitants, the measures taken by Liberals in favour of the final abolition of slavery, and the weak influence of the Catholic Church within the region.[77] If this assertion seems valid in the long run, there is a need to look more closely at the way partisan politics developed over time. In the remainder of this chapter, I analyse the nature of *Costeño* politics in a national context. First, I briefly look at how, during the second half of the nineteenth century, *Costeño* partisan behaviour was muted by the rise of Rafael Núñez to power. Second, I explore *Costeño* electoral behaviour in an attempt to identify the extent to which regional politics coincided with or diverged from national trends. Finally, I look at other factors which have to be considered when dealing with the struggle for power at the local level.

Coastal politics were much shaped by General Juan José Nieto (1804–66), but even more significantly by Rafael Núñez (1825–94).[78] Both belonged to the Liberal party, but both encouraged regional loyalties that overrode partisan sympathies. Early in his career, Núñez served under Nieto's administration in the 1850s, which abolished slavery in Bolívar. As an active Liberal, Núñez had been elected to

[76] P. J. Bustillo, *Mensaje que dirige el Gobernador a la Asamblea* (Barranquilla, 1914), 5. Despite their significance, the study of Colombian elections – like the study of elections elsewhere in Latin America – has received little attention among scholars. See my 'Elections and Civil Wars in Nineteenth-Century Colombia'.

[77] Delpar, *Red against Blue*, 16–21, 41.

[78] Bossa Herazo, *Cartagena independiente*, 128–39. For the role of Nieto in Coastal politics and government, see O. Fals Borda, *El Presidente Nieto* (Bogotá, 1981), and E. Lemaitre, *El General Juan José Nieto y su época* (Bogotá, 1983). See also J. J. Nieto, *Mensaje del Gobernador de Cartajena* (Cartajena, 1852); also by Nieto, *Bosquejo histórico de la revolución que rejeneró al Estado de Bolívar* (Cartajena, 1862).

Congress, and had served as head of the Bolívar government and as Minister in various national cabinets. In 1862 Núñez had carried out Mosquera's decision to confiscate Church property, and in 1863 he attended the Ríonegro constitutional Convention.[79] But in 1875, as already shown, Núñez had come to oppose the Radical wing of the Liberal party then in power. His presidential campaign was supported by a nationwide movement of Liberal dissidents – the *Independientes* – and he received significant support on the Coast. He built up a strong base which took him later to the presidency: the region became a *Nuñista* stronghold of Conservatives and Liberals alike. Coastal Liberals such as Juan Campo Serrano signed the 1886 Constitution.[80] Joaquín F. Vélez, a prominent *Cartagenero* Conservative, was also an ardent supporter of the *Regeneración*, as the *Nuñista* regime, in coalition with the Conservatives came to be known. Although some Liberals in the region were declared opponents of the *Regeneración*, it is undeniable that during his years in power, Núñez could count on strong support from both parties on the Coast.

If party alignments appeared weakened by *Nuñismo* predominance and its attempt to build an alternative to the two traditional parties, the region again showed its Liberal tendencies during successive twentieth century elections. Even during the Conservative Hegemony up to 1930, it is easy to identify the strength of Liberalism in the region. In the 1904 presidential elections, 78 per cent of Coastal delegates in the Electoral College supported Rafael Reyes, despite the *Costeño* origins of the other contender, Joaquín F. Vélez. Although both belonged to the Conservative party, Reyes was regarded as the candidate of compromise by the Liberals, who abstained from presenting their own ticket in this contest. Vélez was perceived as a hardliner, an intransigent closely associated with the Catholic Church. In Bolívar, where Vélez had served as Governor, votes for Reyes outnumbered those for Vélez in all provinces but Sabanalarga. It is possible to argue that despite accusations of electoral wrongdoings the 1904 electoral results in the Coast therefore reflected *Costeño* political sympathies, differing significantly from the national trend.[81] That a strict contest

[79] Park, *Rafael Núñez*, 80; Bossa, *Cartagena independiente*, 134.

[80] *La Reforma Política*, v. 117.

[81] It is a well–known fact that the final decision of the Electoral Board in 1904 was determined by the manipulation of the electoral register by Juanito Iguarán in the Padilla Province. But even without the 45 votes apparently controlled by Iguarán, Reyes still won a comfortable majority among *Costeño* delegates. See E. Lemaitre, *Rafael Reyes* (Bogotá, 1967), 257–67; *El Porvenir*, 22 Apr. 1904.

between two Conservatives could be coloured by Liberal support was even more evident in the 1918 presidential election. Liberals openly backed the candidacy of Guillermo Valencia while opposing Marco Fidel Suárez. The *Unión Liberal* voiced the reasons *Costeño* Liberals had for supporting Valencia: he guaranteed Liberal rights and favoured decentralization.[82] The paper also warned of Suárez's close relationship with the Catholic Church and his clerical approach to educational matters. That year, the Coast again showed a distinctive electoral behaviour: while a national majority of 52.6 per cent gave the presidency to Suárez, 58.9 per cent of Coastal votes supported Valencia. (See Table 6.2.)

The analysis of these results serves, of course, only to identify some trends, as sometimes Liberals abstained from contesting national elections during the Conservative Hegemony. Whenever they decided to compete with their own candidates, as in 1922 and in 1930, the results were blurred by official fraud and corruption.[83] Nevertheless, even in these elections Liberal majorities were already recognized in some areas, without dispute. In Atlántico, for example, both Liberal candidates were recognized as obtaining clear majorities in 1922 and 1930. On both occasions, the Liberals captured the major urban and commercial centres, while Conservatives could count only on the distant rural areas of Southern Bolívar. In 1930, while Liberal Enrique Olaya Herrera lost to Conservative Guillermo Valencia in Magdalena and Bolívar, he won in Santa Marta, Ciénaga, Cartagena, Aracataca, El Banco, Sincelejo, and Magangué.[84] This visible Liberal majority in some areas during the national elections prior to 1930 is easier to identify in the results of local elections, where Liberals were more constantly active. By 1916, Liberals ruled Barranquilla's city council; a year later, they had the majority in the *Asamblea* of Atlántico. In the 1923 municipal elections, Liberal gains throughout the Coast were significant.[85] But even when Liberal electoral gains were not visible, those who ruled during the Conservative Hegemony were well aware

[82] *Unión Liberal,* 18, 23 Oct. 1917 and 6, 8, 17, 27, 29 Nov. 1917; American Consul to Department of State, Barranquilla, 16 Feb. 1918, NAUS/ 821.00/406.

[83] *Los partidos políticos en Colombia* (Bogotá, 1922), 73–115, 265–76. Allegations of electoral corruption are well documented in Ministerio de Gobierno, Asuntos Electorales, ANC.

[84] *El Pequeño Diario* and *La Patria*, 11, 14 Feb. 1930.

[85] 'Municipal elections in Bolívar', Cartagena, 9 Oct. 1923, NAUS/ 821.101/1.

that they were governing a population whose loyalty lay by and large with the Liberal party.[86]

TABLE 6.2 *Presidential Elections in Coastal Departments, 1914–1946 (No. of votes and percentages)*

Year	Candidates	Bolívar	Magdalena	Atlántico	% Coast	% Colombia
1904	Reyes	168	93		78.1	44.5
	Vélez	68	4		21.5	44.4
	Others	1	0		0.4	11.1
1914	Concha	43,993	8,666	5,576		
	Esguerra	1,453	1,646			
1918	Suárez	10,072	4,824	1,671	36.7	52.6
	Valencia	18,097	4,945	3,509	58.9	41.5
1922	Ospina	32,261	11,515	4,723	61.4	62.4
	Herrera	16,141	9,224	5,142	38.6	37.6
1930	Olaya	17,987	10,489	8,860	33.3	45.0
	Valencia	49,084	16,147	3,749	62.0	39.0
	Vásquez	3,320	966	936	4.7	26.0
1942	López	54,726	29,980	25,010	66.0	59.0
	Arango	27,948	16,423	12,109	34.0	41.0
1946	Turbay	17,822	17,610	6,234	20.0	32.0
	Gaitán	55,454	20,361	31,044	50.0	26.0
	Ospina	32,814	19,040	11,789	30.0	42.0

Source: Colombia (registraduría), *Historia electoral colombiana* (Bogotá, 1988), 115–20.

This became all the more evident after 1930. As electoral results for the Lower Chamber between 1931 and 1949 demonstrate, Liberal majorities in the Coast were above the national average (see Table 6.3). The Liberal electorate that emerged after 1930 also showed some interesting variations when compared to national trends: first, it was closer to the *Lopista* faction of the party, and later overwhelmingly in favour of Jorge E. Gaitán. In both cases, this behaviour can be mainly explained by the attention given by both Gaitán and López to labour politics, in particular, to the problems of the banana zone and the Magdalena river. A brief look at the 1942 and 1946 presidential contests serve to illustrate these points.

In the 1942 presidential election, there were no outstanding

[86] See e. g. Carbonell to Concha, Barranquilla, 21 Jan. 1918, AJVC, Box 1, and Suárez to Atlántico Governor, Bogotá, 16 Nov. 1918, Copiador, Libro Segundo, 4–5, AMFS.

TABLE 6.3 *Elections in Coastal Departments to the Cámara de Representantes, 1931–1949*

Year	Party	Atlántico	Bolívar	Magdalena	% Coast	% Colombia
1931	Liberal	10,724	15,602	8,559	61.7	51.0
	Conservative	2,675	10,331	8,642	38.3	49.0
1933	Liberal	15,827	29,153	24,303	77.4	62.4
	Conservative	2,642	5,492	12,076	22.6	37.6
1939	Liberal	10,059	42,964	20,344	72.6	62.6
	Conservative	5,674	13,117	8,856	27.4	36.9
	Others					0.5
1941	Liberal	22,376	45,937	20,489	73.0	63.8
	Conservative	6,675	16,968	9,290	27.0	35.7
	Others					0.5
1943	Liberal	26,210	47,713	26,628	72.2	64.4
	Conservative	7,308	20,990	9,414	27.1	33.8
	Others	1,046			0.7	1.8
1945	Liberal	26,580	57,440	20,066	74.0	62.9
	Conservative	5,603	17,283	7,992	22.0	33.6
	Communist	140	1,532	4,197	4.0	3.2
	Others					0.3
1947	Liberal	31,212	85,717	34,001	68.6	54.7
	Conservative	11,323	37,409	18,449	30.5	44.4
	Socialists		781		0.3	0.8
	Popular Front			1,391	0.6	0.1
1949	Liberal	36,252	72,763	40,135	65.8	53.5
	Conservative	11,047	44,683	21,693	34.2	46.1
	Communist					0.4

Source: Colombia (Registraduría), *Historia electoral colombiana* (Bogotá, 1988), 178–86.

differences between the national results and those of the Coast. Support for Alfonso López Pumarejo was stronger on the Coast than in the rest of the country, despite an active *antilopista* Liberal faction in the region. During his first administration (1934–8), after he had become President in an uncontested election, his programme had appealed to a large proportion of Coastal population. The commercial élite of Barranquilla were pleased with the President's official opening of Bocas de Ceniza in 1935. However, what strengthened López's popularity in the region were his policies towards the labour movement, in particular his mediating role in disputes where the interests of workers from along the Magdalena river and the banana zone were involved. Torres Giraldo, who participated as an organizer in the 1934 strike on the banana zone, described the President's attitude:

> What does López do? He orders the Minister of War to offer an Army airplane to the union leaders so they could travel from the banana zone to Bogotá. Union leaders are not only invited to join the negotiating table but they are housed in decent accommodation while the State continues to pay their salaries for as long as the talks last.[87]

Later, in 1937, the government introduced a bill in Congress aimed at intervening in the banana industry. That same year, the American manager of the United Fruit Company was sent to prison on corruption charges.[88] Similarly, López's role had been crucial for the achievements of Fedenal – the strong communist-led union federation along the Magdalena river – during the 1937 strike. Thus when López decided to run again for President to succeed Eduardo Santos (1938–42), he found ready support on the Coast. As early as May 1940, the Barranquilla City Council proclaimed his candidacy.[89] On 14 January 1941, López spoke to the crowds in the Paseo de Bolívar in Barranquilla, where he launched his campaign after returning from abroad. 'Social policy will bring peace to the republic', he told 135 Liberals who attended the welcoming banquet at the Prado Hotel the following day. Two months later, elections for members of *cámaras* and *asambleas* took place: in Barranquilla, the *Lopistas* Alberto Pumarejo and Juan B. Barrios secured a comfortable majority over their Liberal opponent Cristobal Navarro.[90] Yet the campaign was not running that smoothly. After López's unofficial nomination, an anti-re-election campaign within the Liberal party, led by the Atlántico Senator Pedro Juan Navarro, was soon spreading nationwide. In January 1941 the Bolívar *Representante* Alfonso Romero Aguirre organized a Liberal convention in Magangué to launch the candidacy of Carlos Arango Vélez.[91] Arango Vélez, who like López had family links on the Coast, ran against López later with the support of the Conservative party.[92] In July 1941 Navarro was elected President of Congress where

[87] Torres Giraldo, *Los inconformes*, v. 12–13. See also ibid., 2–3.

[88] A. Tirado Mejía, *Aspectos políticos del primer gobierno de Alfonso López Pumarejo, 1934–38* (Bogotá, 1981), 223–8. Mass demonstrations took place in Ciénaga in support of the government's bill; see ibid., 224. See A. Tirado Mejía (ed.), *Estado y economía: 50 años de la reforma del 36* (Bogotá, 1986), 279–87.

[89] *La Prensa*, 14 May 1940.

[90] *La Prensa*, 15, 16 Jan., 17 Mar. 1941.

[91] Romero Aguirre, *Confesiones de un aprendiz*, 128–31.

[92] *La Prensa*, in Barranquilla, portrayed Arango Vélez as a *Costeño* candidate; *La Prensa*, 17 Dec. 1941.

he obtained Romero Aguirre's election as *Contralor General de la República*, a key position in the bureaucratic machinery. In the Barranquilla Conservative newspaper *La Prensa*, Aquiles Arrieta edited a *Página liberal anti-reeleccionista.* It was a bitter campaign that in the region was also encouraged by the Liberal opposition to the dominant *Lopista* faction led in Barranquilla by López's relative Alberto Pumarejo.[93] It was also an unsuccessful one. As Table 6.2 shows, the support for López in the elections left no doubts about where Coastal preferences lay.

In 1946 the region again showed distinctive electoral behaviour, this time differing substantially from the national pattern. Whereas the overall result gave the presidency to the Conservative candidate Mariano Ospina and a split Liberal party gave the majority of its votes to Gabriel Turbay, 50 per cent of the Coastal electorate supported the dissident Liberal Jorge Eliecer Gaitán. Gaitán won in all three departments, but the margin of his victory was larger in Atlántico and Magdalena than in Bolívar. (See Table 6.2). Gaitán's popularity in the region could be traced back to the 1928 banana strike, when his intervention in Congress on behalf of the workers gained him a national reputation. Shortly after the strike, Gaitán had travelled to Barranquilla, Santa Marta, and Ciénaga, where he was made guest of honour by the city council.[94] He toured the banana region, met strikers, gave interviews to the regional press, and went back to Bogotá, to deliver his famous attack on the Abadía government. In Congress, Gaitán dramatized the December events achieving quick political success. By September 1929, both *Senado* and *Cámara* had passed a bill demanding the retrial of those imprisoned, including union leaders and communist agitators. Most of them were soon released. 'Gaitán freed them after nine months', a participant in the 1928 strike gratefully recalled fifty years later.[95] After his role in the banana crisis, no other national leader except López Pumarejo could match Gaitán's reputation in the region. In his capacity as a lawyer, Gaitán kept in contact with labourers in the Coast. In 1934, for example, he visited Barranquilla to give professional assistance to the Asociación de Empleados.[96] As *Ministro de Trabajo*, a post that Gaitán used to strengthen his links

[93] Romero Aguirre, *Confesiones de un aprendiz*, 140.

[94] Torres Giraldo, *Los inconformes*, v. 130; J. A. Osorio Lizarazo, *Gaitán, vida, muerte y permanente presencia* (Buenos Aires, 1952), 116–17.

[95] Josefa María Blanco interviewed in Arango, *Sobrevivientes de las bananeras*, 99.

[96] Carbonell, *La quincena política*, ii. 145.

with urban workers, he toured the Coast in 1943. *Semana* would later recall how the Minister Gaitán 'travelled down the Magdalena river angrily speaking out against the misery of the people who live by the river, against intestinal parasites, and malaria, against the floods'.[97] As early as April 1944, there was an organized movement in Barranquilla working for Gaitán's candidacy, involved in propaganda activities including a daily one-hour radio programme.[98] Leaders of Fedenal, who decided to support Turbay, learnt how distant they were politically from the majority of their members when the electoral results gave such a comfortable victory to Gaitán.

In addition to partisan activities, the emergence of labour movements also gave a national dimension to regional politics. María Cano toured the Coast in 1928.[99] Several other labour leaders from the Andean interior, such as E. Mahecha and I. Torres Giraldo, were directly involved in organizing strikes in the banana zone. Work stoppages in the Caribbean ports were quick to spread along the river with far-reaching national consequences. Furthermore, labour politics in the region were characterized by their radical stance and the landmarks they left in the history of the Colombian labour movement. The general strike that took place in Barranquilla in 1910, together with the 1918 strikes in Cartagena, Barranquilla, and Santa Marta, have been regarded as pioneering in terms of labour demands in twentieth-century Colombia.[100] The national impact of the 1928 banana strike helped to topple the Conservative regime. Deals achieved by the banana unions and Fedenal were a prelude to the development of a national social security system.

Although anarchists, communists, and social-democrats achieved significant influence in some unions, it would be a mistake, however, to see the labour movement of this period as disassociated from traditional party politics. J. Martínez, a leader in the 1918 strikes, was a member of the Liberal party; a certain Linares, a Dominican involved in organizing labour in the banana zone, was closely linked to the Magdalena politician J. I. Díaz Granados; A. Badel, later Bolívar Governor, presided over the organization of María Cano's tour of the Coast; in their early political careers, liberals such as A. Romero

97 *Semana*, 4 Nov. 1946.

98 See R. E. Sharpless, *Gaitán of Colombia: A Political Biography* (Pittsburgh, 1978), 107.

99 *La Prensa*, 23 Feb. 1928; Torres Giraldo, *Los inconformes*, iv. 61–2.

100 M. Archila, 'La clase obrera colombiana, 1886–1930', in Tirado, *Nueva Historia de Colombia*, iii. 222; Torres Giraldo, *Los inconformes*, iii. 70–2, 125.

Aguirre and S. Bossa were active participants in labour union congresses.[101] The development of events in the banana zone, following the outcome of the 1928 strike, showed how quickly national party politics became embroiled in social conflicts. Shortly after the strike was repressed, M. F. Robles and R. Campo, lawyers from Magdalena, started a press campaign blaming the national government for the casualties, while the Liberal Senator Lanao Loaiza raised the issue in Congress. They were joined by the Barranquilla press, including the Conservative papers *La Nación* and *La Prensa*, and the campaign was echoed in Bogotá. Soon Gaitán was touring the banana region and capitalizing on the mismanagement of the strike. According to Torres Giraldo, who had accompanied María Cano on her Coastal tour early in 1928, most labourers in Magdalena looked to the socialist agitators as 'lieutenants marching at the vanguard of the masses'. They were useful negotiators with the American company and local banana planters. But when it came to national politics, to the aspiration of ending the Conservative regime, 'in dealing with the great battle, it is clear that they would follow the leadership of generals Morán, Socarrás, and other well-known [Liberal] warriors'. Thus, Torres Giraldo concluded, 'Liberalism flourished in Magdalena and, for the common workers, revolutionary socialism was a Liberal stimulant'.[102] With the rise of Olaya to power in 1930, a strengthened Liberal party intensified its activities in the labour unions. Leaders such as Torres Giraldo lamented the 'electoral heritage which is a burden on the labour movement', while criticizing the new developments as 'diversion towards official "legalism"': 'the reformist wing . . . judged the importance of all union organization by the acquisition of a brand-new legal status and the presence of a legal adviser'.[103] To be sure, state recognition of unions dated from the Conservative regime but the number of organizations which were granted legal status increased rapidly after 1930. More significant perhaps was the direct intervention of the President in labour affairs, particularly during the López Pumarejo administration. His role as mediator in disputes such as those in the banana zone and in the Magdalena river, together with

[101] See A. Carbonell to Concha, Barranquilla, 14 Jan. 1918 and Nicolás Dávila to Concha, Santa Marta, 4 May 1918, in AJVC, Boxes 1 and 3 respectively; Torres Giraldo, *Los inconformes*, iv. 5, 46, 61; and Romero Aguirre, *Confesiones de un aprendiz de estadista*, 20.

[102] Torres Giraldo, *Los inconformes*, iv. 64–5; Arango, *Sobrevivientes de las bananeras*, 37.

[103] Torres Giraldo, *Los inconformes*, iv. 262, iii. 177.

Gaitán's activities, strengthened the position of the Liberal party among labourers in the Coast.

Partisan politics, and their electoral struggles, therefore encouraged nationwide allegiances through the role that the two parties – Liberal and Conservative – have historically played in Colombian politics. It is possible to suggest, as H. G. Nicholas has done for the United States, that elections played a unifying role in an otherwise diverse country.[104] However, that *Costeño* politics were framed in a national context does not deny the existence of distinctive regional political behaviour. In certain periods, as when Núñez was in power or during the second decade of this century, regional loyalties seemed to overcome partisan rivalries. Yet national party politics also took root in the region, although *Costeño* behaviour at the polls slightly differed from the national trend in the 1942 presidential elections, and differed significantly in those of 1904, 1918, 1930, and 1946. All in all, there emerges a picture of a region politically more Liberal in its outlook and less deferential to the Catholic Church. By the 1930s, its is also possible to identify an electorate in the growing urban and commercial centres ready to be mobilized by leaders such as López Pumarejo and Gaitán.

If politics at the national level were characterized by traditional loyalties to the conflicting parties, at the regional level politics were riven with cleavages among local factions and characterized by patronage, where family ties, friendship, and gratitude often conditioned the nature of partisan activities. The picture would be incomplete without looking at these features of political life.

Conflicts among factions within the parties were often so intense as to override party rivalries. Thus deals between Conservatives and Liberals in local elections, over *asambleas* and *concejos*, and over the distribution of state patronage were a commonplace of local politics. In Atlántico, Carbonell's faction counted on the support of Liberal groups to challenge Insignares' during the second decade of this century. Pumarejo's main opponent was Navarro, a member of his own party, backed by 'the most numerous and the least disciplined element [of the Liberals], as well as the most ignorant'.[105] In Magdalena, General Manjarrés led a Conservative group traditionally opposed by General Iguarán and, in turn, both competed with other

104 H. G. Nicholas, *The Nature of American Politics* (Oxford, 1986), 65.

105 See NAUS/ RG84: Records of the American Legation in Bogotá, general correspondence, Barranquilla consular district, vol. 8, 8 Apr. 1931.

Conservatives, who eventually formed a third group. Vargas, Bossa, and Gómez Fernandez led rival Liberal factions in Bolívar.[106] These are just a few examples of some of the most prominent factions in the struggle for power within the parties. Mergers, divisions, and the emergence of new factions were frequent occurrences. In some provinces, political factions were identifiable family groups. When J. M. Valdeblánquez described the *Conservadores históricos* in Magdalena, he identified them by their family names: 'In Ríohacha, the Labordes, Iguaranes, Barros, Valverdes, . . . and in the Province: the Lacouture, Dangones, Ariza, Cotes.'[107] S. Bossa was the head of an influential Liberal faction in Bolívar, whose network was essentially based on family ties. The conditions for such features of political development were provided by the dominance of extended family networks with low population density. However, members of the same family belonging to opposing factions were not exceptional.

Sources of political power were varied. Undoubtedly, some politicians had strong links with the cattle industry, which was after all the most important economic activity in the region. Landowners and cattle traders – Conservatives such as F. Burgos and D. Martínez, or Liberals such as P. Castro Monsalvo and R. Támara – were actively involved in politics. P. Castro Monsalvo, a rural entrepreneur, was Magdalena Governor, member of Congress, and Minister of Communications and Agriculture.[108] Congressmen often supported cattle interests in both the *Cámara* and *Senado.*[109] However, political developments did not always favour cattlemen. When Striffler visited Plato in the 1870s, he observed the bitterness of cattle *hacendados* over the high price they had to pay for political disturbances in their province: 'They all complain about the forced loans that are often imposed on them.'[110] Cattle associations, such as the Sociedad de Agricultores de San Marcos and the Federación de Ganaderos de Bolívar, also complained about the treatment they received from politicians and legislative bodies.[111] As a pressure group, cattlemen

[106] See J. M. Valdeblánquez to Ospina, Santa Marta, 8 and 22 May 1922, AGPNO; A. Romero Aguirre, *Confesiones de un aprendiz de estadista* (Bogotá, 1949), 73–7; and *La Lucha*, 21 Mar. 1934.

[107] J. M. Valdeblánquez, *Biografía del señor General Florentino Manjarrés* (Bogotá, 1962), 20.

[108] See Castro Monsalvo, *Un campesino previno al país*, 3, 10, 18, 22.

[109] *Ganadería de Bolívar* (Sincelejo, 1935), 801–23.

[110] Striffler, *El río Cesar*, 24.

[111] *RNA* (Feb. 1912), 305, and (June 1913), 809; *Ganadería de Bolívar* (Sincelejo, 1935), 768.

were not effectively united. Their power was limited by their own fragmentation and their regional scope. Taxes on cattle exports, agreements to import livestock from Venezuela, government hesitation in supporting the development of the meat packing-house in Coveñas, all these revealed the lack of political power of Coastal cattle interests at the national level.

Other rural economic activities sought to forward their interest in politics. In northern Magdalena, where the United Fruit Company was often accused of sponsoring corruption, the banana industry tried to exert its influence upon state legislation and institutions. Some local banana growers achieved considerable political power. Nevertheless, the relationship between politicians and *bananeros* – the American company in particular – was essentially a conflictive one. Opposing interests clashed in the Magdalena Asamblea and in Congress, and they took sides during the labour conflicts of the 1920s and the 1930s.

Despite the apparent predominance of a rural economy in the region, urban life in river- and seaports and also in small towns and villages was of paramount importance for political activity. As seats of local government, towns exercised control over state resources which, under conditions of scarcity, became all the more significant. Merchants, small industrialists and artisans, builders, lawyers, doctors, teachers, and labourers, were all affected by political developments. There was a political hierarchy attached to towns not always linked to economic success. In spite of its decline, Cartagena, for example, preserved its political ascendancy over the region well into the twentieth century. However, economic growth caused the emergence of new centres of power which challenged traditional hierarchies. Barranquilla, Ciénaga, Sincelejo, and Magangué were respectively gaining in importance over Cartagena, Santa Marta, Montería, and Mompox. In all towns, traditional and modern alike, politics were conditioned by the degree of access to state resources which, in turn, required manoeuvring in elections, skilful knowledge of how public administration functioned, and the necessary links with the outside world, other regional towns where the centres of power were located and with the central government. Thus politics were often a full-time occupation, and state patronage an important source of political strength. Successful politicians had usually devoted a long career to mastering the intricacies of power and climbing up the political ladder. As J. M. Valdeblánquez pointed out, for men such as General Iguarán, 'politics was his only vice'. Iguarán, political boss of the Padilla province in

Magdalena, knew the state inside out: he had held the posts of *Alcalde*, *Prefecto*, *Gobernador*, *Concejero Municipal*, *Diputado*, *Representante*, and *Senador* among others in a long public career.[112] His electoral skills were outstanding. In addition, his ability to deal with the Guajiro tribes, which in the 1920s still occasionally challenged the state, enhanced his political power.

A training in a liberal profession usually provided a background for a political career, as was the case of successful politicians such as Rafael Núñez, Felipe Angulo, Abel Carbonell, Manuel Dávila Florez, Francisco Escobar, Pedro Juan Navarro, and Alfonso Romero Aguirre.[113] Not all politicians shared the same backgrounds. They were as varied as their sources of power. In the larger towns and ports, higher levels of education and continuous contact with the outside world produced a breed of political leaders also distinguished by their impeccable white linen suits, such as L. Patrón and A. Pumarejo. Politicians from rural towns were more commonly like the *cacique* in Sucre as described by *El Tiempo*: '. . . He always wears trousers and jackets of ordinary cheap drill, . . . a coloured shirt without a collar, sandals, a straw hat pulled down over his face; he has never worn socks . . . He is a man of few words because of his poor command of language.'[114]

The extent of political power that could be exercised differed significantly from town to town. Hardly any politician was able to wield power over the whole region. Rafael Núñez was an exception. Through his national stature, and skilful handling of different regional interests, Núñez managed to build up a political base that extended throughout the Coast. In general, however, what prevailed was a weak balance of power, conditioned by the loose character of the coalitions among the different factions engaged in the competition to control scarce state resources. Besides, the emergence of important new urban centres, competing with each other and challenging the traditional cities, meant a further fragmentation of power.

112 J. M. Valdeblánquez, *Historia del Departamento del Magdalena y del territorio de la Guajira* (Santa Marta, 1964), 160; J. M. Vesga y Avila, *Perfiles colombianos* (Bogotá, 1908), 55–7.

113 Biographies of *Costeño* politicians are scarce, but see J. P. Llinás, *Felipe Angulo y la Regeneración* (Bogotá, 1989).

114 *El Tiempo*, 12 Feb. 1923, in Villegas and Yunis, *Sucesos colombianos*, 443. See also López, *Esbozos y atisbos*, 111–20, and Romero Aguirre, *Confesiones de un aprendiz*, 10.

8. Conclusion: Region, Nation and *Costeño* Politics

'The multiplicity of local powers means that we cannot benefit from any accumulation of our strengths', Rafael Núñez had insisted in 1889.[115] In spite of his efforts to centralize power, the expansion of the Colombian state had to be accommodated to the circumstances of a vast and fragmented territory where the interests of scattered populations often pulled in different directions.

The Coastal *departamentos* and *municipios* were financially weak, which made them dependent on the national budget. Yet this did not make the region politically dependent on the central government. Congress played a significant role in channelling national resources, and congressmen from all Colombian regions, including the Coast, distributed the spoils of the national budget to the dismay of Ministers of Hacienda. Although presidents had the power to appoint and remove heads of local government, they had to try to avoid alienating regional feelings. Moreover, at the local level, governors had to deal with elected bodies over which the central government had little control. In contrast to many of the *jefes políticos* of *Porfirian* Mexico, Coastal governors were in general natives of the region. Only very exceptionally were figures from other parts, such as Jose María Obando, named to posts in the Coastal provinces. Furthermore, while it does not seem that these occasional appointments were met with any strong regional disapproval during the nineteenth century, they would have probably caused public outrage had they been made during the twentieth.

Thus the consolidation of the nation-state did not take place as a linear process where regions disappeared to give way to an homogeneous and dominant national polity. In addition to the survival of an effectively decentralized political life, the expansion of the powers of the central state faced serious barriers, which this chapter has illustrated by showing the problems in implementing conscription and curtailing contraband trade. Those few who believed that the Army was an appropriate institution for encouraging national integration could find no allies for their cause in the Colombian Caribbean, since avoidance of conscription was the rule. In turn, the extent of contraband trade – besides testing the strength of the state – meant that

[115] Núñez, *La reforma política*, iii. 160.

a large number of Coastal inhabitants managed to avoid most national taxation.

'I wish that the Coast would get its independence, and create its own State', says a character in Manuel María Madiedo's *Nuestro siglo XIX* of 1868.[116] This is not the first or the last time that one finds expressions of this sort. However, the aim of *Costeño* regionalism was far from that of creating its own state. More often than not, it was a reaction against what was considered as an exclusion of the Coast from the main trends of national development. In this sense, *Costeño* regionalism essentially sought to strengthen links with the national polity, not weaken them. Regionalism in the Coast was not a consistent phenomenon. When it surfaced, it always left behind a legacy of *Costeño* rhetoric and a few concrete achievements. Traditionally, the existence of regionalism has been interpreted as a barrier to national integration.[117] Yet what seems to have given rise most frequently to the *Costeño* version was the manner in which national integration took place as, for example, with decisions about national transport policies. This would suggest a need to re–examine regional cleavages and regional alliances, and their role in processes of national integration. In this context, it would probably be useful to differentiate between different types of regionalism and identify its diverse nature. Did *Antioqueño* regionalism have the same aims as its counterpart on the Colombian Caribbean?

Given all the circumstances mentioned above, it should come as no surprise that in 1949 the *Costeño* politician Alfonso Romero Aguirre, attacking the legacy of Rafael Núñez, wrote: 'we are far from being a nation'.[118] Yet his own political career was, from its early stages, framed in a national context. As a schoolboy, Romero Aguirre had contributed to the establishment of a *Sociedad Infantil 'Rojas Garrido'*, a gathering of friends who shared an enthusiasm for Rojas Garrido and Vargas Vila – both Vargas Vila and Rojas Garrido were heroes of the Liberal party, but neither was a *Costeño*. Romero Aguirre studied in Bogotá in the Colegio Mayor del Rosario, and later in the Universidad Externado, before a successful career in Congress. That he showed concern over Coastal affairs and identified himself as a *Costeño* did not contradict his deep involvement in national life. Thus after surveying

116 Madiedo, *Nuestro siglo XIX*, 347.

117 See e. g. M. Palacios, *Estado y clases sociales en Colombia* (Bogotá, 1986), 87.

118 Romero Aguirre, *Ayer, hoy y mañana del liberalismo colombiano: Historia de la regeneración* (Bogotá, 1949), 119.

national politics, and somewhat in contradiction to his previous statement, Romero Aguirre acknowledged in a *Renanian* fashion, 'we have a nation . . . because we wish to'.[119] What he did not acknowledge explicitly was that politics, from the very early days of the republic, had been partly responsible for creating that desire for a nation. His own politics were those of the Liberal party, to which the Coast gave most of its sympathies, and those of its national leaders and ideologues. Yet one must question the extent that such figures enjoyed real national authority. Romero Aguirre recalls a meeting in Cartagena with the Liberal party leader Alfonso López Pumarejo to discuss local politics. At one point, he made explicit his disagreement with the national leader and threatened to leave the meeting. 'You – damn it! – want to prevail over the Liberal leadership', López Pumarejo rebuked him. To which the Bolívar politician answered, 'You – damn it! – have failed to recognize the work of the party convention in Bolívar.'[120]

119 Romero Aguirre, *Ayer, hoy y mañana*, 124.

120 A. Romero Aguirre, *Un radical en el Congreso* (Bogotá, 1949), 67.

Conclusion

In 1914 General Benjamín Herrera visited his banana farm, Colombia, to inspect the disastrous results of the venture. Mismanagement and lack of drainage and irrigation had all contributed to poor yields and a low-quality product. A final blow to the farm was a hurricane which destroyed a large number of the best bananas. 'This is a disgrace ... worse than a military defeat', Herrera exclaimed, while he lamented: 'why did I reject so many good suggestions to invest my wife's capital in cattle in Bolívar?'[1]

Not all banana plantations suffered the fate of Herrera's. On the contrary, from the last decades of the nineteenth century onwards, the banana proved to be a suitable crop for Coastal conditions. Frustrated experiences in other products motivated shifts to bananas in Northern Magdalena, a tendency further encouraged by the influx of foreign capital. Although the presence of the United Fruit Company was the focus of recurrent conflict, there is little doubt that bananas were a stimulus to economic growth. They assisted the recovery of Santa Marta. Ciénaga, Aracataca, and Fundación experienced sudden booms. Migrants from all over the Coast and the Andean interior poured into the banana zone in search of new opportunities, not only on the banana plantations but also in a wide range of activities which were springing up out of the banana trade. Regional capital, including *Barranquillero* interests, was invested in banana production. A few banana planters moved to Barranquilla, where they invested part of their profits. Merchants and industries from Barranquilla also benefited from a growing market in the banana zone. Banana production, however, required capital investment in irrigation and drainage, managerial skills, labour efficiency, and sufficient working capital to meet frequent destruction by hurricanes. Hence General Herrera's hesitation: cattle or bananas?

For many on the Coast cattle proved to be the most appropriate choice. Throughout the period, the cattle industry grew steadily, forming a regional market and, in turn, integrating the region into a wider national market. The Coast itself was a major consumer of beef, cheese, tallow, and hides. A larger demand came from the Andean markets, where the Medellín fair played a significant role. Hides and

[1] Luna Cárdenas, *Un año y otros días*, 112, 120–1, 127, 172–4.

livestock also found their way to external markets, although attempts to develop a meat-packing industry for exports failed. Above all, stock raising was a widespread activity, affording a livelihood to a large number of people. Given the conditions of land, capital, and labour, it was the activity best suited to most rural areas. The majority of cattlemen concentrated on the expansion of their herds, although a few of them also reinvested their profits in other agricultural ventures, urban development, banking, and even industry. Barranquilla, Cartagena, Valledupar, Magangué, Montería, and Sincelejo benefited from a growing cattle trade.

The rise and consolidation of Barranquilla, after the inauguration of the railway to Sabanilla in 1871, was a major stimulus to regional growth. The achievements of this city were undoubtedly impressive. From being an insignificant village it became the main Colombian port, and by the 1920s the second largest Colombian city, although it was soon to be displaced to third position by Medellín. Trade encouraged the emergence of an industrial sector. Its early success led to the belief, as voiced by Luis Ospina Vásquez, that modern Colombian industry would primarily locate on the Coast, given its easy access to imported raw materials and the open mentality of its entrepreneurs.[2]

All these accomplishments were due, in part, to the existence of a merchant community which was ready to incorporate immigrants, foreigners, and nationals alike, to support new ventures and to fight against adverse conditions, thus developing a civic ethos which still characterized Barranquilla in 1950. The successful establishment of Scadta and the struggle to open Bocas de Ceniza were just two enterprises which identified Barranquilla with progress. Some *Barranquilleros* such as Fernando E. Baena resented the fact that the growth of the city owed so little to the national government. 'This city has achieved progress without outside support,' Baena stated, albeit with some exaggeration, in 1941.[3]

The handling of foreign trade had originally stimulated growth in Barranquilla. In turn, Barranquilla's development encouraged further economic activities in the region. Foodstuffs – including beef, rice, sugar cane, and fruits – were produced to meet an increasing urban demand. Raw materials from the Coast – cotton, leather, tallow, timber – were significant in giving initial impetus to emerging industries. Coastal agriculture, however, faced obstacles which often proved

[2] Ospina Vásquez, *Industria y protección*, 376.

[3] *La Prensa*, 27 Nov. 1941.

insurmountable. Backward technology, transport problems, lack of drainage and irrigation, shortage of capital and labour hampered agricultural development.

In spite of these difficulties, the Colombian Caribbean experienced significant changes between 1870 and 1950, while it was a major contributor to the national economy. The region supplied the Andean interior with food and raw materials. Caribbean ports were the main outlets for Colombian foreign trade. Exports of bananas, livestock, and hides contributed to the external sector of the economy. Immigrants from the interior were employed in the banana plantations and also joined, though in small numbers, the growing Coastal urban centres. By 1950, two of the five largest Colombian cities, Barranquilla and Cartagena, were on the Caribbean. By then Coastal population represented 16.7 per cent of the national total, although population density on the Coast – with the exception of Atlántico – was still the lowest among Colombian departments.

The pace of change varied from province to province, conditioned by scant resources. Growth was certainly uneven. It was against this background of scarcity that the gradual process of transformation took place, accelerating during the first decades of this century. By the mid-1920s, however, the Barranquilla business community noticed worrying signs threatening to slow down the rhythm of growth. The opening of the Panamá Canal had encouraged the rise of the Pacific port of Buenaventura. While roads and railways were built to link the producing areas of the interior with Buenaventura, communications between the Andean regions and the Caribbean were restricted to the Magdalena river. Coffee exports were diverted towards the Pacific route. Trade through the Caribbean ports, which hitherto had been a major stimulus for growth, suffered relative decline.

Problems were exacerbated by the Depression, although by the mid-1930s there were signs of recovery. Banana exports were again on the rise. The opening of Bocas de Ceniza strengthened Barranquilla's foreign trade. Industrial development took on new life. Whether or not this growth had a solid base was soon to be tested by the hardship of the 1940s. Sigatoka disease severely damaged the banana plantations; exports were halted. Labour problems in the banana zone together with worsening relationships between the government and the United Fruit Company had convinced the latter to pursue a policy of gradual abandonment of its Colombian plantations. The large sugar *Ingenios*, which had been growing despite their financial difficulties, slipped finally into bankruptcy, incapable of competing with the more efficient sugar industry of Valle del Cauca. The closing down of the *Fábrica de Tejidos Obregón* was the most evident sign of the shortcomings of Barranquilla's industrial development. Barranquilla itself could not cope with the demands of an increasing urban population. The city's attempt to resort to foreign capital was met with frustration, due both to the Second World War and the general low credit standing of Latin America. To add to Barranquilla's worries, the works in Bocas de Ceniza were a disappointment. Bocas de Ceniza was described by Gabriel García Márquez in 1951 as '1,330 tons of rust'.[4] The crisis of the Magdalena river reached a peak, determined by the lack of efficiency of river companies, by labour conflicts and poor navigation conditions.

By 1950 the Coast was suffering from increasing isolation from the main trends of national development. 'Barranquilla is . . . an island', Rafael Obregón had remarked a decade earlier, describing how distant the region felt from the Andean interior.[5] This was, above all, physical isolation as a consequence of poor transport. In 1956, in suggesting an ambitious *Plan Decenal* for the region, Karl Parrish Jr. acknowledged the errors of Barranquilla, and of the Coast in general, in not having appreciated the importance of surface transport: 'We have to acknowledge our poor understanding of the basic problem of Barranquilla fifteen or twenty years ago, namely that the lack of land transport within the Atlantic Coast and between this region and the interior of the Republic has painfully slowed down our economic development.'[6]

During the nineteenth century the Coast and the interior shared significant economic interests. Customs duties, mostly collected in Caribbean ports, were the main sources of national income. Merchant houses from the Coast traded in the most important export commodities of the country. Shipping companies – with steamers, *bongos*, and *champanes* providing practically the only means of transport, together with the pack-mule – had their headquarters in Coastal ports. But as the economy expanded based on coffee production, transport developed towards the Pacific, and the industrial sector grew faster in the more densely populated Andean regions, Coastal interests tended to clash

[4] G. García Márquez, 'Viacrucis de Bocas de Ceniza', *El Espectador*, 9 Mar. 1955, in Gilard (ed.), *Gabriel García Márquez: Entre cachacos*, ii. 518.

[5] *La Prensa*, 12 May 1941.

[6] K. Parrish Jr., *Segundo plan decenal* (Barranquilla, 1957), 4.

with those from the interior. In 1941 *La Prensa* suggested the creation of an 'axis Cartagena–Barranquilla–Santa Marta' to oppose what was called the 'axis Medellín–Manizales–Cali'.[7]

The rise of Coastal regionalism was a political consequence of increasing isolation. *Costeño* feelings had been strongly expressed during the 1875 presidential campaign, but once Rafael Núñez had gained power, they subsided as regional interests were satisfied. During the second decade of this century, there was some resentment against the central government, reaching its peak in 1919 after the organization of the Liga Costeña, as it was felt that the region was losing out. The presidential elections of 1922, by exacerbating the partisan struggle, somehow dampened regionalist feelings. *Costeño* regionalism none the less frequently returned to the political agenda giving support to issues related to the cattle sector, cotton production, industrial development and transport, the latter being the most significant source of regional cleavages. The Atlantic Coast, however, was far from being homogeneous, both economically and politically, although efforts were made to encourage stronger regional integration. In 1955 José Raimundo Sojo observed: 'The *Costa* must . . . face the country and the centralist forces in the capital as a solid and opulent bloc, whose demands ought to be given priority.'[8]

Costeño regionalism was often the expression of regional weakness; it was used as an efficient tool to gain access to national resources. A poor fiscal base could not make for a politically strong region. Political centralization gave the national government some degree of control over the Coast, although it required much tact and skill to interpret regional politics without alienating the local population. Barranquilla, which grew economically to become a focus of regional development, was slow to gain the status of a centre of political power. Under these circumstances, the Coast gradually lost direct influence over national economic policy-making. After 1918, scarcely a single *Costeño* was appointed to the *Ministerio de Hacienda*. Instead, they were conspicuously placed in the less important *Ministerio de Guerra* and *Correos y Telégrafos*, and later responsibilities in the newly established *Ministerio de Agricultura*.[9]

This does not mean that the region lost all bargaining power. Coastal politicians concentrated their activities in Congress, where they had

[7] *La Prensa*, 26 Jun. 1941.

[8] Sojo, *Barranquilla, una economía en expansión*, 192.

[9] A. González Díaz, *Ministros del Siglo XX* (Bogotá, 1982), 3-118.

some degree of success in influencing the distribution of national funds towards the region. These efforts were scattered, and they often led to clashes of interests within the Coast. What was more evident was the lack of any regional leadership with ambition to achieve national political power: there was no Rafael Núñez during the first half of this century.

The picture is far from complete, and the above summary has merely underlined some of the central issues which emerge from the wide scope of this book. Given the broad range of topics and the long time period covered, inevitably not all questions have received a definitive answer. Overall, this study has basically aimed to provide a history of the Atlantic Coast region which, by viewing it as an ensemble and readdressing its significance to Colombian history, could stimulate further research. In so doing, this book has also made substantial revisions to several stereotypes which have become commonplace in the scant references to the Atlantic Coast in Colombian historiography.

I have argued that, whatever the level of agricultural development, its shortcomings cannot, as hitherto assumed, be attributed to an expanding cattle industry which supposedly grew at the expense of a peasantry interested in arable agriculture. Cattle raising was not an exclusively large-scale operation. Its dimensions were not that large if compared to similar operations in cattle countries such as Argentina. Raising livestock was a generalized activity which grew out of the safer and even higher returns that it offered to many in the region, given the conditions of land, capital, and labour together with better market opportunities. It involved cattle ranchers of different sorts, including 'peasants', whose herds varied in size, in a complex process where the stock changed hands several times before reaching the final consumer. There developed to some degree a division of labour, often accompanied by regional specialization, which implied that cattlemen's interests were not always consonant. There is obviously a need to assess the development of the cattle industry itself, its achievements and its shortcomings under regional circumstances.

Without resorting to geographical determinism, this book has also found it necessary to address the problems of physical conditions, relevant in particular to the development of agriculture when both capital and labour are scarce resources. These difficulties partly explain the slow development of products such as cotton, rice, sugar, and cacao. They also partly explain the enthusiasm for the cultivation of bananas, where the input of foreign capital and the returns of a growing external trade encouraged investment in drainage, irrigation, and transport. It also made possible the development of a labour market, by means of higher wages which other crops could not afford. Although the available information does not allow for a definitive cost-benefit analysis, this book has suggested that the expansion of the banana trade, encouraged by the involvement of the United Fruit Company, was a stimulus for regional economic growth. By using the 'enclave' model and assuming that this designation excuses the need for any deeper analysis, traditional interpretations of the United Fruit Company on the Colombian Coast have neglected the study of how the banana industry actually worked and of the impact it had on the regional and national economies.

In spite of the importance of both pastoral and arable agriculture, there is also a need to readdress the picture which portrays the region as being overwhelmingly rural, with a population mostly devoted to subsistence farming. By 1870, and even earlier, a significant proportion of Coastal population was involved in trade and river transport. This should not be surprising since a large number of Coastal towns and important cities were located by the sea and by the rivers. As these towns and cities grew, other activities followed – boatbuilding, carpentry, shop-keeping, shoe-making, and even the professions. Townsmen not rural landowners were found advancing money for future crops to cultivators. It was the town not the rural estate which was the centre of political power and social status – though this did not either impede townsmen from acquiring rural property or keep rural landowners out of politics, not that either move provided any guarantee for success. However basic life in towns and cities was, it was more attractive than the hardship of the rural world in the tropics, and the risks involved in agriculture.

The development of the Colombian Atlantic Coast during the period under study was far from being stagnant. The Coastal urban hierarchy, for example, experienced significant changes. Older colonial centres of power suffered relative decline to give way to emerging urban centres which challenged traditional values while offering new economic, social, and political opportunities. The fact that by 1950 Barranquilla had lost its original dynamic should not detract from the long and steady period of growth that this town underwent after the mid-nineteenth century, or the impact it had over regional development.

Above all, what I hope emerges from this book is the picture of a region with distinctive features, which has merited detailed study to understand the Atlantic Coast *per se*, and its significance to Colombian history. The Coastal population shared, in general, a 'place of common living' marked by particular geographical characteristics. In addition, economic circumstances gave the Coast some degree of coherence. Politically, the Coast also showed distinctive behaviour – in electoral results and partisan activities, for example. Regional identity was also, at times, manifested in the various expressions of a *Costeño* regionalism, overcoming internal disputes. As a region with its own interests, the Coast frequently clashed with other Colombian regions, although the relationship between the Coast and neighbouring regions was not always one of conflict. Nevertheless, regional cleavages and regional alliances were major forces behind economic development and the consolidation of the national state in Colombia.

Appendix I

Exports and Imports through the Port of Barranquilla, 1873–1950 (in ton)

Year	Exports	Imports
1873	14,198	
1874	16,255	
1875	16,738	
1876	11,169	11,352
1877	11,229	7,140
1878	14,398	11,654
1879	15,258	15,173
1880	14,922	14,191
1881	15,862	
1882	15,624	
1883	20,199	
1884	13,856	
1885	5,029	
1886	13,438	
1887	14,985	10,077
1888	18,179	11,867
1889	16,164	17,260
1890	20,067	21,803
1891	20,020	25,768
1892	23,025	20,475
1893	19,206	28,094
1894		
1895		
1896		
1897	27,055	39,893
1898		
1899		
1900	10,403	15,358
1901		
1902		
1903	37,073	38,076
1904	43,581	37,232
1905	28,133	41,644
1906	33,514	30,552
1907	30,658	33,552
1908	28,675	38,836
1909	30,357	30,907
1910	28,072	42,122
1911	29,898	46,306
1912	37,972	59,977
1913	41,376	66,478
1914		
1915		
1916	57,295	55,596
1917		39,683
1918		22,302
1919	66,929	
1920		
1921		
1922	73,851	66,667
1923	79,794	106,314
1924	78,086	106,052
1925	69,632	165,430
1926	86,238	238,917
1927	83,914	243,792
1928	74,558	320,809
1929	69,985	263,784
1930	80,388	163,316
1931	77,888	107,807
1932	76,244	85,543
1933	87,849	106,499
1934	84,266	129,617
1935	59,692	127,545
1936	84,132	167,314
1937	94,778	158,625
1938	87,817	186,737
1939	79,319	221,189
1940	88,328	146,254
1941	61,979	153,247
1942	90,595	63,103
1943	119,012	85,852
1944	123,239	122,756
1945	119,044	198,693
1946	112,090	259,002
1947	97,243	411,446
1948	91,417	331,832
1949	84,211	297,276
1950	121,712	403,032

Sources: Figures for years 1876–80: Despatches from U.S. Consuls in Sabanilla, 1856–1884, NAUS, film T426; 1873–75 and 1881–1905: *PP*, 42, CII (1895), 133; 44, XCV (1898), 19–20; 45, LXXXI (1901), 590; 45, LXXXVIII (1905), 214 and 220; 59, CXXIII (1906), 755; 1906–13 and 1916: *RCCoB* (18 November 1916), 1 (31 May 1917), 9; 1917–18 (imports): Bell, *Colombia, a Commercial and Industrial Handbook*, 208; 1922–23, 1925, 1927, 1929, and 1936, *BME* (Barranquilla, March 1932), 26; 1919, 1941–50(exports), *Anuario General de Estadística* (Bogotá, 1932, 1946, 1949, and 1952), 382, 277, 267, and 1010 respectively; 1924, 1926 and 1928: Carbonell (ed), *Anuario Comercial pro-Barranquilla*, 106; 1935: Contraloría, *Geografía ecónomica de Colombia. Atlántico*, 207; 1939–50 (imports) and 1939–40 (exports): Sojo, *Barranquilla, una economia ín expansion*, 14–5.

Appendix II

Heads of Government in the Colombian Atlantic Coast, 1870–1950

Year	Bolívar	Magdalena	Atlántico
1870	R. Santodomingo V.	M. Dávila G.	
		J. M. Campo Serrano	
		M. Cotes	
1871	A. del Real	C. Cayón	
	R. Santodomingo V.		
1872	P. Blanco G.	I. Díazgranados	
	M. E. Corrales		
1873	R. Santodomingo V.	J. I. Díazgranados	
	M. E. Corrales		
	R. Santodomingo V.		
	M. E. Corrales		
	E. Baena		
1875		J. Riascos	
		J. A. Granados	
		M. Salzedo Ramón	
		M. Dávila G.	
1876	M. González C.		
	E. Baena		
	R. Núñez		
	M. González C.		
1877	R. Núñez	L. A. Robles	
	M. González C.		
	R. Núñez		
1878	B. Noguera		
	R. Núñez		
1879	M. González C.	J. M. Campo Serrano	
	B. Noguera		
1880	R. Urueta	J. A. Vengochea	
	B. Noguera		
1881	M. Laza G.		
1882	V. García	P. A. Lara	
1883	F. de P. Manotas	M. Salzedo Ramón	
1884	V. García		
	M. A. Núñez R.		
1885	J. N. Mateus		
1886	J. M. Goenaga	L. S. Cotes	
1887	H. L. Román	M. Salzedo Ramón	
	J. M. Goenaga		
1888		R. Goenaga	

Year	Bolívar	Magdalena	Atlántico
1889		E. C. de Barros	
		R. Goenaga	
1890	E. Gutiérrez de P.	P. F. de Castro	
	H. L. Román		
1893	L. Patrón	J. M. Campo Serrano	
	H. L. Román		
1894		L. A. Riascos	
1895	J. F. Vélez	C. Campo	
1896	E. Gerlein	F. E. Escobar	
		J. A. Alarcón	
1897		J. M. Campo Serrano	
1898	J. E. Osorio	A. Cotes	
	E. Gerlein		
	J. V. Aycardi		
1899	Ricardo Núñez	F. Manjarrés	
	F. A. Gómez P.		
	J. M. Goenaga		
1900	P. Carbonell	J. M. Iguarárn	
1901		J. Gnecco Laborde	
		J. R. Méndez	
1902		F. Vergara Barros	
1903	L. Vélez R.	M. A. González	
	J. F. Insignares		
1904		J. G. Coronado	
1905	L. Patrón R.	E. Solano	D. A. de Castro
	E. L. Román	S. Ceballos	
	C. Piñeres	L. S. Cotes	
	E. L. Román		
1906	J. M. Pasos	L. J. Barros	
1907	M. M. Torralbo	G. Bermúdez	
		L. J. Barros	
1908	J. Martínez A.	F. Vergara B.	A. R. Osorio
		G. Bermúdez	J. F. Insignares
		R E. Travecedo	
		T. Goenaga	
1909	J. U. Osorio	F. Vergara B.	
	J. M. de la Vega	J. M. Campo	
1910		P. A. Bruges	D. Carbonell
1911	R. Calvo C.	C. Bermúdez	A. del Río
		Manuel G. Angulo	

Year	Bolívar	Magdalena	Atlántico
1912	J. A. Gómez R.		
1913		J. M. Campo	R. M. Palacio
		P. A. Infante	P. J. Bustillo
1914	R. Rodríguez D.	R. de Armas	T. Goenaga
1915			A. Carbonell
1917	E. Arrázola		
1918	J. Martínez A.	N. Dávila	J. F. Insignares
			J. U. Osorio
1919		T. Goenaga	G. Martínez A.
		G. Bermúdez	
		L. Riascos	
		M. Campo	
1922	F. A. Gómez P.	J. A. Benavides	J. F. Insignares
	E. L. Román	J. Campo S	E. González
1923	V. Martínez R.		
1924		H. Molina	
		J. M. Núñez R.	
		N. Dávila	
		R. Robles	
1925	L. Pérez U.		
1926	E. Arrázola	J. B. Cormane	
		J. Ceballos	
1928	F. Lequerica	J. M. Núñez R.	J. U. Osorio
	H. A. de la Vega	M. Mendez B.	
1929		G. Bermúdez	
1930	R. Pupo V.	R. Goenaga	A. Pumarejo
	H. Grau	F. Ospina M.	
1931	L. P. Angulo	R. Goenaga	J. B. Fernández
	J. M. de la Espriella	M. J. de Mier	
		M. A. Zúñiga	
		J. Lanao Tovar	
1932			J. P. Manotas
1933	R. Támara	R. Campo A.	
		R. Castañeda	
		L. E. Ovalle	
1934	N. Franco P.	M. Dávila P.	N. Llinás V.
		R. Lanao L.	
1935	C. del Castillo	C. Pupo M.	J. M. Blanco N.
	M. F. Obregón	F. Ospino	
		J. I. González	
		L. R. Robles	
		J. A. Garizábal	
1936	H. A. de la Espriella	R. Pinedo S.	R. Blanco de la R.
	A. Badel	P. Castro M.	
		F. Parodi	

Year	Bolívar	Magdalena	Atlántico
1938	M. F. Obregón	M. F. Caamaño	J. A. Donado V.
1939		J. I. Vives	
1940			J. R. Lafaurie
1941	N. Pineda		
	M. Lengua		
	D. López E.		
1942	F. de P. Vargas V.	M. Guerra	R. Blanco de R.
1943		A. Fuentes	
1944	N. Franco P.	J. B. Barrios	
		P. Castro M.	A. Pumarejo
		R. Vives	
		E. Valencia	
1945	E. Bossa	F. Parodi	
	S. González G.	N. Brugés	
		L. Cabello	
1946	J. Pupo V.	J. Peña	J. M. Blanco N.
1947	J. G. de la Vega	A. Mora	
1948	A. A. Torres G.	Joaquín Campo Serrano	
		G. Vides J.	
1949	R. P. de Hoyos	J. M. Riveira D.	
	A. Araújo G.	A. Escobar C.	
1950	A. de la Vega	J. A. Benavides M.	
	R. Cavelier		

Sources: Bossa Herazo, *Cartagena Independiente*, 184–203; Alarcón, *Compendio de historia*, 433–435; Valdeblánquez, *Historia del departamento del Magdalena*, 309–309; de Castro, *Ciudades colombianas del Caribe*, 144; A. Bernal (ed), *Barranquilla, su pasado y su presente* (Barranquilla, 1946), 200–201.

Appendix III

Colombian Exchange Rates (pesos per dollar)

Year	Pesos	Year	Pesos	Year	Pesos
1905	1.04	1925	1.01	1946	1.75
1906	1.06	1926	1.01	1947	1.75
1907	1.01	1927	1.02	1948	1.76
1908	1.08	1928	1.02	1948	1.76
1909	1.05	1929	1.03	1950	1.96
1910	0.97	1930	1.03		
1911	0.99	1931	1.03		
1912	1.01	1932	1.05		
1913	1.02	1933	1.24		
1914	1.04	1934	1.62		
1915	1.08	1935	1.78		
1916	1.04	1936	1.75		
1917	1.01	1937	1.76		
1918	0.94	1938	1.78		
1919	0.93	1939	1.75		
1920	1.12	1940	1.75		
1921	1.17	1941	1.75		
1922	1.09	1942	1.75		
1923	1.05	1943	1.75		
1924	1.00	1944	1.75		
		1945	1.75		

Source: *El Banco de la República. Antecedentes, evolución y estructura* (Bogotá, 1990), 122, 366, 417.

Bibliography

1. Archival Sources

Barranquilla

Archives of the Parrish Family (APF). Uncatalogued collection of letters, pamphlets, and general papers related to the family business, 1904–50.

Bogotá

Archivo Nacional de Colombia. (ANC).
Ministerio de Industrias: correspondencia de baldíos, vols. 3, 10, 12, 16–18, 21, 27, 36, 37, 46, 52; 1873–1929.
Ministerio de Gobierno. Asuntos electorales, 1903–27.
Academia de Historia de Colombia.
Archivo de José Vicente Concha (AJVC). In correspondence, 1902–30.
Archivo de Enrique Olaya Herrera (AEOH). In correspondence, 1930–34.
Archivo del Congreso.
Cámara de Representantes. Memoriales y solicitudes, 1919.
Copiador de Marco Fidel Suárez, 1917–19. One volume of letters. Family collection (AMFS).
Papers of the Laserna Family. Deeds related to the rural estates *Don Diego* and *La Esperanza*.
Sociedad de Agricultores de Colombia. Actas, 1917–27.

Cartagena

Academia de Historia de Cartagena: Archivo de la Gobernación de Bolívar (AGB). Uncatalogued official papers but classified in boxes by years, 1870–1930.
Banco de la República. Información Económica Trimestral (IET). One volume of reports on the economy of Bolívar, by the 'Sección de Investigaciones Económicas', 1946–50.

London

Public Record Office. Foreign Office (FO), general correspondence, series 55, 1880; series 371, 1920–50, and Embassy and Consular Archives, series 135/8, 1900–43.

University College

Archives of the Bank of London and South America (BOLSA):

Anglo-South American Bank. Bogotá, Santa Marta, Cartagena, and Barranquilla, various in and out letter books, 1921–35.

Bank of London and South America. Barranquilla, out letter book, 1925–32.

Commercial Bank of Spanish America, Bogotá, in and out letters, 1921–28.

British Film Institute. My Macondo (dir. D. Weldon, Channel Four, 1990).

Medellín

Fundación Antioqueña para los Estudios Sociales

Archivo de la Sociedad Agriícola del Sinú. (ASAS):

Correspondence, 1912–50.

Movimiento de Ganado, 1913–1950.

Libro de Compradores de Ganado, 1924–33.

Feria de Medellín, 1930–50.

Libro de Actas.

Archivo del General Pedro Nel Ospina (AGPNO):

In correspondence, 1922–26. Copiador. Out correspondence, 1924.

— Archivo Ospina Hermanos (AOH): Copiador. Out correspondence, 1890–92.

Universidad de Antioquia

Archivo de Carlos E. Restrepo (ACER):

Out and in correspondence, 1910.

Oxford

Bodleian Library

Corporation of Foreign Bondholders Council: the newspaper cuttings of the Council of Foreign Bondholders in the Guildhall Library, London. Films 1411, Colombia, 1870–1947.

Malcolm Deas's private collection (MDC):

Indice Notaría Primera de Barranquilla, 1815–1900.

Indice Notaría Primera de Santa Marta, 1857–1905.

Indice Archivos notariales de Plato, Magdalena, 1876–1938.

Indice Notaría de Ciénaga, 1827–1941.

Valledupar

Archivo de la Notaría Unica, 1868–72, 1919, 1930, and 1940.

Washington

National Archives of the United States (NAUS)

Department of State:

General records of the Department of State (Record Group 59). Despatches from US Consuls in Santa Marta, 1870–83, Ríohacha, 1870–83, Cartagena, 1870–1906, and Sabanilla, 1870–84, Microfilms T427, T425, T192, T426, respectively.

State Decimal File, 1910–44.

Records of the Foreign Service Posts of the Department of State, (Record Group 84). Consular posts records, general correspondence from US Consuls in Santa Marta, Barranquilla, and Cartagena.

Department of Agriculture:

Records of the Foreign Agricultural Service (Record Group 166). Narrative Agricultural Reports (NAR): copies of agricultural reports submitted by US consular officers, agricultural attachés, agricultural commissioners, and special agents in Colombia 1904–45.

Department of Commerce:

Records of the Bureau of Foreign and Domestic Commerce (Record Group 151).

Reports of commercial attachés, 1931–40.

2. Official Publications

Reports, Memoirs, and Other Documents

Colombia

AGUDELO, F., *Informe dado por el Gobernador de Barranquilla* (Barranquilla, 1869).

Atlántico (Departamento), *Documentos relacionados con el empréstito y contratos suplementales celebrados entre el municipio de Barranquilla y la Central Trust Company of Illinois* (Barranquilla, 1925–32).

Anuario Estadístico de Colombia (Bogotá, 1875).

Anuario General de Estadística (Bogotá, 1934).

BLANCO DE LA ROSA, R., *Mensaje del Gobernador del Atlántico a la Asamblea departamental* (Barranquilla, 1937, 1938).

BORELLY, R., *Informe del Alcalde de Barranquilla al señor Gobernador del Departamento* (Barranquilla, 1945).

BUSTILLO, P. J., *Mensaje que dirige el Gobernador del Atlántico a la Asamblea Departamental* (Barranquilla, 1914).

CARBONELL, A., *Mensaje que el Gobernador del Atlántico presenta a la Asamblea del Departamento* (Barranquilla, 1918).

Censo de Población de la República de Colombia levantado el 14 de octubre de 1918 (Bogotá, 1923).

Censo general de la población de Colombia levantado el 1 de marzo de 1912 (Bogotá, 1912).

Contraloría General de la República, *Geografía ecónomica de Colombia. Bolívar* (Bogotá, 1942); *Geografía ecónomica del Atlántico* (Bogotá, 1936); *Primer censo industrial de Colombia, 1945. Departamento del Atlántico* (Bogotá, 1947); *Síntesis estadística de Colombia, 1939–1943* (Bogotá, 1944).

DEL CASTILLO, C., *Mensaje del Gobernador del departamento de Bolívar* Cartagena, 1935).

De Tomás Eastman al Consejo de Ministros (Bogotá, Jan. 1911).

Empresas Públicas Municipales, *Informe de la Junta Administradora* (Barranquilla, 1936, 1937).

GONZÁLEZ, E., *Mensaje del Gobernador del Atlántico a la Asamblea Departamental* (Barranquilla, 1928).

Informe de Francisco Javier Balmaseda, Presidente de la Junta Central de Agricultura (Cartagena, 1879).

Informe del Gobernador del Magdalena a la Asamblea (Santa Marta, 1939).

Informe del Ministro de Gobierno (Bogotá, 1912).

Informe del Ministro de Guerra al Congreso (Bogotá, 1911).

Informe del Ministro de Hacienda al Congreso (Bogotá, 1884, 1898, 1910, 1912–13, 1915, 1919–21, 1938, 1942, 1949, 1951). (Title varies).

Informe del Ministerio de Obras Públicas al Congreso: Documentos (Bogotá, 1919).

Informe del Presidente del Estado Soberano del Magdalena (Santa Marta, 1868).

Informe del Secretario de Gobierno al Gobernador del Atlántico (Barranquilla, 1933).

Informe del Secretario de Hacienda (Santa Marta, 1919, 1920).

Informe que rinde la Comisión de Presupuesto al Concejo de Barranquilla (Barranquilla, 1924).

Informe que rindió a la honorable Cámara de Representantes la Comisión designada para visitar la zona bananera del Magdalena (Bogotá, 1935).

Junta Coordinadora del Puerto, *Historia de una gran obra* , n.d.

LAFAURIE, J.R., *Mensaje del Gobernador del Atlántico* (Barranquilla, 1942).

Memoria del Gobernador de Ríohacha (Ríohacha, 1843).

Memoria del Ministro de Agricultura al Congreso (Bogotá, 1961).

Memoria del Ministro de Gobierno (Bogotá, 1925, 1929).

Memoria del Ministro de Obras Públicas al Congreso (Bogotá, 1926–7, 1930, 1931).

Memoria del Secretario de Gobierno al Gobernador de Bolívar (Cartagena, 1888, 1914, 1936) (Title varies).

Memoria del Secretario de Hacienda de Bolívar (Cartagena, 1914, 1936, 1937).

Memoria que presenta el Secretario de Instrucción Pública al Señor Gobernador del departamento (Cartagena, 1896).

Mensaje del Gobernador del Atlántico (Barranquilla, 1936).

Mensaje del Presidente constitucional a la Asamblea Legislativa (Cartagena, 1883).

Mensajes e informes del Gobernador del departamento de Bolívar (Cartagena, 1917).

Ministerio de Industrias, Anexos a la memoria de 1924 (Bogotá, 1924).

Ministerio de Obras. *Compilación de estudios. Conceptos e informes elaborados por el Consejo de Vías de Comunicación y la Comisión de Tarifas Ferroviarias y Ferrocarriles* (Bogotá, 1932); *Documentos relacionados con el Ferrocaril de Santa Marta* (Bogotá, 1923).

Misión de Rafael Reyes a los departamentos de la Costa Atlántica y Antioquia (Bogotá, 1908).

MURILLO, D., *Memoria del Secretario de Hacienda de Bolívar* (Cartagena, 1936, 1937).

NIETO, J. J., *Mensaje del Gobernador de Cartajena a la Cámara Provincial* (Cartajena, 1852).

NÚÑEZ, R., *Mensaje del Presidente Constitucional* (Bogotá, 1882, 1888).

OBREGÓN, M. F., *Memoria de Gobierno* (Cartagena, 1934).

PÉREZ, J. M., *Esposición del Gobernador de Mompox a la Cámara Provincial* (Mompox, 1853).

Policía Nacional, *Codificación de leyes y decretos ejecutivos sobre extranjeros* (Bogotá, 1928).

PRADO VILLANUEVA, F., *Informe del señor oficial de estadística de la oficina de tabaco* (Cartagena, 1937).

Registraduría, *Historia electoral de Colombia* (Bogotá, 1988).

RIASCOS, L., *Informe del Gobernador del Magdalena* (Santa Marta, 1920).

ROMÁN, H. L., *Mensaje del Gobernador del Departamento a la Asamblea* (Cartagena, 1896).

SALZEDO RAMÓN, M., *Informe del Gobernador del Magdalena* (Santa Marta, 1888).

SANTODOMINGO VILA, R., *Informe del Presidente constitucional del estado soberano de Bolívar* (Cartagena, 1871).

Santos Cabrera, J., *Informe al señor Gobernador* (Cartagena, 1934).

Vengochea, M.A., *Mensaje que el Presidente del Magdalena dirige a la Asamblea Legislativa* (Santa Marta, 1869).

United Kingdom

Department of Overseas Trade, *Report on the Finance, Industry and Trade of the Republic of Colombia* (London, 1922).

Garnett Lomax, J. (Department of Overseas Trade), *Republic of Colombia: Commercial Review and Handbook* (London, 1930).

Lee, C. A. A. (Department of Overseas Trade), *Report on the Conditions in the Republic of Colombia* (London, 1924).

Parliamentary Papers: 'Report on the port of Carthagena for the three years ending December 31, 1845' 31, LXIV (London, 1847), 330–5; and similar reports for the trade and commerce of Sabanilla, Barranquilla, Cartagena and Santa Marta, in 27, LX (1868–9); 29, LXV (1871), 209–10; 29, LXVII (1873), 909–17; 27, LXV (1873), 44–5; 35, LXXVI (1875), 362–4; 35, LXXVI (1875), 378–80; 36, LXXIII (1883); 34, LXXXI (1892), 754–6; 42, CII (1895), 117–45; 37, LXXXV (1896), 281–95, and 463–89; 44, XCV (1898), 17–26; 45, LXXXI (1901), 581–91; 45, LXXXVIII (1905), 215–21; 59, CXXIII (1906), 739–55; 42, LXXXVIII (1907), 625–43; 49, CX (1908), 761–73; 47, XCI (1911), 296–303.

'Report by Mr Bunch, Her Majesty's Chargé d'Affaires, on the Financial Condition of the United States of Colombia', 28, LXI (London, 1868–9), 3–6; and similar reports in LXVI (1874), 47–57; LXXIV (1874), 365–78; 35, LXXXIII (1887), 607–11; CIII (1888), 389–95; 32, LXXVIII (1889), 587–613; 49, XCVIII (1904), 593–628; 44, XCIII (1909), 519–34.

'Report on Agriculture in Colombia', 36, C (1888), 633–50.

'Report on the Railways of Colombia by Mr Victor Huckin, Acting British Consul–General at Bogotá', 38, XCV (1910), 3–57.

'Report on the condition and Prospects of British Trade in Colombia', 28, LXVIII (1913), 554–84.

'Report on an Excursion to the Sierra Nevada de Santa Marta to Investigate the Cultural Capabilities of the District', XC (1893–4), 139–55.

Imperial Economic Committee, 'Report of the IEC on the "Marketing and Preparing for Market of Foodstuffs Produced" in the Overseas Parts of the Empire', 12 (1926), 240–69.

Scopes, L. A., *Economic and Commercial Conditions in Colombia* (London, 1950).

SULLIVAN, W. J., (Department of Overseas Trade), *Report on the Commercial and Economic Situation in the Republic of Colombia* (London, 1925).

United States of America

BELL, P. L., (Department of Commerce), *Colombia: A Commercial and Industrial Handbook* (Washington, 1922).

Department of Commerce, *Statistical Abstract of the United States* (Washington, 1943).

Department of State, *Monthly Consular Report (MCR)* (Washington, 1881–1906).

PORTER, H. C., (Department of Agriculture), 'Cotton in Colombia', *Foreign Agricultural Service* (December 1971).

US Tariff Commission, *Agricultural, Pastoral and Forest Industries in Colombia* (Washington, 1945).

WYLIE, K., (Department of Agriculture), *The Agriculture of Colombia* Washington, 1942).

Periodicals

Anales de la Cámara de Representantes (Bogotá, 1913–15, 1921–7).
Anales del Senado (Bogotá, 1908, 1912–29).
Anuario Estadístico de Medellín (Medellín, 1938–50).
Anuario General de Estadística (Bogotá, 1932–50).
Boletín Municipal de Estadística (Barranquilla, 1928–34).
Bolívar, Gaceta Departamental (Cartagena, 1919).
Diario de Bolívar (Cartagena, 1875–84).
Diario Oficial (Bogotá, 1924, 1925).
Gaceta de Bolívar (Cartagena, 1870–74).
Registro de Bolívar (Cartagena, 1885–1907).

3. Contemporary Books, Memoirs, Articles, and Pamphlets

ABELLO, J., *El departamento del Atlántico* (Barranquilla, 1915).

ACOSTA, J., *Manual del navegante* (Barranquilla, 1945).

ADAMS, F. U., *Conquest of the Tropics* (New York, 1914).

ALARCÓN, J. J., *Compendio de historia del departamento del Magdalena* Bogotá, 1963).

ARANGO, CARLOS (ed.), *Sobrevivientes de las bananeras* (Bogotá, 1981).

ARMENTA, A. L., *La renta de salinas maritimas. Sus defectos y el modo de corregirlos* (Barranquilla, 1914).

BADEL, D., *Diccionario histórico geográfico de Bolívar* (Corozal, 1943).

BAENA, F., and VERGARA, J. R., *Barranquilla, homenaje del Banco Dugand* (Barranquilla, 1922).

Banco Comercial de Barranquilla, 1905–1955 (Barranquilla, 1955).

Banco de Barranquilla, *Informes y balance general presentados por la Junta Directiva a la Junta General de Accionistas en sus sesiones ordinarias de 24 y 26 de Julio de 1889* (Barranquilla, 1889, and similar reports dated Jan. 1890 and July 1899).

Banco Dugand, *Informe de la Junta Administradora a la Asamblea de accionistas* (Barranquilla, 1920).

The Barranquilla Railway and Pier Company, Ltd. (London, 1928).

BERGER, J., *Memoria detallada de los estudios del río Magdalena, obras proyectadas para su arreglo y resumen de su presupuesto* (Bogotá, 1926).

BERNIER, A., *Datos sobre el territorio guajiro* (Ríohacha, 1911).

BLACK, MCKENNEY, and STEWART, *The Bocas de Ceniza and the Magdalena River to Barranquilla, Colombia* (Washington, 1921).

BOY, H., *Una historia con alas* (Madrid, 1955).

BRICEÑO, S., *Geografía militar de Colombia* (Bogotá, 1955).

CARBONELL, A., *La quincena política* , 5 vols. (Bogotá, 1952).

CARBONELL, A. L. (ed.), *Anuario comercial pro-Barranquilla* (Barranquilla, 1936).

CASTAÑEDA ARAGÓN, G., *El Magdalena de hoy* (Santa Marta, 1927).

CASTRO MONSALVO, P., *Un campesino previno al país* (Bogotá, 1972).

CORRALES, M. E. (ed.), *Efemérides y Anales del Estado Soberano de Bolívar* (Bogotá, 1892), iv.

CORTÉS VARGAS, C., *Los sucesos de las bananeras* (Bogotá 1979).

CROWTHER, S., *The Romance and Rise of the American Tropics* (New York, 1929).

CUERVO MÁRQUEZ, L., *Geografía médica y patológica de Colombia* (Bogotá and New York, 1915).

DE CASTRO, A., *Ciudades colombianas del Caribe* (Barranquilla, 1942).

DE GREIFF OBREGÓN, L., *Semblanzas y comentarios* (Medellín, 1955).

DE LA TORRE Y MIRANDA, A., 'Noticia individual de las poblaciones nuevamente fundadas en la provincia de Cartagena', in J. P. Urueta ed.), *Documentos para la historia de Cartagena* (Cartagena, 1894), iv.

DE NARVAEZ Y LA TORRE, A., 'Relación o informe de la Provincia de Santa Marta y Ríohacha, por lo que respecta al estado actual de su comercio, haciendas y frutos. . . (1788)', in A. B. Cuervo (ed.), *Colección de documentos inéditos sobre la geografía y la historia de Colombia* (Bogotá, 1982), ii. 175–202.

DIAZ, A., *Sinú, pasión y vida del trópico* (Bogotá, 1935).

DIAZ, A. M., *Compendio de Geografía de Colombia* (Barcelona, 1907).

Escrituras y estatutos de la Compañía Urbanizadora El Prado Barranquilla, 1920).

EXBRAYAT, J., *Reminiscencias monterianas* (Montería, 1939).

FAWCETT, W., *The Banana, its Cultivation, Distribution and Commercial uses* (London, 1921).

Ferrocarril de Santa Marta, *Escritos de la prensa y el país y documentos varios relacionados con la empresa* (Barranquilla, 1911).

Ferrocarril de Santa Marta, *Exposición que al honorable Congreso de 1915 hace el gerente de la Compañía* (Bogotá, 1919).

FRANCO, P. E,. *Mis andanzas en la guerra de los mil días* (Barranquilla, 1964).

GERSTL, O., *Memorias e historias* (Caracas, 1974).

GNECCO LABORDE, J., *Nociones de geografía del departamento del Magdalena* (Santa Marta, 1896).

GOENAGA, J. M., *Colonización de la Sierra Nevada de Santa Marta* (Bogotá, 1911).

GOENAGA, M., *Lecturas locales. Crónicas de mi vieja Barranquilla* (Barranquilla, 1953).

— (ed.), *Acción costeña* (Barranquilla, 1926).

GÓMEZ PICÓN, R., *Magdalena, el río de Colombia* (Bogotá, 1945).

GRAU, E., *La ciudad de Barranquilla en 1896* (Barranquilla, 1896).

GREGG, E. S., 'Trading in the Tropics', *Economic Geography*, 1 (Oct. 1925), 396–401.

GUBEREK, S., *Yo vi crecer a un país* (Bogotá, 1987), 2 vols.

Historia gráfica de la Urbanización de El Prado (Barranquilla, 1945).

International Institute of Agriculture, *International Trade in Meat* (Rome, 1936).

— *World Cotton Production and Trade* (Rome, 1936).

JONES, C. F., 'Agricultural Regions of South America', *Economic Geography*, 5 (1929).

LANAO LOAIZA, R., *Las pampas escandalosas* (Manizales, 1936).

La prensa asociada y el Ferrocarril de Santa Marta (Bogotá, 1911).

LEMAITRE, D., *Soledad Román de Núñez: Recuerdos* (Cartagena, 1938).

Libro azul de Colombia (New York, 1918).

LLERAS RESTREPO, C., *Crónicas de mi propia vida* (Bogotá, 1983), i.

LÓPEZ, A., *Problemas colombianos* (Paris, 1927, repr. Medellín, 1976).

— *Idearium Liberal* (Paris, 1931).

Los partidos políticos en Colombia (Bogotá, 1922).

LÓPEZ, E. (ed.), *Almanaque de los hechos colombianos* (Medellín, 1919).

LUNA CÁRDENAS, A., *Un año y otros días con el General Benjamín Herrera en Aracataca* (Medellín, 1960).

MADIEDO, M. M., *Nuestro siglo XIX* (Bogotá, 1868).

MÁRQUEZ, A. J., *Saludo a Barranquilla* (Barranquilla, 1913).

MARTÍNEZ APARICIO, A., and Niebles, R. (eds.), *Directorio Anuario de Barranquilla* (Barranquilla, 1892).

MATTAR, A., *Guía social de la colonia árabe en Colombia* (Bogotá, 1945).

MONSALVE, D., *Colombia cafetera* (Barcelona, 1927).

NAVARRO, P. J., *El problema del Magdalena. El Ferrocarril de Santa Marta y la falta de cumplimiento de la Compañía inglesa* (Bogotá, 1915).

— *El parlamento en pijama* (Bogotá, 1935, 1943), 2 vols.

'The New Barranquilla', *The American City Series*, 5B (Washington, 1928).

New Granada Canal and Steam Navigation Co., *Remarks on the Canal or 'Dique' of Carthagena, New Granada, and its Navigation by Steam* (New York, 1855).

NIETO, J. J., *Bosquejo histórico de la revolución que rejeneró al Estado de Bolívar* (Cartagena, 1862).

— 'Geografía histórica, estadística y local de la provincia de Cartajena . . . descrita por cantones' *Boletín Historial* , 34/6 (Apr. 1918).

NÚÑEZ, R., *La reforma política* (Bogotá, 1945–50), 8 vols.

ORTEGA DÍAZ, A., *Ferrocarriles colombianos* (Bogotá, 1923).

— *Ferrocarriles colombianos: Legislación ferroviaria* (Bogotá, 1949).

ORTEGA TORRES, J. J. (ed.), *Marco Fidel Suárez: Obras* (Bogotá, 1966).

PALACIO, J. H., *Historia de mi vida* (Bogotá, 1942).

— *Historia de mi vida* , 2 (Bogotá, n.d., possibly 1991).

— *La Historia de mi vida. Crónicas inéditas* (Barranquilla, 1992).

PALMER, J. P., 'The Banana in the Caribbean Trade', *Economic Geography* 8 (1932).

PARRA, A. *Memorias* (Bogotá, 1912).

PARRISH Jr., K. C. *Segundo Plan Decenal* (Barranquilla, 1957).

PEARSE, A. *Colombia, with Special Reference to Cotton.. Being the Report of the Journey of the International Cotton Mission through the Republic of Colombia* (London, 1926).

PÉREZ, F., *Jeografía de Colombia* (Bogotá, 1863), 2 vols.

PLATT, R. P., 'Railroad Progress in Colombia' *Geographical Review*, 16 (1926).

POSADA-GUTIÉRREZ, J., *Memorias histórico-políticas* (Bogotá, 1971), iii.

Primera asamblea nacional de estadística agropecuaria (Bogotá, 1939).

RASH-ISLA, E. (ed.), *Directorio comercial pro-Barranquilla* (Barranquilla, 1928).

RASH-ISLA, E., and RASH-ISLA (ed.), *Guía comercial de Barranquilla* (Barranquilla, 1910).

REICHEL-DOLMATOFF, G. (ed.), *Diario de viaje del P. Joseph Palacios de la Vega entre los indios y negros de la Provincia de Cartagena en el Nuevo Reino de Granada, 1787–1788* (Bogotá, 1955).

REBOLLO, P. M., *Memorias* (Barranquilla, 1956).

RENNER, G. T., 'Colombia's Internal Development', *Economic Geography* III (1927).

RESTREPO, C. R., *Orientación Republicana* (Bogotá, 1972), 2 vols.

REYNOLDS, P., *Banana Chart Manual* (New York, 1927).

ROMERO AGUIRRE, A., *Confesiones de un aprendiz de estadista* (Bogotá, 1949).

— *Un radical en el Congreso* (Bogotá, 1949).

RUEDA VARGAS, T., *El Ejército Nacional* (Bogotá, 1984).

SAMPER, J. M., *Ensayo sobre las revoluciones políticas y la condición social de las repúblicas colombianas* (1861) (Bogotá, 1984).

SÁNCHEZ SANTAMARÍA, I. M., *Geografía comercial y ecónomica de Colombia* (Bogotá, 1928).

SARASÚA, J., *Recuerdos de Barranquilla* (Barranquilla, 1988).

SILVESTRE, F., *Descripción del Reyno de Santa Fe de Bogotá (1789)* (Bogotá, 1968).

SOJO, J. F., *El Club Barranquilla* (Barranquilla, 1942).

SUNDHEIM, A., *Vocabulario costeño o lexicografía de la región septentrional de la República de Colombia* (Paris, 1922).

TAYLOR, C., 'Settlement Zones of the Sierra Nevada de Santa Marta, Colombia', *Geographical Review* , 21 (1931), 539–58.

The Basis of a Development Program for Colombia (Baltimore, 1950).

This is Barranquilla (n.p., 1954).

TODD, J. E., *The World's Cotton Crops* (London, 1915).

TORRES GIRALDO, I., *Los inconformes* (Bogotá, 1973–4), 5 vols.

United Fruit Company, *A Short History of the Banana and a Few Recipes for its Use* (Boston, 1904).

United Fruit Company (Medical Department), *Annual Report* (Boston, 1920–29).

URIBE URIBE, R., 'El banano', *Revista Nacional de Agricultura* (Bogotá, 1 May 1908), 5–105.

URUETA, J. P., and DE PIÑERES, E. G., *Cartagena y sus cercanías* (Cartagena, 1912).

VALIENTE, F., *et al.* (eds.), *Cartagena ilustrada* (Cartagena, 1911).

VARELA MARTÍNEZ, R., *Economía agrícola de Colombia* (Bogotá, 1949).

VEDOVELLI-BRAGUZZO, C., *Programma di una societa per azioni per la colonizzazione di 2,000,000 di pert met di terreni concessi del governo colombiano nella Sierra Nevada di Santa Marta* (Milano, 1892).

VERGARA Y VELASCO, J. J., *Nueva geografía de Colombia* (Bogotá, 1901).

VESGA Y AVILA, J. M., *Perfiles colombianos* (Bogotá, 1908).

WATT, G., *The Wild and Cultivated Cotton Plants of the World* (London, 1907).

WILSON, C. M., *Empire in Green and Gold: The Story of the American Banana Trade* (1947).

4. Newspapers and Journals

El Agricultor (Bogotá, 1879, 1881, 1883, 1889, 1894).

Alef (Santa Marta, 1939).

Bank of London and South America, *Monthly Review*, later published *Fortnightly Review* (London, 1916–29, 1944–48).

Board of Trade Journal (London, 1898, 1899).

Boletín Industrial (Barranquilla, 1873).

British and Latin American Trade Gazette (London, 1920).

Colombian Trade Review (London, 1921–2).

El Debate (Barranquilla, 1921).

La Defensa (Barranquilla, 1915).

El Día (Barranquilla, 1919).

Diario del Comercio (Barranquilla, 1923).

El Estado (Santa Marta, 1931, 1934).

Ganadería de Bolívar (Sincelejo, 1932).

El Heraldo (Cartagena, 1883).

El Heraldo (Barranquilla, 1938).

Heraldo de la Costa (Barranquilla, 1919).

El Heraldo Nacional (Santa Marta, 1917).

El Imparcial (Barranquilla, 1919).

La Lucha (Sincelejo, 1934).

Mundo al Día (Bogotá, 1929).

El Nacional (Barranquilla, 1945).

Panamá Canal Record (August 1917).

La Patria (Cartagena, 1930).

El Pequeño Diario (Magangué, 1916,1918).

El Porvenir (Cartagena, 1904, 1910, 1911).

La Prensa (Barranquilla, 1932–4, 1938, 1940–2, 1946).

El Rayo (El Banco, 1916, 1919).

República (Barranquilla, 1919).

Revista de Colombia (Bogotá, 1873).

Revista de Ganadería (Bogotá, 1939).

Revista de la Cámara de Comercio de Barranquilla (Barranquilla, 1916–45).
Revista Nacional de Agricultura (Bogotá, 1905–39).
El Tiempo (Bogotá, 1919).
La Union Comercial (Cartagena, 1916).
Union Liberal (Cartagena, 1917).
El Universal (Barranquilla, 1919).
Vagos, Maleantes y Rateros (Barranquilla, 1937–8).

5. Travel Books and Guides

BATES, H. W., *Central America, the West Indies and South America* (London, 1878).
BINGHAM, H., *A Journal of an Expedition Across Venezuela and Colombia* (London, 1909).
BOLINDER, G., *We Dared the Andes* (London, 1958).
BONNEY, C. V. R. (ed.), *Legacy of Historical Gleanings* (Albany, NY, 1875).
CAMERON, C., *Woman's Winter in South America* (London, 1910).
CANDELIER, H., *Río-Hacha et les Indiens Goejires* (Paris, 1893).
CANÉ, M., *En viaje, 1881–1882* (Paris, 1884).
CARNEGIE-WILLIAMS, R., *A Year in the Andes or a Lady's Adventure in Bogotá* (London, 1882)
COCHRANE, C. S., *Journal of a Residence and Travels in Colombia During the Years 1823 and 1824* (London, 1925).
The Colombian Railways and Navigation Co., *Visit Colombia* (London, 1930).
CREVAUX, J., *Voyages dans l'Amérique du Sud* (Paris, 1883).
CUNNINGHAME GRAHAM, R., *Cartagena and the Banks of the Sinú* (London, 1921).
CURTIS, W. E., *The Capitals of Spanish America* (New York, 1888).
DAWE, M. T., *Account of a Journey down the Magdalena River, Through the Magdalena Province and the Peninsula of Goajira* (Bogotá, 1917).
D'ESPAGNAT, P., *Recuerdos de la Nueva Granada* (Bogotá, 1942).
DUFFIELD, A. J., *Recollections of Travels Abroad* (London, 1889).
EARLY, E., *Ports of the Sun* (Boston, 1937).
EDER, P. A., *Colombia* (London, 1913).
FARSON, N., *Transgressor in the Tropics* (London, 1937).
FOREST, A. S., *A Tour Through South America* (London, 1913).
GÓNGORA ECHENIQUE, M., *Lo que he visto en Colombia* (Madrid, 1936).
GOSSELMAN, C. A., *Viaje por Colombia, 1825 y 1826* (Bogotá, 1981).
HAMILTON, J. P., *Viajes por el interior de las provincias de Colombia* (Bogotá, 1955).

HOLTON, I., *New Granada: Twenty Months in the Andes* (New York, 1857, and London, 1957).

HUMBOLDT, A. VON., *Personal Narrative of Travels to the Equinoctial Regions of America* (London, 1853), iii.

ISHERWOOD, C., *The Condor and the Cows* (London, 1949).

JUAN, G., and DE ULLOA, A., *Voyage to South America: Describing at Large the Spanish Cities, Towns, Provinces, on that Extensive Continent* (London, 1806).

KOEBEL, W. H. (ed.), *Anglo-South American Handbook* (London, 1921).

LEVINE, V., *Colombia* (London, 1914).

MOLLIEN, G., *Viaje por la república de Colombia en 1823* (Bogotá, 1944).

NILES, B., *Colombia, Land of Miracles* (New York and London, 1924).

PARRISH, R. H., *An Iowan's View of Colombia, South America* (n.p. 1921).

PEARSON, H. C., *What I Saw in the Tropics* (New York, 1906).

PEÑA, P. A., *Del Avila al Monserrate* (Bogotá, 1913).

PÉREZ, F., *Episodios de un viaje* (Bogotá, 1946).

PETRE LORAINE, F., *The Republic of Colombia: An Account of the Country its People, its Institutions and its Resources* (London, 1906).

POWLES, J. D., *New Granada: Its Internal Resources* (London, 1863).

RECLUS, E., *Colombia* (Bogotá, 1958).

— *Viaje a la Sierra Nevada de Santa Marta* (Bogotá, n.d.).

— *Mis exploraciones en América* (Valencia, 1910).

ROBINSON, W., *A Flying Trip to the Tropics* (Cambridge, Mass., 1985).

ROMOLI, K., *Colombia: A Gateway to South América* (New York, 1941).

ROTHLISBERGER, R., *El Dorado* (Bogotá, 1963).

SAINT GAUTIER, S. M., *Voyage en Colombie* (Paris, 1893).

SAFFRAY, D., *Viaje a Nueva Granada* (Bogotá, 1948).

SCRUGGS, W., *The Colombian and Venezuelan Republics* (Boston, 1905).

SCHENCK, F. VON., *Viajes por Antioquia en el año 1880* (Bogotá, 1953).

SIMMONS, F. A., 'On the Sierra Nevada de Santa Marta and its Watershed', *Proceedings of the Royal Geographical Society*, 3 (London, 1881).

— 'Notes on the Topography of the Sierra Nevada de Santa Marta', *Proceedings of the Royal Geographical Society*, 1 (London, 1879).

STRIFFLER, L., *El río San Jorge (1880)* (Montería, 1958; new edn., Barranquilla, 1993).

— *El río Cesar. Relación de un viaje a la Sierra Nevada de Santa Marta en 1876* (n.d., possibly 1882). The prologue was written in San Marcos in 1882.

— *El río Sinú* (Montería, 1922; new edn., Barranquilla, 1993).

THOMSON, N., *Colombia, the Country to Watch* (London, 1927).

TROLLOPE, A., *The West Indies and the Spanish Main* (London, 1859).

6. Other Books, Articles, and General References

ABEL, C., *Politica, iglesia y partidos en Colombia* (Bogotá, 1987).

— and LEWIS, C., *Latin America, Economic Imperialism and the State* (London and Dover, 1985).

ALTER, P., *Nationalism* (London, 1989).

ANDERSON, B., *Imagined Communities* (London, 1983).

ANGULO VALDES, C., 'El departamento del Atlántico y sus condiciones físicas', *Revista Geográfica* (Barranquilla, Dec. 1952).

ARCHILA, M., 'Barranquilla y el río: una historia social de sus trabajadores', *Controversia* 142 (Bogotá, Nov. 1978).

— 'La clase obrera colombiana, 1886–1930', in A. Tirado Mejía (ed.), *Nueva Historia de Colombia*, iii.

ARDANT, G., 'Financial Policy and Economic Infrastructure of Modern States and Nations', in C. Tilly (ed.), *The Formation of National States in Western Europe* (Princeton, 1975).

ARRÁZOLA, R., *Palenque, primer pueblo libre de América: historia de las sublevaciones de los esclavos de Cartagena* (Cartagena, 1970).

ARRUBLA, M. (ed.), *La agricultura colombiana en el siglo XX* (Bogotá, 1976).

— and URRUTIA, M. (eds.), *Compendio de estadísticas históricas de Colombia* (Bogotá, 1970).

Aspectos pólemicos de la historia colombiana del siglo XIX (Bogotá, 1983).

BACCA, R. I., 'El modernismo en Barranquilla', *Boletín Cultural y Bibliográfico*, 30/33 (1994).

BAKER, C. J., *An Indian Rural Economy, 1880–1955: The Tamilnad Countryside* (Oxford, 1984).

BARNHART, D. S., 'Colombian Transport and the Reforms of 1931: An Evaluation', *Hispanic American Historical Review* (Feb. 1958).

BARRAN, J. P., and NAHUM, B., 'Uruguayan Rural History', *Hispanic-American Historical Review* , 64/4 (1984).

BASTOS DE AVILA, F., *Immigration in Latin America* (Washington, 1964).

BAUER, A., 'Rural Workers in Spanish America: Problems of Peonage and Opression', *Hispanic American Historical Review*, 59/1 (1979).

BEJARANO, J. A., *El régimen agrario de la economía exportadora a la economía industrial* (Bogotá, 1979).

— 'La historia de las ciencias agropecuarias hasta 1950', *Ensayos de historia agraria colombiana* (Bogotá, 1987).

— *Economía y poder* (Bogotá, 1985).

BELL, G.(ed.), *El caribe colombiano* (Barranquilla, 1988).

BELL-VILLADA, G. H., *García Márquez: The Man and his Work* (Chapel Hill, NY, and London, 1990).

BERGQUIST, C., 'En nombre de la historia: una crítica disciplinaria de Historia doble de la Costa de Orlando Fals Borda', *Huellas* (Aug. 1989).

BERGERON, L. (ed.), *La croissance regionale dans l'Europe Mediterranénne: 18e–20e siècle* (Paris, 1992).

BERNAL SALAMANCA, R., *Las condiciones económico-sociales y el costo de la vida de la clase obrera en la ciudad de Barranquilla* (Bogotá, 1948).

BERROCAL HOYOS, J., *La colonización antioqueña en el departamento de Córdoba* (Montería, 1980).

BEYER, R. C., 'Transportation and the Coffee Industry in Colombia', *Inter-American Economic Affairs* , 2/3 (1948).

BISHKO, C. J., 'The Peninsula Background of Latin American Cattle Ranching', *Hispanic American Historical Review*, 32/4, (Nov. 1952).

BLANCO BARROS, J. A., *El norte de Tierradentro y los orígenes de Barranquilla* (Bogotá, 1987).

BONIVENTO, J. A., *Aspectos socioeconómicos del departamento del Magdalena* (Bogotá, 1963).

BOSSA HERAZO, D., *Cartagena independiente: Tradición y desarrollo.* (Cartagena, 1967).

BOTERO, F., and GUZMAN BARNEY, A., 'El enclave agrícola en la zona bananera de Santa Marta', *Cuadernos Colombianos*, 11 (Bogotá, 1977).

BOURGOIS, P. I., *Ethnicity at Work: Divided Labor on a Central American Plantation* (Baltimore and London, 1989).

BRAUDE, H. W., 'The Significance of Regional Studies for the Elaboration of National Economic History', *The Journal of Economic History* (Dec. 1960), 588–596.

BREW, R., *El desarrollo económico de Antioquia desde la independencia hasta 1920* (Bogotá, 1977).

BROWN, J., *Agriculture in England: A Survey on Farming, 1870–1947* (Manchester, 1987).

BULMER-THOMAS, V., *The Political Economy of Central America since 1920* (Cambridge, 1987).

BURGOS PUCHE, R., *El general Burgos* (Bogotá, 1965).

BUSHNELL, D., *Eduardo Santos y la política del buen vecino* (Bogotá, 1984).

BUTLIN, R. A., 'Regions in England and Wales, 1600–1914', in R. A. Dodgshon and R. A. Butlin, *An Historical Geography of England and Wales* (Cambridge, 1990), 223–54.

CARVALLO, G., *El hato venezolano, 1900–1980* (Caracas, 1985).

CASTRO MONSALVO, P., *Un campesino previno al país* (Bogotá, 1972).

COLON, C. E., *La rebelión poética de Luis Carlos López* (Bogotá, 1981).

CROSSLEY, J. C., and GREENHILL, R., 'The River Plate Beef Trade', in D. C. M. Platt *Business Imperialism, 1840–1930* (Oxford, 1977).

CURTIN, P. D., *Death by Migration: Europe's Encounter with the Tropical World in the Nineteenth Century* (Cambridge, 1989).

DAVIES, P. N., *Fyffes and the Banana: A Centenary History, 1888–1988* (London, 1990).

DAVIES, R. R. G., *Airlines of Latin America since 1919* (London, 1984).

DEAS, M., *Del poder y la gramática* (Bogotá, 1993).

— 'The Fiscal Problems of Nineteenth-Century Colombia', *Journal of Latin American Studies*, 14/2 (Nov. 1982).

— 'La influencia inglesa y otras influencias en Colombia, 1880–1930', in A. Tirado (ed.), *Nueva Historia de Colombia* (Bogotá, 1984).

— 'Algunas notas sobre el caciquismo en Colombia', *Revista de Occidente*, 127 (Oct. 1973).

— 'Poverty, Civil War and Politics: Ricardo Gaitán Obeso and his Magdalena River Campaign in Colombia, 1885', *Nova Americana* , 2 (1979).

— 'La presencia de la política nacional en la vida provinciana, pueblerina y rural de Colombia en el primer siglo de la República', in M. Palacios (ed.), *La unidad nacional en América Latina: del regionalismo a la nacionalidad* (Mexico, 1983).

DE BARRANQUILLA, J. A., *Así es la Guajira: Itinerario de un misionero-capuchino* (Bogotá, 1953).

DE LA PEDRAJA, R., 'La Guajira en el siglo XIX: indígenas, contrabando y carbón', *Desarrollo y Sociedad* (Bogotá, June 1981).

DEL CASTILLO, N., *El primer Núñez* (Bogotá, 1971).

DELPAR, H., *Red Against Blue: The Liberal Party in Colombian Politics 1863–1899* (Alabama, 1981).

DICKINSON, R. E., *The City Region in Western Europe* (London, 1967).

DOMAR, E., 'The Causes of Slavery or Serfdom: A Hypothesis', *Journal of Economic History*, 30 (1970).

DOYLE, M., *Empires* (Ithaca, NY, and London, 1986).

DUNCAN BARETTA, S. R., and MARKOFF, J., 'Civilization and Barbarism: Cattle Frontiers in Latin America', *Comparative Studies in Society and History* (1978).

ELLIS, F., *Las transnacionales del banano en centroamérica* (San José, 1983).

Empresas Varias de Medellín, *Ferias de ganados, 25 años* (Medellín, 1974).

ESCALANTE, A., Geoeconomía del algodón, *Revista Geográfica*, 1/1 (Barranquilla, 1952).

EXBRAYAT, J., *Historia de Montería* (Montería, 1971).

FAJARDO, D., *Haciendas, campesinos y políticas agrarias en Colombia, 1920–1980* (Bogotá, 1986).

FALS BORDA, O., *Capitalismo, hacienda y poblamiento en la Costa Atlántica* (Bogotá, 1976).

— *Historia de la cuestión agraria en Colombia* (Bogotá, 1975).

— *Mompox y Loba* (Bogotá, 1980).

— *El Presidente Nieto* (Bogotá, 1981).

— 'Réplica a Bergquist: Comentarios a la mesa redonda sobre la Historia Doble de la Costa', *Huellas* (Dec. 1989).

— *Resistencia en el San Jorge* (Bogotá, 1984).

— *Retorno a la Tierra* (Bogotá, 1986).

— *La insurgencia de las provincias* (Bogotá, 1988).

— 'Influencia del vecindario pobre colonial en las relaciones de producción de la Costa Atlántica colombiana', *El agro en el desarrollo histórico colombiano* (Bogotá, 1977).

FAWCETT, L. L., 'Lebanese, Palestinians, and Syrians in Colombia', in A. Hourani and N. Shehadi (eds.), *The Lebanese in the World* (London, 1992).

FISHER, C., *The Reality of Place* (London, 1965).

FRIEDEMANN, N., *Ma ngombe: guerreros y ganaderos en Palenque* (Bogotá, 1979).

GARCÍA, J. J., *Epocas y gentes* (Bogotá, 1977).

GASPAR, J. C., *Limón, 1880–1940: Un estudio de la industria bananera en Costa Rica* (San José, 1979).

GIBERTI, H., *Historia económica de la ganadería argentina* (Buenos Aires, 1981).

GILARD, J. (ed.), *Gabriel García Márquez: Obra periodística* (Barcelona, 1982).

— 'El grupo de Barranquilla', *Revista Iberoamericana*,128–9 (July–Dec. 1984).

— (ed). *Alvaro Cepeda Samudio: En el margen de la ruta* (Bogotá, 1985).

GILBERT, E. W, 'The Idea of Region', *Geography*, 45 (1960).

GILHODES, P., 'La Colombie et l'United Fruit Company', *Revue Française de Science Politique*, 17 (Apr. 1967).

GILMORE, R. L., and HARRISON, J. P., 'Juan Bernardo Elbers and the Introduction of the Steam Navigation in the Magdalena River', *Hispanic American Historical Review* (Aug. 1948).

GONZÁLEZ DÍAZ, A., *Ministros del siglo XX* (Bogotá, 1982).

GONZÁLEZ, L., *Invitación a la microhistoria* (Mexico, 1973).

GORDON, L. B., 'Human Geography and Ecology in the Sinú Region of Colombia', *Ibero-Americana*, 39 (Berkeley, 1957).

GRUNWALD, J., and MUSGROVE, P., *Natural Resources in Latin American Development* (n. p., 1970).

GUHL, E., 'Ambiente geográfico-humano de la Costa Atlántica', *Revista Geográfica*, 1/1 (Barranquilla, 1952).

HALL, R. B., 'The Geographic Region: A Resumé', *AAAG: A Conference on Regions*, 30/3 (1935).

HARTSHORNE, R., *Perspective on the Nature of Geography* (London, 1963).

HARVIE, C., *The Rise of Regional Europe* (London and New York, 1994).

HAVENS, E., and USANDIZAGA, E., *Tres barrios de invasión* (Bogotá, 1966).

HELMSING, A. H. J., *Firms, Farms and the State in Colombia* (Boston, 1988).

HERRERA SOTO, R., and ROMERO CASTAÑEDA, R., *La zona bananera del Magdalena* (Bogotá, 1979).

HILL, P., *Development Economics on Trial* (Cambridge, 1989).

HOBSBAWM, E., *Nations and Nationalism since 1780* (Cambridge, 1990).

HORNA, H., 'Transportation, Modernization and Entrepreneurship in Nineteenth–century Colombia', *Journal of Latin American Studies*, 14/I, 33–54.

JAMES, P., *A Geography of Man* (Boston, 1949).

JAMES, P. P., 'Toward a Further Understanding of the Regional Concept', *AAAG: A Conference on Regions*, 30/3 (1935).

JOHNSON, D. C., *Santander* (Bogotá, 1984).

JONES, C. A., *International Business in the Nineteenth Century: The Rise and Fall of a Cosmopolitan Bourgeoisie* (Brighton, 1987).

KALMANOWITZ, S., *Economía y nación* (Bogotá, 1982).

— *El desarrollo de la agricultura en Colombia* (Bogotá, 1982).

— 'El régimen agrario durante el siglo XIX', *Manual de Historia de Colombia* (Bogotá) ii.

KEPNER, C. D., and SOOTHILL, J. H., *The Banana Empire: A Case Study of Economic Imperialism* (New York, 1935).

KIMBLE, G. H. T., 'The Inadequacy of the Regional Concept', in L. D. Stamp, and S. W. Wooldridge (eds.), *London Essays in Geography* (London,1951).

KUETHE, A., 'La campaña pacificadora en la frontera de Ríohacha, 1772–1779', *Huellas* (Apr. 1987).

LAMOREAUX, N., *The Great Merger Movement in American Business, 1895–1904* (Cambridge, 1985).

LEBERGOTT, S., 'The Returns to U.S. Imperialism, 1890–1929', *Journal of Economic History* (June 1980), 229–52.

LEGRAND, C., 'El conflicto de las bananeras', *Nueva Historia de Colombia*, 3 (Bogotá, 1989).

— *Colonización y protesta campesina en Colombia, 1850–1950* (Bogotá, 1988).

LEMAITRE, E., *Breve historia de Cartagena* (Bogotá, 1979).

— *Historia general de Cartagena* (Bogotá, 1983), 4 vols.

— *Rafael Reyes* (Bogotá, 1967).

— *El general Juan José Nieto y su época* (Bogotá, 1983).

LEURQUIN, P., 'Cotton Growing in Colombia, Achievements and Uncertainties', *Food Research Institute Studies*, 6/1 (1966).

LEVINE, R., *Pernambuco in the Brazilian Federation, 1889–1937* (Stanford, Calif., 1978).

LIEVÁNO AGUIRRE, I., *Rafael Núñez* (Lima, 1944).

LLERAS REstrepo, C., *La estadística nacional: Su organización, sus problemas* (Bogotá, 1938).

LLINÁS, J. P., *Felipe Angulo y la regeneración* (Bogotá, 1989).

LÓPEZ MICHELSEN, A., *Esbozos y atisbos* (Bogotá, 1980).

LORENTE, L., 'La ganadería bovina en Colombia', in A. Machando, (ed.), *Problemas agrarios colombianos* (Bogotá, 1986).

Los estudios regionales en Colombia: el caso de Antioquia (Medellín, 1982).

LOVE, J. H., 'An Approach to Regionalism', in R. Graham, and P. Smith, (eds.), *New Approaches to Latin American History* (Texas, 1974).

— *Rio Grande do Sul and Brazilian Regionalism, 1882–1930* (Stanford, Calif., 1971)

— *Sao Paulo in the Brazilian Federation* (Stanford, Calif., 1980).

— 'Federalismo y regionalismo en Brasil, 1889–1937', in M. Carmagnani (ed.), *Federalismos latinoamericanos* (Mexico, 1993).

LUCENA, M., 'Las nuevas poblaciones de Cartagena de Indias, 1774–1794', *Revista de Indias* (Sept.–Dec. 1993).

MCCANN, T. P., *Am American Company: The Tragedy of the United Fruit Company* (New York, 1976).

McFarlane, A., *Colombia Before Independence: Economy, Society, and Politics under Bourbon Rule* (Cambridge, 1993).

— 'Comerciantes y monopolio en la Nueva Granada: el consulado de Cartagena de Indias', *Anuario Colombiano de Historia Social y de la Cultura*, 11 (Bogotá, 1983), 43–70.

— 'Cimarrones and Palenques: Runaways and Resistance in Colonial Colombia', G. Heiman (ed.), *Out of the House of Bondage: Runaways Resistance and Marronage in Africa and the New World* (London, 1986).

McGreevey, W. P., *An Economic History of Colombia, 1845–1930* (Cambridge, 1971).

Machado, A., *Politicas agrarias en Colombia, 1900–1950* (Bogotá, 1986).

Madrid Malo, N., *Barranquilla, el alba de una ciudad* (Bogotá, 1986).

Masefield, G. B., *A Handbook of Tropical Agriculture* (Oxford, 1970).

May, S. and Plaza, G., *The United Fruit Company in Latin America* (Washington, 1958).

Meisel, A., 'Esclavitud, mestizaje y hacienda en la provincia de Cartagena, 1553–1851', *Desarrollo y Sociedad* (Bogotá, July 1980).

— (ed.), *Historia ecónomica y social del Caribe colombiano* (Bogotá, 1994).

— and Posada-Carbó, E., *Por qué se disipó el desarrollo industrial de Barranquilla. Y otros ensayos de historia ecónomica de la Costa Caribe* (Bogotá, 1993).

— and Posada Carbó, E. 'Los bancos de la Costa Caribe, 1873–1925', in F. Sanchez Torres (ed.), *Ensayos de historia monetaria y bancaria de Colombia* (Bogotá, 1994).

Melo, J. O., 'La república conservadora, 1880–1930', *Colombia hoy* (Bogotá, 1985).

Miller, S., 'Mexican Junkers and Capitalists Haciendas, 1810–1910: The Arable Estate and the Transition to Capitalism Between the Insurgency and the Revolution', *Journal of Latin American Studies* 22/2 (May 1990).

Minta, S., *García Márquez: Writer of Colombia* (New York, 1987).

Mommsen, W., and Osterhammel, J. (eds.), *Imperialism and After* (London, 1986).

Moreno de Angel, P., *Antonio de la Torre y Miranda: viajero y poblador* (Bogotá, 1993).

Mörner, M., *Adventurers and Proletarians: The Story of Migrants in Latin America* (Paris, 1985).

— *Region and State in Latin America's Past* (Baltimore and London, 1993).

MORSE, R. ,'Trends and Patterns of Latin American Urbanization, 1750–1920', *Comparative Studies in Society and History*, 4 (1974).

NEWTON, W. P., 'International Aviation Rivalry in Latin America, 1919–1927', *Journal of Inter-American Studies*, 7 (July 1965).

NICHOLS, T., *Tres puertos de Colombia* (Bogotá, 1973).

— 'The Rise of Barranquilla', *Hispanic American Historical Review* 34 (2 May 1954).

NIETO ARTETA, L. E. *Economía y cultura en la historia de Colombia* (Bogotá, 1962).

— *El café en la sociedad colombiana* (Medellín, 1971).

OCAMPO, J. A., *Colombia y la economía mundial, 1830–1910* (Bogotá, 1984).

— and MONTENEGRO, S., *Crisis mundial, protección e industrialización* (Bogotá, 1984).

ORTEGA TORRES, J. J., *Marco Fidel Suárez: Obras* (Bogotá, 1966, 1980), ii and iii.

OSORIO LIZARAZO, J. A., *Gaitán, vida, muerte y permanente presencia* (Bunos Aires, 1952).

OSPINA VÁSQUEZ, L., *Industria y protección en Colombia, 1810–1930* (Medellín, 1955).

— *El Plan agrario* (Medellín, 1963).

OWEN, E. R. J., *Cotton and the Egyptian Economy, 1820–1914* (Oxford, 1969).

PALACIOS, M., *Estado y clases sociales en Colombia* (Bogotá, 1986).

— (ed.), *La unidad nacional en América Latina: Del regionalismo a la nacionalidad* (Mexico, 1983).

— *El café en Colombia* (Bogotá, 1979).

— 'La fragmentación de las clases dominantes en Colombia, una perspectiva histórica', *Revista Universidad Nacional de Colombia* (Medellín, Jan.–Mar. 1980).

PALACIOS PRECIADO, S., *La trata de negros por Cartagena de indias* (Tunja, 1973)

PARK, J. W., *Rafael Núñez and the Politics of Colombian Regionalism 1863–1886* (Baton Rouge La., 1985).

— 'Preludio a la Presidencia: Rafael Núñez, Gobernador de Bolívar, 1876–1879', *Boletín de Historia y Antiguedades*, 63 (Oct.–Dec., 1976).

PATIÑO, V. M., *Historia de la actividad agropecuaria en la América equinoccial* (Cali, 1965).

PEÑAS GALINDO, D. E., *Los bogas de Mompox* (Bogotá, 1988).

PENSO, URQUIJO, E., 'Aspectos agroeconómicos del Atlántico', *Revista Geográfica*,1 (1952).

PERREN, R., *The Meat Trade in Britain, 1840–1914* (London, 1978).

POSADA-CARBÓ, E., *Una invitación a la historia de Barranquilla* (Bogotá, 1987).

— 'La ganadería en la Costa Atlántica colombiana, 1870–1950', *Coyuntura Ecónomica*, 18/3, (Bogotá, 1988).

POUNDS, N. J. G., *An Historical Geography of Europe, 1800–1914* (Cambridge, 1985).

PRIETO, F., and SOLER, Y., *Bonanza y crisis del oro blanco, 1960–1980* (Bogotá, 1982).

RAMÍREZ, A. de J., *Monografía del municipio de Villanueva* (Barranquilla, 1971).

RANDALL, S. J., 'Colombia, the United States, and Inter-American Aviation Rivalry, 1927–1942', *Journal of Inter-American Studies and World Affairs* , 14 (1972).

RAUSCH, J. *The Llanos Frontier in Colombian History, 1830–1930* (Albuquerque, 1993).

REICHELL-DOLMATOFF, G., *Datos histórico-culturales sobre las tribus de la antigua gobernación de Santa Marta* (Bogotá, 1951).

RENAN, E., *Qu'est–ce qu'une nation?* (Paris, 1882).

RESTREPO, J., and RODRÍGUEZ, M., 'Los empresarios extranjeros de Barranquilla, 1800–1900', *Desarrollo y Sociedad* (Bogotá, May 1982).

REVOLLO, P. M., 'Las inundaciones del río Magdalena', *Revista Geográfica* 1 (Barranquilla, 1952).

REYES POSADA, A., *Latifundio y poder político: la hacienda ganadera en Sucre* (Bogotá, 1978).

RIPPY, F., *The Capitalists and Colombia* (New York, 1931).

ROBERTS, B., *Cities of Peasants* (London, 1978).

— 'State and Region in Latin America: The View from Below', in Cedla, *State and Region in Latin America: A Workshop* (Amsterdam, 1981).

ROBINSON, G. W. S., 'The Geographical Region: Form and Function', *The Scottish Geographical Magazine*, 69/2 (Sept. 1953).

ROMERO AGUIRRE, A., *Ayer, hoy y mañana del liberalismo Colombiano. Historia de la Regeneración* (Bogotá, 1949).

ROMERO, J. L., *Latinoamérica: las ciudades y las ideas* (Mexico, 1976).

ROSEVEARE, G. M., *The Grasslands of Latin America* (Cardiff, 1948).

ROTBAUM, I. C., *De Sefarad al Neosefardismo* (Bogotá, 1977).

SCOBIE, J. R., *Secondary Cities of Argentina* (Stanford, Calif., 1988).

— 'The Growth of Cities', in L. Bethell (ed.), *Latin America: Economy and Society, 1870–1930* (Cambridge, 1989).

SETON-WATSON, H., 'Unsatisfied Nationalism', *Journal of Contemporary History*, 6 (1971), 3–13.

SHARPLESS, R. E., *Gaitán of Colombia: A Political Biography* (Pittsburgh, 1978).

SLATTA, R., *Cowboys of the Americas* (New Haven and London, 1990).

SMITH, A., *National Identity* (London, 1991).

SOJO, J. R., *Barranquilla, una economía en expansión* (Barranquilla, 1955).

SOLANO, S. P., and CONDE, J., *Elite empresarial y desarrollo industrial en Barranquilla, 1875–1930* (Barranquilla, 1993).

THOMSON, G., *Puebla de los Angeles: Industry and Society in a Mexican City, 1700–1850* (San Francisco and London, 1988).

THORP, R., and BERTRAN, G., *Perú, 1890–1977* (London and Basingstoke, 1978).

TIRADO MEJÍA, A., *Aspectos políticos del primer gobierno de Alfonso López Pumarejo, 1934–38* (Bogotá, 1981).

— (ed.), *Estado y economía: 50 años de la reforma del 36* (Bogotá, 1986).

TOVAR PINZÓN, H., *Grandes empresas agrícolas y ganaderas* (Bogotá, 1980).

URRUTIA, M., *The Development of the Colombian Labour Movement* (New Haven and London, 1969).

VALDEBLÁNQUEZ, J. M., *Historia del departamento del Magdalena y del territorio de la Guajira* (Bogotá, 1964).

— *Biografía del señor General Florentino Manjarrés* (Bogotá, 1962).

VARELA MARTÍNEZ, R., *Economía agrícola de Colombia* (Bogotá, 1949).

VÁSQUEZ. T. M., *La gobernación de Santa Marta, 1570–1670* (Seville, 1976).

VIDAL DE LA BLACHE, P. *The Personality of France* (London, 1928).

VILLEGAS, J., and YUNIS, J., *La guerra de los mil días* (Bogotá, 1979).

WHITE, J., *Historia de una ignominia* (Bogotá, 1978).

WHITTLESEY, D., 'The Regional Concept and the Regional Method', in P. E. James and C. F. Jones (eds.), *American Geography: Inventory and Prospect* (Syracuse, 1954).

WILLIAMS, R., *Novela y poder en Colombia, 1844–1987* (Stanford, Calif., 1977).

WIRTH, J., *Minas Gerais in the Brazilian Federation, 1889–1937* (Stanford, Calif., 1977).

YOUNG, E. van (ed.), *Mexico's Regions* (San Diego, 1992).

ZAMBRANO, F., 'La navegación a vapor por el Río Magdalena', *Anuario Colombiano de Historia Social y de la Cultura*, 9 (Bogotá, 1979).

ZAMOSC, L., *The Agrarian Question and the Peasant Movement in Colombia* (Cambridge, 1986).

Index

7. Unpublished Theses and Other Documents

CARBONELL INSIGNARES, E., 'Apuntes sobre la colonia china en Barranquilla', Barranquilla, 8 July 1979.

HARRISON, J. P., 'The Colombian Tobacco Industry, from Government Monopoly to Free-Trade', Ph.D. thesis, University of California, 1951.

KROGZEMIS, J., 'A Historical Geography of the Santa Marta Area, Colombia', Ph.D. thesis, Univesity of California at Berkeley, 1967.

MONTENEGRO, S., 'Producción del algodón en Colombia, 1900–1930', n.d.

PALOMINO, A., *et al.*, 'Anteproyecto acerca de la reconstrucción de la racionalidad económica de la Sociedad Agrícola del Sinú', Universidad de Antioquia, Medellín, 1985.

RESTREPO ZEA, R. N., 'Evaluación de la capacidad de la Feria de ganados y posibilidades de nuevos servicios', Medellín, 1984.

SOLANO, S. P., 'Orígenes de la industria en Barranquilla: Fábrica de Tejidos Obregón', Barranquilla, 1989.

URICOCHEA, F., 'Resabios tribales y cosmopolitanismo periférico, Bogotá y Cartagena en 1910', paper given at the IV Congreso de Historia Colombiana, Tunja, Dec. 1983

WHITE, J., 'The United Fruit Company in the Santa Marta Banana Zone, Colombia: Conflicts of the 20s', B. Phil., Oxford, June 1971.

YODER, L. O., 'The Cattle Industry in Colombia and Venezuela', MSc. thesis, University of Chicago, 1926. .